W9-BDA-006

The American
Immigration Collection

Americans in the Making

WILLIAM CARLSON SMITH

Arno Press and The New York Times

NEW YORK 1970

Reprint Edition 1970 by Arno Press Inc.

LC# 70-129414

ISBN 0-405-00568-7

The American Immigration Collection—Series II

ISBN for complete set 0-405-00543-1

Manufactured in the United States of America

AMERICANS IN THE MAKING

THE NATURAL HISTORY OF THE ASSIMILATION OF IMMIGRANTS

THE CENTURY SOCIAL SCIENCE SERIES

EDITED BY

EDWARD ALSWORTH ROSS, *University of Wisconsin*

CONTEMPORARY SOCIAL MOVEMENTS, by Jerome Davis.
PRINCIPLES OF SOCIOLOGY, Third Edition, by Edward A. Ross.
FIELD WORK AND SOCIAL RESEARCH, by F. Stuart Chapin.
POVERTY AND DEPENDENCY, Third Edition, by John L. Gillin.
ORGANIZING THE COMMUNITY, by Bessie A. McClenahan.
EDUCATIONAL SOCIOLOGY, by David Snedden.
SOCIOLOGY FOR TEACHERS, by David Snedden.
EDUCATIONAL APPLICATIONS OF SOCIOLOGY, by David Snedden.
THE DEVELOPMENT OF SOCIAL THEORY, by J. P. Lichtenberger.
FUNDAMENTALS OF SOCIAL PSYCHOLOGY, Second Edition, by Emory S. Bogardus.
OUTLINES OF SOCIOLOGY, Revised Edition, by Edward A. Ross.
THE ENVIRONMENTAL BASIS OF SOCIETY, by Franklin Thomas.
MEANS OF SOCIAL CONTROL, by F. E. Lumley.
CRIMINOLOGY AND PENOLOGY, Revised Edition, by John L. Gillin.
REGIONAL SOCIOLOGY, by Radhakamal Mukerjee.
THE NEGRO IN AMERICAN LIFE, by Jerome Dowd.
CULTURAL EVOLUTION, by Charles A. Ellwood.
CULTURAL CHANGE, by F. Stuart Chapin.
SOCIOLOGY OF RURAL LIFE, by Horace B. Hawthorn.
RACE CONTACT, by E. E. Muntz.
PROBLEMS OF THE FAMILY, Revised Edition, by Willystine Goodsell.
COMMUNITY PROBLEMS, by A. E. Wood.
SOCIAL PROBLEMS, Revised Edition, by John L. Gillin, C. G. Dittmer, and R. J. Colbert.
SOCIAL PROGRESS, by J. O. Hertzler.
TESTS AND CHALLENGES IN SOCIOLOGY, by Edward A. Ross.
VILLAGE AND OPEN-COUNTRY NEIGHBORHOODS, by Walter E. Terpenning.
SOCIAL PATHOLOGY, Revised Edition, by John L. Gillin.
THE PROPAGANDA MENACE, by F. E. Lumley.
LEADERS AND LEADERSHIP, by Emory S. Bogardus.
CONTROL IN HUMAN SOCIETIES, by Jerome Dowd.
THE STUDY OF MAN, by Ralph Linton.
SOCIAL INSTITUTIONS, by Lloyd V. Ballard.
METROPOLIS: A STUDY OF URBAN COMMUNITIES, by Howard Woolston
AMERICANS IN THE MAKING, by William Carlson Smith

OTHER VOLUMES ARRANGED

THE CENTURY SOCIAL SCIENCE SERIES

AMERICANS IN THE MAKING

THE NATURAL HISTORY OF THE ASSIMILATON OF IMMIGRANTS

BY

WILLIAM CARLSON SMITH, PH.D.

PROFESSOR OF SOCIOLOGY, LINFIELD COLLEGE

AUTHOR OF "THE AO NAGA TRIBE OF ASSAM: A STUDY IN ETHNOLOGY AND SOCIOLOGY," AND "AMERICANS IN PROCESS: A STUDY OF OUR CITIZENS OF ORIENTAL ANCESTRY"

D. APPLETON–CENTURY COMPANY
INCORPORATED

NEW YORK LONDON

389

PRINTED IN THE UNITED STATES OF AMERICA

Dedicated

to

the memory of my

Father and Mother,

who, as immigrants, helped
to give me an understanding and
appreciation of Americans
who are in the making

EDITOR'S INTRODUCTION

What goes on in the souls of immigrants into this country, is, I believe, presented as well in this book as it ever will be. For the author has drawn upon a host of illuminating studies that have come out since the turn of the century. Compare what is now known about the Americanization process with what was known in nineteen hundred!

There are parts of the world where an immigrating element spins about itself a cocoon in which it may remain for centuries, retaining its own speech, religion, and folkways. That even happened here when we were merely a string of British colonies—witness the Pennsylvania Germans! Now, why is it that the time arrived when an immigrant group could not thus encyst itself and continue its old-world type of life? Because a distinctive American culture had grown up and we were unwilling to bestow citizenship and the ballot upon strangers in our midst to whom they had no meaning.

Many things impinged upon our immigrants that were not parts of this culture. I mean misunderstanding, ridicule, intolerance, swindling, industrial oppression, police persecution, etc. For American culture by no means comprises all the features of American life as the immigrant met them, but only that which goes on with the approval of the more intelligent, self-conscious Americans, that which is collectively approved and intended. Many of the harrowing experiences of the foreign-born with our petty officials and public agencies, whose business is to do justice and protect the weak, were quite unknown to such Americans until the residents of the social settlements made them acquainted with the facts. Yet naturally the immigrant charged all these impositions and wrongs against "America."

The immigrants assumed that, since this is a "free country" they would have no difficulty in reconstituting here their old-world life. On the other hand, the self-conscious Americans assumed that, of course, once the immigrants understood the nature of the great social experiment going on here, they would be glad to share in it. Often both were disappointed, yet no one was to blame; nothing else could have happened. But all praise to those agencies which are helping Americans to understand what's on the mind of the immigrants and immigrants what's on the mind of the Americans.

Would it have been better if we had not *forced* the child of the immigrant into the American public school, where the teacher was unsympathetic with un-American ideas and institutions while the pupils were intolerant of foreign food, dress, and ways? Some will reply: "No, since the stage of assimilation in which we now find ourselves is inevitable, it is better to 'have it over with' in a single generation than to 'prolong the agony' through a series of generations." Others will observe: "There would have been far less anguish, moral wreckage, and social damage if the strain of Americanizing had been distributed among children, grandchildren, and great-grandchildren."

There is room here for honest difference of opinion.

EDWARD ALSWORTH ROSS

TABLE OF CONTENTS

PREFACE

This is not a *history* of immigration. It is an endeavor to set forth the *natural history* of the assimilation of immigrants to America; it aims to present the more general aspects of the assimilative process which are common to all groups. In doing this, no attempt is made to record minute details relative to any or all the arrivals from every land—that is not necessary.

It has been the author's purpose to select sufficient significant data to depict the processual aspect of the situation. The selections have been more or less arbitrary and might as well have been made from other groups. To be sure, restrictions were placed on the range of choice by the kind of materials available. Intimate personal documents, such as letters, diaries, autobiographies, and life histories, have been used as extensively as possible and these are strictly limited in quantity.

It is also true that such sources have serious limitations in *quality* as well. Immigrant autobiographies usually have been written by sensitive, self-conscious intellectuals who are not necessarily random samples of their compatriots. Nevertheless, they are closer to actuality than elaborate statistical tables interpreted through eyes that are afflicted with the myopia of nationalism. Since such interpreters are not "participant observers" they are in grave danger of assuming that they are viewing the overt behavior of the immigrant exactly as the alien himself does. This assumption, however, is an erroneous one. The interpreter of the mind of the immigrant must be on his guard against this "psychologist's fallacy." Life histories, many of which have been secured through personal interviews, are less restricted to the intelligentsia and thus are more typical of the groups they represent. Diaries which are not meant for publication tend to be closer to reality than the published autobiographies of literary persons. Personal letters are one of the good, if not the best, sources of material on the immigrant. Many letters have been written by persons who may, only by a process of stretching, be called literate. Nevertheless, they reveal much. *The Polish Peasant in Europe and America* by W. I. Thomas and Florian Znaniecki exemplify the value of immigrant letters. Despite shortcomings, personal documents are invaluable aids in understanding immigrants as well as other persons—they penetrate the protective masks which we see.

Thus far insufficient attention has been paid to the accumulation and preservation of personal documents. Much of the available literature is polemic—immigrants are either good or bad. A change, however, is noticeable and literature on immigrants is becoming interesting, fascinating—even human. The various state historical societies have not as yet done much to exploit the resources in this fruitful field, while certain immigrant organizations have devoted more energy to self-laudation than to historical research. There are indications, however, of a deepening interest, and we may expect better results in the near future. The work of the Norwegian-American Historical Association is particularly commendable as evidenced by the publications issued thus far. When the historians accumulate these valuable source materials, we shall be in a position to study the immigrant to better advantage.

The author's interest in this study has not been motivated by any desire to start a reform movement. It has been his purpose to *understand*—to study immigrants as *persons*, as *human beings*, instead of regarding them as mere statistical units, as scum of the "melting pot," or as scape-goats for our sins and shortcomings.

The writer is indebted to many persons who have made this study possible. He appreciates the coöperation of a considerable number of immigrants and their children who contributed their life histories which have been used freely. He is grateful to Miss Mildred Grey Smith of William Jewell College for her painstaking care in typing the first copy of the manuscript, to Miss Catherine Stover of Linfield College for her typing of the volume in its final form, and to Miss Julia Blanchard of Linfield College for assistance in reading the proof sheets. To the editor, Professor Edward Alsworth Ross, he owes a debt of gratitude for a number of valuable suggestions which came from his critical reading of the manuscript.

In addition, acknowledgment is made to the writer's wife, Veda Esther Smith, for her invaluable contribution through her encouragement and discriminating criticism of the manuscript in its various stages of preparation. Besides the acknowledgments made in the text, thanks are also due to the following:

THE AMERICAN ACADEMY OF POLITICAL AND SOCIAL SCIENCE, for material by Kate H. Claghorn from *Annals of the American Academy,* Vol. XXIV.

THE AMERICAN MERCURY, and the author, for material from "An Immigrant Father," by Anthony M. Turano, *The American Mercury,* Vol. XXVII.

AMERICAN SOCIOLOGICAL SOCIETY, for material from "Nationality and Crime," *American Sociological Review,* Vol. I.

D. APPLETON-CENTURY COMPANY, INC., for material from *The Immigrant and the Community,* by Grace Abbott; *On New Shores,* by Konrad Bercovici; *The Emigrants,* by Johan Bojer; *Seventy Years of It, The Old World in the New,* and *Principles of Sociology,* by E. A. Ross; *Community Problems,* by A. E. Wood; "An Arkansas Epic," by Bruno Roselli, *The Century Magazine,* Vol. XCIX. To publisher and author for material from "Sons of Immigrants Remind Us," by Rose C. Feld, *The Century Magazine,* Vol. CXV.

ATLANTIC MONTHLY, for material from "Race Factors in Labor Unions," by William Z. Ripley, *Atlantic Monthly,* Vol. XCIII.

AUGSBURG PUBLISHING HOUSE, for material from *History of the Norwegian People in America,* by O. M. Norlie; *Amerika-Breve,* by P. A. Smevik.

THE BURTON PUBLISHING COMPANY, for material from *Americanism in Americanization,* by B. K. Baghdigian.

THOMAS ČAPEK, author, for material from *The Čechs in America.*

THE CARNEGIE CORPORATION OF NEW YORK, for material from *The Immigrant's Day in Court,* by Kate H. Claghorn; *America Via the Neighborhood,* by John Daniels; *Adjusting Immigrant and Industry,* by W. M. Leiserson; *Memorandum on Participation, Prepared by the Americanization Study, 1919; The Immigrant Press and Its Control,* by R. E. Park; *Old World Traits Transplanted,* by R. E. Park and H. A. Miller; *Justice and the Poor,* by R. H. Smith; *A Stake in the Land,* by P. A. Speek.

COLUMBIA UNIVERSITY PRESS, and the author, for material from "A Study of Assimilation Among the Roumanians of the United States," by Christine A. Galitzi, *Columbia Studies in History, Economics, and Public Law.*

CHRISTOPHER PUBLISHING HOUSE, for material from *The Italian Immigrants in Our Courts* and *The Italian Contribution to American Democracy,* by John H. Mariano; *Social and Religious Life of Italians in America,* by E. C. Sartorio.

F. S. CROFTS AND COMPANY, for material from *Introduction to Sociology,* by Wilson D. Wallis.

THE CROWELL PUBLISHING COMPANY, and the author, for material from "Spiritual Unrest," by Ray Stannard Baker, *American Magazine,* Vol. LXVIII.

THOMAS Y. CROWELL COMPANY, for material from *Hull House Maps and Papers,* by Jane Addams; *Our American Music,* by John Tasker Howard.

GEORGE M. DAY, author, for material from *The Russians in Hollywood.* (Permission also acknowledged from The University of Southern California Press.)

DORRANCE AND COMPANY, Philadelphia, Pa., for material from *From Steerage to Congress,* by Richard Bartholdt.

E. P. DUTTON AND COMPANY, INC., for material from *Seventy Years of Life and Labor,* by Samuel Gompers; *Caste and Outcast,* by Dhan G. Mukerji; *The Jews of Today,* by Arthur Ruppin.

WM. B. EERDMANS PUBLISHING COMPANY, for material from *The Dutch Settlement in Michigan,* by Aleida J. Pieters.

A. B. FAUST, author, for material from *The German Element in the United States.*

GEORGE T. FLOM, author, for material from *A History of Norwegian Immigration to the United States.*

FOREIGN LANGUAGE INFORMATION SERVICE, and Temple Burling and Evelyn Hersey, authors, for material from *The Interpreter,* Vols. IV, IX, XI.

THE FRIENDSHIP PRESS, for material from *Sons of Italy,* by Antonio Mangano; *The Oriental in American Life,* by A. W. Palmer.

FUNK AND WAGNALLS COMPANY, for material from *Children of Loneliness,* by A. Yezierska.

HARCOURT, BRACE AND COMPANY, INC., for material from *The Story of American Dissent,* by John M. Mecklin.

HARPER AND BROTHERS, for material from *Carmella Commands,* by Walter S. Ball; *Immigrant Farmers and Their Children,* by E. deS. Brunner; *An American Business Venture,* by Henry A. Dix; *Social Psychology,* by J. K. Folsom; *Principles of Sociology,* by E. T. Hiller; *Peasant Pioneers,* by K. D. Miller; *Peder Victorious,* by O. E. Rölvaag; *The Story of Religion in America,* by William W. Sweet; *American Minority Peoples,* by Donald Young.

HARVARD UNIVERSITY PRESS, for material from *Children Astray,* by S. Drucker and M. B. Hexter; *The Italian Emigration of Our Times,* by Robert F. Foerster.

HEARST MAGAZINES, INC., for material from "The Land of the Too Free," by Konrad Bercovici, *Good Housekeeping,* August, 1935.

D. C. HEATH AND COMPANY, for material from *Immigration and Race Attitudes,* by E. S. Bogardus; *Immigration and Assimilation,* by H. G. Duncan.

E. T. HILLER, author, for material from *Rural Community Types,* by E. T. Hiller, F. E. Corner, and W. L. East.

HAMILTON HOLT, author, for material from *Life Stories of Undistinguished Americans.*

HENRY HOLT AND COMPANY, for material from *The Range of Social Theory,* by Floyd N. House; *Our Natupski Neighbors,* by Edith M. Miniter; *The Frontier in American History,* by Frederick J. Turner.

K. C. HOLTER, for material from *The Scandinavian-American,* by A. O. Fonkalsrud.

IOWA STATE HISTORICAL SOCIETY, for material from *The British in Iowa,* and *Hollanders of Iowa,* by Jacob Van der Zee.

THE JEWISH INFORMATION BUREAU, for material from *In a Strange Land,* by Vladimir Korolenko.

MARSHALL JONES COMPANY, for material from *On Becoming an American,* by Horace Bridges.

ROBERT KUTAK, author, for material from *A Bohemian American Village.*

MRS. LILLIAN M. LARSON, for material by the late Laurence M. Larson from *American Historical Review,* Vol. XL.

LITTLE, BROWN AND COMPANY, for material from *An American Saga,* by Carl Jensen; *Mental Conflict and Misconduct,* by William Healy.

LIVERIGHT PUBLISHING CORPORATION, for material from *The Gentleman from the 22nd,* by Benjamin Antin; *Culture and Democracy,* by Horace M. Kallen.

LONGMANS, GREEN AND COMPANY, for material from *Immigration,* by Lawrence Guy Brown; *The American Colonies,* by Marcus W. Jernegan.

HENRY R. MARESH, author, for material from *Czech Pioneers of the Southwest,* by Estelle Hudson and Henry R. Maresh.

MICHIGAN HISTORICAL SOCIETY, for material from *Michigan Historical Collections,* Vol. XXXIX.

MINNESOTA HISTORICAL SOCIETY, for material from *Minnesota History,* Vol. X, by G. M. Stephenson.

YOUEL B. MIRZA, author, for material from *Myself When Young.*

MISSOURI HISTORICAL SOCIETY, for material from *Missouri Historical Review,* Vol. XII.

THE NATION, for material from "The Greatest Jewish City in the World," by Konrad Bercovici, *The Nation,* Vol. CXVII; "Second Generation Aliens," by Eugene Lyons, *The Nation,* Vol. CXVI.

NATIONAL COMMITTEE FOR MENTAL HYGIENE, for material from "Conflicts of Cultures and Children's Maladjustment," *Mental Hygiene,* Vol. XVII.

THE NEW REPUBLIC, for material from *New Republic,* October, 1934; "Rise of the New American," *New Republic,* Vol. XXX.

NORWEGIAN-AMERICAN HISTORICAL ASSOCIATION, for material from *Publications of the Norwegian-American Historical Association: Studies and Records,* Vol. II; *The Changing World,* by Laurence M. Larson.

C. T. PIHLBLAD, author, for material from "The Kansas Swedes," *Southwestern Social Science Quarterly,* Vol. XII.

POWELL AND WHITE, for material from *The Slavic Immigrant Woman,* by B. O. Pehotsky.

PSYCHOLOGICAL CLINIC PRESS, for material from "Foreign-Born Parentage and Social Maladjustment," *Psychological Clinic,* Vol. XIX.

G. P. PUTNAM'S SONS, for material from *Ireland in America,* by Edward F. Roberts; *Some Aspects of Italian Immigration to the United States,* by Antonio Stella; *Recollections of an Immigrant,* by Andreas Ueland.

RANDOM HOUSE, for material from *The Italians of New York,* Federal Writers' Project.

DOROTHY REED, author, for material from *Leisure Time in Little Italy.*

REPUBLIC PUBLISHING COMPANY, for material from *Youth in Conflict,* by Miriam Van Waters.

FLEMING H. REVELL COMPANY, for material from *The Broken Wall, The Immigrant Tide, From Alien to Citizen, On the Trail of the Immigrant,* by E. A. Steiner.

THE RONALD PRESS COMPANY, for material from *An Introduction to Sociology,* by Carl A. Dawson and Warner E. Gettys; *Human Migration,* by Donald R. Taft.

CARL M. ROSENQUIST, author, for material from *The Swedes in Texas,* unpublished dissertation.

THE RYERSON PRESS, for material from *A Search for America,* by F. P. Grove.

THE RUSSELL SAGE FOUNDATION, for material from *Immigrant Gifts to American Life,* by Allen H. Eaton; *What Is Social Case Work?,* by Mary Richmond; *The Social Work Yearbook,* 1935, 1937.

CHARLES SCRIBNER'S SONS, for material from *The Sabbath in Puritan New England,* by Alice Morse Earle; *The Marginal Man: A Study in Personality and Culture Conflict,* by Everett V. Stonequist.

STATE HISTORICAL SOCIETY OF WISCONSIN, for material from *Proceedings of the State Historical Society, 1901, 1907; Wisconsin Magazine of History,* Vols. VIII and XIX.

BUREAU OF PUBLICATIONS, TEACHERS COLLEGE, COLUMBIA UNIVERSITY, for material from *The Yiddish Press—An Americanization Agency,* by Mordecai Soltes.

STANFORD UNIVERSITY PRESS, for material from *Modern Samoa,* by Felix M. Keesing.

FREDERICK A. STOKES COMPANY, for material from *Imported Americans,* by Broughton Brandenburg.

THE SURVEY ASSOCIATES, INC., for material by Alice Bennett from *The Survey,* May 1, 1909; "Of the Second Generation," by John Valentine, *The Survey,* Vol. XLVII; acknowledgments are due both to publisher and author for material from the four following: "Of Horologians Here and There," by John P. Gavit, *Survey Graphic,* Vol. II; "Behind Our Masks," by Robert E. Park, *Survey Graphic,* Vol. LVI; "Americanizing Husbands," by Cecilia Razovsky, *The Survey,* Vol. LIV; "Jim's Own Story," by Pauline V. Young, *The Survey,* Vol. LIX.

W. I. THOMAS, author, for material from *The Polish Peasant in Europe and America,* Vols. I and II.

THE TORCH PRESS, for material from *How a Dane Became an American,* by T. M. Nielsen.

C. M. PANUNZIO, author, for material from *The World Tomorrow.*

UNIVERSITY OF CHICAGO PRESS, for material from the *Proceedings of the National Conference of Social Work,* by Sophonisba Breckenridge, John Collier, Julius Drachsler, Ida L. Hull, Mary E. Hurlbutt, W. W. Husband, John A. Lapp, Robert E. Park, Josephine Roche, and E. H. Sutherland; *Immigration: Select Documents and Case Records,* by Edith Abbott; "Occupational Succession of Hungarians in Detroit," by E. D. Beynon, *American Journal of Sociology,* Vols. XXXIX and LXI; material by E. D. Beynon in *American Journal of Sociology,* Vol. XXIX; *Social Problems and Social Processes,* edited by E. S. Bogardus; *Suicide,* by Ruth S. Cavan; "Cultural Marginality in Sex Delinquency," *American Journal of Sociology,* Vol. XXXIX; *Backgrounds of Swedish Immigration,* by Florence E. Janson; "A Study of Marriage in a Finnish Community," by John I. Kolehmainen, *American Journal of Sociology,* Vol. XLII; material by Robert E. Park from *American Journal of Sociology,* Vol. XXXIII; *The City* and *Introduction to the Science of Sociology,* by R. E. Park and E. W. Burgess; *In Pennsylvania German Land, 1928–1929,* by Jessie L. Rosenberger; "Lithuanian Immigrants," by J. S. Roucek, *American Journal of Sociology,* Vol. XLI; *The Gang,* by F. M. Thrasher; *The Ghetto,* by Louis Wirth; *Pilgrims of Russian-Town,* by Pauline V. Young; "The Russian Molokan Community in Los Angeles," by Pauline V. Young, *American Journal of Sociology,* Vol. XXXV; *The Gold Coast and the Slum,* by Harvey M. Zorbaugh.

THE UNIVERSITY OF ILLINOIS, for material from *The Scandinavian Element in the United States,* by Kendrick C. Babcock.

UNIVERSITY OF NORTH CAROLINA PRESS, for material from "The Ghetto and the Slum," by A. W. Lind, *Social Forces,* December, 1930; "Culture Conflict and Delinquency," by Louis Wirth, *Social Forces,* Vol. IX; "The Reorganization of Jewish Family Life in America," by Pauline V. Young, *Social Forces,* Vol. VII.

THE COMMONWEATH REVIEW, University of Oregon, for material from "The Basques in Oregon," by Cressman and Yturri, *The Commonwealth Review,* March, 1938.

UNIVERSITY OF SOUTHERN CALIFORNIA PRESS, for material from "Occupational Attitudes of Orientals in Hawaii," by Andrew W. Lind, *Sociology and Social Research,* Vol. XIII; "The Problem of Becoming Americanized," by Joseph S. Roucek, *Sociology and Social Research,* Vol. XVII; "Rural Immigrant Communities," by J. A. Saathoff, *Sociology and Social Research,* September–October, 1931.

THE VIGO PRESS, for material from *The Italians in America,* by G. E. Schiavo.

JOHN WILEY AND SONS, INC., for material reprinted by permission from *Immigrant Backgrounds,* by H. P. Fairchild, published by John Wiley and Sons, Inc.
DANIEL J. WILLIAMS, author, for material from *The Welsh of Columbus, Ohio.*
LOUIS WIRTH, author, for material from *Culture Conflicts in the Immigrant Family,* unpublished dissertation.
YALE UNIVERSITY PRESS, for material from *Ireland and Irish Emigration to the New World,* by W. F. Adams; *Greek Immigration to the United States,* by H. P. Fairchild.

WILLIAM CARLSON SMITH

AMERICANS IN THE MAKING

THE NATURAL HISTORY OF THE ASSIMILATION OF IMMIGRANTS

CHAPTER I

CAUSES OF IMMIGRATION

If we take a panoramic view of the hordes of immigrants that have poured through our ports of entry during the past two centuries, certain questions arise. Why did they come? What forces loosened them from their old moorings?

Human beings are anchored to their natal localities by family ties, by the graves of their ancestors,[1] by property interests, and by sentimental associations. Held by these bonds, it is far easier to remain in one's home environment than to go away. Removal usually necessitates considerable habit derangement thereby causing distress. Hence, men do not migrate without reason. To discover the causes of these shiftings is difficult. Chronicles of the exploits of kings and nobles are sterile sources. The student must go to the humble dwellings of the peasants on the land and to the cottages of the fisher-folk on the fiord for his materials. The life of the commoners was not deemed worthy of record, except fragmentarily, and even then the accounts were warped by prejudice.[2]

Both expulsive and attractive forces were in play. Conditions in the homelands developed unrest. This dissatisfaction, coupled with the attractions—real or imagined—beyond the Atlantic, broke old bonds and migration resulted. The causes were complex and usually no one factor impelled the migrant to leave his country. In this mass movement certain general or fundamental causes operated but there were also many personal elements peculiar to individuals. A son or daughter left because of friction with un-

[1] George A. Gordon, a Scottish immigrant, writes of "a weary-footed lassie" with a bundle on her back and one in her hand as she was leaving Scotland. In one of the parcels she was carrying with her some turf from her mother's grave. *My Education and Religion* (Houghton Mifflin Company, Boston, 1925), pp. 132–33.

[2] Cf. George M. Stephenson, *A History of American Immigration* (Boston, 1926), p. 7. Also Edith Abbott, *Historical Aspects of the Immigration Problem* (Chicago, 1926), pp. 11–198.

sympathetic parents; a girl went away to avoid marriage with the man her parents had chosen; a youth who had lost status because of a petty misdemeanor, sought a new start far from the venomous tongues of local gossips; a girl fled to avoid scandal; a young man, grown weary of working for his father without compensation and with less freedom than a hired hand, yet loath on account of sharp class distinctions to hire out in the neighborhood where he was known, hoped to lose himself in America. For these and a thousand other reasons, men and women determined to leave their old homes. No attempt will be made to present all the concrete factors in the situation, but in the following pages the most outstanding causes will be considered.

A. Dissatisfaction with Conditions in the Homeland

The religious factor. In early years the religious factor was prominent. It gave us the New England Puritans. It entered into the early development of Pennsylvania. The Germans, who settled at Germantown in 1683, were religious refugees, mainly from the Palatinate. In Germany and along the Rhine, all groups but the Catholic, Lutheran, and the Reformed were outlawed. George Fox and William Penn spread their ideas throughout this area where the Pietists had prepared the soil for Quakerism. Penn advertised Pennsylvania widely with the result that English Quakers, Scotch and Irish Presbyterians, German Mennonites, and French Huguenots, who had suffered persecution, came in considerable numbers.[3] Some Finns emigrated from Russia because of the religious situation. The rise of Methodism in England exerted an influence. The Wesleys and Whitefield, apostles of this new sect, exposed the dry formalism of the established church and emphasized the dignity of the individual at a time when human life had become cheap because of the newly-risen factory system. America, vaunted as a land not only of economic opportunity but also of religious freedom, attracted many who had been touched by the new gospel.[4]

[3] Cf. Albert B. Faust, *The German Element in the United States* (New York, 1927), Vol. I, p. 30; Frank Reid Diffenderffer, *The German Immigration into Pennsylvania* (Lancaster, Pa., 1900), pp. 16–22; W. K. Knittle, *Early 18th Century Palatine Emigration* (Philadelphia, 1937).

[4] Cf. G. M. Stephenson, *op. cit.*, pp. 17–18.

Religious oppression about 1870 was one of the expulsive forces responsible for the migration of thousands of southern Slovaks into the coal and steel regions of Ohio, Indiana, and Illinois.[5]

Religious persecutions, which began in the thirties under the revival of an old Napoleonic law in Holland, were the primary and fundamental causes of the emigration of the Dutch to Michigan in 1847.

> It is quite possible, however, that if other factors had not also come into play the Hollanders would have remained at home, for they revered the House of Orange and loved their country. For the time being at least, freedom of worship was granted, if only by favor, and not as a right. They could look forward, therefore, to a time of peace and, perhaps, complete liberty might ultimately be theirs by right. Famine and poverty, however, were more insistent.[6]

The majority of Armenians in the United States are refugees from persecution.[7] They, a Christian group, suffered at the hands of the Mohammedan Turks. The Armenians made contacts with American missionaries and educators in the Near East and thus they looked toward America as a haven of refuge. Likewise the Syrians of the province of Lebanon, who were predominantly Christian, felt the sting of Turkish oppression. The massacre of Christians in 1860 furnished the initial impulse for emigration from Syria.[8]

Few countries have been as free from religious persecution as Norway, yet intolerance has not been unknown.[9] The established church, never favorably disposed toward dissenters and separatists, at times joined hands with the state to suppress heresy. In the early nineteenth century, the followers of the lay preacher, Hans Nielsen Hauge, were persecuted. The Quakers, thorough-going separatists, would have nothing to do with Lutheran doctrines and practices. When pressure was used to bring conformity, they in-

[5] Cf. Konrad Bercovici, *On New Shores* (New York, 1925), p. 11.

[6] Aleida J. Pieters, *The Dutch in Michigan* (Grand Rapids, 1923), p. 31.

[7] Cf. M. Vartan Malcom, *The Armenians in America* (Boston, 1919).

[8] Morris Zelditch, *The Syrians in Pittsburgh*, unpublished dissertation, University of Pittsburgh, 1936.

[9] George T. Flom, *A History of Norwegian Immigration* (Iowa City, 1909), p. 74.

vestigated rather thoroughly the advantages offered by America.[10]

"Religion as a cause of emigration from Sweden is a factor historians cannot ignore, however much they may differ as to its relative importance." [11] In the first half of the nineteenth century, a separatistic movement called "The Great Awakening" developed and out of this grew a conflict with the state church which came to be a major cause of emigration to America. This dispute

> acted as a selective factor. . . . . The desire for religious freedom furnished a strong motive for emigration only among those who were deeply religious. For those to whom religion was of little significance, outward conformity to the rules of the church did not prove more than mildly irksome. It would follow, therefore, as it actually has, that a disproportionate percentage of the emigration from Sweden was made up of the most enthusiastic members of the dissenting sects or of the deeply religious members of the Lutheran Church who were dissatisfied with the lack of spirituality within that organization.[12]

The spiritual aridity of the state church and its attitude toward the dissenters is indicated by the following letter:

> As long as I could swear, dance, drink a little, and answer well at the church examinations—which I always did—I was greatly praised by the reverend fathers. But when I left the sinful life and took Christianity seriously, with the Bible as my guide in life and action, I was threatened with imprisonment on bread and water. Since the seaman, F. O. Nelson, was exiled in 1850 for his faith, thousands have gone into voluntary exile on account of the persecutory diligence of the clergy.[13]

[10] Cf. Olaf M. Norlie, *History of the Norwegian People in America* (Minneapolis, 1925), pp. 114–15; Kendrick C. Babcock, *The Scandinavian Element in the United States* (Urbana, 1914), p. 23; George M. Stephenson, *Religious Aspects of Swedish Immigration* (Minneapolis, 1932).

[11] G. M. Stephenson, *Religious Aspects of Swedish Immigration* (1932), p. 9. Quoted by permission of the publisher, The University of Minnesota Press, Minneapolis, Minn.

In another connection Stephenson wrote: "We shall not stray far from the truth if we regard the men in the vanguard as non-conformists in political, religious, social, and economic matters." *American Historical Review,* XXXI (July, 1926), 709.

[12] Carl M. Rosenquist, *The Swedes of Texas,* unpublished dissertation, University of Chicago, 1930.

[13] "Utvandrarnes egna upgifter," *Emigrationsutredningens Bilaga* (Stockholm, 1908), Vol. VII, p. 168. Hereafter references to this source will be given: *Emi-*

Even after persecution had ceased, the dissenters were obliged to pay taxes to support an institution from which they derived no benefit. They were also subjected to other annoying discriminations,[14] particularly as to marriage. Until 1873 there was no legal marriage for citizens not affiliated with the state church. Since the Baptists would not allow their children to be confirmed, they could not be legally married. Prior to the legalization of civil marriage in 1873, the children born of Baptist marriages were illegitimate in the eyes of the law.

During the persecution America became a symbol of freedom to the dissenters in Sweden. Baptist papers regarded emigration as providential and encouraged it. Prior to the Civil War, Baptist congregations in America were scattered and poor, but they aided their persecuted brethren in the homeland and did much to encourage expatriation.[15]

The Jews in Russia,[16] subjected to many indignities, sought refuge in the United States by the tens of thousands. Political and economic discriminations, however, were enforced against them because of their religion. Jews had lived in Russia for many generations, but at the partition of Poland near the end of the eighteenth century the Jewish question arose. With the addition of Poland to her territory, Russia acquired several million Jews, so that nearly half of the world's Jewry lived under the Russian flag. Almost from the outset governmental policies toward the new subjects were repressive. They were restricted in their residence to certain western provinces, known as the "Pale of Jewish Settlement."

grationsutredningens Bilaga, VII. All the excerpts have been translated from the Swedish by Dr. Carl M. Rosenquist of the University of Texas.

[14] Cf. *ibid.*, p. 152.

[15] Cf. G. M. Stephenson, *Religious Aspects of Swedish Immigration,* pp. 89–91.

[16] On the emigration of Jews from Russia, the following works may be consulted: R. Beazley, N. Forbes, G. A. Birkett, *Russia from the Varangians to the Bolsheviks* (Oxford, 1918); Carlton J. H. Hayes, *A Political and Social History of Modern Europe* (New York, 1916), Vol. II; Charles D. Hazen, *Europe Since 1815* (New York, 1929), and *Modern European History* (New York, 1919); J. Salwyn Schapiro, *Modern and Contemporary European History* (Boston, 1923); E. R. Turner, *Europe Since 1870* (Garden City, 1923); Willis M. and Ruth West, *Story of World Progress* (Boston, 1931); *Reports of the Immigration Commission,* Vol. IV. (This report is the most complete on the causes, of emigration from Russia.) For the Ukrainians, cf. Wasyl Halich, *Ukrainians in the United States* (Chicago, 1937), p. 15.

Rigid limitations were placed on the number who might attend the schools and universities. They had to serve in the army but could not become officers. They had to pay all the ordinary taxes as well as special ones levied against them. At times edicts were issued which seemingly gave them certain privileges, but shortly these were followed by discriminations and harsh measures that finally culminated in the Kishinev massacre of April 19–21, 1903, a bloody prelude to later events. The outbreak of the Russo-Japanese War and the first indications of an organized revolution boded ill for the Jews. The peasants had no enthusiasm for the carnage in which they were forced to participate, and when the Russian army met with reverses, the bureaucratic agitators spread propaganda that the Jews had forced Russia into the contest with Japan in order to profit thereby. The government, on the verge of a breakdown under revolutionary attacks, was eager to divert attention from its own incompetencies and shielded itself through the deliberate organization of Jewish massacres.[17] A special government office printed literature inciting the populace against the Jews and sent out instructors in the art of the *pogrom*.[18]

The emigration of Jews, particularly from Russia, differs from that of the other Russian peoples and cannot be attributed to the same causes. It is also far different from the emigration of any group from any other country. This movement was not the outcome of some deep economic phenomenon. Russia was sparsely populated and there was considerable demand for the services of skilled artisans. Thus the Jews left Russia, not because opportunities were lacking but because the government deprived them of the most elemental conditions of security. Jewish emigration has been closely related to political conditions. When Alexander III [19] ascended the throne in 1881 and inaugurated a definite anti-Jewish policy, a great New Exodus began.[20]

[17] Cf. Samuel Joseph, *Jewish Immigration to the United States* (New York, 1914), p. 67.

[18] *Reports of the Immigration Commission,* Vol. IV, p. 279. Cf. R. Beazley, N. Forbes, G. A. Birkett, *op. cit.*, p. 532.

[19] J. S. Schapiro, *op. cit.*, p. 532.

[20] Cf. Abraham Cahan, *The Rise of David Levinsky* (New York, 1917), pp. 60–61.

Nevertheless, except for some Jews,[21] few European immigrants have come to America in recent decades because of religious conditions in the homelands.

The political factor. Love of liberty has been an element in the peopling of America. Nearly every European country has sent us a quota of political idealists [22] who preferred democracy to monarchy. "The rumor of a virgin land where the oppressed might dwell in peace drew together a population varied, but rich in the spirited and in idealists." [23] Ideas relative to freedom in America penetrated far-distant areas where the common people suffered privations. According to an American social worker, "In a Siberian hut from which four sons had gone forth to America to seek their fortune, I saw tacked up a portrait of Lincoln cut from a New York newspaper. Even there they knew what Lincoln stood for, and loved him." [24]

Political discontent has been conspicuous in the immigration of the Irish.[25] It has also played a part in the migration of Poles from Germany and Austria. Similarly, political conditions in Turkey have added to our population.[26] Russia lost many emigrants because of political oppression.[27] It was a factor in the emigration

[21] Cf. Horace M. Kallen, *Culture and Democracy in the United States* (New York, 1924), pp. 76–77.

[22] According to Giovanni E. Schiavo, political exiles have always been the superior immigrants. Political conspirators have usually been educated persons of distinction drawn largely from the upper classes. They have been idealists and not opportunists. In Italy the movements for independence from 1802 to the agitations before the World War were led by students, professors, and aristocrats. *The Italians in America before the Civil War* (New York, 1934), pp. 211–12. Cf. E. Abbott, *op. cit.*, pp. 54–55.

[23] Edward Alsworth Ross, *The Old World in the New* (New York, 1914), p. 14.

[24] *Ibid.*, preface.

[25] Cf. William Forbes Adams, *Ireland and Irish Emigration to the New World from 1815 to the Famine* (New Haven, 1932), pp. 2–3.

[26] A Syrian immigrant reported: "My father had a small farm from which we earned a bare living. . . . . When the tax collector, a Turk and a Mohammedan who hated us Christians, came to collect in our village, the tax charged against my father was $6.00. We had no such sum, of course, and my father pleaded our inability to pay it. The collector pulled out his revolver and threatened to come back with soldiers if we did not pay up. Then he suddenly spied our horse. Without a word he seized the horse and went off with it, shouting back that this would pay the tax." M. Zelditch, *op. cit.*

[27] Cf. A. S. Blackwell, *The Little Grandmother of the Russian Revolution: Reminiscences of Catherine Breshkovsky* (Boston, 1917), for an account of oppression under the Czarist régime.

of Finns, Lithuanians, and Poles. Since the Russian government officially oppressed the Jews, the political element must be considered one cause of Jewish immigration.[28]

The Parliamentary Reforms of 1866 in Sweden which introduced a high property qualification for voting created discontent among the disfranchised lower classes. This situation was contrasted with conditions in the United States where

> every Swedish immigrant was eligible to vote as soon as he was naturalized. . . . . He entered eagerly into his new political rights and assisted in the organization of many a county in the territories and new states of the West. . . . . Social and political equality were often the subjects of his letters to his friends and relatives in Sweden.[29]

Desire to be free from tyrannical oppression of petty princes, who improverished the people through heavy taxation to support an extravagant and corrupt government, induced many intellectual and patriotic Germans to emigrate to America.[30] Carl Schurz, who became a prominent figure in American politics, was a political refugee from Germany. He spent some time in London but concluded that America would afford a better opportunity for the realization of his ideals.[31] Governmental injustice led Frederick Steines to leave the fatherland he ardently loved. In 1834 he submitted his resignation to the school authorities in these words:

> Since the year 1820 I have been teacher of the school here. Now the hour has come when I must sever the bonds that have officially bound me. As citizen and in my official and military relations to the state I have

[28] Benjamin Antin pictorializes the conditions which led many Jews to emigrate. "If you could have seen us gathered together in that hovel, the nickelodeon! If you could have seen the way we drank in and swallowed those pictures! If you could have seen us there shaking, trembling, electrified with the emotion of it all! If you could have heard us shout, 'That's where my brother is!' 'That's where I am going, God willing—some day that's where I am going!' America! Where there are no Cossacks' whips to beat you down. America! Where there is no one to break into your house at night. No drunken brawler to rush in and demand you or your sister or your few pennies, or the miserable stock of groceries out of which you make a living. No one to burn and pillage and curse and bully you if you refused." *The Gentleman from the 22nd.* (New York, 1927), p. 12.

[29] Florence E. Janson, *The Background of Swedish Immigration, 1840–1930* (Chicago, 1931), p. 18.

[30] *Missouri Historical Review,* XII (October, 1917), 5. Cf. A. B. Faust, *op. cit.*

[31] Cf. Carl Schurz, *The Reminiscences of Carl Schurz* (New York, 1907).

had so many bitter experiences, which in my opinion an upright citizen of the Prussian state ought not to have been subjected to, that I find myself compelled to make a change. Since I see no opportunity for a betterment of conditions here, I have resolved to migrate to North America.[32]

The struggle of Bohemia against Teutonic domination has been a long one and at the close of the Thirty Years War the Bohemian people were crushed under the Hapsburg heel.[33] The Bohemian spirit, however, was not broken and in the opening of the nineteenth century a number of concessions were wrung from the Austrian throne. The fight was continued against the hostile government, but after the failure of the revolutionary movement of 1848, a number of leaders found it expedient to flee the country. These were the pioneers of the Bohemian (or Czech) immigration to America. Between 1850 and 1870 a steady stream of Bohemians flowed to the rich lands of Nebraska, Iowa, Wisconsin, and Texas.[34]

Untoward political conditions in Hungary augmented our population. Governmental policies, in large measure, were shaped by the land-owning nobility. Suffrage was limited to the propertied and official classes who were, for the most part, Magyars. As late as 1810,[35] "out of a total population of 20,886,000 in the Hungarian kingdom, there were not more than 1,000,000 voters and . . . . out of 413 members of the Chamber of Deputies . . . . , there were only seven non-Magyars." Furthermore, an eligible Slovak citizen imperiled his own safety when he took part in an election. If a Slovak was sent to Parliament he would often be unseated for having advocated an unauthorized policy in his election speeches.[36] The undemocratic open ballot and property qualifications for vot-

[32] *Missouri Historical Review,* XIV (October, 1919), 457.

[33] Cf. W. M. and R. West, *op. cit.,* p. 354.

[34] Cf. C. J. H. Hayes, *op. cit.,* Vol. II, pp. 123–44; Estelle Hudson, and Henry R. Maresh, *Czech Pioneers of the Southwest* (Dallas, 1934), pp. 38–39, 386; Eleanor E. Ledbetter, *The Slovaks of Cleveland* (Pamphlet) pp. 7–8; J. Salwyn Schapiro, *Modern and Contemporary European History,* pp. 427–36; *Proceedings of the State Historical Society of Wisconsin,* 1901, p. 159.

[35] From Carlton J. H Hayes, *A Political and Social History of Modern Europe,* Vol. II, p. 434. By permission of The Macmillan Company, publishers.

[36] Cf. Mary L. Zahrobsky, *The Slovaks in Chicago,* unpublished dissertation, University of Chicago.

ing aided the nobles in holding large tracts of land. As a result the peasants were unable to secure enough arable land to maintain themselves after paying the excessive taxes. Hence large numbers responded to more alluring prospects in other lands.[37]

Social factors. Social distinctions which set a stigma of inferiority upon certain classes and persons have been important factors in our immigration. The Magyars in Hungary, for some time, seemed to overlook nothing that would humiliate the Slovaks and other minority groups.[38] After 1847 education, elementary or higher, in their own languages was proscribed. Furthermore, they were even forbidden to speak or read books and papers in their vernaculars.[39] Another offensive factor was the policy of renaming places. The old historic names were abolished and new Magyar ones substituted. Resentment against these stigmatizing practices led many to emigrate to America.[40]

Even though Norway abolished nobility in 1814, a titled aristocracy has continued to exist; the lines between the upper and lower classes, between the rich and the poor, have been tightly drawn. The custom which obliged those of lowly estate to pay deference to the gentry [41] became repugnant to many ambitious boys and caused them to migrate to America.[42]

[37] Huldah F. Cook, *The Magyars in Cleveland* (Pamphlet). Cf. J. S. Schapiro, *op. cit.*, pp. 131–35. Cf. *World's Work,* XLI (January, 1921), 270–73.

[38] Cf. Emily Greene Balch, *Our Slavic Fellow Citizens* (New York, 1910), p. 118; C. D. Hazen, *Europe Since 1815,* pp. 391–92. An experience of Michael Pupin with a railway conductor indicates the attitude of Austrian officialdom toward the Serbs. *From Immigrant to Inventor* (New York, 1923), p. 26. Cf. B. Antin, *op. cit.*, pp. 59–60; Henry A. Dix, *An American Business Venture* (New York, 1928), pp. 22–25, for a comparison of Russian class distinctions with American democracy.

[39] The Lithuanians were in much the same plight in Russia as the government entered upon a program of Russification. In 1864 an edict forbade the printing of books and periodicals in the Latin type which had been in use for some three centuries. Finally the Lithuanian language could no longer be taught in the schools. All these measures were enforced strictly and an administrative official, without court proceedings, could imprison or deport to Siberia anyone in whose possession was found a calendar or prayerbook in the Lithuanian language. Cf. Fabian S. Kemesis, *Co-operation among the Lithuanians in the United States of America* (Washington, D. C., 1924), p. 9.

[40] M. L. Zahrobsky, *op. cit.*

[41] Cf. G. T. Flom, *op. cit.*, p. 72.

[42] The following may be considered typical of many prosperous Norwegian farmers in the Northwest. "His thoughts went out; they went far back into the

Class distinctions in Sweden led to much discontent.[43] Peasants and laborers resented the condescending attitude of the gentry who held the high positions in every community. The reaction to the homeland situation is presented by an emigrant of 1881.

If I should go to Sweden now and enter your office, I should hold my cap or hat in hand and bow and scrape and call a plain bookkeeper "my lord," etc., while here in America a worker and an officer are regarded as equals. Why even our honored President [Theodore] Roosevelt does not look upon me with contempt whether I take my hat off or not when I talk with him.[44]

Desire to escape compulsory military training has been an incentive to migration from many lands. Portuguese men in considerable numbers emigrated to avoid service in the army. Even though the economic status of the Portuguese peasant was low, he looked with disfavor upon three years in the barracks.[45] The law of 1874 which subjected all residents in Russia to military service was the immediate cause of emigration of both Mennonite and non-Mennonite colonists.[46] A Dutch immigrant wrote:

In Holland every able-bodied man is numbered. If his number is drawn . . . . he must begin serving his six years, either in the army or navy. My number was drawn just as I was most enthusiastic about my work. I felt as if my entire life was ruined, and that I had suddenly been deprived of my freedom. For some time rumors and tales of America had come to my ears, and, with the army service staring me in the face, and

past—the times he had known. His breast heaved, his beard bristled, his right hand clenched into a fist. For he remembered the lad who had stood under the stars and yearned out, yes, out. . . . . How he burned to escape, and how he was tortured because all means of escape were closed. He felt choked by all the straitened conditions in the home town. Every place he turned, a 'superior' stood in his path! The 'superior,' yes! Limbs of Satan they were. . . . . He was held down. No one cared about him, considered him no more than a worm." Quoted by Sigrid Moe in *The Norwegian-American Novel,* unpublished dissertation, University of Chicago.

[43] Cf. F. E. Janson, *op. cit.,* pp. 19, 60–61.

[44] *Emigrationsutredningens Bilaga,* VII, p. 178. "Here we have rich men; here we have learned men, here we have smart men; here we have work bosses, who sometimes abuse us—but *lords* we have none." *Ibid.,* p. 144.

[45] Donald R. Taft, *Two Portuguese Communities* (New York, 1923), p. 94.

[46] Cf. Cornelius C. Janzen, *Americanization of the German-Russian Mennonites in Central Kansas,* unpublished dissertation, University of Kansas; *Kansas Historical Collections,* XI (1909–1910), 489–91.

being young and adventurous, it did not take me long to decide to migrate to America.[47] I did not come steerage, but bought a third class passage.[48]

Two to three years in the army, in the prime of life, was distasteful; that stood in the way of a satisfactory vocational adjustment.[49] A Swedish immigrant shows how military service has an economic bearing: "The poor, unfortunate peasants can not without almost unlimited sacrifices bear this burden, for they must not only bear the burden of increased taxes, but it so happens that when one most needs his sons at home they must go off to training."[50] The result is that the United States has gained a large number[51] of the most enterprising.[52] To be sure, passage money from the United States and cheap travel made it easier for the less ambitious to go.

[47] According to Stephenson, "It was not so much that the average young man was unwilling to serve his country, but rather that he rebelled against the haughty and starchy military caste." *The Religious Aspects of Swedish Immigration* (1932), p. 439. Quoted by permission of the publisher, The University of Minnesota Press, Minneapolis, Minn.

[48] *Unpublished life history*. Cf. E. Hudson and H. R. Maresh, *op. cit.*, pp. 173–74; *Emigrationsutredningens Bilaga*, VII, p. 245; *Proceedings of the State Historical Society of Wisconsin*, 1901, p. 159; *Ibid.*, 1907, p. 265; *Wisconsin Magazine of History*, VIII (1925), 395–97; W. Halich, *op. cit.*, p. 17.

[49] Cf. Marcus E. Ravage, *An American in the Making* (New York, 1917), p. 49.

[50] *Emigrationsutredningens Bilaga*, VII, p. 191.

[51] "In confirmation of the statement, made editorially in 1903 by an influential paper, that the cause of the great increase of emigration was the extension of the period of military service, may be cited the upward trend of emigration following the enactment of such legislation in 1885, 1892, and 1901. Although in most cases application for permission to emigrate by men of military age was a mere formality, it is significant that among the emigrants the number of young men of the age just previous to that of eligibility to service was disproportionately large. Moreover, the parish records bear witness that many departed without even the formality of making application for permission. . . . The question most frequently asked at the Gothenburg Bureau of the National Society Against Emigration by visiting Swedish-Americans was: 'If we decide to stay, will we be exempted from military service?' Most of them declared that they would return to the United States rather than submit to military service." G. M. Stephenson, *Religious Aspects of Swedish Immigration* (1932), pp. 440–41. Quoted by permission of the publisher, The University of Minnesota Press, Minneapolis, Minn.

Pastor Carl W. Andeer of Sorunda, Sweden, superintendent of the Augustana Synod Immigrant Home in Boston from 1900 to 1905, stated that there would sometimes be between seven and eight hundred men leaving Sweden on a single boat to escape military service. *Ibid.*, p. 441. Cf. also p. 439.

[52] Cf. F. E. Janson, *op. cit.*, p. 19.

CHAPTER II

CAUSES OF IMMIGRATION
(*Continued*)

The economic factor. The causes of immigration are complex. Religious, political and various social factors cannot be ignored, but a careful analysis makes it evident that the economic component is undoubtedly the most important; the majority of the immigrants came in order to get a better living.[1] The religious and political aspects bulked larger in the "old" immigration than in the "new." At times and in certain areas, economic discontent was accentuated by religious and political unrest. According to the *Reports of the Immigration Commission*,[2] "Immigration from Europe is not now (1910) an absolute economic necessity and, as a rule, those who emigrate to the United States are impelled by a desire for betterment rather than by the necessity of escaping intolerable conditions." [3] In the words of Emily G. Balch, "Given an open sluiceway,

[1] "While the grounds of emigration are in the main economic, it is a mistake to suppose that poverty is its cause in the sense that the greater the poverty of a man or district the greater the impulse to emigration. Poverty, especially settled poverty, to which people have adjusted themselves and which finds expression in a low standard of living and perhaps in physical deterioration is not an initiating force. Rather, it means stagnation and lack of any margin of energy for new undertakings.

"It is when the habitual balance of family budgets is disturbed that a sense of poverty incites to emigration. The misadjustment may be due to a cutting down of income by some disaster or it may be due to an increase of wants. The result is the same. And this awakening of new wants is a characteristic of our time, affecting one backward and lethargic region after another. It is extremely contagious and the news that it is anywhere possible to earn more and to live better calls slumbering forces of energy and unrest into sudden life. Emigration will then result if there is any opening which promises any improved circumstances." E. G. Balch, *op. cit.*, p. 50.

A fairly well-to-do Swiss family migrated to Wisconsin because the homeland did not offer an assured economic future to the children. *Wisconsin Magazine of History*, XIX (1935–1936), 190.

[2] Vol. I, p. 25.

[3] "The pioneers of this country may have come here in pursuit of spiritual liberty only. Tens of thousands, hundreds of thousands, may have come here because of love of adventure only. But the great bulk of the population here have come to better their material circumstances, because of work that could be obtained here quicker than in the home country, because of land that could be got cheaper than elsewhere and worked to greater advantage. . . . . The subconscious motto of life

men are bound to pour to the place where land, grain, and meat cost least in terms of hours of energy."[4]

But to consider the economic phase merely from the point of view of ability to command the necessities of life or even some luxuries is not sufficient. A bank account can do more; it can purchase social status. An Italian immigrant recalls his mother's anticipation of improved status in the home community when his father would return from America laden with riches.[5] "She would tell me how we would have a house, which I always desired, and two pigs and how our neighbors would all respect us, and the *signori* in the town would even deign to talk to us sometimes."

Miss Balch recounts the improved status of an emigrant girl who, after her return to Croatia, bought back the ancestral plot of ground.

> Many girls are very fortunate in America. For instance this very day a family is coming home. The wife was poor and ill-favored. Relatives sent her money for the journey to America and there she married a poor and very humble sort of man. By work and saving they have got together $6,000 in thirteen years. And they have six children and with them are now returning. In those days she was poor, ridiculed, alone; now she is well-to-do, respected, the mother of a family. The women are full of curiosity about her. At noon they were all in the street in hopes of seeing her but in vain. She and her family are staying in Fiume and will come tonight, perhaps. My housekeeper is her godmother and so awaits her happy godchild with much pleasure for she is to offer her, for purchase, a large meadow which once belonged to the parents of her godchild, but which they were obliged to sell. I think that would be a very pleasant feeling, to be able to buy back again a piece of land lost in one's father's time, and to let the happy grandchildren jump and play about where once the poor grandfather worked and whence misfortune drove him away to die.[6]

of most of the people is *ubi bene, ibi patria;* where it is well, there is my fatherland." K. Bercovici, *op. cit.*, pp. 5–6.

[4] E. G. Balch, *op. cit.*, p. 54.

[5] From Pascal D'Angelo, *A Son of Italy* (New York, 1924), p. 50. By permission of The Macmillan Company, publishers. One immigrant said, "Each one hoped to get rich, return to Hungary, buy much land and live like a gentleman." S. C. Newman, *Immigrant Adjustment of the Hungarians in Lorain, Ohio,* unpublished dissertation, Oberlin College, 1934. Cf. D. R. Taft, *op. cit.*, p. 95.

[6] E. G. Balch, *op. cit.*, p. 185.

Status and class distinction mean more in the older European countries than in America and, as a result, great sacrifices are made to gain standing in the community. Miss Balch describes the struggle in Moravia:

> A peasant in this village commonly owns three horses and a peasant's social standing is largely measured by his stock. A "horse peasant" so outranks an "ox peasant," I was told elsewhere, that a man often keeps a pair of horses at an economic loss for the sake of the prestige.[7]

To win status in the home community many immigrants endure grinding hardships in America. Schiavo says of the Italians:

> On arriving in the new country, they swear to impose upon themselves all sorts of sacrifices, by limiting their personal expenses to the minimum in order to hasten the realization of the dream of a happy and moneyed return. Therefore, if their way of living in the crowded tenement house of the American cities has been found objectionable, it is to be ascribed to this proposed economy, which is carried to the extreme limit of the imaginable.[8]

We may now consider briefly the conditions in some of the countries which sent immigrants to America.

1. *Conditions in England.* A number of factors in England had an economic bearing and as such exerted an influence upon emigration to the United States.

(a) *Population pressure.* In certain areas of England the population increased as much as 15 per cent in a decade while there was no corresponding industrial expansion to absorb the surplus man power. Inevitably this decreased wages and the attendant suffering was a driving force in the emigration movement.[9]

(b) *Agricultural conditions.* In the early years of the nineteenth century the lot of the agricultural laborer came to be less and less desirable. With an oversupply of workers, wages dropped to a low level. The gradual spread of enclosures so the worker had no common lands on which to keep a cow, some chickens and geese,

[7] *Ibid.*, p. 41.

[8] Giovanni E. Schiavo, *The Italians in Chicago* (New York, 1928), p. 42. Quoted from *Hull House Maps and Papers.*

[9] Cf. Stanley C. Johnson, *History of Emigration from the United Kingdom* (London, 1913), p. 44.

reduced still further the standard of living. Moreover, the introduction of certain farm machinery lowered the demand for labor. Consolidation brought a gradual increase in size of farms and coincident with this the landlords raised rentals. These conditions resulted in a deep agricultural slump lasting from 1816 to 1822. In the beginning of the thirties another depression aggravated the situation and this led to a heavy emigration of farm laborers. Furthermore, the practice of converting farm lands into sheep pasturage forced large numbers out of the agricultural areas and in the year 1801 thousands sailed for America.[10]

(c) *The Poor Law*. Prior to the amendment of the Poor Law in 1834, the inadequate wages of farm workers were supplemented by parish funds. Landlords then evicted tenants who were likely to seek assistance, in order to escape taxes that would be assessed against their lands for poor relief. These ejected families gravitated into the nearby open villages where the small farmers were taxed heavily for their support. Because of this, many parishes raised funds to send the charity seekers to America.[11]

(d) *Factory system*. The beginnings of large-scale emigration from England is coincident with the rise of the factory system. Under the new order, impersonal relations developed and conflicts between laborer and employer resulted. As factory-made goods were poured into the world market, fluctuations in trade brought periods of unemployment. As machinery was developed, skilled hand-workers were often thrown out of work. Women and children could operate the machines and thus wages were forced down.[12]

(e) *Conditions in other lands which affected England*. Between 1825 and 1830 the Irish, who were passing through a period of acute depression, crossed the Channel and flooded the industries of England with cheaper labor. As a result of this immigration, wages in one district fell nearly 50 per cent in eight years.

During the Napoleonic Wars England made great gains in the

[10] Cf. S. C. Johnson, *op. cit.*, pp. 44–47.

[11] Cf. G. M. Stephenson, *A History of American Immigration,* p. 16; S. C. Johnson, *op. cit.*, pp. 41, 46–47.

[12] Cf. G. M. Stephenson, *A History of American Immigration,* pp. 12–13; S. C. Johnson, *op. cit.*, pp. 53–57.

industrial field but, with the cessation of hostilities, other European countries began to develop manufactures and thus many trades suffered from unemployment between 1836 and 1845.[13]

(f) *Results*. These conditions brought discontent and many looked to America for relief. Samuel Gompers wrote of this disquietude as it appeared in his boyhood. His father was a cigar-maker. He himself had to begin work at the age of ten because earning a livelihood was becoming increasingly difficult as expenses mounted with the growing family. Meantime they heard more and more about the United States, while London seemed utterly unresponsive to all efforts to improve their condition.[14] According to Gompers, the English wage earners used to sing:

> To the west, to the west, to the land of the free,
> Where the mighty Missouri rolls down to the sea;
> Where a man is a man if he's willing to toil,
> And the humblest may gather the fruits of the soil.
> Where children are blessings and he who hath most
> Has aid for his fortune and riches to boast.
> Where the young may exult and the aged may rest,
> Away! far away, let us hope for the best
> And build up a home in the land of the west.[15]

Many, then, turned to emigration as the only escape from misery, and the human stream which flowed westward across the Atlantic swelled to large volume.

2. *Conditions in Ireland*. The lot of the Irish in the nineteenth century was an unhappy one. Dissatisfaction with governmental policies brought insurrections and riots which were stamped out by harsh measures. Restraints on trade and industry made it difficult to earn a livelihood. Absentee landlordism and the movement for consolidation of holdings led to the eviction of large numbers from their farm plots. These various factors combined to reduce the peasants to such dire poverty that they barely existed.[16] Then, to

[13] Cf. S. C. Johnson, *op. cit.*, pp. 54, 57.

[14] Cf. *Seventy Years of Life and Labor* (New York, 1925), Vol. I, pp. 18–21.

[15] *Ibid.*, p. 19. Andrew Carnegie told Gompers that this song inspired his father to leave Scotland for America. Carnegie refers to the song in his *Autobiography* (Boston, 1920), p. 25.

[16] An Irish immigrant who landed in America in 1888 wrote of his childhood. "It was not an unusual sight to see the children of our neighborhood scratching the offal

cap the climax, came the potato famine of 1847. With a dense population [17] and limited industrial opportunities Ireland had become a one-crop country in which the potato was the staple article of food.[18] Starvation and death stalked through the land and fear of a like fate led thousands to leave their country. An exodus commenced then which has never been paralleled in the history of emigration.[19] More than one and one half million people left Ireland for North America between January 1, 1847, and December 31, 1854, of whom a vast majority made the United States their new home.[20]

One must, however, speak guardedly of the "potato famine." The impression is usually given that the famine of 1845 was the only one. There had been others, one as early as 1728, and much the same features—disease, death, thinning of population, and consequent reallotment of land—appeared in all of them. Yet there had been comparatively few departures. The Irish, with a deep attachment to the soil, hesitated to leave—they stayed and died. Furthermore, shipping facilities were inadequate and many could not go away even though they wished to do so. Gradually, however, changes came. Ocean transport was improved and cheap-

in the dunghills and the gutterways for scraps of meat, vegetables and refuse. Many times I have done it myself." He wrote about the poverty of his family and about going to bed hungry many times. Still he said: "If there was any misery in my life at this time, I neither knew nor felt it. I was living the life of the average boy of my neighborhood, and had nothing to complain of. Of course, I was in a chronic condition of hunger, but so was every other boy in the alley and on the street." From *From the Bottom Up* by Alexander F. Irvine, copyright, 1909, 1910, by Doubleday, Doran and Company, Inc., New York, pp. 3, 8. Cf. E. Abbott, *op. cit.*, pp. 68–72.

[17] In 1821 the density of population in Ireland was greater than in any other European country. W. F. Adams, *op. cit.*, p. 4.

[18] "From 1815 to 1845 the cotter relied almost wholly upon his potato patch for subsistence, and his holding was rarely used for any other purpose than the raising of potatoes for himself, his family, and his pig. The pig was his one regular source of income, and as such an important figure in Irish economy. The old saying 'the pig pays the rent' was an exaggeration, however. The price of pork on the hoof remained fairly low throughout most of the period after 1815, and though the animal usually paid a part of the rent he could not pay it all, and in lean years did so only at the expense of hunger and almost starvation for his owner." *Ibid.*, p. 18.

[19] S. C. Johnson, *op. cit.*, p. 50.

[20] It is interesting to note that while the British endeavored to attract their subjects to other parts of the Empire, the Irish have shown a disinclination to settle in any of the possessions. Furthermore, while the English are rather self-satisfied and slow to become naturalized in the United States, the Irish do not hesitate in renouncing their allegiance to Great Britain.

ened. Inducements were offered to prospective immigrants and favorable reports from Irish in America turned the scales in favor of emigration when two successive crop failures brought distress again.[21]

3. *Conditions in Scotland.* The emigration from Scotland was smaller than from England and Ireland, but economic conditions led many to embark for North America. The conversion of large tillable areas into sheep pastures, the depression in agriculture, and the collapse of the kelp industry and other industries brought distress to large numbers. Andrew Carnegie [22] recalled the hard times in Scotland. There was much agitation and denunciation of monarchical and aristocratic government. With the introduction of steam machinery, trade grew worse for the small manufacturers. When relatives in Pittsburgh sent a favorable report concerning conditions in America to Carnegie's father, he left Scotland in 1848.

4. *Conditions in the Scandinavian countries.* At different times various factors induced Scandinavians to emigrate. Indian corn and tobacco were articles of commerce which attracted Swedes to the shores of the Delaware. Trade, however, soon gave way to religion, but at no time did the latter constitute a primary cause. Economic pressure proved to be the most potent factor in the exodus. Between 1866 and 1870, a financial depression led to heavy migration from Norway.[23] Among other things,

> Lower class farmers were caught, too, in the reaction of the railroad building of 1865–1869. Extended railroad construction, much inflation of property values and constantly increasing loans met the natural check. Norway found herself too small a country, too restricted in resources, to keep up the pace she had set, and the smaller farmer felt the reaction. So poverty and dissatisfaction with the office-holding class drove the Norwegians to America.[24]

[21] Cf. W. F. Adams, *op. cit.; American Historical Review,* XXXIII (April, 1928), 579–92.

[22] *Op. cit.,* pp. 9–19, 25.

[23] Cf. G. T. Flom, *op. cit.,* pp. 66–69; O. M. Norlie, *op. cit.,* p. 106.

[24] Alfred O. Fonkalsrud, *The Scandinavian-American* (Minneapolis, 1915), pp. 35–36. A good picture of the hard economic struggle in Norway is found in Johan Bojer, *The Emigrants* (New York, 1925), pp. 39–49.

The hope of larger returns for one's labor was the mainspring in the emigration from Sweden. Other factors entered in, but had the economic situation been satisfactory these other annoyances would probably have been endured.[25] Periods of economic distress, crop failures,[26] unemployment, low wages, and the difficulty of securing loans, linked with the demand for labor at higher wages in America, and the attraction of the millions of acres of cheap virgin land fed the "America fever" which swept parish after parish. "Going to America was not an 'industry'; it was a contagious disease." [27]

5. *Conditions in Portugal.* According to Donald R. Taft, the forces attracting the Portuguese to the United States seemed to be chiefly economic. They did not seek religious freedom, political liberty, or educational opportunity. Doubtless, the glamor of America allured them in some measure, but, in the main, they sought the United States because of better opportunities in industrial employment or in independent farming, while over-population and mistaken politico-economic governmental policies at home drove them from behind.[28]

6. *Conditions in Italy.* The majority of our Italian immigrants have come from southern Italy where centuries of misrule and oppression reduced the peasant population to a state of abject poverty. Prior to the wars of liberation which resulted in an united

[25] A Swede who emigrated in 1881, wrote: "When I was nine my parents moved to Stockholm. . . . . What I remember from this time is that I both froze and starved. At twelve I began to haul wood and hay to Stockholm. This work ought to have brought in enough so that I need not have starved, but many times we children had to go to bed hungry. Hope it will soon be a reality, this Sweden of dreams and promises, which is promised in the newspapers. I believe and know to a certainty that thousands of emigrants longingly await the hour of its birth. But from the Sweden that is, O Lord God, deliver me!" *Emigrationsutredningens Bilaga,* VII, p. 163.

[26] Cf. G. M. Stephenson, *Religious Aspects of Swedish Immigration* (1932), p. 103. According to one report, "If the emigration from this region at the close of the Civil War seemed like an exodus, in 1868 it was a stampede. . . . . From April to September, 1868, rain fell only two or three times and then for only two or three hours in all. Everything was scorched by the sizzling heat; trees were burned black and died. The lean cows roamed at large. Houses and farms were deserted. The unripe rye was chopped up, dried in ovens, ground into flour, and made into bread. When even this scanty fare was denied, the people ate grass." G. M. Stephenson, *John Lind of Minnesota* (1935), p. 6. Quoted by permission of the publisher, The University of Minnesota Press, Minneapolis, Minn.

[27] G. M. Stephenson, *A History of American Immigration,* p. 31.

[28] D. R. Taft, *op. cit.,* pp. 95–96.

and independent Italy, the rulers paid not the slightest attention to the welfare of the people. Absentee landlords, whose holdings dated back to feudal times, together with the Roman Church, made it exceedingly difficult for the peasants to wring a bare existence from the soil. In the summer when fruits and vegetables were abundant the peasant did not face actual hunger, but in the winter one meal a day was the rule in many a peasant home. In addition to the high rents and low wages, the church made heavy demands on the income, and, if there was anything left, it was taken by the tax collector.

> Italy entered the world of nations a poor country, with all the needs but few of the resources of a modern European state. She has made rapid strides . . . . in creating a first-class army and navy, building thousands of miles of railroads, in matters of public health, in education, in encouraging art, music, and physical training, but all these require vast sums of money, and these she has raised by an established and minute system of taxation which Professor Villari calls "Progressive taxation, topsy-turvy—the less a man has the more he pays." On the theory that each must do his share equally, all necessities are taxed and all luxuries exempted. . . . . The rich landlord pays no tax on his riding horses, but the poor peasant is taxed for his donkey, his necessary beast of burden. Works of art, are, of course, exempt, while the peasant must pay a tax on everything he raises and everything he buys. Under such circumstances it is almost impossible to save and to rise in the world.[29]

Probably the economic factor has bulked larger in emigration from Italy than from any other European land. The country has been densely populated and the resources have not been sufficient, or at least not adequately developed, to support a large and growing population. The emigration has been well-nigh an expulsion.[30]

The Italian knew that his life in the new world would not be an easy one, "but the desire to change his economic status was by far much stronger than any obstacle that he was to overcome." [31] Health conditions also have been an important consideration in

[29] Antonio Mangano, *Sons of Italy* (New York, 1917), pp. 99–100.

[30] Cf. Robert F. Foerster, *Italian Emigration of Our Times* (Cambridge, 1919), pp. 47–48; Federal Writers' Project, *Italians in New York* (New York, 1938), pp. 3–4.

[31] G. E. Schiavo, *op. cit.*, p. 22.

Italy, but even this had a decided economic bearing. According to Francesco S. Nitti,

> The territory of Italy is very small, but it is rendered still smaller. . . . . The fertile plain in many places is . . . . rendered unproductive by the malaria. Two millions of Italians . . . . are ill of the malaria every year, and agriculture is consequently often rendered impossible in those places where it would produce most. The scarce territory becomes still more limited.[32]

7. *Conditions in Greece.* "It may be said without exaggeration that the economic factor [33] is the determining cause of all emigration from Greece." [34] But conditions differ widely from those in Ireland, Italy, Russia, and other countries. There is little abject poverty in Greece. The land is fertile and there is no want of the actual necessities of life. But Greece is backward industrially and wages are low. Hence the Greek came because he could earn more money in the United States. Prior to 1891, the immigration from Greece was very light, but at that time there was a sudden increase. This was due to an industrial depression which came when the all-important currant industry failed and disorganized an industrial system that was lacking in diversification.[35]

8. *Conditions in Russia.* In the main, religious discriminations were responsible for the departure of the Jews from Russia, but even this had economic consequences. The Jews were excluded from the soil and were thus forced to become city dwellers. Since they were restricted in their residence to certain areas, they could not locate where they might carry on their urban occupations to the greatest advantage. There were severe handicaps against them in the professions. When the government took over the railways, Jewish employees of all grades were dismissed. When the sale of intoxicants became a state monopoly, many thousands of Jews lost their means of livelihood.

[32] Quoted in *Reports of the Immigration Commission,* Vol. IV, p. 152.

[33] Cf. Henry Pratt Fairchild, *Greek Immigration to the United States* (New Haven, 1911), pp. 59–60.

[34] *Reports of the Immigration Commission,* Vol. IV, p. 401.

[35] Thomas Burgess, *The Greeks in America* (Boston, 1913), p. 17.

As a result of these restrictions, distressing economic conditions prevail among the Hebrews in many towns and cities, and when to this is added the occasional outbreaks against them, resulting in the destruction of life and property, there is a double cause for emigration. Undoubtedly the anti-Jewish outbreaks have been the direct cause of a considerable part of the Hebrew emigration from Russia, but on the other hand, the movement closely resembles the emigration from other European countries, which is almost entirely the result of economic conditions in such countries and in the United States. This is particularly noticeable in the movement following the depression of 1907–1908 in the United States. In 1907 the immigration of Hebrews from Russia to the United States was 114,932, but in common with practically all immigrant peoples, there was a great decrease in the two following years.[36]

The chief force behind the exodus of peasants from western Russia has been economic necessity. Not one but several conditions conspired to make their situation unsatisfactory. Since there were no industries to absorb the increase in population, an unduly large number were dependent on the soil. Antiquated methods of farming brought relatively meager returns from the small holdings. Consequently, in certain densely populated areas, the means of support were insufficient. Emigration either to Siberia or to the United States, therefore, became highly desirable.[37]

9. *Conditions in other countries*. The Dutch immigrants of 1847 reacted against religious oppression, but this alone would not have caused them to emigrate; desire to better their economic state was a powerful influence.[38] A bitter struggle for existence was the prime reason impelling many to leave Finland.[39] Likewise a Swiss colony settled in Wisconsin because the mountain sides of Switzerland begrudged them a satisfactory livelihood.[40]

[36] *Reports of the Immigration Commission,* Vol. IV, p. 272. Cf. Harry Jerome, *Migration and Business Cycles* (Washington, 1926), for the cyclical fluctuations in the current of migration.

[37] *Reports of the Immigration Commission,* Vol. IV, pp. 265–71.

[38] A. J. Pieters, *op. cit.,* p. 7. Cf. G. M. Stephenson, *A History of American Immigration,* p. 55.

[39] Eugene Van Cleef, *Finland—The Republic Farthest North* (Columbus, Ohio, 1929), p. 190. Cf. John Wargelin, *The Americanization of the Finns* (Hancock, Michigan, 1924).

[40] *Proceedings of the State Historical Society of Wisconsin,* 1811–1879, pp. 413–17.

The religious motive brought immigrants from Germany in the early years. Between 1815 and 1852 a considerable number of political refugees came to our shores. After 1852, however, when the movement assumed the nature of a stampede, the economic pressure far outweighed all others.[41]

Religious and political causes were important in Bohemian immigration, but with a large number the desire to improve their economic condition was the final determinant.[42] Publication in the Bohemian newspapers of highly colored reports about the discovery of gold in California drew approximately 25,000 Bohemians to the United States.

[41] Cf. A. B. Faust, *op. cit.*, Vol. I, pp. 582–91.

[42] E. Hudson and H. R. Maresh, *op. cit.*, p. 123; Robert I. Kutak, *A Bohemian-American Village* (Louisville, 1933), pp. 8–11; Thomas Čapek, *The Čechs in America* (Boston, 1920), pp. 28–29, 33–34; Willa Cather, *My Antonia* (Boston, 1926), pp. 102–03; *Proceedings of the State Historical Society of Wisconsin,* 1901, pp. 148, 159. For other groups see Joseph S. Roucek, "Lithuanian Immigrants in America," *American Journal of Sociology,* XLI (January, 1936), 447–48; J. S. Roucek, "The Yugoslav Immigrants in America," *ibid.,* XL (March, 1935), 602; J. A. Saathoff, *The Eastfriesians,* unpublished dissertation, State University of Iowa; George Adam Smith, *Syria and the Holy Land* (New York, 1918), pp. 35–41; Daniel J. Williams, *The Welsh of Columbus, Ohio* (Oshkosh, Wisconsin, 1913); W. Halich, *op. cit.*, p. 15.

CHAPTER III

CAUSES OF IMMIGRATION
(*Concluded*)

In the preceding chapters the religious, social, political, and economic circumstances in the homelands which functioned as causes in emigration were considered. These conditions, however, were balanced against those on the other side of the Atlantic. Hope of a better lot in a new land sharpened dissatisfaction with things in the home village. This chapter will treat more specifically the attractions of America.

B. Stimulations from America

General information. While the state of affairs in the homeland was such as to create unrest and act as an expulsive force, many allurements were pulling in the direction of America. Information was secured from various sources. Some first learned about America from their school geographies. Many read every available book. America was the main topic of conversation in homes and everywhere. Carl Schurz reminisces:

> Things American were eagerly discussed by my father and uncles. I heard for the first time of that immeasurable country . . . . , of that young republic where the people were free, without kings, without counts, without military service, and, as was believed in Liblar, without taxes. Everything about America that could be procured was eagerly read. . . . .
>
> The men in our family circle revelled in the log-cabin romance . . . . and it wanted but little to induce the men . . . . to try their fortunes in the New World. Although the resolution was not at the time carried out, America has always remained a favorite topic of conversation. Later every member of my family did emigrate.[1]

[1] From *The Reminiscences of Carl Schurz,* by Carl Schurz, copyright, 1907, by Doubleday, Doran and Company, Inc., New York, Vol. I, p. 29. Cf. E. Abbott, *op. cit.*, pp. 90–91, 129–72.

In like vein an Italian concurs:

My father's brother was very ambitious and at the same time very dissatisfied with conditions as they were. He used to go into the village quite frequently and listen to the talk at the saloons and inns. At these places there was much talk of America and its wonderful opportunities. The thought of coming to America was with him for some time and finally one day he surprised us by his decision that he and a group of other men were leaving within the week for America.[2]

The returned emigrant. The emigrant returning to his native heath has been a great promoter of emigration.[3] He was a conspicuous figure in the home community.[4] He wore American clothes, had new ideas which he expressed freely, did not bow and scrape before superiors,[5] but most important of all was the American money which jingled in his pockets. He boasted about his success and well-being in his adopted country and as he dangled his heavy gold watch-chain he advertised American prosperity in terms that could not be misunderstood. The young man who had prospered in the new world returned to his home where he became a missionary of a new gospel. As he moved leisurely about the old village, he spoke words of wisdom to his admiring listeners. The appearance and bearing of the returned emigrant were irresistible.[6] Andreas Ueland recalls the contagion spread by one of these visitors.

[2] Unpublished life history.

[3] Cf. *From the Bottom Up,* by Alexander F. Irvine, New York, 1914, p. 9. Cf. George M. Stephenson, *John Lind of Minnesota* (Minneapolis, 1935), pp. 5–6. D. J. Williams, *op. cit.,* pp. 46–47; M. Zelditch, *op. cit.;* Hamilton Holt, *The Life Stories of Undistinguished Americans* (New York, 1906), pp. 82–83; Bartalan Barna, "From Hungarian Banker to American Pastry Merchant," *World's Work,* XLI (January, 1921), 207; W. Halich, *op. cit.,* pp. 15–17.

[4] In Italy they jestfully call the returned immigrant "an American." He is a marked man. He wears an American suit, hat, and shoes, and smokes an American pipe. But the greatest change in him is the fact that he has money—more than he ever had before. He advertises the good fortune that awaits the seeker in the new world. Cf. Stefana Miele, "Why and How I Became an American," *World's Work,* XLI (January, 1921), 204.

[5] "He was a rash man, indeed, who would refuse to remove his hat upon meeting a pastor—this was a luxury in which only a reckless returned immigrant would indulge in order to advertise the emancipation that citizenship in the American republic had conferred upon him." G. M. Stephenson, *The Religious Aspects of Swedish Immigration* (1932), p. 3. Quoted by permission of the publisher, The University of Minnesota Press, Minneapolis, Minn.

[6] Bojer gives an excellent description of a Norwegian emigrant who returned to his native village. *Op. cit.,* pp. 23–24.

He infected half the population in that district with what was called the America fever and I who was then the most susceptible caught the fever in its most virulent form. No more amusement of any kind, only brooding on how to get away to America. It was like a desperate case of homesickness reversed. Mother was appealed to with all the arguments I could think of, such as that I would escape being drafted as a soldier and would surely soon return.[7]

Kendric C. Babcock recounts the influence of an emigrant who returned to Norway in 1835 after spending ten years in the United States.

Whatever may have been the results of his visit . . . . personally, they were of far-reaching importance to the emigration movement in western Norway. From near and from far . . . . people came . . . . to talk with this experienced and worldly-wise man about life in New York or in Illinois. . . . . The "America fever" contracted in conference with Slogvig and men of his kind was hard to shake off. The accounts of America given by this emigrant visitor were so satisfactory, that when he prepared to go back to the United States in 1836 a large party was ready to go with him.[8]

E. A. Steiner tells of the influence of a returned emigrant upon him. Among other things he talked about Abraham Lincoln. Since a man, whose first name was Jewish, had risen to the presidency, it seemed that there were no handicaps against Jews in America. One can imagine the effect it had upon a Jew who, even though a young boy, must have known something about the discriminations against his people.[9]

Usually, however, it was not a general report of the conditions in America that proved interesting but a concrete recital of the informant's success—the success of one of their own number. Ueland

[7] *Recollections of an Immigrant* (New York, 1929), pp. 22–23.

[8] *Op. cit.*, pp. 31–32. Cf. O. M. Norlie, *op. cit.*, p. 137; *Proceedings of the State Historical Society of Wisconsin*, 1898, p. 162. According to G. M. Stephenson, "Many of the students (of Bethel Baptist Theological Seminary) emigrated to the United States and served as pastors; some of them after serving apprenticeships in American free churches, returned to utilize their experience in Sweden and incidentally stimulated emigration." *The Religious Aspects of Swedish Immigration* (1932), p. 88. Quoted by permission of the publisher, The University of Minnesota Press, Minneapolis, Minn.

[9] Cf. Edward A. Steiner, *From Alien to Citizen* (New York, 1914), p. 22.

wrote of a Norwegian immigrant who had come into prominence in America. "The good people of Evanger were very proud of Senator Nelson,[10] as well they might be. Why, that poor little boy from their poor little parish had got to be almost president of the United States!" [11]

As a rule the immigrant who met with a modicum of success in America tended to exaggerate rather than to minimize his accomplishments in the adopted country. He compared the conditions in America to the disadvantage of the homeland.[12] Surrounded by admiring listeners the returned emigrant was tempted to stretch the truth.[13] He boasted about his success and tried to make an impression on his former cronies. Nor was it all empty show; [14] more than the big cigar in his mouth, the big ring on his finger, the big gold watch in his pocket, was the fact that the returned emigrant was unwilling to work in the fields at thirty cents a day; he was able

[10] U. S. Senator Knute Nelson of Minnesota.

[11] *Op. cit.*, p. 174.

[12] Cf. M. E. Ravage, *op. cit.*, pp. 18, 20–21, for an interesting case.

[13] A Norwegian gave the following report to his old pals in the home village: "The earth over there is so rich that you can eat it instead of cream-porridge; and when you sow oats or barley, up come sweet apples or a crop of oranges. The potatoes are as yellow as the yolk of an egg, and taste like raisins, and you can get a square meal whenever you want it for the trouble of stepping outside your door." J. Bojer, *op. cit.*, p. 55.

A returned emigrant, in the inn of an Alpine village, compared the slow ways of the natives with the speed of America: "In America the trains go so fast that they can't stop to take on passengers; they just have hooks with which they are caught as the train flies past. They have reaping machines . . . . to which a dozen horses are hitched, and the grain is cut, threshed, ground to flour and baked, in a few minutes. All you have to do is to touch a button and you can get bread or cake as you choose." Edward A. Steiner, *The Immigrant Tide, Its Ebb and Flow* (New York, 1909), pp. 63–64.

[14] According to the Immigration Commission, "a man who left a little village in Transylvania in 1904 with the proceeds of the sale of two head of cattle came back two years later with $500 and was the source of a genuine fever of emigration among his acquaintances. . . . . It is not to be wondered at that young men of spirit and ambition should want to emulate successful friends." Vol. IV, p. 58.

When the Filipinos, who had been working on the sugar plantations of Hawaii, returned to their own islands wearing silk shirts and with money with which to buy land, the homefolk saw visible signs of success and were stimulated to follow their example. The Filipinos were recruited in the Philippine Islands and their passage to Hawaii was paid by the sugar planters. But in the summer of 1927 this process was too slow and a group of Filipinos chartered a ship and came to Hawaii even though they had no assurance of work on their arrival.

Cf. F. E. Janson, *op. cit.*, p. 16, for the experiences of Swedish immigrants who returned to their native land.

to accumulate property; he had money on display; and while he dispensed information and inspiration he was often willing to back his words with loans to prospective emigrants. The living example of such prosperous men, scattered through the villages of Europe, induced a restless spirit in many neighbors and led them to emigrate to America.[15]

Letters and books written by immigrants. Letters of immigrants to home folks were effective stimuli to emigration. They brought a considerable number of Belgians,[16] Czechs,[17] East-friesians,[18] Hungarians,[19] Irish,[20] Swedes,[21] Swiss,[22] and others.[23] The Immigration Commission reached the conclusion that "it is entirely safe to assert that letters from persons who have emigrated to friends at home have been the immediate cause of . . . . the greater part of the remarkable movement from southern and eastern Europe to the United States." [24] Naturally periods of industrial depression in the United States have reversed the in-

[15] Cf. Jeremiah W. Jenks and W. Jett Lauck, *The Immigration Problem* (New York, 1926), pp. 20–21.

[16] *Collections of the State Historical Society of Wisconsin,* XIII (1895), 395.

[17] E. Hudson and H. R. Maresh, *op. cit.*

[18] J. A. Saathoff, *op. cit.*

[19] S. C. Newman, *op. cit.*

[20] "Insofar as the state of America affected Irish emigration these letters were the greatest single agency." W. F. Adams, *op. cit.*, p. 101.

[21] G. M. Stephenson, *John Lind of Minnesota* (1935), pp. 5–6; by permission of the publisher, The University of Minnesota Press, Minneapolis, Minn. Hans Mattson, *Reminiscences: The Story of an Immigrant.* (St. Paul, 1891), p. 297. "Emigration from Sweden began in earnest in the decade of the forties, when the first 'America letters' found their way back. . . . . These letters made a tremendous impression . . . . at a time when a new world . . . . was dawning in literature and in the press. Into this realm of the idealist the 'America letters' fell like leaves from the land of Canaan. They were not only read and pondered by the simple and credulous individuals to whom they were addressed, and discussed in larger groups in homes and at markets and fairs and in crowds assembled at parish churches, but they were also broadcast through the newspapers, which, unwittingly or not, infected parish after parish with the 'America fever.' The contents of these documents from another world were so thrilling and fabulous that many editors were as glad to publish them as were the recipients to have them published. The result was that the most fanciful stories were circulated about the wonderful country across the Atlantic—a land of milk and honey." George M. Stephenson, "America as the Land of Canaan," *Minnesota History,* X (September, 1929), 238. Cf. Hamilton Holt, *op. cit.*, p. 83.

[22] *Wisconsin Magazine of History,* VI (1922–1923), 317–33.

[23] E. Abbott, *op. cit.*, pp. 22–49, 75–78; *Norwegian American Studies and Records,* V, 14–29; VII, 47–52; VII, 23–57; W. Halich, *op. cit.*, pp. 15–16.

[24] *Reports of the Immigration Commission,* Vol. IV, p. 57. Cf. *Wisconsin Magazine of History,* III (1919–1920), 3.

fluence of these communications. "At such times intending emigrants are quickly informed by their friends in the United States relative to conditions of employment and a great falling off in the tide of emigration is the immediate result." [25]

According to Babcock, old settlers from Norway bear witness to the great attraction of these letters relating American experiences and telling about conditions. It is reported of one immigrant that

> he spoke in terms of high praise of American legislation, equality, and liberty, contrasting it with the extortion of the Norwegian official aristocracy. He counselled all who could to come to America. . . . . Of this and other letters . . . . , copies were made by the hundred and circulated in the Norwegian parishes and many of the early immigrants have stated that they were induced to emigrate by reading these letters. . . . .[26] These letters scattered through western Norway from 1830 to 1840, were as seed sown in good ground.[27]

The stimulus of these narratives was not restricted to the recipients because the documents usually circulated throughout the village [28] and even beyond. According to a Swedish immigrant, the accounts "were full of hope and great expectations for the future, and people came from far and near to read these letters. Copies were made and read to crowds of people upon public occasions in the surrounding country. All the information about America, then, was gained from letters." [29] Often they were printed in the local newspapers.

[25] *Reports of the Immigration Commission,* Vol. IV, p. 57.

[26] The religious factor exerted some influence in connection with immigration from the Scandinavian lands, but "What early strength it had was soon lost in a greater impetus, the subtle attraction of letters homeward bound from countrymen who had already emigrated. . . . . Reluctant to engage in required military training, the young men of the country read letters, pamphlets, and newspapers describing the glories of the new country, then embarked for America." A. O. Fonkalsrud, *op. cit.,* pp. 34–35.

[27] K. C. Babcock, *op. cit.,* p. 30. Cf. *Proceedings of the State Historical Society of Wisconsin,* 1898, p. 162; *Wisconsin Magazine of History,* IV (1920–1921), 14; XII (1912–1913), 21–22; XV (1931–1932), 356–69; XIX (1935–1936), 300.

[28] Cf. Vladimir Korolenko, *In a Strange Land* (New York, 1925), pp. 6–9; Michael Gold, *Jews Without Money* (New York, 1930), p. 100.

[29] C. J. A. Ericson, "Memories of a Swedish Immigrant," *Annals of Iowa,* VIII, No. 1, p. 2. Cf. G. T. Flom, *op. cit.,* pp. 61–62; 69–70; 80–81; O. M. Norlie, *op. cit.,* pp. 125–26; A. Cahan, *op. cit.,* p. 61; V. Korolenko, *op. cit.,* pp. 6–7, 8–9.

No great stretch of the imagination is required to picture the results of letters from America when bad political conditions in Germany produced so much unrest in the thirties of the last century. On February 17, 1834, a German immigrant wrote of his pride in being a free citizen. He invited his parents to join him in America.

There will be inconveniences for all of us to face, but if you wish to see our whole family living in the same country, a country where freedom of speech obtains, where no spies are eavesdropping, where no wretched simpletons criticise your every word and seek to detect therein a venom that might endanger the life of the state, the church, and the home, in short, if you wish to be really happy and independent then come here and become farmers in the United States. Here you will find a class of beings that think sensibly, and that still respect the man in man. Oppressive military systems and exorbitant taxation are foreign to this country. Nature has blessed this land abundantly. Here one fully enjoys what one earns, here no despots are to be feared, here the law is respected, and honest citizens do not tolerate the least infringement or interference by human authority.[30]

When a person or family had become restless, the arrival of an "America letter" quite frequently hastened a decision as was the case with these Roumanians:

In the meantime, father had letters from his brother who immigrated to Omaha, Nebraska, where he had become wealthy in taking up a homestead, upon which a town was later built. So each time a letter came we started to plan to go to America, to the land of opportunities. This was the land of adventure, freedom of religion, no military service, free to go and come, and live as you wanted to. Our plans crystallized into immediate action, upon my receiving summons from the government office to report within a short time for active duty for a three-year period in the army.[31]

[30] *Missouri Historical Review,* XIV, No. 1 (October, 1919), 230. Cf. George W. Spindler, *The Life of Karl Follen* (Chicago, 1917), pp. 84–85, for an impression of America. To the Jews in Russia, the "America letter" often brought a new hope. It brought tidings from a land "where there are no Cossacks, no kings, no oppressors. . . . . Where there is neither hunger nor suffering." B. Antin, *op. cit.,* pp. 8–9.

[31] Unpublished life history. A Swiss immigrant woman in Kansas remembers a letter her father received from his brother who had emigrated to America. When the letter arrived her father was on the roof of the house sweeping the dust off the shingles to keep the water supply from the winter's snow clean in the cistern. He threw the broom to the ground and exclaimed that the next tenant might have the privilege

In certain areas the influence of the America letters swept through the population like an epidemic. Many, carried away by the excitement, departed for America even though they were under no economic pressure; they did not want to remain behind when all their friends had left. As a result whole districts were depleted of their young folk.[32]

Letters were usually filled with glowing accounts of conditions in America. In contrast to the life of the old country, with its poverty and hardships, any slight success here meant much to them and they delighted in telling about it.[33] "We eat beef with onions and ripe cream. Of ripe cream, we drink an unbelievable amount. We consume ripe cream as freely as you eat clabber milk at home." [34] An Eastfriesian notified his kinsmen:

We are glad that we are in America and we have no desire to return to Germany. Here with a little work it is easy to earn enough to buy white bread while there it was hard to earn enough to buy black bread. This is the promised land for every German who is willing to work. Forty acres of good land may be bought for fifty dollars, land that is good as the best clay soil in Eastfriesland. I am earning ninety-six dollars the first year and will get one hundred and fifty dollars next year. Wubke (the girl) earns sixty dollars this year, and she will get eighty dollars next year. We eat meat three times a day and nice white bread.[35]

A Swede commented on the mail that came from his relatives.

They wrote letters home in the most glowing terms describing the country and the opportunities for the poor man in this New World, as it was called. These letters contained such sentences as the following:

of sweeping the roof because they were now leaving for America. Elise Dubach Isely, *Sunbonnet Days* (Caldwell, Idaho, 1935), p. 19. Cf. *The World Today,* XIV (January, 1908), 53, for the effect of a letter on a Lithuanian.

[32] Cf. F. E. Janson, *op. cit.*, p. 16.

[33] Cf. William I. Thomas and Florian Znaniecki, *The Polish Peasant in Europe and America* (New York, 1927), for letters written to relatives in Poland. A slight success receives considerable attention.

[34] Paal Morck, *Amerika-Breve Fra P. A. Smevik* (Minneapolis, 1912), p. 104. Translated from the Norwegian by W. C. Smith. According to Ueland, "letters were coming back from the poor immigrants telling how much land they had acquired and how they fared on pork, eggs, and white bread every day, instead of in Norway (as they used to say) 'one day on soup and herring and the next day on herring and soup.'" *Op. cit.*, p. 21.

[35] J. A. Saathoff, *op. cit.*

"The farmers here do not know how many chickens or how many hogs they own, as these run at large. We are allowed to go and gather all the eggs we want; likewise they let us milk their cows and keep all the milk we want. As soon as we can buy a cow it can run at large in grass two feet high! We can mow all the hay we want—all free! All our bread is white, being made from bolted wheat flour. We get two kroner (fifty-four cents) for a day's work, and in harvest time four kroner and all you want to eat! This is surely the Promised Land!" [36]

A letter from a Polish immigrant girl in Chicago is illuminating. Undoubtedly the fact that she, a scrub-girl and not a guest, used Palmer House stationery made an impression back home.

And now I write you how I am getting along. I am getting along very well, very well. I have worked in a factory and am now working in a hotel. I receive eighteen (in our money thirty-two) dollars a month, and that is very good.

If you would like it we could bring Wladzio over some day. We eat here every day what we get only for Easter in our country. We are bringing over Helena and brother now. I had $120 and I sent back $90.

I have no more to write, only we greet you from our heart, dearest Olejniczka . . . . and all our acquaintances we greet. Good-by for the present, sweet good-by.[37]

Any slight improvement in status would be reported with enthusiasm. One immigrant woman exulted that in America chickens, cows, and human beings did not have to live huddled together in mud huts. But most important was the fact that all to herself she had a room with a door and no one might enter without her permission. There, like a king in his palace, she could say to would-be entrants, "Come in" or "stay out." [38]

Very often the letters contained remittances and this money spoke eloquently.

[36] C. J. A. Ericson, *op. cit.*, p. 2. A Dutch immigrant agrees closely: "The boarding houses are wonderful. I have a room of my own, and three times a day, coffee, or tea with sugar, bread, butter, meat, fish, potatoes, greens, and now since Easter, many eggs,—beer, cider, and other drinks are here in abundance! . . . . The writer stated that he had agreed to write after he had been in America a year, but declared that he could not wait so long to tell of the blessings of the new country." A. J. Pieters, *op. cit.*, pp. 37–38.

[37] *Immigrants in America Review,* II (April, 1916), 58.

[38] Cf. *Century,* CI (November, 1920), 74.

The cottage of the recipient becomes at once the place to which the entire male population proceeds, and the letters are read and re-read until the contents can be repeated word for word. When instances of this kind have been multiplied by thousands, it is not difficult to understand what impels poor people to leave their homes.[39]

Many letters contained steamship tickets [40] for relatives or friends. It was difficult, often impossible, in southern or southeastern Europe to save enough money to purchase a steerage ticket to America, no matter how strong the desire might be. To the immigrant in the United States, however, such an amount was a comparatively small matter, and this made it possible for many to emigrate.[41]

In the same category with the "America letter" is the book written by the immigrant for circulation in the homeland. An immigrant from Sweden called attention to this stimulus: "Then I received a book to read about America and thus I caught America fever, as it is called. It was the 17th of March, 1869, when I left dear Old Sweden." [42] According to Flom, these books exerted a great influence.

The "America fever" had not yet taken hold of the people, many would not give credence to mere hearsay, but after a while a couple copies of Rierson's book about Texas came to the district. "Now we have the printed word to go by," it was said, and many of the doubters soon were converted to the orthodox faith in the land of promise beyond the great ocean. And as a result, many began to emigrate.[43]

Gottfried Duden, one of the early German immigrants to Missouri, wrote a book, *A Report of a Journey to the Western States of North America* (Elberfeld, 1829), in which he pictured life in

[39] *Reports of the Immigration Commission,* Vol. IV, p. 57. According to Hans Mattson, the large sums of money sent home each year lightened the burdens of poor relatives and friends. Because of these remittances many, who had looked forward to nothing but an old age in the poor-house in Sweden, were enabled to provide brighter futures for themselves in America. *Op. cit.,* p. 298.

[40] Cf. V. Korolenko, *op. cit.,* pp. 8–9.

[41] H. P. Fairchild quotes an interesting letter which brought steamer passage. *Op. cit.,* pp. 93–94.

[42] *Emigrationsutredningens Bilaga,* VII, p. 150.

[43] G. T. Flom, *op. cit.,* p. 87. Cf. *ibid.,* pp. 85–88.

America in contrast with conditions in Europe.[44] Thousands of Germans read the book. The political unrest and economic depression of that day had caused many Germans to look beyond the Atlantic and, now, Duden's book pointed to the trans-Mississippi regions with their opportunities. "Presently a veritable Teutonic invasion poured itself down the Ohio valley and through the gates of New Orleans to populate not only great areas of Missouri, but also, even more preferably, the non-slave states to the north." [45]

In 1842 *A Brief Historical, Statistical, and Descriptive Review of East Tennessee, United States of America, Developing its Immense Agricultural, Mining, and Manufacturing Advantages, with Remarks to Immigrants* by J. Gray Smith, a Naturalized Citizen of the United States of America, was published in London. This book described Tennessee in glowing terms. Conditions in America were in every way superior to those back home in England.

> With all these advantages in favor of America, where is the ultimate hope of the poor, forlorn, heart-broken English operative? Twenty years ago, the writer was in Lancashire, and never can he forget the distress that prevailed for years amongst the hand-loom weavers—it required no tongue to tell their tale; their image was that of famine, helpless and hopeless, the mother the picture of despair, and the children that of the miserable; their pallid countenances have been visible to him 'mid the abundance of the far West, and it requires no magic to recall them amidst the splendour of the modern Babylon;—those men must long since have gone "to their long homes, where the weary are at rest," for the canker-worm of famine and death was then upon them.[46]

Frequently, as we have seen earlier, conditions in America were pictured as rosier than they actually were.[47] Some, who met with

[44] *Missouri Historical Review,* XII, No. 1 (Oct., 1917), 1. Cf. E. Abbott, *op. cit.,* pp. 56–61.

[45] *Missouri Historical Review,* XII, No. 1 (October, 1917), 8. In 1834 a German "visited Missouri and went to Duden's place in order to see *where* and *how* that one lived, who with magic power had lured hordes of sons of Germans from their dearly beloved, but oppressed and mistreated fatherland, who with magic pen had clothed this wilderness with such a pleasing and attractive garment." *Ibid.,* p. 71.

[46] P. viii.

[47] An extreme case was recorded by Faust: "The booklet pretends to give the impressions recorded in letters of Swiss settlers located in South Carolina. . . . . The pleasures of house and home on large acreage are emphasized. The land literally flows with milk and honey—the cows roaming about on perfect pasturage all the

disillusionments, were unwilling to make admissions and write the truth. Hence, highly colored reports of salary, position, and prospects of success went back home. A waiter in a hotel would send a photograph of himself, seated in an automobile, wearing a heavy watch chain and a big, cheap ring. They would think he was rich and his two cousins would take the next boat for New York.[48]

These glowing accounts led many to expect entirely too much in America and bitter disillusionments resulted. On the other hand, the fertile imaginations of the readers in the home lands read into the documents more than the writers had intended them to mean. Many German immigrants, who met with disappointments, heaped the blame upon Duden. His accusers became so numerous that he prepared a defense in which he strongly advised against indiscreet emigration. He declared that his first book had been written for intelligent people and he regretted that he had not used hieroglyphics so that its readers would have been fewer.[49]

The powerful influence of these communications from America may be inferred from attempts in Sweden to counteract them.

At a book auction at the courthouse in the autumn of 1890 I bought a lot of books, among which I found one with the title, *The Truth about America.* I have long since forgotten the author's name, but no doubt he was one of your predecessors in the work of putting the brakes on emigration.

This book contained a mass of the most outrageous lies about America, of the same sort one may read from time to time in our society-preserving newspapers at home and which, it is believed, will scare the simple Swedes

year round, and honey being found abundantly in hollow trees. Wild turkeys are found in flocks of 500, geese—that some of the farmers possess in flocks to the number of 200—furnish choice feather beds. As for game, the bisons put their heads through the windows of the log cabins waiting to be shot; the wolves are by no means as large as the European, and can be tamed. The taste of venison in Carolina far surpasses anything in Europe, the bears are smaller and frequently seen herding with the swine. The alligator has no terrors, it is diminutive in comparison with the crocodile of the Old World, and the Indians and negroes use its tail for food. The danger of overpopulation which is the main cause for emigration in Switzerland, can never exist in Carolina. . . . .

"The book seems to have been so seductive in its effects that it called forth a reply, written perhaps under the auspices of the Town Council of Bern." A. B. Faust, *op. cit.,* Vol. 1, pp. 63–64.

[48] Cf. T. Burgess, *op. cit.,* p. 20.

[49] Cf. A. Cahan, *op. cit.,* p. 95.

as one scares little children with bugbears. It is forgotten that the average Swede has as much knowledge of American conditions as do authors and journalists. As before indicated, the book in question painted America in colors quite as black as any medieval priest could have painted the residence of Old Nick himself. It occurred to me and to others who read the book to reflect on the motives which lay back of it, and we came to the conclusion that it was first and foremost to frighten people away from emigration and secondly to make the common people contented with conditions in Sweden. How successful it was may be seen from the fact that all the farmers' sons of the village, to whom I lent the book, accompanied me to America the following year.[50]

Stories and myths. When a certain modicum of fact trickled back to the homelands, when the poor and downtrodden received reports of the successes of friends or relatives in America and when they, with their own eyes, saw the returned emigrants who had bought land and lived in, to them, almost unbounded luxury, they were ready to believe almost anything. The situation as described by an Italian immigrant was fertile soil for the growth of fantastic stories: [51]

Previously, there was no escape; but now there is. In the old days men from our highlands did go down into the marshes of Latium to harvest and earn some extra money. And there they sickened with malaria and came back ghosts of their former selves. But now there was escape from the rich land-owners, from the terrors of drouth, from the spectre of starvation in the boundless Americas out of which at times people returned with fabulous tales and thousands of liras—riches unheard of before among peasants.

Furthermore their imaginations were given rein and they spun extravagant myths about the land far across the seas. The following account by a Persian furnishes excellent material for stories that almost outstript tales from the *Arabian Nights.*

My uncle Shmuel has written marvelous things of America. The streets there are lighted by a "new night sun," so bright that one can play

[50] *Emigrationsutredningens Bilaga,* VII, p. 218. Cf. *American Historical Review,* XXXI (July, 1926), 715–17.

[51] From Pascal D'Angelo, *A Son of Italy* (New York, 1924), p. 48. By permission of The Macmillan Company, publishers.

marbles by it in the depth of night. One rides, not in carriages nor on camels or horses, but in trains of wagons that, with nothing to push or to pull them, go faster than a bullet from a gun.

The men come to hear the letter and wonder: "Can man create a sun to shine by night? Can wagons laden with men and animals move of themselves, with neither oxen nor horses to pull them?" [52]

The following account by an American-born man of Swedish parentage gives an idea of exaggerations current in Sweden in the early eighties when immigration from that country was at its height. "My mother told me that in those days stories circulated in the home village about the wonderful opportunities in America. There they could make a living easily; fat pigs, with sharp knives sticking in their sides, would run up to a person and say, 'Cut and eat.' " [53]

[52] Youell B. Mirza, "Across the World to 'Yankeedonia,' " *Asia,* XXII (April, 1922), 267. Abraham Mitrie Rihbany, an immigrant from Syria, tells of the way his imagination ran riot when he began to think about America. *A Far Journey* (Boston, 1914), pp. 165–66.

[53] That this same myth circulated widely and was potent in emigration may be inferred from a quotation from a handbook and guide for emigrants which was published in England in 1844. "It is a mistaken notion, if people suppose the hogs run about streets there, already roasted, with a fork stuck in their backs, crying, 'Come, eat me!' Here has been one great cause of failure and disappointment." J. Van der Zee, *The British in Iowa* (Iowa City, 1922), p. 22.

In Bohemia it was known that "gold in California grew on the sides of the hills like the antlers of deer; that the fences generally were made of bologna sausages, and pigs ran about ready roasted with carving knife and fork sticking in their backs, inviting all to slice off the juicy sirloin." *Wisconsin Magazine of History,* VIII (1925), 395. Many emigrants from Norway had much the same idea, which later found humorous expression in the song about Ole Bull's colony in Pennsylvania:

In Oleana, that's where I'd like to be, and not drag the chains of slavery in Norway. . . . .
In Oleana they give you land for nothing, and the grain just pops out of the ground. . . . .
The grain threshes itself in the granary while I stretch out at ease in my bunk. . . . .
And little roasted piggies rush about the streets politely inquiring if you wish for ham. . . . .
And the cows they milk and churn and make cheese just as skilfully as Else my sister. . . . .
And the calves they kill and flay themselves and turn to veal roast faster than you can take a drink. . . . .
You bet, they give you two dollars a day for carousing; and if you are good and lazy, they'll probably give you four. . . . .
And we all stalk about in velvet suits with silver buttons, smoking meerschaum pipes which the old woman fills for us. . . . .
And every last one of us plays upon the fiddle, and dances a merry polka; and that's not so bad! . . . .

An immigrant Pole records a myth which, with slight variations, was spread afar.

The stories about America, as I remember them, were mostly fantastic. For instance, all one had to do was to walk along the streets with a shovel in one's hands and gather as much money as one pleased. The streets and pavements were covered with plush rugs.[54]

In view of the vague ideas many had concerning America, flights of fancy might be expected.[55] These distorted accounts and myths, because of their very vagueness, appealed to the imagination, and, by way of comparison, the situation in the homeland became all the more intolerable. When these stories pictured the fabulous wealth accumulated by the humble cotter's son on his 160-acre farm in Wisconsin, then the small plots of land in the old village seemed even smaller than before. When these fanciful romances showed how persons of humble origin and of lowly status had risen to positions of prominence in the far-away country, then discontent

Publications of the Norwegian-American Historical Association: Studies and Records, II (1927), 11–13.

[54] Unpublished life history. Practically the same story is reported by Elizabeth Hasanovitz. "All of them were immigrants who had come to the land . . . . where people 'shovel gold' as Tina, the dark-eyed, charming little Italian had dreamed. She came over here with her father and two brothers to shovel up a lot of money and then return to Italy. . . . . They had dreamt of carrying money back with them to buy a villa and live like real decent people do." *One of Them* (Boston, 1918), p. 72.

According to an Italian immigrant, "It was said of a man that after he landed in New York and was walking down the street, he saw a five dollar gold piece but gave it a kick saying, 'If I start to pick up money now, I'll be loaded before I'll be ready to go home.' " Unpublished life history. When Michael Pupin was bound for America he heard immigrants on the ship relate stories of incredible successes of their relatives in the new land. *From Immigrant to Inventor* (New York, 1923), p. 39. A story in Roumania was to the effect that in America people could dig into the streets anywhere and find gold. The poorest ragpicker in America lived better than a Roumanian millionaire. M. Gold, *op. cit.*, p. 102, Cf. J. Bojer, *op. cit.*, p. 51.

A Norwegian immigrant song which was published December 14, 1842, contains these words: "There the horses are shod with silver, and the carriage wheels mounted with silver, too; and gold, why, that is spread all around you. All you need do is to pick it up." *Publications of the Norwegian-American Historical Association: Studies and Records,* II (1927), 6.

[55] An Irish immigrant wrote: "I remember one sturdy Irishman who spoke to me one night asking, quite seriously, how many American Indians a white man would be allowed to kill without getting into trouble in New York City." From *Fourteen Years a Sailor,* by John Kenlon, copyright, 1923, by Doubleday, Doran and Company, Inc., New York, p. 125. Cf. Jacob A. Riis, *The Making of an American* (New York, 1901), p. 23, for some interesting ideas about America.

and restlessness increased while the "America fever" grew apace.

Steamship agents. Ticket agents for the steamship companies furnished another important inducement to immigration. The steerage traffic was a lucrative one, and, as a result, the transportation companies had thousands of agents in Europe whose business it was to stimulate emigration. Nothing was left undone to create a restlessness in the peasants by setting before them the advantages and the glories of America. Circulars describing in glowing terms the promises of America were widely distributed in the Scandinavian countries.[56] A prospectus often portrayed the prosperity of settlers for some time resident in America. Letters from successful Scandinavians were frequently printed and distributed broadcast.[57] According to A. B. Faust [58] the steamship agents practiced much fraud in Germany. The "newlanders," as they were called, carried letters from acquaintances, perhaps from some one of the same village now settled in America, prosperous and anxious that his friends should share his happiness. These documents were often forged so skillfully that he whose handwriting had been imitated acknowledged it to be his own. Such practices deceived even those who were not credulous. Many of these agents were returned emigrants who had met with some success in America. Hence their words carried weight.

While the steamship agent operated for many years in northwest Europe, he developed his activities very largely in connection with the "newer" immigration.[59] The ease and comfort of recent

[56] Land companies, and even several states, coöperated with the steamship companies in this advertising in the rural press of Sweden after the Civil War. They adopted the policy of reaching the emigrant in his home where they supplied him with land maps and illustrated booklets. He was met at American ports by agents and often escorted to his destination by a guide who spoke his own language. F. E. Janson, *op. cit.*, p. 15. Cf. Harold F. Peterson, "Early Minnesota Railroads and the Quest for Settlers," *Minnesota History,* XIII (1932), 25–44.

The states of Wisconsin, Minnesota, Iowa, and Dakota carried on extensive advertising campaigns. *Wisconsin Magazine of History,* III (1919–1920), 3–29. Kansas also advertised. Alfred Bergin, *Lindsborg* (Rock Island, 1909), p. 12.

[57] G. T. Flom, *op. cit.*, p. 79.

[58] *Op cit.*, Vol. I, p. 62. Cf. H. P. Fairchild, *op. cit.*, pp. 90–92 for methods used by agents in Greece.

[59] There was no steamship agent with a sufficiently vivid imagination to tell the Pilgrim Fathers that Plymouth Rock was plastered with five pound notes, Cf. C. Hedger, *Immigrants in America,* II (July 1, 1916), 26.

travel has been an important element in the situation; emigrants could go easily to America, amass wealth and then return in comparative luxury.

Furthermore, since the transportation of steerage passengers was purely and simply a commercial undertaking, the brokers were not particularly interested in selecting settlers. In fact, selling tickets to "birds of passage" brought a more lucrative business because they traveled back and forth with the seasons—they would work in America as long as the weather permitted and then spend the winters in the mild climate of southern Europe. This insured not only west-bound but east-bound traffic as well.[60]

[60] Cf. E. Abbott, *Immigration: Documents and Case Records*, pp. 201–02.

CHAPTER IV

FIRST IMPRESSIONS OF AMERICA

The majority of immigrants to America idealized our country; here they expected all their fondest hopes and ambitions to be realized. They saw everything as desirable and beautiful; it was the land of freedom, of opportunity, and of unbounded wealth—all of which would be theirs without effort.

A. First Experiences

First reactions. Many an immigrant was thrilled at the prospects before him when, at his journey's end, he saw the Statue of Liberty. The first glimpse of the land of his dreams thus enraptured this immigrant from Ireland.

The approaches to New York harbor, to one who sees them for the first time, are like the opening of a book. It seems to unfold itself, page after page, and gradually as you get inside you are face to face with a noble panorama setting forth the wonders of God and the works of man. All the emigrants on the ship lined the sides of the vessel and noted every detail as we approached the shore. I, myself, was almost overcome with emotion at being actually in America, but my feelings were nothing compared to those of a number on board who were at last, after years of privation and suffering, rejoining those who had gone before.[1]

Likewise an immigrant from India rejoiced when he landed in San Francisco.

America at last! The seventeen days of Asiatic steerage seemed like the experience of another man the very moment the immigration authorities gave me permission to enter the United States. The reverence that I felt for this country was so great that nothing short of falling on my knees and kissing its soil would have sufficed to express my feelings.[2]

[1] From *Fourteen Years a Sailor,* by John Kenlon, copyright, 1923, by Doubleday, Doran and Company, Inc., New York, p. 127. Cf. M. Pupin, *op. cit.*, pp. 37–38.

[2] Dhan Gopal Mukerji, *Caste and Outcast* (New York, 1923), p. 165. Cf. J. A. Riis, *op. cit.*, p. 21; A. M. Rihbany, *op. cit.*, pp. 183–86; Etsu Inagaki Sugimoto, *A*

Such are the feelings of many who come. All too often, however, soon after landing on the soil which they practically worship, they meet with experiences that begin to raise doubts and questions.[3] "But Americans," wrote Mukerji, "are a strange people! No sooner did they see that I had such feelings for their country than they began to knock it out of me in a very unceremonious fashion." [4] Some who come to America with the idea that almost everything may be had for the asking, or even without asking, receive severe shocks. This Persian's dream castle was rudely crushed to earth.

No sooner have we left New York than a pleasant young man enters the car with his arms full of boxes, which he distributes to the passengers. We open our boxes and find them full of candy. This is generous America! Gratefully we begin to eat the chocolates. But in a few minutes the young man returns and asks for the boxes. When the young man finds that the candy is half eaten, he is very angry and refuses to accept the boxes and demands payment. I try to speak to him in English, but he cannot understand me. We pay for the candy. Even in America, things are not given away.[5]

Many of those influenced by highly colored reports about America were disillusioned when faced by realities. In the words of a Polish immigrant, "America, as I saw it for the first time, was disappointing. According to the stories, I expected to find wagons with golden wheels, horses with golden horseshoes." [6] Hopes were

Daughter of the Samurai (New York, 1925), pp. 160–74, 175–220; and G. W. Spindler, *op. cit.*, p. 83, for interesting reactions to America.

[3] According to Edward J. Corsi, the America of fact proves to be quite something else. "It dawns upon the immigrant with his landing at Ellis Island, chilling him to the marrow of his bones. It presents no streets paved with gold, no fortunes easily acquired, no liberty unrestrained. On the other hand, its offering is hard, incessant labor and bitter struggle. . . . . This America is variable, disappointing, not as ideal as imagined. Its impression on the newly arrived is a discouraging one. It compels him to work long hours in steel mills . . . . live segregated in mining towns, with no opportunities to learn English, to read, study, distinguish. It subjects him to injustices and misunderstandings in court . . . . continual cheating by 'banker,' 'boss,' 'lawyer,' and 'promoter.' It offers no protection from the thousands of abuses practiced on the 'ignorant foreigner.' The wonderful impression . . . . turns to a psychic disappointment at the end of a few years of work in our factories." "The Voice of the Immigrant," *The Outlook*, CXLVII (September 21, 1927), 89.

[4] *Op. cit.*, p. 165.

[5] From *Myself When Young*, by Youell B. Mirza, copyright, 1929, by Doubleday, Doran and Company, Inc., New York, pp. 230–31.

[6] Unpublished life history.

dashed for many Germans who believed that they would find a paradise in the New World and that riches would come with but little effort. "Constant work, a simple and frugal mode of living, and the all-pervading solitude are simply horrifying to them.[7] They find a strange language, different customs and manners, deceptive people. . . . . They find that the absolute condition of success, prosperity and contentment is hard work." [8] America, too, failed to fulfill this Italian's anticipations.

All the time I hear about the grand city of New York. . . . . I hear such fine words like "liberty," "democracy," "equality," "fraternity," and I like these high principles. The people say it is the country where you are your own boss, where you may receive money on your word, where there is trust and confidence, so that America looks like a blessed country . . . . and my heart develop big admiration and a great, noble sentiment for America. I arrive in New York. You think I find here my ideal? . . . . It is difficult for me to explain my disgust. The next day I feel like to come back to Italy.[9]

Mistreatment by officials. Harsh treatment by immigration officers [10] all too often dispels the newcomers' illusions about America. Abraham Cahan testified to this. In contrast to the gruff officials in his home country he had expected to find cordiality and refinement here. Their icy inhospitality, however, made them not a whit better than the Cossacks of Russia.[11] "The treatment at Ellis Island," wrote an immigrant from Switzerland, "was the most difficult to comprehend for me in my new experiences. I understood then why they called it 'the isle of tears.' " [12] An Italian immigrant concluded that the reception at the port of entry, the discomfort,

[7] O. E. Rölvaag, *Giants in the Earth* (New York, 1927), depicts this phase of the life among the Norwegian immigrants in the Dakotas. Cf. also, O. M. Norlie, *op. cit.*, p. 125.

[8] Excerpt from diary of Herman Steines, May 26, 1834, quoted in *Missouri Historical Review,* XIV (1919), 440.

[9] *Red Cross Magazine,* XIV (September, 1919), 45. Cf. George A. Linhart, *Out of the Melting Pot* (privately published, 1923), pp. 30–31; Silvio Villa, *The Unbidden Guest* (New York, 1923), pp. 130–44, especially pp. 130–31.

[10] For an excellent description of the treatment of immigrants at Ellis Island some twenty-five or more years ago, see Broughton Brandenburg, *Imported Americans* (New York, 1904), chapter 18.

[11] Cf. A. Cahan, *op. cit.*, p. 89.

[12] Unpublished life history.

and the harshness did not give the immigrant a favorable introduction to America.[13]

The treatment of immigrants is much the same be it at Ellis Island, New York, or Angel Island, San Francisco. A Chinese girl, who came from the Malay Peninsula to attend an American university encountered a trying situation on reaching San Francisco. Years later even the mention of it would fill her with indignation.

They sent me to Angel Island! What do you think of that! It hurt my pride! I felt like a prisoner! My father paid five hundred dollars gold for my passage from Singapore to San Francisco. I was a first-class passenger. It was not right to send me to Angel Island. My mission teacher went with me. It was after four o'clock in the afternoon when we got there. A man said, "You will have to stay here all night till morning, then you can see the officer." I said, "I will not stay here. I will see the officer now. Where is he?" He knew I was very angry. I wanted to go back to the Malay Straits and never come to the United States if everybody was mean like that. I went to see the officer. I walked up to him. I did not look pleasant. I was very angry. I looked proud and I said, "I want to know from you why I have been sent here. I am not a coolie." That is what I said. He made a nice speech, said it was a law to protect all Chinese girls. But I just looked at him. He let me go. But when I remember how I was sent to Angel Island, I don't need jacket, I don't need coat, I am too hot all over! [14]

Many, after leaving the immigration station, had unpleasant contacts with the police. An Italian who landed in New York without any friends slept on a bench in a park. A patrolman beat him into insensibility and took him to the police court. He found it exceedingly difficult to reconcile such brutal treatment with that which he had expected in the land of the free.[15]

Encountering unfriendliness. It is not only at the hands of the immigration officials and the police that they receive harsh treatment, but others as well act toward them in an unfriendly and

[13] Stefana Miele, "America as a Place to Make Money," *World's Work,* XLI (December, 1920), 204–05. Cf. Peter Roberts, *The New Immigration* (New York, 1912), pp. 18–48.

[14] Survey of Race Relations, 267–A.

[15] Cf. Antonio A. Arrighi, *Antonio the Galley Slave* (New York, 1911), p. 193. Cf. Constantine M. Panunzio, *The Soul of an Immigrant* (New York, 1921), pp. 73–74, for a similar experience. Also E. A. Steiner, *op. cit.*, pp. 136–65.

even cruel manner.[16] American behavior perplexed a young Hungarian:

It is rather difficult to comprehend for a newly arrived immigrant the disinterestedness with which he is regarded by Americans. It was rather shocking the distrustfulness carried all along the line, the absolute absence of showing sympathy to your neighbor. The first few months were quite disappointing.[17]

A Japanese who had come to the United States to enter one of our universities wrote of his reception.

A few days after I landed in San Francisco in the fall of 1920, I was strolling along on Market Street, sight seeing here and there. I became so interested in the way the Americans decorated their show windows. As I was watching the show windows, four Americans, two young men and two women, passed by me, when one of them said to me, "Hey, skibby, get out of my way," and pushed me purposely against the curb. Such persons are few, so I let it go without saying a word. On the following day we were again insulted and embarrassed in the same manner as before. As we were slowly strolling along the street, a passer-by in an automobile called out, "Hello, skibby-do-bo-bo, how's Togo?" I was somewhat blinded but I simply couldn't get over the insult and realized at that moment that I was in a country without ideal principles. Over and over again I have been insulted in the same manner, but I have always tried to forget it.[18]

On the other hand, many are accorded a warmth of welcome on arrival. "My reception in New York was surprisingly friendly," wrote a woman from France. "American women know how to receive friends, how to make them feel at home." [19]

[16] George A. Gordon, an immigrant from Scotland, concluded on the basis of his early experiences that "man's inhumanity to man is nowhere more potent and cruel than in the first years of an immigrant's life." *Op. cit.*, p. 138.

[17] Unpublished life history.

[18] *Survey of Race Relations.* The experience of a Chinese in Australia, where he made his first contacts with the Euro-American culture, is quite to the point. Cf. Hwuy-Ung, *A Chinaman's Opinion of Us and of His Own People* (New York, 1927), p. 14.

[19] Unpublished life history. This woman arrived shortly after the War when there was a friendly feeling toward France and her people. Immigrants from Northern Europe, in the main, receive better treatment than those from southern and southeastern Europe. Says an English woman: "We were cordially treated by the officials at Ellis Island and were shown every courtesy. My father took us with him before

Impressiveness of our material civilization. Certain aspects of the situation impress the newcomers and make them almost awe-stricken. They find practically everything in America new and different. Particularly do they marvel at the mechanical and engineering aspects of our life.[20] A Jewish immigrant remembers his first impressions.

How wonderful everything seemed to us in New York! The West Shore Hotel . . . . looked like a palace. Bananas, running water, electric lights, hansom cabs, shoe shining stands—these were some of the queer things we beheld for the first time in our lives. . . . . Back in Krementchug, there were not at that time any elevators, no gas, no running water. . . . . Yes, the contrast in our environment was so great as to make us feel that we were now in a world which was not real.[21]

Immigrants from areas of slow movement were confused by the speed and hustle in America. "The place was full of activity," observed a Puerto Rican who landed in New York. "I became nervous to see people move so fast. The horses were too big." [22] "I had never in my life seen a place that showed so many outward evidences of hustle," agreed an Irishman. "The people seemed to be actually on the run most of the time, and I thought at first that they were actually chasing each other about the streets." [23] A Hungarian thus records his first impressions:

The most interesting thing in America was the speed—the speed of automobiles in the streets, the express in the subway, and at the very landing a sort of escalator that was carrying the baggage down instead of the

the examining board. . . . . The official patted my baby sister's golden curls and said, 'Too bad we don't have more of your kind entering.' We felt welcome. We sensed a feeling of friendship." Hannibal G. Duncan, *Immigration and Assimilation* (Boston, 1933), p. 537.

[20] When Jacob Riis first saw an American woodcutter swing a "double-bitter" axe, he was filled with admiration both for the man and the axe. "I wished myself back in Copenhagen just long enough to tell the numbskulls there, who were distrustful of American tools, which were just beginning to come into the market, that they did not know what they were talking about." From *The Making of an American*, by Jacob A. Riis (New York, 1901), p. 43. By permission of The Macmillan Company, publishers.

[21] H. A. Dix, *op. cit.*, p. 14. Cf. H. G. Duncan, *op. cit.*, pp. 555, 575–76.

[22] *Survey of Race Relations*, 47–A.

[23] From *Fourteen Years a Sailor*, by John Kenlon, copyright, 1923, by Doubleday, Doran and Company, Inc., New York, p. 130.

porters. There were all sorts of machinery. The eight years preceding my coming to America were spent in small resort places, far away from large cities and my starting in New York at the American speed, punching time-clocks, riding subways, was quite a blow. No European can picture America quite as it is before seeing and working in it.[24]

Repellent force of ugliness. Urban ugliness and squalor revolt some who come to our shores. To be sure, they usually are introduced to the most undesirable sections of our cities. A group of immigrants from Holland landed in Baltimore. They, who had been accustomed to orderly, well-kept highways in city and town, were repelled when they saw chickens, hogs, and cattle running loose upon the muddy streets of this large American city.[25] The ugliness of Chicago disturbed Steiner.[26] His first walk in New York was a nightmare to Ravage.[27] To an immigrant from Finland, New York was repellent. The disorder which he observed everywhere made him homesick.[28]

Disappointment in work conditions. The majority of the immigrants come here with the expectation of working with their hands, but many have found it difficult to secure work. An Irish immigrant, who landed in New York in 1888, related his experience concerning employment.

I had come here with the usual idea that coming was the only problem —that everybody had work; that there were no poor people in this country, that there was no problem of the unemployed. I was disillusioned in the first few weeks for I tramped the streets night and day. I ran the gamut of the employment agencies and the "Help Wanted" columns of the papers. It was while looking for work that I first became acquainted with the Bowery. . . . . It was there that I first discovered the dimensions of the problem of the unemployed, and my first great surprise in the country was to find thousands of men in what I supposed to be the

[24] Unpublished life history. Cf. Hwuy-Ung, *op. cit.*, p. 24, for reaction of a Chinese to occidental speed.

[25] Cf. Jacob Van der Zee, *The Hollanders of Iowa* (Iowa City, 1912), p. 50.

[26] *From Alien to Citizen*, p. 161.

[27] *Op. cit.*, pp. 66–68, 166. After his first depressing experience, Ravage began to compare the conditions in his homeland with those he found in America. *Ibid.*, pp. 82–83.

[28] Kalle Makinen, "The Land Where a Man is Free to Work," *World's Work*, XLI (January, 1921), 274.

most wonderful Eldorado on earth, workless, and many of them homeless.[29]

When work is secured, the conditions may not be at all attractive. Many, like this Italian, had no conception of the hardships they must endure in the occupational field.

For eleven years I had worked in a jewelry shop, sitting down all day and doing very light work. When I came to America I had to work in a shoe shop doing all kinds of work, loading and unloading cars of leather, pasteboard, and cases, and wheeling coal to the furnace. My hands nice, clean, and tender became full of blisters and my body broken. America is not the same as the men in our country pictured it to us. The first two or three years it is hell and 50 per cent would walk back to their native country if they had the price and courage to face the town gossip.[30]

B. Culture Shocks

These elements which have been considered thus far are, after all, more or less external and do not cause the real problems. As immigrants with their home-land traditions come in contact with the American culture system, they experience grievous shocks. Ravage was bitterly disappointed in America. This was not necessarily due to the drab, sordid, or toilsome life of the immigrant as he saw it, but because his whole old-world soul, which had been conditioned by a deep-rooted and ancient heritage, clashed at once with the spirit of America.[31]

Cultural differences. Cultural divergences, ranging all the way from food habits to religion, oftentimes produce inner conflicts and cause embarrassments that develop sensitiveness and self-consciousness. Amusing later, but disconcerting at the time, were the initial experiences of a Greek woman with American food. At her first dinner in a hotel a tall vase, filled with what she considered to be strange, greenish-white flowers, stood in the middle of the

[29] From *From the Bottom Up,* by A. F. Irvine, copyright, 1909, 1910, by Doubleday, Doran and Company, Inc., New York, p. 82. Cf. William I. Thomas, *The Unadjusted Girl* (Boston, 1923), pp. 59–60, for the experiences of a Jewish immigrant girl. John Cournos, *Autobiography* (New York, 1935), pp. 131–35.

[30] Unpublished life history.

[31] Cf. M. E. Ravage, *op. cit.,* pp. 60–61.

table. She took one and fastened it to her dress. When she left the dining room the other diners nudged each other and stared at her. A maid, suppressing a giggle, informed her that she was not wearing a flower but the stalk of a vegetable called celery.[32] Christmas, which plays such a prominent part in our American life and which has a number of deep-rooted practices, does not have the same meaning to all immigrants. Our Christmas celebrations impelled an Oriental to say that

everything seemed such a strange combination of the spiritual and material that I was lost. The star on the tree and the thought of unselfish giving were beautiful, but little was said of either—except in church; and just beneath the star were festoons of popcorn and cranberries—things we eat. Indeed, except for the gaiety of giving and receiving gifts, most things especially belonging to the day seemed to be only the serving of certain kinds of food and the very inartistic and peculiar custom of hanging in a prominent place the garments of the lowest part of the body for the purpose of holding gifts of toys and jewelry or even candy and fruit. That was a custom difficult for a Japanese to understand.[33]

Sad experience taught a Japanese our American custom of locking doors.

One of the new experiences that I could not understand was about "key." In America the people have many keys, while in Japan few people have a key. In a Japanese family in Japan, there is one front key; the people never carry as many keys as American people. Most of the trunks or boxes and rooms are unlocked, except the official room and safety box. When I came to Los Angeles and stayed at the church, my friends and members of the church frequently advised me always to lock every room and every trunk, and the doors of the house. I could not understand why it was so necessary in such a civilized Christian country as America. Even in Japan there was no necessity to do so; and I was not so afraid of thieves as they were anxious for me. But the chance by which I learned about the key problem came. About two months after I arrived in this city, I had stolen two gold watches (value $200) and a new Eastman

[32] Demetra Vaka Brown, *A Child of the Orient* (Boston, 1914), pp. 259–61. Cf. A. M. Rihbany, *op. cit.*, pp. 200–01; Hwuy-Ung, *op. cit.*, pp. 3, 16–18, for the reaction of a Chinese after his first contact with western practices.

[33] From *A Daughter of the Samurai*, by Etsu I. Sugimoto, copyright, 1924, by Doubleday, Doran and Company, Inc., New York, pp. 208–09.

kodak ($75) from my room, because I carelessly unlocked my back door and was studying English in the front room. Then I felt that America is a "key" country as well as a country of democracy and money. Of course, "key" itself means distrust for others.[34]

Many immigrants feel a keen sense of loss as they are uprooted from their old *milieu* and transplanted to an entirely different situation.[35] Some of our practices, if followed, would lower the status of the immigrant and thus create serious mental conflicts. A Chinese girl came from Singapore to attend an American university. She was fortunate in securing a room in the home of a faculty member who had been a missionary in China. Shortly after her arrival she underwent a most trying experience when the professor took her to the cafeteria for a meal. She could not bear the idea of carrying a tray—that was a matter for servants and entirely beneath her dignity. Furthermore, she could not understand how a university professor could possibly condescend to carry a tray.

Where the cultural differences are widest, there come the greatest shocks. The north Europeans find more that is familiar, or closer to their own customs, than do those of southeastern Europe, while the Oriental, who is farther removed culturally than the European, is more disturbed by our practices. Usually the area of greatest disturbance is that of the relationships between the two sexes and the position of woman. It is here that we find an outstanding dissimilarity between the Orient and the Occident. Rihbany pointed out the reactions of illiterate Syrian peddlers to this aspect of American life. They had observed the greater individual freedom and concluded that Americans lived in complete detachment. Even within the same household each one was a law unto himself.

"Hear and I will tell you," said Abdu, especially to new arrivals from Syria, "in this country the husband and wife live each one alone. He has his room and she has hers, and, if anything the man has to mind.

[34] *Survey of Race Relations,* 69–A.

[35] The German who comes here even under the most favorable circumstances gives up much, and he should not be criticized because this loss grieves him sorely. The greatest deprivation is that he, in the fullest sense of the word, is stripped of *Deutschtum*. During the first years of residence in America, this loss is distressing. Adults feel it more or less all through the years. Cf. *Missouri Historical Review,* XIV (1919), 440.

They say that he has to knock at her door like a stranger, and she doesn't have to let him inside if it doesn't suit her. He has to say 'Shkooz me,' which means 'Forgive me'!" . . . .

"Ya, Allah [O God], what customs! Give me Syria and its submissive women." [36]

Rihbany, himself, was perplexed by the position accorded women in America. He was astonished to see the wife of a minister preside with grace, dignity, and supreme authority at the table. It appeared that his host was completely under the domination of his wife and he questioned the advisability of giving a woman so much power.[37]

A Japanese was impressed by the "lady first" in contrast to the "man first" practice of his country.

In Japan, daughters and boys are generally segregated, especially at the marriageable age. The wife respects her husband and obeys him. The man who is too kind or blindly loves his wife is called "Sainorogi" (Sai=wife; norogi=dull, blind or stupid, namely, the man who is stupid or too sweet on his wife). In America, all men seemed to me as "Sainorogi," though are they strictly so? Most of the Japanese men in America, it seemed to me, were well Americanized in "lady first" custom, but I thought it was not caused by the admiration of the American custom, but by the deficit of Japanese women and handicaps for their marriage.[38]

Likewise another Japanese on the Pacific coast encountered the "lady first" custom.

When I was riding in a street car a nicely dressed young lady got on the car hurriedly. I noticed that she was trying to get through the restless crowd which was standing at the rear end of the car. An old man in the crowd was pushed away by this lady, so the man said to her, "What are you trying to do, lady?"

"I am trying to get through, of course. What did you think I was trying to do?" was her answer.

"Woman of America talks," I said to myself.

[36] A. M. Rihbany, *op. cit.*, p. 214.

[37] *Ibid.*, pp. 259–61. Cf. Hwuy-Ung, *op. cit.*, pp. 9–10, 18–20, for the reaction of a Chinese to the position of woman in the occidental cultural system.

[38] *Survey of Race Relations*, 69–A.

Ladies were all seated in the car, but there was not a lady who was kind enough to offer a seat to the aged person.

Average American women have common sense. They do not always stay home but like outside activities as well as men. They do not hesitate to talk even about politics because they believe in equality.

A Japanese woman usually stays at home and tries to keep out of outside activities. She does not talk much because she can't.[39]

A Chinese girl from Singapore was perplexed by the American commingling of sexes.

I was very much shocked on the train from San Francisco to Los Angeles when a black man they called a porter came into the car to make down the beds and men slept in the same car! Now what do you think of that? In Malaysia, we have a compartment to ourselves. I thought this was a very strange country—this United States.[40]

Of her first visit to the beach and to a park this same girl wrote:

I nearly died of fright; I thought all those men and women were bad. Bare arms, bare legs—fat arms, fat legs! I said to my friend, "I do not like that, bare legs, bare arms in this big crowd. Take me home please. I would rather stay in my room all day than go to parks and see heads in laps, parasol up behind, men and women on grass side by side—it is shameless!" I asked my friend what she went to such a place for, and she said, "For walk and good air." I said, "I do not need walk and good air."

The use of cosmetics by women has distressed many immigrants. "What shocked me most about America," wrote a Filipino, "was the way the young women painted their lips and faces and the use of face powder in front of the public. There is no privacy in the application of paints and face powder." [41] "In Malaysia," said a Chinese girl, "only bad women use rouge but here I see good girls use it—at least, they are considered good, respectable girls." To a Polish Jewess the use of cosmetics was repulsive.

I cannot even now, on the tenth year of my living here, comprehend how it is possible for a woman with brains to paint her face—and for a

39 *Survey of Race Relations*, 352–A.
40 *Survey of Race Relations*, 267–A.
41 *Survey of Race Relations*, 291–A.

man with brains to tolerate, even enjoy it. From what I saw before I came here I thought that paint on the faces was used for two purposes: (1) by a performer on the stage, to enable the audience to see his features, and (2) by a woman who has nothing but her body to offer to the world and must, necessarily, make herself noticeable.[42]

Another offensive habit of American women is that of gum chewing. E. A. Steiner was greatly disturbed when he learned that young women in America chewed gum.[43] Chewing gum and eating candy on the street are particularly distasteful to the Japanese.

The most interesting things about America as I saw them for the first time were the "busyness" of the daily life, kissing in public, walking together, necking in the public park, eating candies and fruits on the street as they walked, and eating dinner without taking off their hats in the restaurants. These struck me the very first because such acts in Japan are considered immoral and disgraceful.[44]

Development of self-consciousness. The upshot of these various experiences is that the immigrant becomes self-conscious and reserved; he develops an uneasiness in the presence of Americans and tends to avoid them; he withdraws into himself. He begins to realize that, while he is in, he is not of, America.[45] Overcome by a feeling of desolation the immigrant's thoughts inevitably turn to the homeland. "I longed for my home," wrote a Russian Jewess, "with my devoted family. I longed for my early days surrounded with friends. I longed to be once more the ambitious 'schoolmistress' surrounded by her pupils—sweet little girls with staring eyes, questioningly fixed on their teacher."[46] Loneliness and intense yearning for France were the lot of this immigrant woman:

When I first came here, with my French attitudes, ideas, traditions, my reactions to new conditions were amusing to spectators. I knew some English, but hardly enough to understand or to make myself understood. Had it not been for my husband, I would have gone home or

[42] Unpublished life history.
[43] *From Alien to Citizen,* p. 61.
[44] *Survey of Race Relations,* 349–A.
[45] Cf. A. M. Rihbany, *op. cit.,* pp. 200–04.
[46] E. Hansovitz, *op. cit.,* p. 308. Cf. Elias Tobenkin, *Witte Arrives* (New York, 1916), pp. 14–15; Riis, *op. cit.,* pp. 25–26, 43–45; C. M. Panunzio, *op. cit.,* pp. 114–16; M. E. Ravage, *op. cit.,* pp. 230–34.

died of homesickness. Everything that was French became dear to me. I begged mother to send me newspapers, books. I wrote regularly to all my friends and waited anxiously for their letters which brought to me a little of France. Once a friend enclosed in her letter a little bit of the soil of France [47] and I cried over it.

Sometimes, when thinking of home I would feel such despair that my husband would want to call the doctor. I would read my French books over and over again in a loud voice just to hear French. I forgot all the grievances I had against French politics, or church, or government. France, to me, appeared as the fairest country. My thoughts, my affections were hers.[48]

Nostalgia and a sickening sense of inferiority, at times, become so over-powering that they lead to withdrawal from the world and finally to suicide. Willa Cather tells of a Bohemian family that settled in Nebraska where there were no others of their nationality. The father, a violinist, longed for his old friends with whom he played at weddings and dances in the home village. On the lonely western prairie he looked sadly at his violin and pined away—he took his own life before the end of the first winter.[49]

The attitudes of native Americans are in large measure responsible for the dejection of the newcomer. The most obvious things about the immigrant, the things inevitably seen first, are those aspects of his life in which he differs, or seems to differ, most from ourselves. The great variety of words which we use to describe the divergent manners indicates how interesting those differences are. We designate them as queer, quaint, outlandish, foreign, alien. We are usually not concerned—not at any rate at first—with what we have in common with the stranger we meet. Neither is he. It is on the basis of the diversities that his self-consciousness and our own

[47] Poignantly, a British woman wrote: "Then came homesickness with the arrival of my trunk. On opening it, I found the last thing I packed on that June morning ages ago when I left England. The morning had been wet and I had walked in the dear old meadow for the last time. On my return, I removed my walking boots, wrapped them hurriedly in paper, and thrust them into my trunk. Here they were, and on the soles of them was a handful of earth, the soil of my beloved homeland. I kissed it again and again, while my mother laughed at me with wet eyes." H. G. Duncan, *op. cit.*, p. 538.

[48] Unpublished life history.

[49] W. Cather, *op. cit.*, p. 102.

develop. Since, however, we live in our own cultural *milieu,* we have a decided advantage, while he becomes lonely.[50]

Our first impression of any foreign people is that they all look alike. The title of a song, "All Coons Look Alike to Me," which was common several decades ago, gives terse expression to this idea. Probably that is the reason we are so prone to determine our attitudes toward a whole race on the basis of a limited experience with a single representative of that group. All Italians are "Dagoes"; all Chinese are "Chinks." "Seemingly, Americans fail to distinguish between the educated immigrant and the peasant class," wrote a Russian immigrant. "I have lived here thirty years but have had no opportunity to meet people of education." [51] Similarly, another immigrant regretted this lack of discrimination.

> The Americans do not understand the foreigner because they do not know anything about him. Girls say to me, "I just hate Greeks; they are so dirty." When I ask them what Greeks they have known, they tell me they have seen them in the shoe-shining parlors. When I ask them whether they have seen any Greek merchants or Greek doctors, they have to say, "No." [52]

It is only gradually that individuals begin to stand out from the general mass; their faces begin to show expression; and they, as we say, become more and more human. One of the most interesting discoveries that we make when we first meet alien people is that, different though they may seem, when we become acquainted with them they are found to be human just like ourselves. The experience of a teacher in Texas, in a school with a number of Mexican pupils, is to the point.

> I had never associated with any foreigners or people of another color. Of course, I had been taught in Sunday School and elsewhere about the universality of human nature and the brotherhood of man. If anyone had asked me what I thought of the Mexicans, I would have given the orthodox answers as glibly as anyone else. However, one incident proved conclusively that I had never really considered the Mexicans as human beings. One day little Paulina mischievously pinched the child next to

[50] Cf. Robert E. Park, *Field Studies in Americanization,* mimeographed document.
[51] Unpublished life history.
[52] Unpublished life history.

her and started a free-for-all fight. I scolded her rather severely and she began to cry. It was a surprise and somewhat of a shock to discover that this little black-eyed girl's emotions and feelings were exactly like mine or those of any of the white children in the school.[53]

It requires an effort of the imagination to realize that a pain in one of different race is like a pain in one's own self. Likewise, when we penetrate to the motives behind the conduct and customs of others which at first seemed strange, outlandish, and forbidding, we usually find them to be the motives which would move us in the same situation.

"To comprehend all is to forgive all," says an old proverb. On the other hand, failure to understand opens the way for sinister or even romantic interpretations. We are disposed to attribute something venomous and reprehensible to conduct, or even to facial expression, which we do not fathom. Reams have been written about the trickiness, dishonesty, and depravity behind the stolid countenances of the Japanese. We are prone to be offended by the expression of an emotion with which we, for any reason, cannot sympathize. In fact, it is only so far as we can enter imaginatively into the lives of others that we regard them as human.

The characteristic which we describe as "human" is evidently a matter of degree. Certain things appear more human than others, and the extent to which this is true depends on our ability to discover in others passions and sentiments like our own. It is largely a matter of familiarity.

The persons and faces we know hold few secrets. Therefore, we feel secure and at home among them as we do not among strangers. When a person in a foreign land, or even in a distant city, sees a face, hears a voice, or sees clothing that reminds him of the far-away home, he is irresistibly drawn to it. The tension and restraint of the unfamiliar environment are suddenly relaxed and there is a sense of warmth, of expansion. When the writer was in British India he was always glad to meet some one who spoke "American" English—that was sweeter to his ears than any "English" English. "I sought out the French-speaking people in the

[53] Unpublished document.

little western town I lived in," wrote an immigrant woman. "Most of them I would not have associated with in France, but in this strange land, it did my heart good to talk to them of France." Two Russian immigrants upon arrival had no friends to meet them; they were jubilant on beholding a fellow countryman, even though he was a Jew.

"A Jew! My word, a Jew! May the Lord smite me with lightning if this is not a Jew!" exclaimed Dimma suddenly, pointing to a man in a threadbare coat and a soft hat. With him was a young, well-dressed gentleman, good-looking and not like a Jew at all, yet when he saw the older man's face Matvai was at once convinced that he too undoubtedly was a Jew. More than that; one of their own Jews from Mogilov or Zitomir or Minsk. He looked as if he had just left the Russian market place and changed his garments for foreign clothes. They were so glad to see this man—as if he were one of their near relatives.

The Jew, having noticed the white Svitkas and the sheepskin hats, came up to them with a greeting.

"Well, congratulations on your arrival. How is your health, my friends? I can tell at once that you are my countrymen."

"Well," said Dimma with a triumphant smile, "what did I say? What good folks these Jews are; whenever you need them they are right on the spot." [54]

Abraham Cahan found everything and everyone in New York strange to him. When he saw a cat he was thrilled with joy; that little animal made him feel that he was not entirely lost. In the new environment, however, he was not certain that the cat was real and was tempted to feel its fur to ascertain if it actually was the creature it seemed to be.[55]

Our immigrants are self-conscious and more reserved with us than they are with each other, because they are alien and different. On the other hand, to us they seem alien because they are self-conscious and reserved. It is a vicious circle. Where the radical differences are prominent, the more intense is the self-consciousness and the greater is the social distance which separates the immigrants from the native population.

[54] V. Korolenko, *op. cit.*, p. 38.
[55] Cf. *op. cit.*, p. 88.

CHAPTER V

DISORGANIZATION OF THE IMMIGRANT

A. What Disorganization Is

On every hand social change is ceaselessly going on. There is constant breaking down of the established order and building up of new fabric. Under normal conditions the two processes go on together, bringing about a gradual renewal. At times, however, the innovations produce marked variations from the accepted behavior patterns and abnormalities result. When disorganization sets in there may be a lack of socially sanctioned regulations for directing behavior; the prescripts may be totally inadequate to meet the demands of a social order in process of flux; or there may be approved codes which have become dead letters. Thomas and Znaniecki define social disorganization "as a decrease of the influence of existing social rules of behavior upon individual members of the group." [1] In addition there is also an individual as well as the institutional aspect. According to the same writers, social disorganization in terms of life organization of the individual is "a decrease of the individual's ability to organize his whole life for the efficient, progressive and continuous realization of his fundamental interests." [2] There is a certain relationship between social organization and individual life organization and a corresponding reciprocal dependence of personal disorganization on social disorganization, but there is not any regular and unmistakable connection between the two. Social disorganization may indicate that the rules and institutions prevailing are inadequate and do not correspond to the real attitudes of the members and cannot furnish the latter with an adequate life organization.[3] Disorganized persons actually may have systems of conduct far superior to those of the group.

[1] W. I. Thomas and F. Znaniecki, *op. cit.*, Vol. II, p. 1128.

[2] *Ibid.*, pp. 1128–29.

[3] *Ibid.*, p. 1647.

B. Disorganization and the Immigrant

Introduction. Characteristically the immigrant to the United States passes through a period of disorganization. Even in a well-ordered, stable community, with a homogeneous population which has traditions extending back over several generations, it is difficult to induce all persons to follow the socially approved behavior patterns and there is usually some crime or delinquency. If it is difficult to secure conformity under such conditions, the problem is accentuated in the case of the immigrant. In the homeland he is regulated by his own community, but when he migrates he detaches himself from this influence and the spontaneous and natural pressures no longer control him.[4] Many of his old-world habits do not function in the new-world situation. When he meets a crisis where his old habits fail him, he becomes confused. He cannot follow his established behavior norms and he has not had time to take over the American standards. Hence his conduct is often outlandish because it follows no known pattern; he is an enigma to both natives and to aliens.

It is no easy matter to recognize and follow an American pattern. Edwin H. Sutherland has suggested that the disorganization of the immigrant may be due in a certain measure to "isolation from the private culture of America and contact with the public culture." [5] The immigrant sees America through secondary media such as the newspaper, the moving picture, politics, and business activity where misrepresentation, graft, and the driving of hard bargains in the relentless competition of the business world are the accepted practices. The private culture, that of the intimate and personal phases of family life, is not known to the immigrant.

The immigrant often misapprehends the life about him in Amer-

[4] "One often sees jolly fellows at a dance and in gay company which they did not enjoy at home. That tempts them and so one and another is lost. If a relative is near it is not so dangerous, for the scamp is under some control and one hopes he will become reasonable. But when one who is quite alone gives himself up to the joys of the world, then it goes hard. Thank God such cases are very rare with us. If one goes astray he amends even after years and is not lost." E. G. Balch, *op. cit.*, p. 186.

[5] In Emory S. Bogardus (Editor), *Social Problems and Social Processes* (Chicago, 1933), pp. 54–55.

ica and this may lead to disorderly conduct. In his endeavor to imitate American behavior, he tends to select the more pleasurable aspects—those which will give expression to his suppressed desires.

This misapprehension has become evident in the way alien parents have sometimes used the reform school. Apparently they have regarded it as a free school in which their children might be reared until they would become self-sustaining. A mother with this point of view said to her son:

"Johnnie, you see that street-light? Break the glass! You will be arrested and sent to ———. You will have good things to eat, good clothes and will learn a trade, and when you come out they will give you a new suit of clothes." So Johnnie followed his mother's advice. Everything came out as she said it would, but when he came out he took away more than a new suit of clothes.[6]

The situation is far different from that in the homeland, even if the newcomers settle in a colony, since this colony is merely a loose aggregation of acquaintances, and is quite unlike the highly organized village life at home. Furthermore, the members of the group have changed while in America.

Confusion of standards. Among pre-literates and in peasant groups there is a uniform, harmonious, and consistent set of influences steadily bearing upon the conduct of the individuals. China, until recently, exemplified this situation almost to perfection. The family was dominated by the surrounding community. If any parent was derelict in his duty, this failure was counteracted by the entire group. With such uniform influences, the direction of a person's development was easily plotted. The individual found it exceedingly difficult to depart from the approved standard; he had practically no choice. A boy in China knew that when he attained a certain age a wife would be chosen for him and he would be expected to marry; his occupation would be selected for him in keeping with the position of his family; and his education would follow a fixed pattern. Hence the materials out of which personality developed were practically all prepared in advance; and they could be organized in only one way.

[6] From *The Wayward Child,* by Hannah K. Schoff, copyright 1915. Used by special permission of the Publishers, The Bobbs-Merrill Company. P. 183.

The immigrant in America finds himself in a totally different situation. He rubs shoulders with Americans or other groups of foreigners, who have variant customs and standards, and these multifarious contacts lead to confusion.

He learns to his mortification that his own standards do not fit the new situation and he cannot at once organize a workable scheme from this tangled maze. Such was the problem of the Norwegian with reference to church affiliation.

Norway had only one recognized church in 1825. America had over 100, most of them of the Reformed group. Here was perfect religious freedom with high churchly, low churchly, and broad churchly groups of every description. Here you could belong to church or not, as you pleased. What a strange world to these newcomers of ours who had been compelled to baptize their children and confirm them in the Lutheran faith! But there was some difficulty in knowing just what to do here. Should they join the great throng who did not belong to church? Should they join one of the American churches? If so, which one? Even the Quakers in the party found it difficult to agree as to whether they should be Orthodox, Hicksite, Wilburite or Primitive. Lars Larson remained Orthodox Quaker; Ole Johnson chose the Hicksite brand. Their children became Baptists. The Adventists made a strong bid for their support; they put up a school right in the heart of the Fox River settlement, which is still standing as a witness of missionary zeal. The Baptists and Methodists labored among them both, long and faithfully, but there were a dozen kinds of Baptists and as many Methodist denominations, so it was rather difficult to know which was in the right. Campbellites and Congregationalists, Presbyterians and Episcopalians, all looked upon the Norwegian immigrants as their rightful possession and added to the religious confusion. Possibly the boldest of all . . . . and most successful were the Mormons. . . . . As a concrete illustration of the effects of the religious confusion in America the case of the Rossadal family is typical. Daniel Rossadal was a good man and a good Quaker. He had a large family and no doubt tried to bring them up in the Quaker faith. His descendants are numerous—255—and representative citizens and churchmen. But they are distributed among a great number of denominations, in the following order; beginning with the denomination that has most of them as members—Lutheran, Methodist, Congregationalist, Catholic, Quaker, Campbellite, Mormon. And in addition 40 per cent of them are not known to belong to any church. Such are the conditions in America.[7]

Confusion of cultural standards is a disorganizing influence no matter where it may be. According to E. H. Sutherland, "It has been found in Chicago that the highest rates of juvenile delinquency are not in the heart of a particular foreign section but on the borderline between sections," [8] where no one single standard prevails. Studies made in Honolulu indicate that juvenile delinquency, family trouble, and vice occur with a higher frequency in areas inhabited by a mixture of races with their divergent cultures. "The most striking cases of demoralization—prostitution, bootlegging, drug addiction—are found in the tenements housing the largest variety of racial types." [9] Persons living in such a cultural chaos run a serious risk of being unable to organize their lives to the best advantage.

Loss of status. Since many an immigrant came to America under the influence of stories and myths which exaggerated the advantages of the new country, he expected to acquire wealth easily and become a person of prominence. Instead he suffered a loss in status; he had to do the lowest of common labor, was ignored, and ridiculed for being "queer." The immigrant brings a definite sense of moral worth—he has a certain conception of himself. This status and self-respect depend on the recognition he receives from some group. But he suffers a loss because he cannot bring with him the intimate circle which was the basis of his personality at home. A "greenhorn" is accorded very little standing here even though

[7] O. M. Norlie, *op. cit.*, pp. 190–91. Korolenko indicates the confusion encountered by the immigrant. "How can one find happiness in this Hell where people rush as though mad, over the ground and under the ground and even, God forgive them, through the air; where everything is entirely different from what one is accustomed to at home; where it is impossible to distinguish to what social class a man belongs; where it is impossible to understand a single word of what they say; where baptized Christians are run after by street boys even as a non-Christian, a Turk, would be run after at home?" V. Korolenko, *op. cit.*, p. 52.

[8] *Proceedings of the National Conference of Social Work,* 1927, p. 578. Cf. Thorsten Sellin, *Culture Conflict and Crime* (New York, 1938).

[9] *The Honolulu Advertiser,* June 6, 1932.

he had a high rating in the homeland. Here he may shovel coal or dig sewer ditches. A young man from Germany felt humiliated when he had to perform menial tasks.

A few weeks after landing I was working in a Brooklyn printing office. Think of it! A German high school pupil whose chums had been the scions of aristocracy, learning to set type and worse yet, having to sweep out the office! Bereft of all mercy the foreman stood me up against a compositor's case and showed me how to handle the stick and to "catch" the type. If at that moment some of my former chums had entered the room, I should have felt like creeping into a hole and pulling the dirt after me. The sting of wounded pride was in my heart, a false pride, as I now realize, nurtured by German social conditions. But I was determined to stick.[10]

Similarly, Abraham Cahan felt dejected when he was compelled to peddle oilcloth and shoeblack from a push-cart.[11] Thrilling as were Rihbany's first impressions of the New World, it was at the same time disheartening to learn that in coming to America he had lost, temporarily at least, the status he had enjoyed in Syria as a member of a respected family and as a learned man. In order to live economically he had found refuge in a five-cent lodging house maintained by one of his countrymen in the Syrian colony. Here he would lie awake at night and think of all the good things he had enjoyed among his kindred at home while in the New World he was tucked away in a dingy corner and no one noticed his real worth.[12] Being without money to buy an interest in a store, without knowledge of the English language and having learned from his compatriots that at twenty-two he was too old to learn, the only thing that remained for him was to peddle jewelry and notions. But this was too much—it created a revulsion against having his status lowered. He was a learned man, and to become a peddler was out of the question. He was nauseated by the very sight of the greasy, crude peddlers and under no circumstances would he shoulder the pack. At the mere thought of lowering himself to

[10] Richard Bartholdt, *From Steerage to Congress* (Philadelphia, 1930), p. 24.
[11] *Op. cit.*, p. 109. Cf. *Red Cross Magazine,* XIV (September, 1919), 45.
[12] A. M. Rihbany, *op. cit.*, pp. 194–95.

peddling notions and jewelry, even death lost its terror for him.[13]

The intellectual who analyzes his condition is in a painful situation. In peasant communities of the homeland, the educated man occupies a position of superiority and is highly respected. He reads some language other than the folkspeech and translates it to his fellows. This gives him status in his group. When a member of the intelligentsia comes to the United States he feels that he is conferring an honor on our country. But to the American all immigrants from a certain area look alike; every Italian, be he intellectual or illiterate laborer, is called a "Dago," and given the pick and shovel. This loss of status makes him dissatisfied. He considers it all wrong, develops into a radical, and sets about to reform America. Then he is likely to be labeled "communist" or "anarchist" and be sent back home.

In addition to his personal self-respect, the immigrant has a group self-consciousness; he is aware of the status of his group among others. He also has a national consciousness; he knows the place of his country among the nations of the world.[14]

When the immigrant receives no recognition on account of his own personal worth or because of the status of his group or nation, he is perplexed as was this Bohemian:

When I first came I thought I could not stand it here, so many people would refer to the southern European class and refer to the peasant class of people with great disdain. They seemed to look down upon Europeans from our land. I know that many have a serious misconception of class. Our peasant is a landholder, more nearly compared to the American farmer, and is far from the bottom of the social scale. We have classes of peasants, the half peasant, the quarter and even the eighth

[13] *Ibid.*, pp. 198–99. The story of a Slavic immigrant woman is typical of a considerable number where the transition to America means a fall, not a rise, in social status. Her family were cultivated, well-to-do people. They came to America where, on account of misfortunes, this delicately reared girl had to go into domestic service on a pioneer farm. She married a prosperous Bohemian and their children had the advantages of college. She was glad to hear from her relatives in Europe, but she did not want any of them to see her American environment. She could not forget the degradation of her barefoot, hardworking girlhood. E. G. Balch, *op. cit.*, pp. 224–25.

[14] Cf. M. Pupin. *op. cit.*, pp. 41–42.

peasant with smaller holdings of land. Below them are still lower classes of laborers, cottiers and other workers. As in America the standing is measured by the stock he holds. Our peasant is a link in a long line of family inheritance and tradition which oftentimes runs back many centuries with a name, a reputation to sustain and a posterity. So my blood would boil when many an uneducated person would look down upon me and speak in a condescending way of "Class." For a long time these sarcastic remarks hurt me, and worried me.[15]

Under such conditions, the immigrant may lose his self-respect and turn to anti-social conduct. This unsatisfied desire for recognition is an important factor in the development of immigrant colonies. Rather than be a nobody in an American community, the immigrant intellectual turns to a group of his own countrymen where he may win approbation. He may begin the publication of a newspaper or organize a society by means of which he may acquire status in his own group. Through this means he also has a better opportunity for being accepted by the native-born Americans. Rihbany wrote of organizing the Syrian Scientific and Ethical Society for the mutual benefit of its members and the advancement of the Syrians in general. He was elected vice president and found great satisfaction in serving the organization in various capacities.[16] It was his place in this society which secured him the position of literary editor of the *Koukab America,* the first Syrian paper in America, and this distinction brought a sense of personal expansion, responsibility and dignity. He felt that by virtue of his position as editor he would probably be admitted in due time to the circle of editors of the big New York newspapers and thus be enabled to make contacts with some of the highest and best elements in American life.[17]

Inner conflicts. Immigrants come largely from the lower classes since the upper classes have status in the homeland and have less to gain by emigration. In fact, many would lose through migration.[18] Furthermore, they come largely from the rural sections and

[15] Unpublished life history.

[16] *Op. cit.*, pp. 219–20.

[17] *Ibid.*, p. 229.

[18] An army officer, whose family was well known in Sweden, came to Wisconsin to seek his fortune as a colonist. "He was forced to exchange his chevron-trimmed

small villages. In these areas the mores and behavior patterns grow up spontaneously and require no reflection—the codes are right and must not be questioned. When immigrants come to America and find that their moral codes and behavior patterns do not fit and are even ridiculed, they are torn by conflicts. If these sacred elements in their lives are no longer true and dependable, then all else is false. They slip their anchors and many become utterly demoralized.

Not alone is it their moral codes that suffer, but language, dress, and all their customs, which in the homeland gave them assurance of membership in a homogeneous cultural group, become objects of ridicule. The newcomer meets with sneers and attitudes of disdain which lead him to drop certain traits at once in order to avoid being called a "greenhorn" or other names. Too often this leads to a contemptuous attitude toward his own standards and customs and he turns away from them before he has developed new rules or dependable patterns to follow.

Since immigrants are persons with manners, sentiments, attitudes, and ambitions, they are subjected to what James G. Frazer has described as "perils of the soul." Out of these various disturbing experiences many develop a "sickening sense of inferiority" as they realize their own inadequacies in coping with a new situation. Furthermore, they see little possibility of realizing the hopes they brought. At times this leads to a greater determination to succeed at any cost, but many, in seeking to compensate for this lowered self-esteem, turn to anti-social conduct.

One of the most disturbing factors is the change immigrants observe in their relatives and fellow countrymen who have been in America for some time. Rose Cohen was shocked by her father shortly after her arrival when he bought a piece of watermelon

uniform for a working-man's blouse, and his gilded saber for the rake and spade. . . . . We soon taught him to drive our oxen; to these at times he would give his military commands in a most comical fashion, as if he had been drilling a squad of recruits in a training camp." *Wisconsin Magazine of History,* XIX (1935–1936), 301.

The settler's life may be satisfying to the laborer, but not to the one on a higher social level. To be sure, there was a considerable group of intellectuals who left Germany in the fifties on account of political repression. Many professional men encountered difficulties in adjusting themselves. *Ibid.,* IV (1920–1921), 290.

for her and paid for it on Saturday—the holy Sabbath. In the old country he would not have touched a coin on the Sabbath but would have waited until the following week to make payment.[19] At another time her father brought her great distress.

I found that father was already at home. As I came into the room I saw him resting against the wall, clipping his beard. I was so surprised and shocked to see him actually do this that I could neither speak nor move for some minutes. And I knew that he, too, felt embarrassed. After the first glance I kept my eyes steadily on the floor in front of me, and began to talk to him quietly, but with great earnestness: "You had been so pious at home, Father," I said, "more pious than anyone else in our whole neighborhood. And now you are cutting your beard. Grandmother would never have believed it. How she would weep!" The snipping of the scissors still went on. But I knew by the sound that now he was only making a pretense at cutting. At last he laid it down and said in a tone that was bitter, yet quiet: "They do not like Jews on Cherry Street. And one with a long beard has to take his life into his own hands." [20]

Differences in conduct in those of other races and nationalities may be permissible, even expected, but when a person of one's own blood breaks with the sacred traditions, that is painful—unbearable; that is fruitful soil for inner conflicts.

Growth of individualization. With the break-down of the old patterns of behavior there is an ever-increasing development of individualization. When the traditions which controlled conduct fall into disrepute, the individual is thrown back upon his unschooled impulses. He tends to gratify his own wishes even at the expense of his fellows. Group consciousness gives way to egoistic attitudes. When the peasant comes to America and realizes that he is not expected to regard himself as an inferior, the courtesy which rested on the acceptance of a fixed class status disappears and often his conduct becomes crude and boorish. When members of the lower classes who have bowed and scraped before the aristocrats hear about *equality* and *freedom,* they think they may do exactly as they please. This leads to individualized behavior and

[19] From *Out of the Shadow,* by Rose Cohen, copyright, 1918, by Doubleday, Doran and Company, Inc., New York, p. 78.

[20] From *Out of the Shadow,* by Rose Cohen, copyright, 1918, by Doubleday, Doran and Company, Inc., New York, p. 106.

to license. In Japan the family council is an important instrument of control. Since immigration has been largely an individual matter it has not been possible to call together these councils made up of groups of relatives, and the absence of this regulatory device has caused many to play discordant rôles.

CHAPTER VI

DISORGANIZATION OF THE IMMIGRANT
(*Concluded*)

C. Factors in Disorganization

Mobility. Mobility is a vital element in disorganization. When one transfers from his own group with its mores and behavior patterns to another with a different set, he may lose quickly the standards he carried with him. Migration from place to place produces conflict of cultural values, disorganizes habits when old adjustments are disrupted, and results in maladjustments in the new environment. Not only is that because of leaving the homeland, but it is often a matter of moving about in the United States. Many immigrants, shifting from place to place as casual laborers, make contacts with a variety of culture patterns and cannot feel the steadying influences of any community.[1]

A neighborhood, town or community in which there is a high rate of mobility cannot develop stable behavior patterns. McKenzie found a high correlation between this social flux and juvenile delinquency in Columbus, Ohio.[2] The studies of Thrasher [3] and

[1] "Even when cultures are not greatly different from an external point of view, mobility is attended by greater criminality. Persons who are born in the United States and who migrate into Canada have a rate of conviction for indictable offenses in Canada nearly twice as high as the natives of Canada. Natives of Canada who migrate to the United States have a rate of commitment to prisons in the United States one and one half times as high as the native white population of the United States. Natives of Minnesota, Illinois, Nebraska, and Missouri who migrate into Iowa are committed to the state prison of Iowa four times as frequently in proportion to their population as are persons who are born in Iowa and remain in the state." Edwin H. Sutherland, *Proceedings of the National Conference of Social Work.* 1927, pp. 576–77. Cf. also Edwin H. Sutherland, *Principles of Criminology* (Chicago, 1934), pp. 73, 113–17. Cf. Charles Horton Cooley, *Social Process* (New York, 1918), pp. 180–81, for the importance of intimate association with a group of some sort.

[2] "The Neighborhood: A Study of Local Life in the City of Columbus, Ohio," *American Journal of Sociology,* XXVIII (September, 1921), 166.

[3] Frederic M. Thrasher, *The Gang* (Chicago, 1927).

Shaw [4] bear this out for Chicago. Lind [5] reached the same conclusion in a study of Seattle.

Mobility on the part of the immigrant results in confusion, the weakening of old standards and small opportunity for the development of new codes. Habits can be formed only in an environment which is relatively stable. Any change that brings a marked alteration in the routine of social life tends to break down habits. When the behavior patterns upon which a dependable social life rests are disintegrated, the entire group becomes disorganized. Every new device, every invention, every new idea that in any way affects social life and its routine is a disorganizing influence.[6] As the immigrant moves about in America he is bombarded from all directions by the new and intriguing, and these broadsides unsettle his old habits and behavior patterns.

Isolation. Isolation is an important factor in disorganization. Near as they may be in space, immigrants, nevertheless, may be insulated from the native white population. Social distance is often more effectual than spatial distance in preventing intimate social contacts. Opportunities for making friends with the better element among the native Americans and thereby learning their ways are denied the newcomers; they are left to associate with the unwholesome characters in our city slums. Elizabeth G. Stern reports that the principal of her high school was the first American gentleman to speak to her father—the scholar and dreamer. The ones who had spoken English to him were the bums on the street and the crooked politicians in the ward.[7]

All too often the first American institution with which the young immigrant comes up against is the juvenile court, and then only

[4] Clifford R. Shaw, *Delinquency Areas* (Chicago, 1930). Cf. also National Commission on Law Observance and Enforcement, *Report on the Causes of Crime* (Washington, 1931), Vol. II.

[5] Andrew W. Lind, *A Study of Mobility of Population in Seattle* (Seattle, 1925).

[6] Probably the most demoralizing single instrument of today is the automobile. Its connection with vice and crime is notorious. It extends the radius of possible movement from a fixed abode and thus permits men to carry on many of their activities at a considerable distance from the watchful eyes and gossiping tongues of the immediate neighborhood. The newspaper and motion picture show are conceivably somewhat less demoralizing than the automobile, but nevertheless they are powerful influences.

[7] E. G. Stern, *My Mother and I* (New York, 1917), p. 113.

after he has committed an offense; the adult not infrequently makes his approach through the police court after he has unwittingly peddled without a license. These contacts are usually unpleasant and do very little toward furthering other wholesome relationships. Some, after suffering injuries, receive care where the treatment is far different. Rose Cohen related her experience in a hospital which gave her an insight into American life. It was the first time she had met people beyond the East Side of New York, and they were so different.[8]

Under such conditions it is not surprising that the immigrants at times give way to impulse and even commit crimes. Often they act in self defense and in desperation when they are defrauded and mistreated by the unscrupulous and have no hope of securing justice. It is indeed amazing that they control themselves as well as they do.

D. Indices of Disorganization

Crime. It has often been said and statistics have been used to show that immigrants commit more crimes than native-born Americans. Much of the available statistical data, such as total arrests, convictions, or numbers committed to penal institutions, etc., must be carefully interpreted.[9]

According to the Census of 1910, the number of foreign-born whites committed to institutions as prisoners or juvenile delinquents was twice as large in proportion to their entire population as for the native-born whites.[10] In 1923 the native white prisoners constituted only 53.4 per cent of the prison population and only 54.4 per cent of the total commitments, while 70.9 per cent of the total population belonged to this group. The foreign-born white prisoners constituted 13.8 per cent of the total number of prisoners and 18.7

[8] R. Cohen, *op. cit.*, pp. 233–50.

[9] Cf. Francis J. Brown and Joseph S. Roucek, *Our Racial and National Minorities* (New York, 1937), pp. 697–710; Thorsten Sellin, *Culture Conflict and Crime*, pp. 71–78; Donald Young, *Research Memorandum on Minority Peoples in the Depression* (New York, 1937), pp. 162–71.

[10] Bureau of the Census, *Prisoners and Juvenile Delinquents in the United States* (Washington, D. C., 1910), p. 108.

per cent of those committed as compared with the 19.4 per cent of foreign-born whites in the total population.[11]

These data place the immigrants in an unfavorable light; but the figures are misleading. In the first place, among the immigrants there is an abnormally large proportion of young adults whose crime rate is high in any group. There are comparatively few children and old people. In 1910 only 5.7 per cent of the foreign-born were under fifteen years of age while 36 per cent of the native-born were in this age group. If the adult offenders over fifteen years in both groups are compared, then the foreign-born had only 1.3 times as many commitments as the native whites, instead of 2.0 times without this correction. In the second place the immigrants, particularly the recent ones, settle largely in the cities and the crime rates for all elements are higher in the city. Several studies show that in the cities the foreign-born have a lower rate than the native-born. The Immigration Commission of 1910 came to this conclusion after studying the statistics of several urban areas.[12] Dean Edith Abbott arrived at the same result in a study of Chicago.[13] In the third place, the majority of the immigrants are males and males have a higher crime rate than females.

When these several factors are considered it is found that the seemingly high crime rate of the foreign-born is due to the fact that they are young male adults living in cities.[14] To be fair, male immigrants between twenty and thirty-five should be compared with native males in the same age group.

Investigators who have studied the statistics carefully are unanimous. In 1910 the Immigration Commission concluded:

> No satisfactory evidence has yet been produced to show that immigration has resulted in an increase in crime disproportionate to the increase

[11] Bureau of the Census, *Prisoners, 1923* (Washington, D. C., 1926), pp. 57–69.

[12] *Reports of the Immigration Commission,* Vol. XXXVI, *passim.*

[13] *Report of the City Council Committee on Crime of the City of Chicago,* 1915. Cf. E. H. Sutherland, *Criminology* (Philadelphia, 1924), p. 98, for a table that brings together the results of several studies. Cf. also E. H. Sutherland, *Principles of Criminology,* pp. 73, 113–17.

[14] Cf. Samuel Ornitz, *Haunch, Paunch and Jowl* (New York, 1923), for a picture of the corrupting influences which touch many Jews on the East Side in New York City.

in adult population. Such comparable statistics of crime and population as it has been possible to obtain indicate that immigrants are less prone to commit crime than are native Americans.[15]

Isaac Hourwich concurred in 1912.[16] On the basis of her study of the city of Chicago in 1913, Edith Abbott agreed:

It seems clear, therefore, that the statistics show beyond any question that a larger proportion of crime is committed by the native American, whether white or colored, than by the immigrant. That our immigrants form the criminal element of our population today is clearly a myth which has had a hardy survival owing to our desire to shift responsibility for our own faults. No facts have ever been found to substantiate it.

The record of the immigrant is in fact very much better than the statistics show. The great majority of all those arrested are poor people, and the poorer they are the more liable they are to conviction. . . . . The immigrant is engaged in occupations that easily involve violations of the laws. The peddling and junk business, for example, is largely in the hands of immigrants, and undesigned violations of ordinances (petty misdemeanors) are common.[17] Moreover the immigrant stands a chance that the American does not of failing to understand our laws or the methods of our police or our courts. We have no system in Chicago of official interpreters, and the immigrant, particularly the immigrant from southeastern Europe, is certainly at a disadvantage in a court where he understands no one and no one, except possibly an incompetent interpreter, understands him. Keeping in mind these facts, it is indeed remarkable that all statistics relating to this subject show that in spite of

[15] *Reports,* Vol. XXXVI, p. 1.

[16] "Immigration and Crime," *American Journal of Sociology,* XVII (January, 1912), 478–90.

[17] John Palmer Gavit records an instance where an immigrant was arrested for trying to beautify his surroundings. "I remember . . . . a Chicago landlord who had a Greek tenant arrested for carving the casing around one of the doors in his tenement. The defendant pleaded that the place was unthinkably ugly. In his childhood he could see out of the window from his bed the Parthenon—he was homesick for its loveliness. If anything the landlord should pay *him;* but he had done it as a labor of love; transferring his own priceless memories to the pitiless environment of a Halstead Street hovel. . . . . Very likely the artist went to jail, as have gone countless others who have tried to beautify and make tolerable for the human soul the conditions of life." "Of Horologians Here and There," *Survey Graphic,* XXII (August, 1933), 426.

all handicaps the immigrant has a better crime record than the rest of us.[18]

In 1926 Carl Kelsey came to the same conclusion.[19] The Wickersham Report in 1931 stated that "in proportion to their respective numbers, the foreign born commit considerably fewer crimes than the native born.[20] There has been one dissenting note, to be sure. H. H. Laughlin in his report [21] to the Committee on Immigration and Naturalization of the House of Representatives in 1922 gave a different interpretation, but when several critics [22] pointed out fallacies due to the fact that he had failed to take into consideration the age and sex composition and the rural-urban distribution, he made corrections which brought him to the same conclusion that other investigators reach.

It is often stated that the crimes of the immigrants are more serious than those of the native-born. This is incorrect. According to the report of the Immigration Commission, the native (or American-born) exhibited in general a tendency to commit more serious crimes than did the immigrant.[23] On the basis of data for 1933 [24] the native white males of native parentage had 2.55 times as many commitments per 100,000 males fifteen years of age and

[18] *Report of the City Council Committee on Crime of the City of Chicago*, 1915, pp. 54–55.

[19] "Immigrants and Crime," *The Annals*, CXXV (May, 1926), 165–74.

[20] National Commission on Law Observance and Enforcement, *Report on Crime and the Foreign Born* (Washington, 1931), p. 195. A report for 1933 on prisoners received from courts by nativity gives the foreign-born white a much lower ratio per 100,000 of population 15 years old and over than the native white of native parentage. To be sure, the proportion of the native white population in the so-called "criminal ages" is larger than for the foreign-born white. The immigrants will be found increasingly in the higher age brackets. Hence their ratio of criminality will improve year by year. Bureau of the Census, *Prisoners in State and Federal Prisons and Reformatories, 1933* (Washington, 1935), p. 26. Cf. *Ibid.*, 1931 and 1932, p. 19.

[21] *Analysis of America's Melting Pot*, House of Representatives, 67th Congress, 3d Session, November 21, 1922, Serial 7–C, p. 790.

[22] Cf. H. S. Jennings, *The Survey*, LI (December 15, 1923), 309–12; J. M. Gillman, *American Journal of Sociology*, XXX (July, 1924), 29–48; C. M. Panunzio, *Immigration Crossroads* (New York, 1927), pp. 115–18.

[23] *Reports of the Immigration Commission*, Vol. XXXVI, p. 5.

[24] *Prisoners in State and Federal Prisons and Reformatories, 1933* (Washington, 1935), p. 27.

over as the foreign-born for the crimes of homicide, robbery, assault, burglary, larceny, embezzlement, fraud, forgery, and rape. The fact that a larger proportion of the foreign-born are in local penal institutions than in state institutions indicates the generally less serious character of their offenses.

In large cities a part of the apparent criminality of the foreign-born consists merely of violations of ordinances, which are offenses only because the persons who commit them are not naturalized. Prominent in this class of offenses are street peddling without a license in cities where such licenses are granted only to citizens.[25]

There are certain differences in the criminality of the several immigrant groups. Italians have a high homicide rate but very few are arrested for drunkenness. Irish immigrants have a much lower rate for major offenses but a higher rate for misdemeanors. (There is more drunkenness among the Irish than among the Italians.) Among Finnish immigrants the rate of commitments on account of liquor is high. These variations are due mainly to the persistence of old-world habits in America.[26]

Immigrant criminality is caused almost wholly by conflicts in cultural values. According to the Wickersham Report,

> The immigrant brings with him a well-defined set of habits of thought and behavior, built up from earliest infancy in an environment many of whose characteristics are entirely at variance with law and custom in the United States.[27] Two directions in which the divergence was particularly great were repeatedly discussed by those interviewed. The laws of this country relative to gambling, prostitution, and manufacture, sale, and consumption of beer, wines, and liquors are entirely different from those effective in the nations from which immigrants come. Whatever

[25] E. Abbott, *Immigration: Select Documents and Case Records,* pp. 540–41.

[26] Cf. E. H. Sutherland, *Principles of Criminology,* pp. 114–15.

[27] Konrad Bercovici reports an interesting case. "I remember the surprise on the face of an Armenian who was arrested because he had killed the man who had dishonored his sister.

" 'Why should they arrest me?' he questioned. 'I did no wrong. And besides the man was an Armenian.'

"The killer had been in this country ten years. He had learned enough American to peddle lace and rugs in uptown New York. It was the opinion of most of such people that, while living here, they should be allowed to live as they had always lived in their native lands. What business had America to meddle with them!" *Good Housekeeping,* CI (August, 1935), 156.

laws they have known in these fields provided for regulation, not prohibition. To most of the foreign born it would be quite as logical to forbid the use of tobacco, tea, coffee, candy, or any of the foods and drinks whose intemperate consumption may be injurious as to prohibit beer and wine. These beverages have been and are, for them and their forebears, a normal accompaniment of food from childhood to the grave. They find the attitude of the American prohibitionist incomprehensible. The habits of a lifetime do not readily yield to a "Thou shalt not" for which their experience has given them no rational preparation. The other point of variance frequently mentioned referred especially to immigrants coming from certain specific areas rather than to the foreign-born group as a whole.[28] This was in connection with the custom of carrying weapons. Many immigrants come from districts where a weapon of some sort is almost as indispensable as any other part of a man's attire—where a man expects, and is prepared to defend himself, literally and physically, whenever occasion arises—and where only the weakling appeals to "the law" for redress of personal wrongs. Among some groups many centuries of custom have made it binding upon the men of the family to wipe out in blood any stain brought upon the honor of its women. This is, of course, analogous to the so-called "unwritten law" of the United States, but is said to be still almost universally operative among the members of certain nationality units, notably the South Italian. This habit of carrying weapons inevitably leads to a fatal ending in many cases where flaring anger might have resulted otherwise in nothing more serious than a fistic encounter. . . . .

Another impression mentioned by two or three social workers was in regard to the attitude of the members of some particular national units toward law in general. The nationalities named where those who, for long periods, have been subject peoples. The laws under which they and their ancestors have lived have frequently been oppressive laws imposed by a ruling nation for its own benefit. Natural indignation against such

[28] According to a police officer, "Those Hungarians were mostly young and middle-aged men, away from their families, and bewildered by their strange life and especially by their 'new freedom.' I had a lot of trouble with them toting guns; they didn't understand it was bad. It was not uncommon to have street fights, especially on pay day as the men gathered at the saloons. And I'll never forget the surprise a rookie patrolman used to get when a Hungarian would pop his head from an upstairs window at bedtime and fire his revolver into the air, recklessly emptying it before retiring!" S. C. Newman, *op. cit.* Cf. E. D. Beynon, "Crime and Custom of the Hungarians of Detroit," *Journal of Criminal Law and Criminology,* XXV (January, 1935), 755–74; John Paget, *Hungary and Transylvania* (London, 1839), Vol. I, p. 295 ff.

oppressive legislation unconsciously grew into an attitude of active resentment of all law, and it became almost a patriotic duty to hold law in contempt and to circumvent it whenever possible.

The comparatively low crime rate among the foreign-born which the statistics reveal would, however, seem to indicate that, whatever its cause, disrespect for law is less common among the immigrants of peasant extraction than among persons born and reared within this country.[29]

While no accurate measures are available relative to the amount of crime committed in the homelands by the emigrants, there are indications that their criminality increases in America.[30] Migration from the old place of abode disrupts habits and thus they are without adequate guides for their conduct in the new world.

Demoralization of immigrant girls. A large number of immigrant girls have come to the United States. In the year ending June 30, 1912, there were 93,267 unmarried girls between the ages of fourteen and twenty-one admitted. Some of them went to friends and relatives but many went to live with strangers.

Oftentimes they lived in immigrant homes where there was more or less promiscuous mixing of men and women lodgers. These young men and women came from homes in the rural areas in Europe into an entirely new environment where there were inadequate housing facilities, lack of privacy, and freedom from parental and community restraint. Over-crowding did not necessarily bring disastrous results in the dwellings where it existed, but it tended to develop a certain familiarity and carelessness which brought a loosening of standards. At times, with entire absence of evil intent on the part of either the man or the girl, lack of privacy led to undesirable results.[31]

[29] National Commission on Law Observance and Enforcement, *Report on Crime and the Foreign Born* (Washington, 1931), pp. 166–68.

[30] Cf. W. I. Thomas and F. Znaniecki, *op. cit.*, Vol. II, pp. 1476–78.

[31] Edith Abbott reported a case: "A Polish girl of 19, who has been in America two years, working in a restaurant in Boston, lodges in an apartment of four rooms, where a Polish man and his wife have four men and nine girl lodgers. She came from Europe alone, expecting to be with her father but he had gone to Canada, and she was obliged to find a lodging place and begin to work immediately. She has an illegitimate child by a man who was a lodger in the same house, and who came from the same village in Poland." *Immigration: Select Documents and Case Records,* p. 529.

In addition to unwholesome housing conditions, immigrants usually have lived in the more undesirable areas of the city where the disreputable dance hall and hotel (and in the olden days the saloon) were tolerated. Hence the environment to which the immigrant girl was subjected was fraught with hazards of which she was entirely ignorant. At home the girls attended out-of-door dances and other social activities. In our large cities there was a demand for some excitement and stimulus at the end of a monotonous week. There was danger, however, that the girl's physical and nervous exhaustion and her demand for stimulation would make her an easy victim for the unscrupulous, and in this situation the neighboring dance-hall proprietor tried to attract her to his establishment where her fatigue might lead to ruin.[32] "There are also cases where, under some special strain or excitement, as for example, after a wedding or some other celebration, when liquor has been freely used, the moral barriers are broken down." [33]

Furthermore, immigrant girls are not always safe in their places of work. Polish girls, particularly, in restaurants in Chicago have been in peril. At first they resisted but "often in the end find themselves unfortified against the combination of force and persuasion which is exerted sometimes against them by the restaurant keeper or a fellow employee." [34] Proprietors of many restaurants have been immigrants whose families remained in Europe and thus were without normal social relationships. Immigrant men, however, are not the only offenders, but "American foremen in factories sometimes abuse a power which is more absolute than any man should have the right to exercise over others, and on threat of dismissal the girl submits to familiarities which if they do not ruin her cannot fail to break down her self-respect." [35] Some girls, thinking they would have good homes, have done housework but were betrayed by men in the family. Promise of marriage often has played a part in the downfall of a girl. She was easily victimized through her affections. Desire for response, together with loneliness, lack of

[32] Cf. Grace Abbott, *The Immigrant and the Community* (New York, 1917), p. 72.
[33] *Ibid.*, p. 70.
[34] *Ibid.*, pp. 72–73.
[35] *Ibid.*, p. 73.

knowledge of herself, and long hours of hard, monotonous work were big factors.[36]

Family disorganization. Under American conditions family ties are loosened.[37] Immigrants themselves notice the changes. "There are more divorces among my people in this country than at home," wrote an Armenian. "It is such a terrible thing in the old country that a man would rather suffer or commit suicide than to divorce his wife." [38] Other groups are affected in like manner also.

Not one but several disorganizing situations impinge upon the immigrant family. An imbalance in the sex ratio is one. Since women were fewer there was keen competition for them. "I inform you, dear parents," wrote a Pole, "that not one, but thousands of girls come here to America, get married, live a month or two, and then some scoundrel persuades her and she runs away with him." [39] "At home," wrote Kate H. Claghorn of the Italians, "the church . . . . holds the man fast to his marital duties; on this side, the grasp of the church is loosened, and . . . . there is no organized body of social opinion to take its place in restraining him." [40] Oftentimes men who left their families in the old country have become involved in irregular sex relations. A man might live in adultery with another woman or might marry in the United States without a legal separation. On the other hand advantage has been taken of easy divorce laws in America and the wife in the homeland has been cast off.

Frequently the immigrant totally misunderstands our life and institutions. He observes some superficiality and interprets that as being fundamental. He hears much about divorce in America and concludes that we have no marriage—only temporary relations. He then takes advantage of what he conceives to be the privileges of a land of liberty. "You write me whether I am married," wrote

[36] Cf. *Ibid.*, pp. 73–74.

[37] Cf. J. P. Lichtenberger, *Divorce, A Social Interpretation* (New York, 1931), p. 110; Stuart A. Queen and Delbert M. Mann, *Social Pathology* (New York, 1925), pp. 370–79; R. I. Foerster, *op. cit.*, pp. 390–441.

[38] Unpublished life history.

[39] W. I. Thomas and F. Znaniecki, *op. cit.*, Vol. I, p. 787. Cf. *Ibid.*, p. 784, document 452. Familial relations are broken down as the girl becomes individualized.

[40] "Immigration in Relation to Pauperism," *The Annals*, XXIV (July, 1904), 192–93. Cf. Caroline F. Ware, *Greenwich Village* (Boston, 1935), p. 172.

a boy to his parents in Poland. "Well, no. America is not the old country where it is necessary to marry for your whole life. Here it is not so." [41]

Dependency. Dependency is one measure of disorganization or failure of individuals to adapt themselves to the environment provided for them by the community. Immigrant communities develop in America and in a measure they provide an environment in which their members are able to live. But their influence is limited because, in the main, the immigrants must go outside the colonies for their livelihood.

The Immigration Commission made a study of charity seekers in forty-three cities which included practically all the larger immigrant centers except New York and found that a small percentage of cases represented immigrants who had been in the United States three years or under, while nearly half of all the foreign-born cases were those who had been in the United States twenty years or more. This investigation showed that the recent immigrants, even in times of comparative industrial inactivity, did not seek charitable aid in considerable numbers.[42] On the basis of the available data it appears that not the able-bodied workers and their families but the industrial invalids apply for charity. Since the hazardous occupations are largely manned by immigrants, their opportunities for being injured are many. They are also subjected to all the other uncertainties of our industrial life.

Social tradition is an important factor in the situation. "It is the immigrants who have maintained in this country their simple village religious and mutual aid organizations who have been most able to withstand the shock of the new environment." [43] This idea

[41] W. I. Thomas and F. Znaniecki, *op. cit.*, Vol. I, p. 813. According to H. P. Fairchild, "The liberty of American life in regard to the relations of young people is construed by the Greeks as license. The innocent, friendly comradeship of young people of opposite sexes is something so foreign to their experiences that they do not understand it." *Op. cit.*, p. 206.

[42] *Reports,* Vol. I, p. 36; Vol. XXXIV, p. 40. Raymond Pearl has shown that immigrants from north Europe exceed their quotas in the almshouses while those from southeastern Europe have a better record. *Science,* N.S., LX (October 31, 1924), 394–97. The advanced age of the former is undoubtedly a factor. Since the immigrants from southeastern Europe are more recent arrivals, they have a smaller proportion in the advanced age brackets. Cf. A. Mangano, *op. cit.*, p. 120.

[43] Robert E. Park and Ernest W. Burgess, *The City* (Chicago, 1925), p. 121.

is supported by the Russian Molokans in Los Angeles. Out of a colony of some 5,000, they contributed forty-eight cases of dependency to local relief agencies in the period 1916–1929. "This situation in a group consisting chiefly of unskilled, seasonal laborers is indeed a remarkable commentary upon the efficiency of their mutual-aid institutions. . . . . The mutual-aid principle is at the very foundation of their communal organization. To receive aid from outside is not only considered personally disgraceful but it is regarded as destructive to communal solidarity." [44]

Among the Japanese on the Pacific Coast there has been very little dependency. The Japanese Association has been highly efficient in maintaining the morale of the Japanese and has promoted in a practical way, mainly by educational methods, the efforts of the Japanese people to make their way in the communities where they lived.

Up to this point only one side of social disorganization has been considered, but there is another aspect. Social disorganization affords opportunities for innovations and progress. Where there is no disorganization, there is no growth. A multiplicity of patterns is stimulating and leads to reflection. Since the old habits of the immigrants do not function efficiently in the American environment, they have to think through every step they take. This will bring development, for under such conditions new steps are inevitable. Social disorganization is thus a first condition of progress. While it may lead to delinquency and crime, it may also lead to social reorganization on a much higher level.

[44] Pauline V. Young, *The Pilgrims of Russian-Town* (Chicago, 1932), pp. 73–74.

CHAPTER VII

REORGANIZATION OF THE IMMIGRANT

Under reasonably normal conditions personal and social disorganization tend to be followed by reorganization. This is so general that disorganization and reorganization may be considered aspects of one and the same process. As conditions change so that the old standards cease to function efficiently, new behavior patterns gradually emerge. Certain features of this reorganization grow out of purposeful direction of the entire group, while other readjustments come even in the face of opposition of particular elements in the population. As the immigrant migrates from his old world environment to a radically different social *milieu* he, too, passes through a period of disorganization. Commonly, he begins to reorganize his life and adapt himself to the new situation.

A. Redefinition of the Situation

When the immigrant with his old-country heritages comes to America, he belongs to a world of which we are not a part. He does not understand us, our language, or our conduct. His experiences, ideas, and attitudes are markedly different [1] and he can share only superficially in our public opinion. With such a chasm between the immigrant and ourselves, he cannot participate in the common life—he is lost.

In his native country the immigrant acquired habits unconsciously and so long as they functioned efficiently, he was no more conscious of them than a healthy boy is of his liver. At first the immigrant seeks to participate in our life on the basis of definitions

[1] The immigrant radical differs from the American radical. The American talks about free speech—that is part of the Anglo-Saxon tradition in the struggle for freedom. The immigrant is not interested in free speech in the abstract. He has certain concrete goals—to establish socialism, communism, or bring some other change in the established social order. The Russian radical in the United States talks largely in terms of experiences in the homeland.

of the situation which were satisfactory in the old world. Oftentimes many, perhaps most, of his social habits, do not run smoothly and he becomes painfully conscious of their malfunctioning. Gradually, however, the immigrant begins to redefine the situation; he reflects and deliberates. New codes of conduct and new behavior patterns are evolved which make it possible for him to adjust to the new environment. He carries over certain traits from his old heritage which are combined with elements from the American culture in the development of the new code of conduct.[2] Thus the immigrant is enabled to work out a behavior scheme which relates him to his past experience and by bridging the chasm permits him to participate more fully in American life. Older immigrants function usefully in passing on the *don't's* to the newcomers. Mary Antin tells how her father began to initiate the other members of the family into American ways immediately after they landed. Carefully he explained the word "greenhorn" and instructed them how to act while riding in a cab from the pier. When they arrived at the new home there was need for further enlightenment as their father introduced them to several untried kinds of food, particularly the banana. The five strangers made their first contacts with a rocking chair—they found five different ways of getting into it and as many ways of getting out.[3]

The situation had not been defined for the newcomers and they did not know how to act in the new environment. The father, however, had worked out definitions for himself and knew what was proper under the circumstances.

The immigrant at first has no guide posts to follow, and much of his behavior is not in accord with the best practices. Usually, however, he develops a code to prevent the recurrence of that which is undesirable. He begins to feel the sneers and the shrugs, the pressure of gossip, the press, and the law. The policeman's club

[2] In the old country the Jew will go many miles to get advice from a rabbi even though he may not follow it. In America the rabbi, very often, does not understand the conditions, yet the Jew seeks counsel. For a number of years the *Jewish Forward* in New York devoted several columns to letters of inquiry. The answers to these have, in considerable measure, taken the place of the rabbi's advice. Answers in the *Forward* are not based on the Talmud but on American experience in an endeavor to indicate practical ways of making necessary adjustments.

[3] Cf. Mary Antin, *The Promised Land* (Boston, 1912), pp. 184–85.

and the jail sentence provide experiences which aid him in developing a workable definition of the situation. A child may, on first sight, be able to identify a tiger from a picture, but he cannot learn from the picture whether to pat the tiger on the head or to climb a tree. The immigrant is in much the same predicament with reference to many things in our life. He may have read about America and heard stories about America, but he must come to know it first hand before he learns how to conduct himself. Through his various experiences he gradually evolves a code which regulates his conduct and makes possible his happy adjustment to the new environment. In this process it is not necessary to iron out all the differences and make the immigrant lose his identity completely, but when a thorough understanding of the divergent mores is acquired participation becomes possible.

B. Development of Immigrant Institutions

Immigrant heritages, in considerable measure, are molded by the primary groups and institutions which touched the person in the homeland. Intimate relationships, particularly in the home and neighborhood, give direction to natural propensities present at birth. The child has a disposition for collecting objects. Society defines this activity and out of it comes the idea of property. The child has a propensity for showing off and society sets standards according to which distinctions may be won. He has fears. Eventually the family and the group define what he is to fear and whom he is to hate. In German Poland the Polish boy is to hate the German and in Finland the Finnish boy is to hate the Russian. The child acquires his language in the home and neighborhood and after learning one pronunciation it is difficult to master another. The majority of our immigrants come from rural areas where they learned their habits. In the village there are no general terms; it is *the* doctor, *the* postoffice, *the* teacher, and the townsmen are called by their first names.[4] These are primary group characteristics

[4] An Italian immigrant stated that to him, as well as to many others, Italy was nothing more than the little village in which he grew up. To him it was the little garden, the little hills, the little celebrations, and the little church. H. G. Duncan, *op. cit.*, p. 564. Cf. *Journal of Criminal Law and Criminology*, XXV (January, 1935), 756.

which defined the dispositions and wishes of the immigrants and patterned their behavior.

The immigrant does not exactly import his institutions but he brings his heritages. He looks around for agencies through which he may express himself. He wants security but cannot find that among the natives. He then turns to his fellow villagers where he feels at ease and secure. When several from the same locality in the homeland settle together, no matter what their origin, some of their old institutions grow up spontaneously. It is evident, however, that homeland establishments cannot possibly be revived with their old content and significance because conditions differ—certain ones cannot be set up at all in the new situation. In Japan the family council is an important regulatory device. When any matter of consequence is to be considered, such as the marriage of a daughter, the council made up of relatives convenes and deliberates. Since grandmothers, uncles, and mothers-in-law did not migrate to America in a body it is impossible to call these conclaves. Social machinery which functioned efficiently in the old country fails to fit American conditions so the immigrants develop new instruments to cope with new problems.

In China the family is the fundamental social unit, and their society is organized on a familial basis, but since the Chinese did not come to America as family groups, changes in their communal organization were inevitable. Village and district societies were common in China, but these could not be continued in the same way in America. In California the "Six Companies" developed as a defense measure against the harsh treatment accorded the Chinese and is a distinct product of American conditions. It does, however, have elements carried over from the village organizations of the Orient.

The Chinese tong. In China the *tong* is a society constituted of a kinship group, but in continental United States this has developed in ways quite foreign to the Chinese.

In order to understand the nature of a *tong,* we must know the conditions out of which a *tong* emerges and the forces which maintain it. For a *tong,* like any other organization, is a means for serving certain interests within the limits of a particular social situation. Interest is fundamental in understanding any organization. It is to serve some interest that organizations are formed. However, interests can be served in many ways and by different kinds of organizations. The reason for the formation of a particular organization to serve a general interest cannot be found in the analysis of an interest, and must be sought in the situation. There must be some forces in the social environment which determine the form that an organization is going to take. Therefore, in our study of the *tong*, we must take into consideration the element of interest as well as the element of social environment, and see how they interplay to create the *tong*.

Gambling is deeply rooted in the folkways of the Cantonese, and most Chinese peasants learned to gamble before they came to this country. As gambling is intimately connected with the activities of a *tong*, we had better take it as a point of departure in our analysis.

Here we have one reason for the existence of a *tong*. It exists to make gambling safe from raiding. Gambling alone does not necessitate the organization of a *tong*. The Cantonese have been gambling for ages in China without any idea of a *tong*. It is only when gambling is prohibited and the desire for gambling cannot be ordered to disappear by prohibition that a *tong* situation arises. At this point it would be interesting to compare the *tong* with the gambling syndicates in some American cities. The Chinese *tong*, in a certain sense, is just a miniature of the larger gambling syndicate. . . . . Wherever gambling is prohibited, in a Chinatown as well as anywhere else, organizations arise to accommodate the gamblers. The Chinese *tong* does not necessarily own any gambling houses as an organization, but it owns the right to grant letters patent to all parties who wish to open a gambling house in Chinatown. The *tong*, being sometimes officially empowered by the police, collects all protection money, takes out its percentage, and turns over the purchase price of immunity. If the policeman refuses to be bribed, then the money goes to the watchmen or spies who are in the employ of the *tong*. If either of these methods does not work out smoothly and the gamblers are caught, the *tong* puts up bail for them. . . . .

Gambling is not the only activity of *tongs*. They are also interested in controlling the prostitutes. The existence of prostitutes in Chinatown is, so to speak, normal; at any rate to be expected, in view of the fact that most Chinese immigrants do not have families in the United States. . . . . While the value of Chinese prostitutes is high, the probability of losing them is very great. This is due to the activities of Christian missions. . . . . A single procurer, without the help of an organized force, would be entirely helpless. For standing at the back of the missions are the forces of public opinion and law. In order to make their human property more secure and their financial loss less probable, the owners of prostitutes have to secure the *tong's* protection. Here we have another reason for the *tong's* existence. It performs the function of a vice insurance company. Again we may point out that vice as such does not need a *tong* in order to exist. It is when vice is attacked and the vice interest is in danger that some organization, in this case a *tong,* is brought to function.[5]

The *tong,* however, is gradually dying out because it, an immigrant institution, does not fit the needs of the American-born group. In Hawaii, where conditions differ from those on the Coast, there is no *tong* in the San Francisco sense. *Tong* wars are unheard of in Hawaii.

The Japanese Association. The Japanese Associations on the Pacific Coast have performed an important function in aiding immigrants to make adjustments to American life. They assisted newcomers in dealing with government officials, distributed information relative to the customs and laws of the areas where the immigrants settled, gave legal aid and agricultural guidance, endorsed various certificates and carried on a variety of educational activities. These organizations were not transplanted from the Orient; they evolved from the immigrants' efforts to adjust themselves to new conditions. These associations, on the whole, have been strong, but they are now on the decline because conditions have changed markedly, particularly since the passage of the Exclusion Act of 1924. Since the anti-Asiatic feeling has greatly subsided and the Japanese are receiving better treatment, these organizations are virtually without function. The alien residents have now become well enough acquainted with American life to need little assistance.

C. First-Aid Institutions

Practically every immigrant group has developed some form of organization to assist the newcomer in making his way in the new

[5] C. C. Wu, *Chinatowns,* unpublished dissertation, University of Chicago. Cf. Eng Ying Gong and Bruce Grant, *Tong War* (New York, 1930); Charles R. Shepherd, *The Ways of Ah Sin* (New York, 1923).

world. The purposes of the Hebrew Sheltering and Immigrant Aid Society, as stated in its constitution, may be taken as typical of a number of such agencies.

To facilitate the landing of Jewish immigrants at Ellis Island; to provide for them temporary shelter, food, clothing, and such other aid as may be deemed necessary; to guide them to their destination; to prevent them from becoming public charges and help them to obtain employment; to discourage their settling in congested cities; to maintain bureaus of information and publish literature on the industrial, agricultural, and commercial status of the country. . . .[6]

In addition to these organizations there are certain business enterprises conducted by the most sophisticated and energetic, but not always the most scrupulous, immigrants for the purpose of serving the practical needs of the newcomers. Among these are banks, steamship ticket offices, boarding houses, real estate brokerages, employment bureaus, the padrone system, *et cetera*. Many operators of such agencies have preyed upon their newly-arrived and immigrant fellow countrymen.[7] The immigrant needs assistance at the outset and these agencies are the only ones available to him since many American establishments do not serve him adequately. Certain institutions of this type will now be considered.

Immigrant banks. Many condemnatory pages have been written about immigrant banks [8] for the purpose of securing legislation to close them. Before dealing with this institution, or any other, we should trace its history; we should study the genetic aspect to learn under what conditions it was founded. We cannot correct undesirable features until we know why a certain institution developed. These banks, peculiar to the newer immigration from

[6] William M. Leiserson, *Adjusting Immigrant and Industry* (New York, 1924), p. 279.

[7] For abuses, see G. Abbott, *op. cit.*; *Reports of the Immigration Commission*, Vol. XXXVII, pp. 125–350; R. F. Foerster, *op. cit.*, pp. 390–92. A Federal Writers' Project says of the Italian immigrant: "With his bundle on his back, he was led straight to Mulberry Street. Meekly he went there, a lamb to be shorn, accompanied by some of his more prosperous countrymen who had arrived a few years before him and who were to thrive on his innocence and ignorance." *The Italians of New York*, p. 19.

[8] Cf. B. Brandenburg, *op. cit.*, pp. 21–24; T. Burgess, *op. cit.*, pp. 49–50; H. P. Fairchild, *Immigration* (New York, 1925), pp. 281–85; R. F. Foerster, *op. cit.*, pp. 391–92; *Reports of the Immigration Commission*, Vol. XXXVII.

southeastern Europe, were not found prior to 1880. Immigrants from northwestern Europe, coming to buy land and settle here, had no need for them. We may now consider some of the factors giving rise to the immigrant bank.

1. *Heritages.* (a) *Family system of Slavs.* The Poles and other Slavic immigrants are members of families, not merely unattached individuals. In the homeland the young Poles give all their earnings to their parents and on coming to America they do not sever family ties but send money home with regularity. This changes only after they have developed certain individualistic tendencies under American influences. The immigrant banker is the agent used for making these remittances.

(b) *Desire for status.* Immigrants as well as others are interested in recognition and status. The immigrant who comes to America is not merely seeking money; he is interested in the distinction which money can secure for him. A Polish immigrant makes this plain:

> Yes, I have succeeded in America; but success among new friends is not like success among the old. I think in a year or two I shall return to Paris and Warsaw for a while. It will not cost much. I will get myself a job on the steamship to save my passage fare. It will be sweet to have money —real American dollars—to spend over there.[9]

This man wished to go back to his old village to receive recognition. Had he paid his passage by first class he would not have attracted attention—he might have been snubbed as an immigrant trying to put on airs, but by saving his fare he would have more money to spend among his friends and kinsfolk where it would mean something.

The Italian is interested in land, but a freehold in America does not give him status unless it be in a colony of his compatriots. Land ownership in the old country, however, gives recognition and he practices thrift in order to buy a farm there.[10] Because of this he saves his earnings and places them in care of an immigrant banker.

Large sums of money have been sent home through the immigrant banks.[11] Much has been said to the effect that this has

[9] Unpublished document.

[10] This applies also to others from southeastern Europe.

[11] Cf. *Reports of the Immigration Commission,* Vol. XXXVII, p. 261.

been a loss to the United States, and that these banks should be legislated out of existence. These foreign remittances, however, have not been all loss. The desire to accumulate savings exercised control over the alien's conduct and made him a more dependable and desirable resident in our country; this ideal tended to keep him from becoming disorganized and criminal. Furthermore, the funds transmitted to the homeland increased the demand for American goods. Preferable to the destruction of immigrant banks would have been encouragement to land ownership in America. Instead, exploitation and crookedness in the real estate business were retarding forces.[12]

2. *Conditions in America.* (a) *Repellent factors in American banks.* The immigrants, in the main, are not attracted to the ordinary American banks; they stand in suspicious awe of their magnificent proportions and equipment.[13] Furthermore there has been no disposition among American bankers to solicit patronage among the aliens. On account of the unwarranted amount of clerical work involved in carrying these small accounts for temporary safekeeping, a charge is made. Impatience and an ignorance of foreign languages on the part of bank clerks repel the immigrant depositor. Neither has the United States government through the postal savings system done much to attract business from the group.

(b) *Attractions of the immigrant bank.* The immigrant turns to one of his compatriots for assistance and for advice in various situations. When he has accumulated a sum of money he takes it to a member of his own group, a saloon-keeper, grocer, or ticket agent, who has a safe. He can talk to this man in his own language. Furthermore, this establishment is convenient—it is located in the neighborhood and is open at night and on Sundays, while the

[12] See materials on exploitation in Chapter IV.

[13] A Slovak immigrant banker, in apologizing for the appearance of his banking room, stated that it was necessarily ill kept because the men would come in their working clothes, often covered with mud, frequently intoxicated, which together with smoking and spitting, kept the room in a constant state of disorder. Such a condition would not be tolerated by an American bank. This informant, who had been a banker for nearly twenty years, stated that he had often been urged to move into more pretentious quarters, but had refrained because he knew that if he insisted on cleanliness he would lose business. *Reports of the Immigration Commission,* Vol. XXXVII, p. 216.

regular business hours of the ordinary bank do not conform to his daily work schedule. Furthermore, the banker carries on a variety of other activities. He may forward mail and write letters for the illiterate, cash pay checks, act as interpreter and, at times, as legal adviser. As a notary public he prepares legal documents and assists in the management of property affairs. He often provides board and lodging at a reasonable cost. He is a labor agent and employers go to him for workers.

Usually no direct charge is made for this help but compensation is received, nevertheless. Many bankers deposit their client's money in regular banks and keep the interest; many use the funds in their own businesses. Frequently these services have been rendered in order to attract trade to the regular business of the banker. If he was a grocer, the depositor would generally trade with him and at times charge purchases against his deposit. When the banker was a saloon-keeper he expected his patron to spend money at the bar.[14]

Steamship agent and banker. Between the steamship agent and the immigrant banker there is usually an intimate connection.

> The relation between the two is so close as to warrant the characterization of them as interdependent. Even the casual observer readily learns to associate the term "immigrant bank" with the poster-bedecked office of the immigrant representative of steamship companies. In the mind of the immigrant the two are almost inseparable. To him the steamship agent is the sole connecting link with the fatherland. . . . . Nothing is more natural than that the immigrant should take his savings to the agent and ask that the agent send them home for him. Having made the start, it is natural that he should continue to leave with the agent for safe-keeping his weekly or monthly surplus, so that he may accumulate a sufficient amount for another remittance or for the purpose of buying a steamship ticket to bring his family to this country or for his own return to Europe. It is not long before the agent has a nucleus for a banking business, and his assumption of banking functions quickly follows. The transition is then complete—the steamship agent has become an immigrant banker.[15]

These men who confined their operations to the bank and steamship agency usually were the most intelligent in the immigrant

[14] Cf. E. Abbott, *Immigration: Select Documents and Case Records,* pp. 498–513.
[15] *Reports of the Immigration Commission,* Vol. XXXVII, pp. 212–13.

community. Through their various activities they became mediators; they became persons of influence. Frequently they became politicians and controlled the votes of the group. Oftentimes their influence was extended through the establishment of newspapers. At first, merely advertising sheets, they gradually began to publish news and other items which enhanced the banker's influence.

Since these banks were not under state supervision, many failed. There was no desire to defraud, but the banker was an amateur and knew little about business. Inasmuch as it was not customary to keep separate accounts for depositor and banker, a business reverse often wiped out the entire resources of both.

The padrone system. When the immigrant came to America his first concern was a job. Some, to be sure, had work promised by relatives or others but, contract labor being forbidden, the majority had to make the necessary arrangements after arrival. Since the newcomers did not know the English language and were unacquainted with conditions here, they naturally turned to the labor agent who was usually an immigrant acquainted with American conditions.[16] Out of this welter in the labor market the Italians and Greeks developed the *padrone* system to a high state of efficiency.

> The Five Points (New York City) are the center of that species of slavery exercised by Italian bosses or *padroni*. These fellows know English, hire workmen in herds (being paid by the employers), charge them enormous commissions, having already advanced to many their passage money for the journey from Italy, sell them the necessaries at high prices, and deduct heavy commissions from the savings which they transmit to Italy. "And while workmen fag from morning to evening, the bosses smoke tranquilly and superintend them with rifles at their sides and revolvers at their belts. . . . ." Whoever tells these natives of Avellino, of the Abruzzi, of Basilicata, that they are being cheated, loses his words. "*Signorina,*" they reply, "we are ignorant and do not know English. Our boss brought us here, knows where to find work, makes contacts with the company. What should we do without him?"[17]

[16] Cf. T. Burgess, *op. cit.*, pp. 45–51, for the story of a labor agent; Hamilton Holt, *op. cit.*, pp. 55–57; *Bulletin of the Department of Labor* No. 9, March, 1897, pp. 113–25.

[17] R. F. Foerster, *op. cit.*, p. 326. Cf. H. P. Fairchild, *Greek Immigration to the United States*, pp. 172–73, for the *padrone* system among the Greeks. For the Jap-

The important element in this situation was not the exploitation, but the fact that the newcomer had to make use of an agency of this type; there was no other provision for adjusting him to industry.[18]

D. Mutual Aid Societies

The prevalent or basic type of immigrant organization in most groups is the mutual benefit or fraternal insurance society. Among the Italians, in particular, there has been a veritable mania for these societies. Fertile soil for their growth was found in the so-called "campanilismo" (from *campanile,* the village church belfry), a chauvinistic attachment to the native village.[19] The first association created by the Italians of Chicago was a mutual benefit society.[20] Among the Magyars of Cleveland lodges and societies have been important from the very beginnings of the settlement. "Most of the societies are organized primarily for sick benefit, funeral expense, insurance, or social purposes. Many of them are directly connected with churches and others are branches or locals of larger national organizations." [21] The Czechs of Texas have

anese system, see *Reports of the Immigration Commission,* Vol. XXIV, p. 226. For the Filipinos see Bruno Lasker, *Filipino Immigration to Continental United States and to Hawaii* (Chicago, 1931).

[18] According to an Italian, America wants immigrants as workers but makes no effort to direct them to the places where they are needed. He reached the conclusion that if the alien were a horse instead of a human being he would receive more attention—if a horse is lost, that is a real loss while one immigrant, more or less, makes no impression. At all events, it seems that way to the immigrant. All this tends to strengthen his propensity to settle among his own people and to turn to them for assistance. Cf. *World's Work,* XLI (December, 1920), 205.

[19] According to F. O. Beck, "There are fully 110 such societies in the city (Chicago) and in their membership is to be found 90 per cent of the local Italians. A list of the names suggests that the membership is generally from the same Italian province, and frequently from the same village or town. . . . . Sickness and death benefits are the important features." "The Italian in Chicago," in *Bulletin of the Department of Public Welfare, Chicago,* Vol. II, No. 3, pp. 22–23. Cf. C. F. Ware, *op. cit.,* p. 155. In the early days of the Hungarian settlement in Lorain, Ohio, the lodges were "composed of people from the same localities in Hungary." S. C. Newman, *op. cit.* The Yugoslav organizations have also been based on provincial lines. J. S. Roucek, "The Yugoslav Immigrants in America," *American Journal of Sociology,* XL (March, 1935), 607. Cf. John P. Johansen, *Immigrant Settlements in South Dakota* (Brookings, 1937), p. 14; Adolph B. Benson and Naboth Hedin, *The Swedes in America* (New Haven, 1938), pp. 140–53; W. Halich, *op. cit.,* pp. 77–82.

[20] Giovanni E. Schiavo, *The Italians in Chicago* (New York, 1928), p. 55.

[21] H. Cook, *op. cit.,* p. 25.

organizations for mutual benefit in every section of the state.[22] The Portuguese have benefit societies in rural areas as well as in cities.[23]

We might go on at length and give information relative to other immigrants, but, in the main, the picture would not be changed; there is considerable uniformity in these mutual aid organizations from group to group. The needs of all are practically identical, the conditions here are rather uniform so far as the various immigrants are concerned, and their responses are much the same. There is, to be sure, some variation due to differences in old-world heritages and to situations which they must face in America.[24]

The Japanese boarding-house, one of the variants established in California and other places, has served well in keeping migratory farm laborers from becoming disorganized. In several cities men may go to these houses and fraternize with those from their own localities in Japan. There they find warmth and congeniality. Peter Roberts wrote of this institution: [25]

> One of the best samples of housekeeping I have ever seen was done by 140 Japanese who lived in the House of the Good Shepherd in South Omaha. A board of managers had charge of the affairs of the group. . . . . Each member was bound by a set of rules that secured peace and order. The men were constantly changing, some going and others coming; but the total number in the colony remained about the same. Whatever differences and difficulties arose, they were settled within the group. If any member got into trouble, the colony was back of him to the fullest extent. It was the most perfect organization on the communal basis I have seen.

We may now consider some of the factors which entered into the development of mutual aid societies.

Tradition. The death and burial association was familiar to most immigrants in the home country. "Its origin can be traced to church fraternities, which since the Middle Ages have collected funds for

[22] E. Hudson and H. R. Maresh, *op. cit.*, pp. 344–46.

[23] Cf. D. R. Taft, *op. cit.*, p. 337.

[24] Cf. F. J. Brown and J. S. Roucek, *op. cit.*, for the organizations of the various immigrant groups.

[25] From Peter Roberts, *The New Immigration* (New York, 1912), p. 124. By permission of The Macmillan Company, publishers.

the funerals of their members and occasionally also for help in sickness."[26] While the old-world heritages furnished the model, problems faced by the immigrants in the new world gave the vital impulse.

In the villages of the old world, it has long been in the mores that the primary group is responsible for its own members.

> An appeal to a charitable institution is considered even in Poland a mark of social downfall; it is even more of a disgrace in the eyes of Polish immigrants here because of the feeling of group responsibility which is imposed, or thought to be imposed, by the American *milieu*. The immigrant has been accustomed to see the wider social group hold every narrower social group within the limits responsible for the behavior of every member; the village praises or blames the family as a whole for the activities of an individual, the parish does the same with reference to the village group, the wider community with reference to the parish or village. The American population is supposed to do the same—and, of course, in some measure actually does the same—with reference to the foreign colony in its midst. Every Pole who accepts the help of American institutions is thus considered not only disgraced personally as a pauper, but as disgracing the whole Polish colony.[27]

In China the family and village groups were expected to care for their own members and failure to do so brought censure.[28] As a consequence there are no public charitable institutions in China. In the United States the Chinese make provision for members of their own group and very few appeal to the American agencies for assistance.[29] This heritage is so deeply embedded in the lives of the Chinese that in Hawaii American-born Chinese resented the fact that some of their old men were inmates of a charitable institution. Among the Molokans of Los Angeles it is considered disgraceful to receive aid from outsiders. "When a Molokan man

[26] W. I. Thomas and F. Znaniecki, *op. cit.*, Vol. II, p. 1588.

[27] *Ibid.*, p. 1519.

[28] Cf. Kia Lok Yen, "The Bases of Democracy in China," *International Journal of Ethics*, XXVIII (January, 1918), 197–203; Daniel H. Kulp, *Country Life in South China: The Sociology of Familism* (New York, 1925); Lin Yutang, *My Country and My People* (New York, 1935), pp. 172–213; Y. K. Leong and L. K. Tao, *Village and Town Life in China* (London, 1915), pp. 66–75.

[29] Cf. Carl Glick, "Year of the Monkey," *Colliers*, IC (June 19, 1937), 49–54, for an interesting story of a Chinese in America and the organization that aided him.

dies and leaves a widow with small children, the brotherhood often contributes sufficient money during the funeral feast to pay off the mortgage on the house or to start a substantial savings account to supplement the widow's or the children's earnings."[30]

Old-world heritages relative to death and burial are important factors.

There is evidence showing that back of the familial and communal solidarity of the European peasant is the fear of death and of its attendants and preliminaries—hunger, cold, darkness, sickness, solitude, and "misery." The peasant is strangely indifferent to death, but he fears any irregular features—suddenness, inappropriateness. He wants to die decently, ceremonially, and socially. Since a man's death is usually the most conspicuous incident in his life, attracting the universal attention and interest of the group, since it is the occasion of judgments and speculations on the status of the family—whether they are thereby impoverished, whether they are rich—death and burial are not only the occasion of the natural idealization of the dead, but a means of securing recognition. Immigrant families are notorious for lavish expenditure on funerals.[31]

The letter of a Polish immigrant to his parents is revealing.

Now I inform you, dearest parents, and you, my brothers, that Konstanty, your son, dearest parents, and your brother and mine, my brothers, is no longer alive. It killed him in the foundry, it tore him in eight parts, it tore his head away and crushed his chest to a mass and broke his arms. But I beg you, dear parents, don't weep and don't grieve, God willed it so and did it so. It killed him on April 20. . . . . He was buried beautifully. His funeral cost $225, the casket $60. Now when we win some (money) by law from the Company we will buy a place and transfer him, that he may lie quietly. We will surround him with a fence and put a cross, stone, or iron upon his grave. For his work let him at least lie quietly in his own place.[32]

In previous letters this same man had written that his brother Konstanty received a daily wage of two dollars in the steel mills

[30] P. V. Young, *The Pilgrims of Russian Town*, pp. 72–73. Cf. also p. 74.

[31] Robert E. Park and Herbert A. Miller, *Old World Traits Transplanted* (New York, 1921), pp. 124–25.

[32] W. I. Thomas and F. Znaniecki, *op. cit.*, Vol. I, pp. 789–90.

and that he was insured for $1,000 in an association. In a subsequent letter he wrote that the funeral had cost $300.[33]

American conditions and mutual aid. In the old country a man had a rightful claim upon certain persons who stood in a particular social relationship to him—the nearest relatives and neighbors were first in line. In America, however, these obligations are undertaken vicariously by comparative strangers because those closest to the one in need are not here. Under such conditions this function is assumed not as a natural duty but through necessity in an abnormal situation. In spite of the carry-over of sentiment for the locality in the homeland, a feeling of solidarity develops among immigrants as they are surrounded by strange people in America. Even though the bond of racial or national unity may have been quite vague in the immigrant colony at first, it always becomes evident when one of their number dies. Sickness and accident provoke feelings of sympathy and a willingness to give assistance; they feel duty bound to help any of their countrymen in America.[34]

The conditions of life in America have accentuated the need for mutual aid. The industrial worker who has no productive property and is hired by the day, or at most by the week, has to face more uncertainties than the peasant farmer or even the manor servant who works by the year. In addition to the uncertainty of tenure there is the probability of accident or sickness due to his occupa-

[33] Italian immigrants spend considerable sums on funerals. In the local lodges of the *Unione Siciliana* of Chicago, in addition to sick benefits "a death benefit of $1,000 is paid. The monthly fees of these societies run from 30 to 60 cents. There is also, in all societies, a death assessment, making the average cost of membership from $12 to $15 per year. . . . . Funeral expenses ranging from $50 to $90 are paid, and every member makes a contribution of $2 to the family of the dead member. During the sickness of a member all other members are obliged to visit and assist him, if he lacks a family. . . . . All members are obliged to attend the funeral, under penalty for absence. A band of musicians is always provided." F. O. Beck, *op. cit.*, p. 23.

A study of burial costs by John C. Gebhart in 1928 indicated the burdensomeness of lavish funerals among immigrants. A study of 319 dependent widows receiving grants from the New York Board of Child Welfare showed that Irish widows spent on the average $452 or 44 per cent of their net assets, while Italian widows spent $421 or 50 per cent. John C. Gebhart, *Funeral Costs* (New York, 1928).

[34] It also seems that where the greatest amount of prejudice is directed against a group by the Americans, those immigrants live under more discipline and organize their life more efficiently. On the Pacific Coast there has been most feeling against the Japanese in San Francisco; hence, they have been better organized and disciplined there than in other places.

tion. Since the majority of the immigrants are industrial workers, occupational hazards constantly remind him of the need for protection. On the other hand, under normal conditions in America where their earnings are so much larger than in the homeland, they are both able and willing to help others.

At first mutual aid was more or less haphazard; a collection or subscription would be taken to meet individual cases of distress. Under such conditions the more well-to-do received most requests. These members of the community could not refuse, but as a matter of self protection they were interested in the development of provident organizations whereby the risks could be reduced and the burdens spread over the entire group. An Italian in Birmingham shows how one of these societies came into existence.

> We have been here about thirty years. At first we did not have any society. We used to sit around in stores and talk about things. When any of our friends got sick or had bad luck we used to go down in our pockets and help them. Then we decided to form a society to help one another. Today this society has nearly three hundred members.[35]

In the old world the unreflective communal solidarity was sufficient to provide for all contingencies, but under American conditions the organization of relief becomes necessary. The first-aid institutions such as the boarding house, the labor agency, and the bank are organized for the newcomer and are at his service when he arrives. The mutual-aid society, however, is organized by the immigrants themselves and grows out of reflection on problems they face in the new environment.

Mutual aid and the community. When a mutual-aid society is organized in a colony it is far more than an insurance company. It serves as a center for bringing together all members of the community and thus makes provision for social intercourse. Since this society grew out of a reflective solution to certain problems, it comes to be a natural initiator as well as an instrument for carrying out new plans. This is exemplified by a Bohemian organization on Long Island.

[35] John Daniels, *America via the Neighborhood* (New York, 1920), p. 100.

The C.S.P.S. is primarily a mutual insurance society, which pays sickness and death benefits to its members. . . . . This particular chapter, however, has risen to the larger demands and opportunities of the local situation. Besides conducting a so-called Bohemian school, supplementing the public school, where Bohemian language and history and the principles of free-thinking are taught to the children, the society holds entertainments, lectures, and community gatherings of various kinds. Its members say, "It is our church. Here the young and old come together in common interest." [86]

In this way the mutual-aid society becomes the basic organization of the community, and in a sense these activities may be more important than the insurance function. In the old world peasant society, with its communal solidarity, no such organ is needed, since the traditional institutions and the parish organization make necessary provision for them. Furthermore, because of the homogeneity of the population and the close social cohesion in the village communities, any emergency is handled by the immediate spontaneous coöperation of the entire group, but in America, where everything is strange and the old-world heritages are inadequate guides to behavior, such organizations are highly desirable.

[86] *Ibid.*, pp. 31–32. Cf. W. I. Thomas and F. Znaniecki, *op. cit.*, Vol. II, pp. 1522–23, for a wide range of activities carried on by the mutual-aid society among the Poles.

CHAPTER VIII

REORGANIZATION OF THE IMMIGRANT
(*Concluded*)

E. Cultural Organizations

A number of societies were formed to fill a sort of vacuum in the social and cultural life of the immigrants for which the American milieu had made no provision. In the old country, communal village life provided the needed social satisfactions, but here "despite the daily toil and social contacts with their neighbors of other nationalities, the cultural life of their native land and local communities sought a means of expression . . . . "for auld lang syne.' " [1] The most important organizations of a distinctly cultural character are nationalistic societies, foreign-language schools, athletic, gymnastic, musical, and dramatic societies. There is, however, no hard and fast line between the different types and there is much overlapping. At times a benefit society may have certain educational features or the reverse may be true. Furthermore, the majority of the associations are in some measure interested in the traditional cultures of their groups.[2] Certain ones have been concerned primarily with that phase. The Germania Society of Chicago, for instance, has stressed the spread of German cultural ideals in America.[3] Among the Bohemians, "Societies have been organized and newspapers established with the sole aim of interpreting to

[1] Cf. John A. Fagereng, *Norwegian Social and Cultural Life in Minnesota*, unpublished dissertation, University of Minnesota.

[2] The organizations of the Slovak immigrants bear this out. Even the Sokols whose main purpose is physical training are a fraternal order. The membership in these is large, but it must be remembered that the work in which Slovaks engage is hazardous, the toll of death and bodily injury in them is heavy. Therefore, some form of insurance is important and these fraternities supply that need. In addition, they are educational—they publish official bulletins that disseminate useful information. M. L. Zahrobsky, *op. cit.*

[3] Andrew J. Townsend, *The Germans of Chicago*, unpublished dissertation, University of Chicago, 1927.

Americans Čech ideals; of defending the honor of the Čech name in America. . . . . Every one of them performed some good service, removed some prejudice, added in some way to bringing knowledge of the Čech to America." [4]

A number of organizations are devoted almost exclusively to musical, dramatic, and gymnastic activities.[5]

> The Čech loves song and the choral society offers him an opportunity to sing; so long as the professional stage in America will not grant entrée to the dramas and the comedies of his native playwrights, he will have amateurs act on the amateur stage his kings, his heroes, his peasants, his maids.[6]

The Lithuanians carry on a number of cultural activities in connection with coöperative stores.

> Each co-operative store is also a literary, dramatic, and musical club. In Chicago and elsewhere operas and operettas . . . . have been translated into Lithuanian and sung there. Besides the Lithuanians have their own composers . . . . who have composed numerous operas and operettas as well as songs, which the Lithuanians . . . . have repeatedly produced and performed in their own language.[7]

The Scandinavians have a large number of choral societies. In South Dakota the Norwegian group "is known for its well-trained and competently directed male choruses in many cities and towns." [8]

Gymnastic work stands on a par with music and dramatics in some immigrant groups, particularly among the Germans, Poles,

[4] Thomas Čapek, *The Čechs in America* (Boston, 1920, Houghton Mifflin Company), pp. 259–60.

[5] Cf. F. J. Brown and J. S. Roucek, *op. cit.*, for the various nationality groups.

[6] T. Čapek, *The Čechs in America* (Boston, 1920, Houghton Mifflin Company), p. 254–55. "A newspaper squib attributed to Bohemian men a double life,—tailors by day and musicians by night. . . . . Most of the orchestras of the city are made up largely of Czechs. . . . . The musical society 'Lumir' has maintained its existence continuously from 1867 until the present and has combined forces with 'Hlahol,' a younger organization. These choral societies produce each season an opera by some distinguished Czech composer." E. E. Ledbetter, *The Czechs of Cleveland* (Pamphlet), p. 15. For the Poles, cf. C. W. Coulter, *The Poles of Cleveland,* p. 35; W. I. Thomas and F. Znaniecki, *op. cit.,* Vol. II, p. 1587.

[7] K. Bercovici, *op. cit.*, pp. 232–33. Cf. J. S. Roucek, *American Journal of Sociology,* XLI (January, 1936), 450–51.

[8] J. P. Johansen, *op. cit.*, pp. 15–16.

and Czechs. The Turn Verein had a phenomenal development among the Germans in America. The Alliance of Polish Sokols organized in Chicago in 1894 claimed to federate over four hundred athletic organizations.[9] The Sokol gymnastic organization, founded in 1862 to meet certain conditions in Bohemia, was transplanted to America and in the early days of Bohemian immigration was an important organization. It had two purposes: (1) the improvement of mental and physical health; and (2) the establishment of a free Bohemia. Interest in the independence of Bohemia attracted members. Furthermore, it was an important agency in the social life of the group. When Bohemia won her independence, the immigrant group began to decrease, and the second and third generation members speak English and participate in American activities, so that now the association is on the wane among the Bohemians in Nebraska.[10] In certain communities of South Dakota, however, the Sokol survives, drawing its membership largely from third-generation Czechs.[11]

F. Nationalistic Associations

A number of immigrant organizations in the United States place the home countries at the focus of attention. In groups that represent subject peoples, the main purpose of certain societies has been to foment revolt against the oppressors. This was the dominant motive in the Polish National Defense Committee which was organized several years before the World War.[12] The Korean National Association of America has for its first two objects: "To help the Koreans liberate themselves from the yoke of Japan; to preserve the Korean culture and civilization." The Slovak League, formed in 1909, exerted itself to improve conditions in the homeland. The American Branch of the Czecho-Slovak National Council

[9] C. W. Coulter, *op. cit.*

[10] R. I. Kutak, *op. cit.*, pp. 149–50. What effect will Hitler's seizure of the Sudetenland have on the sokols? It is too early to note any effects as yet.

Likewise certain German organizations in Wisconsin are now lost in the limbo of the past. The music hall has become a room for the Elk Lodge and the spacious "Turnhalle" is used for occasional political meetings. Cf. *The Wisconsin Magazine of History,* IV (1920–1921), 314.

[11] J. P. Johansen, *op. cit.*, p. 26.

[12] Paul Fox, *The Poles in America* (New York, 1922), p. 91.

worked for the dissolution of Hungary during the War.[13] Through the Lithuanian Federation funds were contributed to win the independence of the homeland.[14] The Pan-Hellenic Union was active in defending the rights of Greece among the nations. It raised funds to assist oppressed Greeks in Macedonia, and aided Greece in the Balkan Wars.[15] The welfare of the home countries has been promoted in a number of ways by these societies. Certain Greek organizations in America have given help to their native towns or villages. At times they have aided a school, a church, or a public utility.[16] The Armenian General Benevolent Union was instrumental in sending considerable sums of money home to the unfortunate people in 1925.[17] At present several Chinese organizations are making contributions to aid China in her struggle with Japan.

Shift in nationalistic societies. The constitutional provisions and utterances of certain prominent intellectuals in the nationalistic societies may convince one that the immigrants' chief interest is in the native country. The original idea, however, has dwindled gradually. For some time the Polish National Alliance, for instance, was avowedly Polish, but since Polish patriotism was not a vital matter with the majority of the Poles in America it gradually became a Polish-American institution and began to deal with matters that concerned the immigrants in America. Even though there was a revival of sentiment toward the home country during the War for which the Alliance furnished both men and money, yet the Alliance became increasingly interested in enhancing the prestige of the Polish-Americans. Meanwhile the organization tried to bring America to appreciate her immigrant Poles by calling attention to the contribution the Polish nation had made to the western world.[18]

[13] E. E. Ledbetter, *op. cit.*, pp. 8–10.

[14] K. Bercovici, *op. cit.*, pp. 231–33.

[15] Cf. J. P. Xenides, *The Greeks in America* (New York, 1922), p. 106; H. P. Fairchild, *Greek Immigration to the United States,* p. 121.

[16] J. P. Xenides, *op. cit.*, p. 103.

[17] Schnorhig Balayan, *The Armenians in the United States,* unpublished dissertation, University of Chicago, 1927. Cf. T. A. Hoverstad, *Norwegian Farmers in the United States* (Fargo, 1916), p. 31.

[18] Cf. W. I. Thomas and F. Znaniecki, *op. cit.*, Vol. II, pp. 1582, 1596–99; C. W. Coulter, *op. cit.*, p. 31.

In the main, therefore, immigrants are usually most concerned with their own affairs in America. The National Slovak Society, organized in 1890, for example, has sick and death benefits, assists Slovak students, disseminates Slovak literature and generally acts as a body representative of the whole group.[19] According to E. A. Steiner, this society published a yearbook which devoted many pages to an admirable civic catechism, but the most impressive article was on "Etikette in America." What a picture! Immigrant workers in a steel mill studying American etiquette! [20] Oftentimes the only real interest local units manifest in the homeland comes through stimuli from the national officers. To be sure, organizations composed of immigrants from certain areas in the old world maintain an attachment to particular localities but are not especially interested in larger aspects of the fatherland. This is exemplified by the Norwegians.

A "bygdelag" is a society composed of natives from a "bygd," that is, some particular settlement or group of settlements in Norway and of their descendants in this country. Thus, the Valdris Lag is a society of men and women from Valdris, Norway, ... and the members of Stavangerlaget came from Stavanger city and county.

The objects of the bygdelags are various: (1) to reunite relatives and friends who lived close together in Norway but are scattered far and wide in this land; (2) to foster and preserve the traditions and memories of the ancestral home localities; (3) to collect and publish historical and biographical information both regarding immigrants to America who came from the district which the "lag" represents and also their descendants; (4) to collect charitable and memorial gifts to be given to their ancestral community. . . . . They have built a large number of hospitals, asylums, and rescue ships, established endowments to help the poor and sick and in other ways given concrete demonstrations of their good will to the land of their birth.[21]

[19] M. L. Zahrobsky, *op. cit.*

[20] Cf. E. A. Steiner, *From Alien to Citizen,* p. 115.

[21] O. M. Norlie, *op. cit.*, p. 436. A number of activities considered in the preceding section were carried on by organizations composed of those from the same village or district in the homeland. Frequently Armenian immigrants from a certain village organize, assume the name of the native town, and then send aid to that particular place instead of making contributions to a general fund for Armenia. Balayan, *op. cit.*

The various nationalistic organizations have stressed racial solidarity and cultural preservation, but this does not appear to be a bond sufficiently strong to hold them together. Length of residence in America, especially if the immigrant has made satisfactory adjustments, tends to dull interest in the homeland and the associations gradually decline. On the basis of a study of immigrant societies Dr. Jakub Horak wrote:

> An important cause of the frequent decay and death of foreign societies is that their members are for the most part foreign born. As they become Americanized they may lose interest in the society and drop their membership. Again, the centers in which the foreign born settle undergo rapid change. A given race, closely settled and extensively organized, sooner or later scatters and perhaps surrenders its locality to another—the society decaying and disappearing in the process. Again the native offspring do not generally join the order of their fathers.[22]

According to Thomas and Znaniecki [23] the ideas and ideals of the Polish nationalistic societies proved insufficient bonds to hold the immigrants together and gradually these great associations moved into the limited field of mutual life [24] and health insurance. The Italians have followed much the same pattern.[25] The main object of the Slovak National Societies is now mutual insurance.[26] This trend approximates that of the nationalistic societies in other groups.

G. *Functions of the Immigrant Institution*

Group solidarity maintained. The immigrant institution performs a most important function in maintaining group solidarity.

[22] *Report of the Health Insurance Commission of Illinois,* 1919, p. 530. This is characteristic of the Hungarians of Lorain, Ohio. S. C. Newman, *op. cit.* It also holds true among the Letts. C. J. Bittner, *The Social Heritages of Latvian Immigrants in the United States,* unpublished dissertation, State University of Iowa.

[23] *Op. cit.,* Vol. II, p. 1588.

[24] Cf. E. Hudson and H. Maresh, *op. cit.,* pp. 344–46, for the growth of the insurance function among the Czechs of Texas.

[25] An advertisement in G. E. Schiavo, *The Italians in Chicago,* p. 206, gives the amount of insurance in force by the Italo-American National Union (Formerly Unione Siciliana) on May 1, 1928, as $5,317,900.00; cash assets $176,169.18; death indemnity paid to date $93,000.00. The society had thirty-nine lodges, four thousand adult members and one thousand junior members.

[26] M. L. Zahrobsky, *op. cit.*

There are more than ten thousand local lodges of Czecho-Slovaks, fraternal benefit and religious organizations with more than a million members. This holds the people together (and gives them training in political government). It is this which makes the Czecho-Slovak feel so secure wherever there are others of his own nation. They are not only his neighbors but his brothers of the same lodge, and this binds them even closer together.[27]

Assuredly many of the organizations emphasize their own race, nationality or even locality in the homeland and pay very little attention to things American at first. But that is not all loss. So long as the immigrants work together and keep the homeland memories before them, there is less danger of disorganization and demoralization as they face discouragements and experience painful disillusionments. It is impossible to shift loyalties abruptly and become genuinely interested in America at once. The folk music, the drama, and the literature of the various groups make powerful appeals to them and keep them loyal and true to their own best traditions until they have an opportunity to find themselves and adjust to the new conditions. Participation in these activities also provides a wholesome social life for them. The various organizations make it convenient to consider together matters of interest pertaining to the homeland. But their adjustments to American life call for reflection; they are challenged by the issues they must face. Inevitably their discussions shift from the homeland to deliberation on their own present problems.

Immigrant institutions tend to counterbalance the numerous disorganizing influences in the new environment. This regulative value is made evident by the experiences of the Germans. "The numerous *Turnvereine* and *Gesangsvereine* have been responsible for keeping the German youth on the farm. . . . . The German young man or young girl is more apt to have a complete life within the home than the son or daughter of any other farmer." [28] Park and Miller have written:

The organization of the immigrant community is necessary as a regulative measure. Any type of organization which succeeds in regulating the

[27] K. Bercovici, *op. cit.*, p. 50.
[28] *Ibid.*, p. 190.

lives of its members is beneficial. If you can induce a man to belong to something, to co-operate with any group whatever, where something is expected of him, where he has responsibility, dignity, recognition, economic security, you have at least regulated his life. From this standpoint even the nationalistic societies do more to promote assimilation than to retard it.[29]

Provides for contact with the past. The new immigrant would be utterly lost if he did not find some points of contact with his past. As he joins a group of his fellow nationals, who preceded him to America, he finds certain elements identifying him with his previous life. He usually goes to relatives or acquaintances who provided him with the steamship ticket. He may work for them or board with them for some time. Here among friends in a colony of his countrymen he finds several agencies which have grown up more or less spontaneously to meet the needs of the group. So far as possible there is a tendency to reproduce the institutions and the society of the homeland, but usually changes are made or new instrumentalities are developed to satisfy their wants in the strange situation. Perhaps the "coffee-house" of the Greeks is the nearest approach to an importation; it accompanies them in all their migrations.[30] "The coffee-houses," wrote Fairchild of those in New York City, "are as exact a reproduction of those in Greece—with the exception of the outdoor features—as one could hope to find."[31]

This institution, based on European models, was intended to meet the tastes and habits of the Greeks, Bulgarians and Turks who did not patronize the American saloon and who did not use intoxicants after the manner of certain other European groups. The coffee houses are usually large, well-lighted rooms furnished with small tables and plain chairs. Coffee, tea, cider, ice cream, and various soft drinks are served. Tobacco in its various forms, even to the Turkish pipe, is available. Thomas Burgess described the Greek coffee houses in Lowell, Massachusetts.

[29] R. E. Park and H. A. Miller, *op. cit.*, pp. 289–90.
[30] Cf. J. P. Xenides, *op. cit.*, p. 84.
[31] H. P. Fairchild, *Greek Immigration to the United States*, p. 149.

For his principal means of recreation, the Greek of Lowell, as in most other Greek colonies of any size, has that purely oriental institution, the coffee house. When these were first established in Lowell, the chief of police objected to the Greek vice-consul, but finally agreed to allow them under sufferance. At the end of six months all ban was removed, and the police declared them one of the most beneficial institutions in the city. They are to the Greek what in a certain degree the saloon is to the American laborer, i. e., in its social aspects, without the harmfulness of the saloon. It would be a mighty good thing if our vociferous temperance societies would spend their tongues and pens in establishing and popularizing American coffee houses instead of frenzied prohibition—at which latter spectacle our Greeks are ever wont to jest. Imagine a room, sometimes shabby, sometimes neat, filled with little tables, about which are seated moustached Greeks, talking, joking, playing cards, sometimes singing, poring over newspapers, and smoking cigarettes and drinking their thick, sweet Turkish coffee, served in tiny cups, or perhaps Moxie or some other soft drink. Here are discussed with relish and vivacity and factional intelligence the politics of the community, Greece, the United States. Here is the typical Greek spirit of comradeship and argument.[32]

These externalities are merely visible symbols of other changes. The fact that they discuss American politics and the relations of Americans to themselves is an important factor. Old-world traits enter into the new institutions but rarely are they pure heritages; they are products of the immigrants' efforts to adapt their behavior patterns to American conditions. In general it may be said that immigrant institutions are a continuation and adaptation of the culture patterns of the home country.

Aids in adjustment to the new conditions. While the immigrant institutions provide continuity with the past life of the alien, they also afford contacts with American life. The majority of the immigrants have come from small villages where agriculture was the main occupation. Life in each of these communities was largely self-sufficient. All relationships were with people of their own kind. In America, however, the majority of the immigrants must go out-

[32] T. Burgess, *op. cit.*, pp. 150–52. Cf. H. P. Fairchild, *Greek Immigration to the United States*, pp. 29, 135, 149, 206, 209; J. P. Xenides, *op. cit.*, pp. 46, 84, 88, 89.

side their own groups to earn a livelihood and in considerable measure they must use American products of various kinds. The immigrant institutions assist the newly arrived in his occupational adjustment; they mediate between him and the American group and permit him to make his approaches to the life outside the colony by easy gradients; they provide a refuge to which he may return and find warmth and fellowship after humiliating experiences among strangers; they assist him in working out a definition of the situation which will make life tolerable in the new environment.

The newcomer gains his first impressions of America through contacts with immigrant institutions and these are not like those in the homeland, neither are they thoroughly American. His success in accommodating himself to American life will in a large measure depend upon the efficiency of these agencies which are a syncretism of old and new elements. It is these institutions which will direct his passage from Europeanism to Americanism. A few individuals plunge into the midst of American life and become quite thoroughly assimilated, but others are wrecked in the process. The great majority will belong to the new society which is growing out of old-world elements transplanted to American soil. They will change gradually as this hyphenated group changes and becomes increasingly American. The process is accentuated as the older element in the population decreases relatively in numbers and in influence and as the younger generations make more contacts with typical American attitudes.

H. American Attitudes toward Immigrant Organizations

The characteristic American attitude is that any and all immigrant organizations, institutions and heritages should be "junked." That, however, is a short-sighted policy. In the homeland the immigrants have lived in close-knit groups under primary relationships. In America they are thrown into secondary relations where they become lost. Immigrants can act intelligently only through their own organizations, and they should not be destroyed before something better has been provided. It is not necessarily "un-American" to continue some of these institutions through which the immigrants may realize their wishes. Opposition to them compels their adherents to take a defensive attitude and oftentimes they are continued longer than necessary because of the hostile American attitude. According to Leiserson,

> We have seen . . . . how some American trade unions have held themselves aloof from the immigrant, been indifferent to his interests, neglected to organize him, and even have deliberately excluded him from their ranks. This made the existence of racial and nationalistic organizing bodies all the more necessary, and engendered some antagonism between these bodies and the American trade unions.[33]

While it may be said that the majority of immigrant institutions exercise a wholesome influence, they are not to be commended indiscriminately. They must be considered primarily as devices to help life go on with some measure of success and efficiency in a new environment. At times the old-world heritages are transplanted to a situation which gives the resultant institution an unwholesome turn. But in the main, immigrant institutions function with a fair degree of efficiency in aiding the immigrant to accommodate himself. There is a considerable amount of disorganization, but the situation would be far more acute were it not for these syncretistic institutions to bridge the chasm between the old world and the new.

[33] W. M. Leiserson, *op. cit.*, pp. 294–95.

CHAPTER IX

THE PROCESS OF ASSIMILATION

When the immigrant comes to America he is strikingly unlike the resident population and, on account of these differences, he is more or less isolated. But inevitably he changes, moves out of his isolation, and comes to be increasingly identified with his social group—he becomes assimilated. Assimilation is the end product of the process through which the immigrant passes. We are interested in the immigrant as such until he becomes assimilated. When he has been assimilated and has lost himself in the group we no longer notice him—he has then become an American.

A. Definition of Concept

The concept "assimilation" has been defined in a variety of ways.

The "melting-pot" theory. For many years, after 1909, Zangwill's dramatic parable of the *Melting Pot* symbolized the popular conception of assimilation. In this great American cauldron we could "crystallize millions of aliens, of all nations, habits, and languages, flocking to us from every quarter of the globe, into a new, homogeneous race, better and finer than the world had ever known." [1] In eloquent words William Jennings Bryan pictured the outcome: "Great has been the Greek, the Latin, the Slav, the Celt, the Teuton, and the Saxon; but greater than any of these is the American, who combines the virtues of them all." [2] This was a comforting theory and it was in full accord with the current *laissez faire* ideas.

[1] Madison Grant and Chas. S. Davison, *The Alien in Our Midst* (New York, 1930), p. 230. Cf. also H P. Fairchild, *The Melting-Pot Mistake* (Boston, 1926), pp. 10–11; Isaac B. Berkson, *Theories of Americanization* (New York, 1920), pp. 73–78.

[2] R. E. Park and E. W. Burgess, *Introduction to the Science of Sociology* (Chicago, 1924), p. 734.

The "Americanization" theory. When the United States entered the World War it became evident that thousands, if not millions, of immigrants living in our industrial cities had not been fused in the melting-pot. Then the "Americanization" theory came into vogue.

According to this position, all immigrants should divest themselves of their heritages immediately and take over a standardized American pattern for their lives. "The immigrant's racial inheritance, no matter how much it may mean to him, becomes, upon his arrival in America, a 'foreign' impediment which must be forthwith cast away." [3] In the words of Panunzio,[4]

> Assimilation, as the word itself denotes, aims to make the foreign born similar to Americans in language, dress, customs, religion, and what not. It lays stress upon formal Americanization through naturalization. It insists that all immigrants must at all times use English and must put away their native customs, ideas, and ideals as soon as possible. In other words, assimilation tends to be a standardization.

According to this conception, assimilation was largely a negative process of denationalization. John Collier commented on this idea that it "rather indicates the taking over of the richly variegated cultural life of the many peoples coming to our shores and reducing them all to a deadly, dull Puritan drab." [5]

The idea of conformity is basic in the popular programs of Americanization, or, more correctly, "spurious" Americanization. In the words of Arthur Evans Wood:

> It fosters on the part of the immigrant a barren conformity to dominant trends in religion, politics, leisure, business, consumption and other aspects of American life. Conform in many large and fundamental ways the immigrant must, if he is to survive. That is as a matter of course. But that he should become a Protestant, vote the majority ticket, "root" for the home team, celebrate Mother's day, eat corn flakes, live beyond his income, divorce his wife, and speculate in city lots would not seem to exhaust the nobler opportunities that America holds for him.[6]

[3] J. Daniels, *op. cit.*, p. 3. Cf. I. Berkson, *op. cit.*, pp. 55–72.

[4] From C. M. Panunzio, *Immigration Crossroads* (New York, 1927), p. 254. By permission of The Macmillan Company, publishers.

[5] *National Conference of Social Work*, 1919, p. 729.

[6] Arthur Evans Wood, *Community Problems* (New York, 1928), p. 430.

In addition to *conformity,* the idea of *injection* is stressed by many. The immigrant is to be taught English and civics, he is to commit to memory certain portions of the Constitution, Lincoln's Gettysburg address, and literature filled with sonorous phrases. After he has learned to read he is supplied with patriotic literature, he is given full instructions relative to saluting the flag, and standing when the band plays the national anthem. Franklin K. Lane summarized this program thus: "One part ability to read, write, and speak English; one part the Declaration of Independence; one part the Constitution; one part love for apple pie; one part desire and willingness to wear American shoes; and another part pride in American plumbing will make an American of anyone." [7]

The idea of rigid standardization is preposterous. In a complex society like ours there are religious sects, occupational, trade, or professional groups which have ideas, attitudes, and practices very diverse and they even have languages not wholly intelligible to outsiders. In Chicago the residents in the "Gold Coast" do not understand the dwellers in the adjoining slum, even though they be of old American stock.

It became evident that the Prussian method, or forcing process, was falling below expectations. The naive assumption that American clothes, practices, and customs were superior to all others and the spirit of condescension and coercion aroused a feeling of resentment among the foreign-born and the process of Americanization was actually retarded. Immigrants criticized the idea scathingly. Konrad Bercovici, an immigrant, wrote:

> What is really meant by assimilation is only the acceptance and imitation of Anglo-Saxon civilization, of Anglo-Saxon modes of life, of Anglo-Saxon business methods, of Anglo-Saxon dress and the Anglo-Saxon language. People are considered assimilated or assimilable to that degree with which they are capable of imitating the existing order of things. Such appraisal of assimilatory abilities is false. Only those people assimilate rapidly whose own culture is not very deep, whose own culture is not very valuable. It is comparatively easy for an uncultured in-

[7] Quoted by C. Terence Pihlblad in *The Language Assimilation of a Swedish Community,* unpublished dissertation, University of Missouri.

dividual or group of individuals, whose range of emotion is expressed in their own language in three or four hundred words, to learn these three or four hundred words in any language for the purpose of daily transactions and expression of emotions. But it is difficult for a spiritually higher-minded individual or group of individuals, whose culture is far deeper, needing thousands of words to express more vivid emotions, to learn these thousands of words in another language. The emotionally and culturally low individual does not leave as much behind him, over which to ruminate and think, as the emotionally highly developed individual who is continually wondering whether the new is worth as much as what he has left behind him. The baser metals melt first. They melt at straw-heat.[8]

The "ethnic federation" theory. Social workers in contact with immigrants thereupon formulated the theory of "ethnic federation," which, quite to the contrary, stressed the perpetuation of the cultural heritages of the different groups. According to this theory each group is to maintain its racial and cultural integrity and contribute of its own culture to American life. The resultant American culture then would be a symbiotic relationship of these several cultures existing side by side as distinct entities.[9]

Culture units in such a situation, however, would not remain unchanged; assimilation would fuse them ultimately. This federation would make conditions favorable for assimilation and gradually the separate entities would tend to disappear.

A "sociological" theory. According to Kimball Young, "we may define assimilation as an interactional process by which persons and groups achieve the memories, sentiments, ideas, attitudes, and habits of other persons or groups and by sharing their experiences become incorporated with them in a common cultural life of the nation." [10]

[8] K. Bercovici, *op. cit.*, p. 16. Evidence from a number of sources support this point of view. In India missionaries have usually made greater headway among the preliterates than among high-caste Hindus. The latter have their sacred books and a more complex culture; hence they would have to give up more.

[9] Horace M. Kallen has been one of the leading exponents of this position. See *op. cit.*, and "Democracy versus the Melting Pot," *Nation,* C (1915), 190–94, 217–20; I. B. Berkson, *op. cit.*, pp. 79–93.

[10] From Kimball Young's, *An Introductory Sociology*. Copyright. Used by permission of American Book Company, publishers. New York, 1934, p. 495. Cf. also R. E. Park and E. W. Burgess, *An Introduction to the Science of Sociology,* p. 735,

According to this conception the immigrant is not required to divest himself all at once of his heritages and be recharged completely with Americanism. While it is highly desirable for an immigrant to learn the English language, it is not absolutely necessary in order to act in concert with the native group. In fact, many useful citizens carry on much of their activity through the medium of a foreign tongue. It is a reciprocal process in which both native and alien participate and the result is a mutual enrichment. In this situation the several groups (like the fire and engineering departments of a city government), even though they engage in quite different activities, are coöperating, nevertheless, in a common enterprise. This idea implies that the various population elements are interacting, and that they are being blended into a common purpose. This gives opportunity for originality and individuality which have no place in popular conceptions of assimilation or Americanization. A dead-level like-mindedness is not the end product of this process.

Assimilation is not a static condition. It cannot be measured by any rigidly objective standard. There is no agreement as to what constitutes an assimilated immigrant.[11] We may say in general

and R. E. Park in *Encyclopedia of the Social Sciences* (New York, 1930), Vol. II, p. 281. Panunzio prefers the term *incorporation* to assimilation. He writes: "Incorporation . . . . aims at a natural and normal embodying of immigrants into the whole fabric of American life. It, too, stresses the need of adopting the English language, American standards of living—social and political ideals and methods; it does not, however, demand these as prerequisites, but emphasizes them only as avenues of common and united life. Incorporation, also, grants immigrants the right to use their native languages if they wish and even encourages their teaching the foreign languages to the young and thereby building avenues of broader culture. Further, incorporation teaches the foreign-born to preserve the finer elements of their Old World cultures and to contribute them to the enrichment of American life. Americanization is not a state that can be brought about by force, but a process in which inspiration and a natural give and take are essential; Americanization becomes an atmosphere and not an institutionalizing effort; it is a state of mind created by wholesome attitudes, fair play and normal contacts; a constant growth deriving nourishment, but from broad and permanent social forces; an awakening into a fuller manhood and a larger social attitude." From C. M. Panunzio, *Immigration Crossroads*, p. 250. By permission of The Macmillan Company, publishers.

[11] Some think that Catholics are not Americans; only Protestants are. The Irish people were once foreigners, but now they think that every good American must observe St. Patrick's day. One Chinese failing to get a definition of assimilation, proclaims to his own satisfaction that an assimilated Chinese is one who enjoys the American dish of *chop suey*. C. C. Wu, *op. cit.*

that immigrants have become assimilated when they acquire the sentiments, attitudes, view-points, and behavior patterns of the Americans, and feel at home in the adopted country. Robert E. Park has expressed it thus: [12]

In the United States an immigrant is ordinarily considered assimilated as soon as he has acquired the language and the social ritual of the native community and can participate, without encountering prejudice, in the common life, economic and political. The common sense view of the matter is that an immigrant is assimilated as soon as he has shown that he can "get on in the country." This implies among other things that in all the ordinary affairs of life he is able to find a place in the community on the basis of his individual merits without invidious and qualifying reference to his racial origin or to his cultural inheritance. Assimilation may in some senses and to a certain degree be described as a function of visibility. As soon as an immigrant no longer exhibits the marks which identify him as a member of an alien group, he acquires by that fact the actual if not legal status of a native.

B. Nature of the Assimilative Process

Assimilation is inevitable. No matter what the situation may be, a change takes place in the immigrant who spends some time in America. Many try to steel themselves against any and all influences which may lead to a discarding of elements in the old cultural heritage and an adoption of anything from the new environment. Even then the inevitable happens. The Mennonites in Central Kansas settled in closed communities and tried to retain their national customs and habits through German schools, through religious instruction, and by restricting the association of their youth with Americans. Despite these precautions, however, changes came gradually; they could not stand against American influences.[13]

Their dress was simple and Quaker-like. When the young people began to be a little more free with their clothing, there were church actions against them. When collars and ties came into use there was strong op-

[12] From R. E. Park, *Encyclopedia of the Social Sciences* (New York, 1930), Vol. II, p. 281. By permission of The Macmillan Company, publishers.

[13] Cf. Arthur M. Schlesinger, *The Rise of the City* (New York, 1933), p. 32; A. Bergin, *op. cit.*, p. 7.

position, especially against the detachable collar. Bicycles met the same fate. Another local church went so far as to actually suspend two young men temporarily from membership for the crime of owning and riding a bicycle. Photographs were long considered as wrong, according to the first commandment. For many years the ladies, young and old, had to wear aprons to church, no hat, but only a black shawl or a small hood on the back of the head. Later on plain black hats came into use, but they went only as far as the ante-room of the church and then the black shawls had to take their place. Soon the hats were taken into the church and gradually the current styles were adopted. Instrumental music was long considered wrong even though the homes might have it. In 1914 the ——— church had neither piano nor organ to help in the singing, but an instrument had appeared in 1929.[14]

Leaders, various cultural organizations, and the foreign-language press, although trying to keep immigrants loyal to the old values, have not been conspicuously successful. Park wrote of the Poles:

> In spite of the interest of the Polish intelligentsia in Polish politics its efforts to impart its enthusiasms to the masses are not always successful. We have only to read the accounts which the leaders give in their own press of the difficulties they are having to maintain in this country the language and traditions of the homeland, to realize how glacial and, in the long run, wholly irresistible, under conditions of American life, is the trend toward a common language, a common life, and a common tradition of all the peoples in this country.[15]

[14] C. C. Janzen, *op. cit.* Williams wrote of the Welsh immigrants: "There was a time when the introduction of the innocent and helpful organ into the church worship met with great resistance. Parting the hair was looked upon by older people at one time as a sign of too much pride. The men combed their hair straight down over their foreheads. But the Welsh of today are quite as modern in their personal appearance and as dashy in their habits of dress as any other respectable people in the community. To sing love songs and "coon songs" used to be regarded as very unbecoming to the young, and they were rebuked for it by the elders of the church. Card playing, dancing, theatre going, billiard playing, and bowling met with wholesale condemnation in former days; and even pitching quoits, playing croquet, and other similar amusements by way of recreation, were discouraged in past decades. Today they are not endorsed, but are tolerated even by the leaders of the church. Some church members have billiard tables in their homes, others play cards, and many attend theatres, but most of them are particular in their attendance upon theatres; they attend the best." D. J. Williams, *op. cit.*, pp. 106–07.

[15] *National Conference of Social Work*, 1921, p. 495.

Park and Miller reached the following conclusion:

Assimilation is thus as inevitable as it is desirable; it is impossible for the immigrants we receive to remain permanently in separate groups. Through point after point of contact, as they find situations in America intelligible to them in the light of old knowledge and experience, they identify themselves with us. We can only delay or hasten this development. We cannot stop it. If we give the immigrants a favorable *milieu*, if we tolerate their strangeness during their period of adjustment, if we give them freedom to make their own connections between old and new experiences, if we help them find points of contact, then we hasten their assimilation. This is a process of growth as against the "ordering and forbidding" policy and the demand that the assimilation of the immigrant shall be "sudden, complete, and bitter." [16]

Assimilation a slow process. Assimilation is a slow process. Mere externals, to be sure, can be changed readily, but assimilation goes far deeper and demands more time. "It is unwise to believe," according to Bercovici, "that a multitude of different peoples could have suddenly dropped all their culture, all their traditions, and all their customs, to adopt another culture and other traditions and other customs and habits." [17]

Many berate the immigrant for not taking on American ways immediately. Some aliens have tried certain practices but have found them unsatisfactory. A Chinese immigrant put it this way:

Some fault is found with us for sticking to our old customs here, especially in the matter of clothes, but the reason is that we find American clothes much inferior, so far as comfort and warmth go. The Chinaman's coat for the winter is very durable, very light and very warm. It is easy and not in the way. If he wants to work he slips out of it in a moment and can put it on again as quickly. Our shoes and hats also are better, we think, for our purposes, than the American clothes. Most of us have

[16] R. E. Park and H. A. Miller, *op. cit.*, p. 308. Ludwig Lewisohn, however, declares that assimilation is impossible for the Jew. *Israel* (New York, 1925), pp. 38–39. James Waterman Wise says of the Jew that he is the most assimilated being on the American scene but still he is an alien. He is passionately, at times pathetically, anxious to be accepted and gives up, perhaps, more than anyone else in his effort to refashion himself to fit American conditions. *Jews Are Like That* (New York, 1928), p. ix.

[17] K. Bercovici, *op. cit.*, p. 4.

tried American clothes, and they make us feel as if we were in the stocks.[18]

It is difficult to appreciate the problems which some immigrants face in making their adjustments. For instance, Jews from various areas in Europe differ widely—some can understand each other only by signs and gestures. "Thus many a Jewish immigrant, on landing in the United States, has to undergo a double process of assimilation, first to find his place in the Ghetto, and then to make his way in the new world." [19]

Assimilation is not merely a process of acquiring the new but it also involves a discarding of the old. The immigrant slowly gives up his traditional ideas, standards, and practices and adopts those of the new country. Gradually the sentimental attachments to the old-world heritages relax and new loyalties are developed.

An unconscious process. In the main, the process of assimilation, as Samuel Gompers found, is an unconscious one and the person is incorporated into the life of the new group without being aware of it.

Unwittingly I was reborn to become spiritually a child and a citizen of the United States. . . . . Soon the currents of New York life crept over our Dutch-English threshold. One by one the members of our family group were swept into the life of our new home city. We learned its customs and found its opportunities.[20]

Ernest Bruncken observed that the unconscious Americanization often became evident only when the immigrant returned to his homeland. A number of Germans planned to spend their last days in their ancestral abodes, but many of them soon retraced their steps to the adopted country. They found that the better part of a lifetime spent in the United States had left them more American and less German than they had imagined.[21] Likewise G. E. Schiavo noted that probably the greatest disappointment in the life of the Italian immigrant has been his return to the scenes of his youth.

[18] Hamilton Holt, *op. cit.*, p. 296.

[19] S. Dingol in H. P. Fairchild, *Immigrant Backgrounds* (New York, 1927), p. 124.

[20] S. Gompers, *op. cit.*, pp. 25–26. Cf. Caroline F. Ware, *Greenwich Village* (Boston, 1935), pp. 152–202.

[21] *Proceedings of the State Historical Society of Wisconsin,* 1897, pp. 18–19.

Here, for the first time, he became aware of the great change that had come over him. Attuned, in some measure at least, to the whirlwind of American life he could not adapt himself to the bucolic tranquility of his native village. And so he returned to the promised land with a new outlook upon life. His children should now grow up as Americans. He would provide for their education—the best they would be willing to accept. He might even send them to college.[22] Such experiences are common to all groups.[23]

Assimilation and amalgamation. Assimilation is often confused with amalgamation, since the two commonly go on together whereever different peoples come into contact. Amalgamation is a biological process; it is a mingling of blood and blending of racial stocks through intermating and intermarriage. Assimilation, on the other hand, is a social, cultural, and psychological process; it involves the modification of attitudes, memories, ideals, and the fusion of cultural heritages. Either process may go on without the other: two racial groups may become assimilated without biological intercrossing, or they may lose their racial identities without any assimilation taking place. Usually, however, the presence of either one aids the other. Assimilation is conducive to intermarriage—that is, more frequent attachments develop between those who are closely akin in customs and language. On the other hand, intermarriage makes possible the primary contacts which are favorable to assimilation.

[22] G. E. Schiavo, *The Italians in Chicago,* p. 44.

[23] See A. M. Rihbany, *op. cit.,* pp. 332–33; Louis Adamic, *The Native's Return* (New York, 1933), pp. 3–92; M. Pupin, *op. cit.,* pp. 138–66; C. M. Panunzio, *The Soul of an Immigrant,* pp. 299–329; J. A. Riis, *op. cit.,* pp. 442–43. Demetra V. Brown, *op. cit.,* pp. 288–92, had become so thoroughly Americanized that an Englishman considered her a foreigner when she returned to her native village for a visit; G. E. Schiavo, *The Italians in Chicago,* p. 44; Christine A. Galitzi, *A Study of Assimilation among the Roumanians in the United States* (New York, 1929), p. 228.

CHAPTER X

STAGES IN THE ASSIMILATIVE PROCESS

A study of life histories of immigrants shows that there is a regular or natural order in the assimilative process. We may, for convenience in discussion, break this sequence into a series of stages, but in so doing we must bear in mind that there are no sharp lines of demarcation between them. Usually the assimilative process is said to begin when the immigrant lands in America. It reaches even further back. When the person first becomes actively aware of America, be it through a letter from a kinsman in the New World or through contact with a returned emigrant, he acquires something from beyond the ocean. When he begins to day-dream about America he loosens his sentimental attachments to his traditional world and transfers them in some measure to the land of his dreams.[1] Furthermore, when he decides to emigrate a crisis comes in his life. His time-worn attachments and habits are to be broken off, and at once he is a changed person; he looks at the old life in a different way. Immediately on his arrival in America a reconstruction of his attitudes begins. He can participate in the life of the new society only as he gradually absorbs the cultural materials in the strange environment. A change takes place even though he makes his way at once to a colony of his own countrymen.

Dr. Jakub Horak suggested three stages in the process of assimilation: external, internal, and creative.[2] This classification has considerable merit and we shall adopt it in our discussion.[3]

[1] A. M. Rihbany tells how he made a visible change in preparation for his departure, *op. cit.*, p. 154.

[2] *Assimilation of the Czechs,* unpublished dissertation, University of Chicago.

[3] Christine A. Galitzi, following Vacher de Lapouge, *Les Selections Sociales* (Paris, 1896), has analyzed the process into the following stages: (1) economic or technical—outward conformity, adoption of new ways of earning a living; (2) cultural—adoption of new cultural traits, language, and the modification of old customs; (3)

External assimilation. External assimilation is characterized in the main by a conscious and deliberate adoption of the more outward and superficial elements in the culture of the receiving group.[4] Usually this is denoted as accommodation rather than assimilation. According to Park and Burgess,

> Accommodation has been described as a process of adjustment, that is, an organization of social relations and attitudes to prevent or to reduce conflict, to control competition, and to maintain a basis of security in the social order for persons and groups of divergent interests and types to carry on together their varied life-activities.[5]

When accommodations are made there need not necessarily be any decided change in the groups or individuals in contact; each may maintain its own culture in this side-by-side relationship. "Accommodation," in the words of Kimball Young, "is a form of adjustment in which many of the independent culture patterns of the contending groups are retained." [6]

Accommodation and assimilation usually go on more or less simultaneously. House, in fact, is unable to draw a hard and fast line between the two processes. He defines accommodation as

> a form of adjustment which, normally, takes place earlier and more rapidly than assimilation, strictly so-called, and which, while to be sure it involves inner, psychic changes in the persons affected, is an ad-

ethnic—intermarriage and ultimate amalgamation. C. A. Galitzi, *op. cit.*, p. 165. This inclusion of amalgamation under assimilation may be questioned. While it is true, other things being equal, that amalgamation is favorable to assimilation, it may beget prejudices and hatreds that retard the assimilative process. On the other hand, assimilation may take place without amalgamation. Cf. E. B. Reuter and C. W. Hart, *Introduction to Sociology* (New York, 1933), pp. 355–56.

[4] According to Bercovici, immigrants adapt themselves to the superficialities of life quite rapidly during the first years. Men shave off beards and mustaches and women discard the traditional colored shawls. They learn the few words absolutely necessary in their every-day activities. "But what is deeper than that in a man's soul—traditions, customs, faiths—cannot be evoked, cannot be expressed in the few hundred words . . . . acquired. It is either expressed in one's own language or remains locked in the breast, to take ever deeper roots, or to fester, sore, and gangrene the soul." *Op. cit.*, p. 4.

[5] R. E. Park and E. W. Burgess, *Introduction to the Science of Sociology*, p. 735.

[6] From Kimball Young's, *An Introductory Sociology*, Copyright. Used by permission of American Book Company, publishers. New York, 1934, p. 496. Cf. Carl A. Dawson and Warner E. Gettys, *An Introduction to Sociology* (New York, 1935), p. 301.

justment of a relatively formal and external character as regards the type of relationship set up between the culture groups and their members.[7]

As soon as the immigrant makes his first adjustments, the process of assimilation begins. Park and Burgess state that assimilation is "the process by which the culture of a community or a country is transmitted to an adopted citizen." [8] As soon as the immigrant begins to wear American clothes or when he takes over anything from our life, superficial though it may be, then our culture is being transmitted to the newcomer. With that in view, we shall use the term "external assimilation" rather than accommodation.

Usually the first changes come in dress.[9] "The Roumanians realized that their attire was arousing curiosity, and sometimes even scorn, of people in the streets, because it helped to sort them out as *greenhorns*." [10] A boy from Mexico reported his experience when he entered school in Texas. "It was the custom of Mexican boys to wear suspenders. When I first wore them to school, the boys laughed at them. After a while I got enough money and bought me a belt so I would not have to wear the suspenders." [11] An immigrant woman in Cleveland said that at first the Americans looked at the Czechs as if they were strange animals. They could not understand why this was so, but learned later that it was because of their strange dress, particularly the shawls the women wore over their heads. When they discovered the reason, they began to dress like Americans.[12] An immigrant from Puerto Rico noticed that people looked at him and laughed. "I became self-conscious," he wrote, "and was not feeling well. I asked my friend and he told me all the trouble was with my hat. 'You must buy a

[7] Floyd N. House, *The Range of Social Theory* (New York, 1929), p. 315.

[8] R. E. Park and E. W. Burgess, *Introduction to the Science of Sociology*, p. 734.

[9] S. C. Newman shows that the Hungarians of Lorain, Ohio, change their dress but cling to the old food habits, even into the second generation.

Food belongs to the recesses of the home and not many Americans see that and comment on it. Clothes, on the other hand, are worn on the street where natives may see them and laugh at them. *Op. cit.*

[10] C. A. Galitzi, *op. cit.*, p. 135.

[11] Unpublished document. Cf. J. Cournos, *op. cit.*, pp. 66–68.

[12] E. E. Ledbetter, *op. cit.*, p. 9.

new, stylish American hat, for if you don't they will know that you are a greenhorn!' "[13]

And the magic of American clothes works!

> "You know," continued Dimma, in an animated tone, not listening to Matvai, "after I changed my clothes for these—I bought them at a Jew's store in the market for very little—well, after I changed my clothes and came out on the street a gentleman stopped me and addressed me in English."[14]

A more urgent reason, however, hastened changes in dress.[15] Few immigrants came with reserve funds; hence, employment was necessary to satisfy immediate needs. The clothes of a newcomer, however, were a serious handicap. After being refused repeatedly on his job-hunting rounds, Ravage asked one man the reason. With pungent frankness, after a contemptuous glance at the shabby foreign shoes, he made it known that a greenhorn was not wanted in his store.[16]

Certain other identification marks are removed in the early stages for similar reasons. The beard is a handicap to a Jew who is seeking employment in America. Abraham Cahan was advised to shave, but hesitated for some time. He yielded, however, when a fellow peddler remarked that his down-covered face made him look like a "green one."[17] It is more difficult to remove a beard than to adopt American shoes. The full beard of the Jew had a religious significance. Hence, its removal touched his emotional life; it brought inner conflicts and moral struggles. In Russia, when young Jews in army service sent home portraits of themselves with their faces shaved, the grieved old fathers and mothers would offer

[13] Unpublished life history.

[14] V. Korolenko, *op. cit.,* p. 71.

[15] Immigrants must adopt American tools at once; they are compelled to do this in order to earn a livelihood. This cannot be delayed for the majority must set to work immediately. But in order to get this desired work, it is usually necessary to adopt American dress. For this reason the immigrant yields early to the new environment in the most noticeable aspects of his life. Later on he makes further changes that he may enjoy some of the comforts which the American worker considers indispensable.

[16] M. E. Ravage, *op. cit.,* p. 91. Cf. J. Cournos, *op. cit.,* pp. 66–68.

[17] Cf. A. Cahan, *op. cit.,* p. 111.

special prayers for the renegades and give charity in their names.[18] Aspects of the religious life that do not touch the bread and butter problem in a vital way, change far more slowly.

Mannerisms and gestures which label one as a greenhorn must also go into the discard. Talmud gesticulations made Abraham Cahan the butt of ridicule. He tried hard to overcome this distressingly un-American habit, even to keeping his hands in his pockets while speaking.[19]

Religion changes less readily than clothes. Old-world shoes stand in the way of a job, but religious ideas cannot be seen. Work conditions, however, bring changes in certain traditional practices.[20] Many employers, for instance, will not hire Jews unless they will work on Saturday.[21] The pressure of industry and business have been so strong that the observance of the Sabbath on the seventh day is virtually non-existent outside the ghetto and even within its confines has been greatly modified. The Jewish festival days with their ritualistic celebrations have also been giving way to American holidays.[22]

Economic pressure brings changes in various ceremonial observances and practically wipes some out. In Hungary weddings and other ceremonies sometimes lasted three or more days, but work on a regular schedule in the steel mills of Ohio all but eliminated this custom.[23] Among Roumanians, "The wedding festivities are changed to one day. Who can afford to be merry for three days! The factory closes its doors if you are late fifteen minutes. But what about being absent two or three days?" [24]

[18] Mary Antin, *op. cit.*, p. 245.

[19] A. Cahan, *op. cit.*, p. 327. Cf. M. Pupin, *op. cit.*, pp. 80, 82.

[20] Among the South Italians of New Haven, the economic mores are affecting the religious beliefs and causing certain adjustments in keeping with the new environment. In an agricultural community, staying at home out of respect for the dead could be observed, but not in this industrial center. The men must go back within two or three days in order to hold their jobs. Phyllis H. Williams, *The Religious Mores of the South Italians of New Haven*, unpublished dissertation, Yale University.

[21] Cf. V. Korolenko, *op. cit.*, pp. 59–65.

[22] Cf. Samuel D. Schwartz, *Social Assimilation*, unpublished dissertation, University of Chicago.

[23] S. C. Newman, *op. cit.*

[24] C. A. Galitzi, *op. cit.*, p. 137.

Early in the process of adjustment, the immigrants pay some attention to the English language. Language, however, is intertwined with literature, religion, and sentimental attachments to the homeland, and a shift here frequently creates emotional disturbances. But change must come because speech is intimately connected with the earning of a livelihood. Very often, however, a mere minimum needed in their daily work seems to satisfy.[25]

In spite of a sentimental attachment to the mother tongue, changes have come in language usages in many immigrant groups. As immigrants experienced new situations known to them only in English they were forced to begin thinking in the new language. Since most of the Hungarians in South Lorain, Ohio, came from peasant rural backgrounds they did not know the Magyar words for many urban phenomena which were not a part of their village life in Hungary. Naturally, then they use the English words even when conversing in their own speech.[26]

Language changes come most slowly in connection with religious

[25] It is amazing indeed how far some immigrants can go with a limited vocabulary. A second generation Italian wrote of his father: "With an English vocabulary that did not exceed fifty mutilated words, he managed to transact all his business with the Anglo-Americans. When his stock of merchandise ran short he would telephone to the wholesalers, giving his order in a strange jargon spoken by no one else in the world. With one foot on the floor, and the other on a sack of potatoes, he hid his mouth in the transmitter of the wallphone, and labored ambitiously. Shouting at the top of his voice, he sought to make up in sheer volume for the imperfections of his pronunciation.

" 'Alo! Alo! Me, Martino Turano,' he announced. After repeating his name several times, he stated his needs: 'Senti me wan hindi quort biff (send me one hind quarter of beef), tenne ponti linki sossiggi (ten pounds of link sausage), to hemme (two hams), fiffity ponti liffi lardo (fifty pounds of leaf lard), and so forth. After many repetitions he brought his conversation to a close with 'gooddi byee.'

"It was indeed surprising that he was ever understood. But his dealers, as the time passed, learned to grasp his extraordinary English, and it was seldom that they made a mistake in his orders. If it happened that a new clerk answered the phone, and my father failed to make him understand, he closed patiently with a different phrase: 'Arriti, me come messelfa.'

" 'Some of these clerks are turnips,' he said in Italian. 'They can't even understand their own language.'

"In a few minutes he would harness his lazy bay pony to a squeaky little wagon, and make a visit to the wholesalers. Very soon he was back again, ready for his customers." Anthony M. Turano, "An Immigrant Father," *American Mercury,* XXVII (October, 1932), 222. Cf. A. Cahan, *op. cit.,* p. 104.

[26] Cf. Carl M. Rosenquist, "Linguistic Changes in the Acculturation of the Swedes of Texas," *Sociology and Social Research,* XVI (January-February, 1932), 223.

activities. Nevertheless, alien speech is on the decline.[27] "The old language has practically passed out of the Norwegian Sunday schools and is rapidly being displaced as the language of worship in the urban churches." [28] In churches of the Hungarian colony of Lorain, Ohio, the foreign language is gradually retreating before the steady pressure of English.[29]

Closely related to changes in language is the Americanization of names. Oftentimes an American finds a name unpronounceable and gives the immigrant a more common name. The mine boss refuses to be bothered with "outlandish" names he cannot spell. Lawvensky thus becomes Levine.[30] Among the Mennonites of Kansas [31] "in the hands of ignorant public officials and careless school teachers Grünwald became Greenult, Jost became Yost, Junk became Young." "One Lithuanian family," wrote Emily G. Balch, "explains carefully their real name and adds, 'We are called Bruno just because father was put down in the boss's book under the name of an Italian who had gone away.' " [32]

Some immigrants adopt new names because Americans have difficulty with them. A Russian Jew, Zvenegarodsky, became Rivkin. Some make the changes for financial reasons.[33] "In Penn-

[27] Kutak found the Czech language gradually dying out in Nebraska. *Op. cit.*, pp. 64–148. Cf. Alfred Bergin, *Lindsborg efter Femtio År* (Rock Island, 1919), pp. 146–47 for the Swedes; John I. Kolehmainen, "The Retreat of Finnish," *American Sociological Review,* II (December, 1937), 887–89; *Wisconsin Magazine of History,* I (1917–1918), 265 for the Dutch in Wisconsin.

[28] *American Historical Review,* XL (October, 1934), 77.

[29] S. C. Newman, *op. cit.*

[30] Wojciechowicz, all-American center on the Fordham football team of 1937, became "Wojie" in the press. Fans would have had some difficulty in cheering the heavy-weight champion Jack Sharkey had he used his real Lithuanian name of Juozas Zukauskas.

[31] From Arthur M. Schlesinger, *The Rise of the City.* By permission of the Macmillan Company, publishers. New York, 1933, p. 32.

[32] *Op. cit.*, p. 412. Cf. Maurice R. Davie, *World Immigration* (New York, 1936), pp. 505–10; *Proceedings of the State Historical Society of Wisconsin,* 1907, p. 283.

[33] According to a United Press dispatch: "Families of Irish descent in Roslindale (Boston) were incensed today over what they considered unwarranted use of one of their most famous names. Because of the prominence of Celts in the neighborhood and apparently believing it would help business, a Chinese laundryman has changed his trade name—without legal formality—to 'Yee Murphy.' " *Springfield* (Missouri) *Daily News,* August 28, 1934. A Jewish real-estate operator in a Pacific Coast city found it advantageous to operate under the name "McCarthy Realty Co." On the other hand, foreign-sounding names have a decided advantage in certain situations. Levon West, a skilled photographer, was unable to make any impression upon New

sylvania mining towns one finds Slavs who call themselves by such names as John Smith or Tim O'Sullivan or Pat Murphy, in the effort to make Americans of themselves." [34] "Vancura . . . . by a genial tug at his surname, emerged from out of the purging process as Van Cura. Who would sense in Van Cura a Čech and not a descendant of a Knickerbocker family?" [35] Young people, in particular, alter their names with considerable ease. Foerster comments on the Italian practice:

Giovannina becomes Jenny, Domencia, Minnie, while Giovanni and Giuseppe, luckier, become John and Joe; and illustrious family names, like Aquinas and D'Adamos, have been known to change, by a process surely of magic, into Quinns and Adamses! It is precisely such changes as these, trivial to all appearances, that make the Italian feel himself to be an American and the American to regard him as no longer quite an Italian.[36]

Certain immigrants who have improved their status and wish to forget the past modify their names. Every "reminder of his former condition of servitude and ignorance is shaken off. The 'sky' and 'vitch' are immediately dropped. Solomonovitch becomes Solomon. Stonowsky becomes Stone, Kelesky becomes Kelly. The old name may be discarded entirely and the name of the street or some prominent man adopted." [37]

York editors but after he re-named himself Ivan Dmitri they noticed him and he now takes pictures for the major magazines and national advertisers. *Portland Oregonian,* October 17, 1937. French hairdressers for ladies have prestige in the United States and for that reason many non-French persons adopt French names in order to attract trade. F. J. Brown and J. S. Roucek, *op. cit.,* p. 163.

[34] E. G. Balch, *op. cit.,* p. 412. Cf. E. A. Steiner, *The Immigrant Tide* (Chicago, 1909), p. 22. For changes in names of a number of prize fighters, see *American Magazine,* CXXIII (June, 1937), 107; William Seabrook, *These Foreigners* (New York, 1938), p. 152.

[35] T. Čapek, *op. cit.,* p. 118. Cf. *American Journal of Sociology,* XL (March, 1935), 608–09, for the Yugoslavs.

[36] R. F. Foerster, *op. cit.,* p. 409. Cf. Phyllis H. Williams, *South Italian Folkways in Europe and America* (New Haven, 1938), p. 95.

[37] S. D. Schwartz, *op. cit.* "The changes made in the surnames of Swedish immigrants may be classified as phonetic, translational, translocatory, and geographical. In addition to such more or less radically changed names, many immigrants assumed names that had no connection whatever with their original surnames, which in the case of most Swedish immigrants were patronymics. An example of a phonetic change would be the adoption in America of the name 'Steen' by one whose Swedish name is 'Sten'; if he chooses rather to call himself 'Stone' in his new country, the change in-

An analysis of the name changes in an immigrant group affords one measure of the assimilative process; this criterion, however, must be used with caution.[38] The names bestowed upon children by immigrant parents is a more reliable index to the degree of assimilation reached by the parents than the changes made in their own names. Writes Rosenquist of the Swedes of Texas:

> If the name selected is Swedish and not suited for use in the American environment, the parents are ignorant of or unmindful of the future needs of their child. If they give the child an American name, their sodoing shows a friendly attitude toward assimilation, a wish to make Americans out of their children, and a sufficient knowledge of the American repertoire of names to make a selection. The extent to which Swedish immigrants do choose American names for their children, indicates that they are quite generally motivated by a desire to become Americans as quickly as possible. Their children carry the tendency still further, so that the given names of the members of the third generation show relatively few traces of Swedish influence. . . . The desire of second-generation parents to choose American names often gives some absurd results because of the parents' ignorance of what is really American. Among the extravagant names encountered among the Texas Swedes are the following: Emergina, Orabell, Lenwold, Dorace, and Je Nell.[39]

volved is translational, for 'sten' is the Swedish word for 'stone.' Translocatory name changes are rather common among Swedes in the United States, and an example of this type of change would be furnished by a Carl Fabian Johnson changing his name to Carl Johnson Fabian, or as it would undoubtedly be in its final metamorphosis, Charles J. Fabian. Rather rarely it occurs that the immigrant selects the name of his native estate, village, or even province as his new American surname in which case the change of name is classified as geographical. Many surnames of Swedish-Americans are hybrids involving both the phonetic and translational types of mutation. An example of such a hybrid would be the name 'Seagreen' from the Swedish 'Sjogren,' the two syllables of which latter name mean 'sea' and 'branch' respectively." O. A. Benson, *The Accommodation of the Swede to American Culture,* unpublished dissertation, University of Pittsburgh.

[38] "To conclude that changes in names are invariably a symptom of progress in assimilation would certainly be unwarranted, but admittedly such deliberate mutations do indicate a conscious striving for accommodation. Since the recent immigrant is naturally more aware of his alienage than he who has been in America for some time, the former is much more inclined toward changing his name than the latter. Hence, name changes would seem to imply rather an artificial accommodation than any genuine assimilation." O. A. Benson, *op. cit.*

[39] C. M. Rosenquist, *op. cit.* Cf. C. T. Pihlblad, "The Kansas Swedes," *Southwestern Social Science Quarterly,* XIII (June, 1932), 10; E. B. Reuter and C. W. Hart, *op. cit.,* pp. 360–64, on the Eastfriesians; W. K. Knittle, *op. cit.,* pp. v-vi.

In the process of adjustment there is not only a tendency to take over superficialities but crudities as well. Many of these are consciously copied while some are acquired quite unconsciously. All too often as American brusqueness is adopted the charming manners of the immigrant are lost.[40]

Internal assimilation. The changes made at first are, for the most part, superficial, due to a conscious attempt to copy the most noticeable elements in our culture. At this stage there can be no close contacts with those of old American stock because of the lack of a common language, together with other isolating factors. The changes made are due in considerable measure, to the activities of fellow countrymen in the immigrant colony and through categorical, or mere touch-and-go, contacts with Americans. Gradually, however, more of the language is learned and more intimate contacts are made. The first cultural elements were adopted under the compulsion of necessity—the necessity to get bread—and they were more or less ill-fitting. Many newcomers felt ill-at-ease in our clothes, felt awkward when trying to use our tools, felt tongue-tied when trying to use our language, and almost starved when trying to use our food.[41]

Gradually, however, as closer contacts are made with American life, the immigrants begin to appreciate the meanings of the cultural materials appropriated; the adoptions are slowly but surely integrated into their own lives.[42] Immigrant girls in domestic service have opportunities to see American home life and to learn

[40] Cf. Demetra V. Brown, *op. cit.*, p. 283; E. A. Steiner, *From Alien to Citizen*, pp. 60–61, 204.

[41] A Grecian immigrant woman gave her reaction to American food. "I almost starved before I could learn to eat American food," wrote a woman from Greece. "It seemed to me painfully tasteless; the beef and mutton were so tough, compared to the meat in Turkey, and all the vegetables were cooked in water—while as for the potatoes I had never seen such quantities in my life. We had them for breakfast, for luncheon, and for dinner, in some form or other. Just before we sat down to table the principal said grace, in which were the words, 'Bless that of which we are about to partake.' To my untrained ear 'partake' and 'potatoes' sounded exactly alike, and I wrote home that the Americans not only ate potatoes morning, noon, and night, but that they even prayed to the Lord to keep them supplied with potatoes, instead of daily bread." Demetra V. Brown, *A Child of the Orient* (Boston, 1914, Houghton Mifflin Company), pp. 275–76.

[42] Even in adopting the dress of the group it is not a matter of getting rid of the old abruptly and taking over the new. An American suit on a green immigrant is not entirely American—suit and man do not quite blend.

habits and customs at close range. As a rule they become more sensitive to American influences than do the boys of their own ethnic group, even though the latter may have been longer resident in the United States.[43] Rarely do the boys come in touch with the intimacies of American family life. In general the girls learn the language and master its finer meanings more rapidly than the boys who make their contacts in the factory.

Changes of a subtler and more profound nature come gradually.[44] Accommodations made to surface elements in the new culture make possible closer contacts and deeper penetration into American life. When the immigrant removes the more evident marks of the greenhorn, friendlier attitudes develop toward him and additional avenues of communication open. As he makes initial excursions into the American community, he desires to be a "good" representative of his ethnic group. Unconsciously this brings a marked change over him. According to Park,

> It is an interesting fact that as a first step in Americanization the immigrant ceases to be a provincial and becomes a nationalist. The Wurtemburgers and the Westphalians become Germans; the Sicilians and Neapolitans become Italians, and the Jews become Zionists. The ambition of the immigrant to gain recognition in the American community, "to represent" the national name "well in America," . . . . is one of the first characteristic manifestations of national consciousness and it is because he has been unable to get that recognition as an individual that he seeks it as a member of a nationality. One reason immigrants live in a

[43] An American-born German boy wrote: "Because my mother, who had come here at an early age, spent many years working for American families and becoming acquainted with American modes of living, she did not try to force anything German on us children. To please my father, to be sure, we used the German language. However, at his death (when I was about nine years old) mother discontinued that practice. In California, mother had fine contacts. Coming here some forty years ago she worked in and became acquainted with some of the better first families. Although working as cook, such were the relations between employer and employee at that time that today she is a welcome guest in many a fine home." Unpublished life history.

[44] "The agencies of assimilation work by conditioning the emotions (or fixating wishes) of many individuals to a common stimulus. In the army the daily salute to the colors amid impressive surroundings, while the band plays the Star Spangled Banner, produces a powerful conditioned emotion. This common sentiment serves as a bond of we-feeling between all those who have been in the military service." Joseph K. Folsom, *Social Psychology* (New York, 1931), p. 394.

colony is that they cannot get out, and one reason they establish nationalist societies which seek among other things to represent the old country well in this, is that in this way they can participate in American life. If the immigrant chooses to remain a hyphenated American it is frequently because, only through an organization of his own language groups, can he get status and recognition in the larger American world outside. As a leader in an immigrant community he and the community are enabled to participate in American life in ways which they could not as individuals, unacquainted with the language and with the customs of the country as they are. . . . . If it is true that the immigrant, who arrives here a provincial, takes his first step in Americanization when he becomes concerned about the reputation of his home country in America, it is equally true that the immigrant who remains a provincial remains at the same time farthest removed from American life.[45]

Creative assimilation. At first the immigrant consciously adopts certain cultural elements in order to make the most elementary and necessary adjustments. These acquisitions with little meaning to him at the outset, gradually are woven into his life.[46] His attention is no longer centered upon the adoption of the minimum elements in our culture that will make his life tolerable in the new environment. He can now understand and appreciate fairly well our cultural values.[47] This does not mean that he has uprooted every

[45] *Conference of Social Work,* 1921, pp. 494–95.

[46] Cf. M. Pupin, *op. cit.,* pp. 115–16, for an interesting comment.

[47] This means, among other things, that he can laugh in the right place; a person who does not understand and appreciate a culture will laugh at the wrong time. In 1928 an American film was exhibited by the Anti-Saloon League to a group of school children of oriental ancestry in Honolulu. The film depicted a "Scoff-law" who carried a hip flask and also bought one for his son. Another man of the same type had a daughter who was the very apple of his eye. The young people had a party at which the hip flasks were much in evidence. Finally they went out for an auto ride which was rather wild, ending in a plunge over an embankment that killed the girl. The girl's father was notified by telephone. When he arrived on the scene he was excited and distraught, since he had lost his only daughter. The picture was of a serious nature, well done, and was a touching scene so far as most Americans were concerned. While they did not approve the man's attitude toward the law, yet in this crisis they sympathized with him. But the pupils of oriental ancestry laughed at that scene. A Japanese man would have been stolid in a comparable situation and would have displayed no emotion. This man lost all claim to serious consideration when he so evidently gave way to his emotions. A few months later a group of Japanese students in Honolulu presented the play "The Faithful," which had its setting in the days of the samurai in Japan. Just before the curtain dropped, ten men, kneeling in a row, committed *hara-kiri* (disembowelled themselves with short daggers). This climax was an intense scene so far as the Japanese were concerned—these men had risen to

vestige of his old-world heritage and taken over everything American. Complete assimilation is rarely, if ever, accomplished in one generation.[48] According to Park,[49]

It cannot, however, be assumed that the associations which have erased the external signs of race and nationality have modified to any great extent fundamental cultural and racial characteristics. W. H. R. Rivers' studies in Melanesia convinced him that, with the increasing contacts which the expansion of commerce and peoples has enforced, the whole material culture of a people, including its language and its religious practices, may be swept away without touching what he calls "the essential social structure" of that people's cultural life. Considerations of this kind have raised the question whether the assimilation that is measured in external uniformities of manners, dress, and speech may safely be taken as an index of fundamental national solidarity, or whether it may not in fact represent a more superficial "like-mindedness," a mere veneer covering profound and more or less irreconcilable moral and cultural differences. It is evident that there are grades and degrees of assimilation whether or not we are able to measure them. Furthermore, the conflicts which not only in political but also in personal and family life, have their origin in these divergent cultures lend a special importance to questions raised in regard to the fusion and assimilation that take place on the profounder levels of cultural life.

great heights; they were now with the immortals. But a number of white people in the audience laughed; it seemed ridiculous to them.

In both instances there was laughter at the wrong time; the Orientals did not understand the American film and the Americans did not understand the Japanese play. Cf. Romanzo Adams, "Laughing at the Wrong Place," *Pacific Affairs,* II (July, 1929), 415–17; William C. Smith, *Americans in Process* (Ann Arbor, 1937), pp. 352–53.

[48] According to Rebecca Kohut, there are on record a few cases of Jews who were honestly converted to another faith. Usually, however, when they left their religion it was to escape the tortures of persecution or because of some evident social advantage. *My Portion* (New York, 1925), p. 249. Says R. I. Kutak of a Bohemian group in Nebraska: "As is usually the case in culture conflicts, the ways and means, the external side of life, have yielded more readily than the inner values, the ends of existence. In outward appearance Milligan does not differ from the average American village. The houses are built to the conventional pattern, and their rooms are filled with the typical products of the machine age. However, the people in their American clothing may speak only in the Czech tongue. The latest model radio may adorn the family living room, but remain silent except when an orchestra is broadcasting Bohemian music. The housewife may use a modern electric stove, but the food she prepares is the same as that which pleased her ancestors in some little village in Bohemia." *Op cit.,* p. 156.

[49] From R. E. Park, *Encyclopedia of the Social Sciences* (New York, 1930), Vol. II, p. 282. By permission of The Macmillan Company, publishers.

Differences in background and experience make it difficult, if not impossible, for the several ethnic groups to see eye to eye.

When we speak of the different "heritages" or "traditions" which our different immigrant groups bring, it means that owing to different historical circumstances they have defined the situation differently. Certain prominent personalities, schools of thought, bodies of doctrine, historical events, have contributed in defining the situation and determining the attitudes and values of our various immigrant groups in characteristic ways in their home countries. To the Sicilian, for example, marital infidelity means the stiletto; to the American, the divorce court. And even when the immigrant thinks that he understands us he nevertheless does not do this completely. At the best he interprets our cultural traditions in terms of his own. This is well exemplified in a letter dated May 2, 1907, to President Theodore Roosevelt from an Italian (the writer was at the time in Sing Sing) proposing to make him president of the Black Hand if his candidacy for the presidency at Washington failed. The native American appreciates the "manhood" and the "big stick" of Colonel Roosevelt in their whole context, but the Sicilian identified them with his own *omerta* (literally "manliness").[50]

An immigrant may appear to be participating freely in our national life, but still trivial incidents make it evident that he is not wholly assimilated. For a long time the words, "Land where my fathers died," in "America" troubled Rihbany and he could not sing them. Finally he came to realize that this did not refer to biological fatherhood, but all those who had stood for the ideals which he cherished were his fathers. After that he could sing those words as truthfully and honestly as the line "Land of the Pilgrim's pride." [51]

Marked changes, nevertheless, do come in the more deep-seated attitudes whereupon the immigrant can participate understandingly in our life. He can view our culture in a more objective and rational manner than the one who is provincially-minded. He can more nearly see the shortcomings in our American life and can make contributions from his ethnic group to the development and enrichment of our culture. He does not do this merely to preserve

[50] *Memorandum on Participation prepared by the Americanization Study*, Carnegie Corporation, 1919.

[51] Cf. A. M. Rihbany, *op. cit.*, pp. 285–86.

his cultural heritage in the New World. He is not interested in preserving this particular cultural trait as such, but he offers it for the contribution it may make, knowing full well that, in all probability, it will be changed as it is fused into the American culture pattern.[52]

Proponents of the "Americanization theory" of assimilation have contended that the immigrants should—and would if sufficient Americanism were injected into them—become like Americans. When aliens took over American culture these adopted elements would in no way be modified. That is an untenable position.[53] Park presents a reasonable point of view: [54]

> Recent anthropological discussions of cultural diffusion have emphasized the fact that the cultural traits of the group are not transmitted to another by the mere fact of exchange and use. The inventions and cultural forms of the people may be said to become a part of the culture of another only when, as Malinowski puts it, the adopting culture "has re-evolved the idea, custom, or institution which it has adopted." The Melanesian, to use his illustration, imports and uses matches, but the match has never become a part of Melanesian culture. Similarly an alien may be said to be assimilated not when he has learned to use the language, customs and institutions of his adopted country, but when he has been able to make them his own in some more thoroughgoing way than mere use implies.

Naturalization and assimilation. According to some, naturalization is the climax—when the alien has gone through that formality he has become thoroughly assimilated. The usual procedure of the

[52] "A transplanted trait frequently, though not invariably, functions differently when taken to a new culture. Among most Indian tribes tobacco had a religious significance as well as a social significance. The incense which is burned in the Buddhist temples of China and Japan has, when introduced into European culture, merely an aesthetic significance. Many of the traits connected with our celebration of Christmas were of pagan origin, but they function in our culture as part of a ceremonial or religious complex." Wilson D. Wallis, *Introduction to Sociology* (New York, 1927), p. 377.

[53] "Americanization is not something which corresponds with the moulding of clay into a certain static form. On the contrary, it models the life of America into forms ever new and more adequate. It is dynamic. It makes American life today different from what it was yesterday, and tomorrow different still. It never rests, but moves ever onward. It is not simply imitative. It is creative." John Daniels, *op. cit.*, p. 13.

[54] *Encyclopedia of the Social Sciences* (New York, 1930), Vol. II, p. 282. By permission of The Macmillan Company, publishers.

naturalization court is a very inadequate test of any fundamental assimilation. It is of some value, to be sure. Obviously the declaration to become a citizen, be the motive either sentimental or utilitarian, discloses on the part of the immigrant a desire to identify himself with our American life.[55] Some immigrants are greatly impressed by the naturalization procedure. An Italian wrote:

After I graduated from the University I became naturalized. To me this was the most wonderful thing that I have ever experienced. When the officer explained to us the significance of our becoming naturalized, a new feeling came over me and I realized that I was really a true American.[56]

Michael Pupin, on the other hand, was disappointed because the naturalization procedure was so perfunctory.[57] A clerk collected the fee and handed him the certificate. No one in the great throng that moved through the city hall noticed him. On the following day he received a diploma from Columbia University. The President of the university beamed on him, friends in the audience applauded, friends sent him flowers, many congratulated him, and one old lady kissed him. The gay and colorful commencement exercises made the formality in the naturalization office appear all the more prosaic and unimpressive. One of the ceremonies made him only a Bachelor of Arts while the other made him a citizen of the Republic. Which one should have been the more solemn? [58]

[55] Cf. C. A. Galitzi, *op. cit.*, p. 144.

[56] Unpublished life history.

[57] But more serious are the attitudes toward naturalization and citizenship which normally develop out of experiences with crooked politicians in the big cities. An Italian immigrant said: "These people are without a king such as ours in Italy. It is what they call a Republic, as Garibaldi wanted, and every year in the fall the people vote. They wanted us to vote last fall, but we did not. A man came and said that he would get us made American for fifty cents and then we could get two dollars for our votes. I talked to some of our people and they told me that we should have to put a paper in a box telling who we wanted to govern us." Hamilton Holt, *op. cit.*, p. 60. But these immigrants came to better their economic condition and, if their much-sought-after votes can be traded for a larger loaf of bread, can we rail at them? Cf. also Philip Rose, *The Italians in America* (Garden City, 1922), pp. 80–81.

[58] M. Pupin, *op. cit.*, p. 136. Cf. *Ibid.*, pp. 100–37; E. A. Steiner, *From Alien to Citizen*, pp. 247–49; P. A. Speek, *A Stake in the Land* (New York, 1921), p. 80; C. M. Panunzio, *The Soul of an Immigrant*, pp. 193–200.

CHAPTER XI

FACTORS IN ASSIMILATION

The process of assimilation goes on unobtrusively but inevitably. Under certain conditions its progress is glacial, but under others the stage is set in such a manner as to accelerate the movement. Factors which aid or retard the process will be considered in the two chapters to follow.

A. Physiological Characteristics

Color and physiognomy. Differences in color and physiognomy which set one apart from the native population retard assimilation.[1] Skin color although of no particular significance biologically is highly important sociologically; it is a permanent badge upon which and around which irritations and animosities incidental to human contacts tend to focus.[2] Furthermore, an unpleasant experience with a person of different color is usually more exasperating than a like experience with one of the same color. A football player, whose nose was broken in an inter-collegiate game in which he played against a Negro, said of the incident, "I didn't mind having my nose broken, but I did hate to have it broken by a 'nigger.' " It is also easy for the imagination to exaggerate and impute unfavorable characteristics to the person or group that differs physically.[3] Thus are barriers raised which prevent sympathetic

[1] Cf. Herbert Quick, *One Man's Life* (Indianapolis, 1925), pp. 126–28.

[2] The importance of physical differences is being made evident on the Pacific Coast in connection with the growing boycott on Japanese goods because of her undeclared war in China. Perhaps the worst sufferers are those of American birth. Americans do not ask if a Japanese is citizen or alien. The fact that he has the physical features of the Oriental is the decisive factor and he is treated as if he were responsible for the war. *Japanese-American Courier,* Seattle, December 25, 1937.

[3] To the point is E. A. Steiner's comment, "Where a tint is equivalent to a taint, a crooked nose to a crooked character, and where a peculiar slant of the eyes is taken as unmistakable evidence that the race so marked cannot see straight." *The Broken Wall* (New York, 1911), p. 5.

contacts. Our American experience seems to indicate that we have been able to fuse into our life a great variety of alien customs and characteristics, except for the purely external one of skin color.

The history of California confirms this conclusion. In the days of the Gold Rush people swarmed in from everywhere. When the railway line from Oakland to Ogden, Utah, was completed, an oversupply in the labor market caused pronounced unrest. Many Irish came directly from Ireland, considerable numbers of Latin Americans arrived, but the Chinese differed most and were singled out as the source of all problems. Shortly they became the target for hatreds. This emerging racial consciousness developed into a movement which culminated in the legislation of 1882 whereby Chinese laborers were excluded.[4]

The Japanese also encountered a great wave of antagonism and they now form a rather distinct racial caste. One young woman, who came here as a child, was not accepted even though she became American through and through.

> I unwillingly realized that I was not to be classed as an American. It was one of the most heart-breaking periods of my life. I wanted to be American; I wondered why God had not made me an American. If I couldn't be an American, then what was I? A Japanese? No. But not an American either. My life background is American. My ideals of life, of education, of religion, were all American. I know the Constitution, the oath of allegiance; I knew the history of America from its earliest beginnings. I knew its strength and weaknesses, its drabness and its romance. I loved America and its ideals, because her ideals were my ideals. I used to rise up in wrath against any criticism which might be made against America, my country. But they tell me I am not an American; that I cannot ever be assimilated for no reason which I have ever been able to understand. My looks made me Japanese, yes, but until a few years ago I was Japanese in appearance only. I speak the Japanese language with the faulty enunciation of the white American.[5]

The question of Philippine independence was discussed more or less in the abstract for many years, but when Filipinos with their

[4] Cf. Mary R. Coolidge, *Chinese Immigration* (New York, 1901).

[5] *Survey of Race Relations*, 322–A.

distinctive physical characteristics came in large numbers to California the issue soon came to a head and was settled.[6]

Witness the Negro. Three hundred years in America have not been sufficient to assimilate him. This, however, is not due to the preservation of an African culture or an alien heritage. The Negro is more American than vast numbers of so-called Americans, but still he is considered a representative of an alien race and is not given full entrée into our life. His physical and racial traits, not cultural differences, set him apart from the white population.

Any visible physical differences in the Jew doubtless accentuate his problems of adjustment. Bercovici wrote of a Jew who tried, but was unable, to lose his identity.

He arrived a bearded Talmudical scholar in 1910. Rabbi Glockman was then less than thirty years old. He had a wife and four children, two sons and two daughters. . . . . A year later Rabbi Glockman was still teaching Hebrew in a little after-school Cheder where the Jewish children were sent by their parents so as not to forget that they were Jews. The school was . . . . on the East Side. Two years later with beard a little trimmed, Mr. Glockman owned a Kosher delicatessen store. . . . . The place closed on Friday evening and remained closed till Saturday after prayers. Mr. Glockman was the president of a congregation. Four years later Mr. Glockman was the partner in a shirt-waist factory where they worked on the Sabbath. The beard was completely gone. They lived in the Bronx. Six years later Mr. Glockman smoked on the Sabbath, ate "unclean" food, and was denounced in a strike as the worst exploiter. He employed only Italian labor, and had changed his name to Bell, George Bell, and had moved from the Bronx to Morristown, because there were no Jews there. Eight years later his daughter had married a Gentile. But then the railroad strike broke out. The great Morristown plan, by which the wealthiest commuters manned the trains, entered into vogue. Mr. Bell came to the station every morning with his overalls under his arms, ready to take his place as a scab—to help the country. But Mr. T. and Mr. D. and Mr. F., who were at the head, would not have the Jew with them in the cab. He had to ride as a passenger. They would not even give him the privilege of acting as conductor. Today Mr. Bell is again Solomon Glockman. He lives in Harlem, in the heart of the Jewish district, is a member of the congregation, and

[6] Cf. Bruno Lasker, *op. cit.*

a fanatical Zionist. Even the beard was allowed to grow back, a little trimmed, to its full length. Until the daughter divorced her husband and married a Jew she was not allowed to enter her parents' home.[7]

Since barriers tend to be raised against persons with marked physical differences, it is evident that those who can mingle with the dominant group and not be noticed have a decided advantage; they can participate earlier and more freely in the life which surrounds them.

Age of immigrants. Obviously young immigrants can adjust themselves more readily than older persons with relatively fixed habits.[8] According to Edward Bok, both of his parents found it difficult to make a fresh start in the new country—it was no easy matter to adapt the habits of a lifetime to strange routines. Edward, however, who came at the age of seven, adjusted himself with comparative ease and soon was Americanized to the core.[9] The receiving group usually shows more cordiality toward the young immigrant than to the older, thus making possible the close contacts indispensable to assimilation.

B. Cultural Aspects

Cultural kinship. When the culture of the intruding group is not widely divergent from that of the old residents, the newcomers (unless they arrive in overwhelming numbers) do not excite animosities. Furthermore, they can acquire a reasonable understanding of the practices of the natives in a comparatively short time.

[7] K. Bercovici, "The Greatest Jewish City in the World," *Nation,* CXVII (September 12, 1923), 259. It must not be considered that the physical factor was the only one in this instance. For more than thirty years he had lived a Jew and could not erase all the characterizing marks such as accent, mannerisms, and attitudes which still labelled him a Jew.

[8] Cf. *American Journal of Sociology,* XXXII (September, 1926), 245.

[9] Cf. Edward Bok, *The Americanization of Edward Bok* (New York, 1920), p. 8. The Immigration Commission, on the basis of its study, concluded that ability to use English was a most important factor in assimilation. Moreover, they found that "the ability to speak English is largely dependent upon his age at the time of arrival in the United States." Vol. XXVI, p. 146.

In Milwaukee they found that "the persons who came to the United States before they were fourteen years of age have the largest proportions of English-speaking persons." *Ibid.,* p. 757.

With the period of misunderstanding reduced to a minimum, adjustments and assimilation can go on unhindered.[10]

Immigrants from the north European countries have been, in the main, more readily assimilable than those from other areas.[11] The English, however, are an exception. Even though they are closest to us culturally, a pride, engendered by their lofty imperial position tends to inhibit acceptance of traits from another culture. The Irish on the contrary, assimilate readily.[12] Hatred toward England occasioned an early break in their British connections. Not forgetful of their homeland and wishing to see it free, they evidently considered that more could be done for Ireland as American citizens than as British subjects.

An analysis of the autobiographies [13] or life histories of immigrants makes it evident that those whose cultures diverge most widely from that of America have the greatest difficulties in making adjustments. Pupin the Serbian, Panunzio the Italian, Menikoff the Bulgarian, Rihbany the Syrian, and Jews from different places,[14] such as Ravage, Cohen, Steiner, and Lewisohn, had to overcome great obstacles. Lewisohn has never been able to lose himself in America.[15]

[10] According to Harry Sundby-Hansen, the Norwegian immigrant comes to feel that he has merely transferred to a greater Norway because of the great similarities, particularly so far as local government is concerned. *Norwegian Immigrant Contributions to America's Making* (New York, 1921), pp. 107–09.

[11] Cf. Gustave Koerner, *Memoirs of Gustave Koerner* (Cedar Rapids, Iowa, 1909), for a German immigrant who was readily accepted. He was elected to the Illinois legislature, appointed to the Supreme Court of Illinois, elected lieutenant-governor of Illinois, and was made minister to Spain.

Eleven years after Carl Schurz escaped from Germany he was sent to Spain as minister. Thirty years later he became Secretary of the Interior under President Hayes. *Op. cit.*, Vol. I, pp. 323, 327. Cf. autobiographies of Bok, Bridges, Carnegie, Jensen, Mattson, McClure, Nielsen, Riis, and Ueland. They came from northwest Europe and were accorded a favorable reception. Cf. *Proceedings of the State Historical Society of Wisconsin,* 1897, pp. 101–22, for the assimilation of Germans.

[12] An Irishman, however, says "the Irish have never been thoroughly Americanized. Their American citizenship becomes a great and dear thing to them, but they are still in some sense citizens of Ireland. . . . . The Irish are a partial exception to the rule that America absorbs its immigrants." From *From Dublin to Chicago,* by Geo. A. Birmingham, copyright, 1914, by Doubleday, Doran and Company, Inc., New York, p. 303; cf. pp. 304–06.

[13] See list of autobiographies in bibliography.

[14] Cf. Isaac Friedlander, *Past and Present* (New York, 1919), p. 357.

[15] Samuel Gompers was a Jew, but he came from England instead of Russia. Because of this he was more readily accepted. Cf. *op. cit.*

There are peoples so different in manners and traditions that we are unable to understand them. For instance very few Californians understand the Russian Molokans in Los Angeles.[16] On the other hand, ethnic groups, whose cultures we are unable to comprehend, quite likely find it difficult to make our institutions their own.[17]

Certain practices of immigrants are so different that they arouse disgust, antagonism, hatred. This holds true particularly with reference to the treatment of women and children. Virginians look with contempt upon the behavior of the Czecho-Slovak father in his rôle as head of the family. They disapprove the hard work he requires of his wife and children and the penuriousness with which he treats them—he builds a barn for his stock, but the family must live in a shed.[18] Shaw and McKay gave the reactions of neighbors to an Italian family. One said:

> That's a dago family or some other foreigners. They fight most of the time. . . . . The kid seems purty nice; he'd be all right if they wouldn't beat him all the time. I guess they are like all foreigners, just fighting all the time. . . . . They pound Nick around, want him to work and support the family, I guess. . . . . These foreigners want their kids to work before they're out of the cradle. You ought to throw the old folks in the pen instead of the kids. They don't belong in this country; they don't know how to live here. I wish they'd move out of here. . . . . We don't have much to do with them, only I side with the kids.[19]

In California much unfavorable comment has been made about the hard work done in the fields by the Japanese women and children.[20] That charge is also brought against the Mexicans. The

[16] Cf. P. V. Young, *op. cit.*

[17] Immigrants from the Orient find considerable difficulty in adjusting themselves. "In many matters, the Chinese who have an old world education cannot very well accept the American pattern of life. The new ideas and practices sometimes conflict so sharply with what he considers right and proper that they shock or disgust him." C. C. Wu, *op. cit.*

[18] Cf. E. deS. Brunner, *Immigrant Farmers and Their Children* (New York, 1929), p. 200. Cf. also pp. 92–93, 210; E. G. Balch, *op. cit.*, p. 226; H. Quick, *op. cit.*, pp. 118–20, 186–97.

[19] National Commission on Law Observance and Enforcement, *The Causes of Crime* (Washington, 1931), p. 11.

[20] Likenesses in cultures, on the other hand, open the avenues of communication. Groups that have comparatively high standards of literacy tend to appreciate the

fact that the immigrant women do a certain amount of manual labor classifies them as inferior drudges and American women will not accept them. Under such circumstances there is slight opportunity for the assimilative process to work.

Language. Any participation in organized social activity implies communication, and in human society a collective life and group solidarity are based on a generally accepted speech. A common language is a prime factor in creating a "universe of discourse"—it embodies the cultural symbols which are peculiar to that group.[21] To share a common speech, to be sure, does not necessarily guarantee full and free participation in the life of the group. The experience of the Negro in America bears this out. It is, nevertheless, an instrument of participation. Acquisition of the common speech by the members of an immigrant group may be considered a criterion or rough index of Americanization.

In the main, immigrants from England can be assimilated more readily than others because they can use our language,[22] except for certain Americanisms. Aliens with a Germanic or Romance lan-

educational opportunities offered by our school system. Furthermore, since they appreciate and enter into the spirit of this institution they touch the heart strings of Americans. In California both teachers and school officials sing the praises of the Japanese children and of their parents because of their coöperative spirit. The Japanese came with a tradition favorable to learning and they give every encouragement to their children in school. When compared with certain other groups they have a high rating indeed. This developed in many an amicable attitude toward the Japanese and doubtless tempered in some measure the attack upon them. Throughout the agitation against them, they could feel a certain friendliness of the schools. For data on the anti-Japanese agitation cf. E. M. Boddy, *Japanese in America* (Los Angeles, 1921); Yamato Ichihashi, *Japanese in the United States* (Stanford University, 1932); Eliot Grinnell Mears, *Resident Orientals on the American Pacific Coast* (Chicago, 1928).

[21] When a person masters the language of a people he also takes possession of its culture. If he does not fully appreciate the culture, he does not understand the language. An immigrant from France wrote: "My sister came to this country four years ago. She married an American soon after and went to live on a homestead in Wyoming. There she met no one who could speak French. She learned English rapidly, I mean American English. Now she speaks an abominable French, for she thinks in English. Often she intermixes English words in her French and would much rather speak English. She does not dream of ever going back to France. In her case, acquisition of the vernacular has meant an entire assimilation." Unpublished life history.

[22] Although the Armenians do not come from northwestern Europe they have been accepted fairly well, probably due to the fact that many had learned English in American mission schools in Armenia and Turkey.

guage have less difficulty than those who speak Polish, Russian, Ukrainian, or Czech. Edward Bok, who came from Holland, mastered the English language readily since the Anglo-Saxon has its roots in the Frisian, his native tongue.[23] John Muir and his brother, who came from Scotland as boys, had a minimum of difficulty in making their adjustments since they had learned the language before their arrival.

> The captain [of the trans-Atlantic sailing ship] occasionally called David and me into his cabin and asked us about our schools, handed us books to read, and seemed surprised to find that Scotch boys could read and pronounce English with perfect accent and knew so much Latin and French. In Scotch schools only pure English was taught, although not a word of English was spoken out of school.[24]

Ignorance of our language is an important barrier to assimilation. Undoubtedly the most baffling and embarrassing obstacle the immigrant encounters upon his arrival in America is his inability to use the current speech. Without a common means of communication, full and free interchange of ideas is impossible, and he is left outside the range of influences that would aid his acculturation.

By means of conscious copying the immigrant can accommodate himself to certain externalities of our life. He can learn some of the processes connected with food-getting and go through the forms of much in our everyday activities, but unless he has a more intimate contact with the realities he will remain far distant. He will not appreciate the meaning behind many of the forms that he meets; he cannot use our institutions in the fullest measure for his own benefit and protection. Generally speaking, adherence to a foreign language within a country tends to cocoon an ethnic group and keep it alien.[25]

The slower assimilation of Orientals and immigrants from south-

[23] *Op. cit.*, p. 4.

[24] John Muir, *The Story of My Boyhood and Youth* (Boston, Houghton, Mifflin Company, 1913), p. 57.

[25] On the basis of its study, the Immigration Commission concluded that "the inability to use the language of this country operates to restrict members of non-English-speaking races to residence in foreign colonies and to prevent their assimilation." Vol. XXVI, p. 235.

eastern Europe undoubtedly is due in considerable measure to the wide divergence of their languages from our own.[26] Dr. Jakub Horak concludes that the older people among the Czechs, especially those above twenty-five or thirty years of age, hardly ever master the English language. They acquire a jargon which is neither English nor Czech, while the Germans, Scandinavians, and Dutch learn to speak English rather fluently. It is not, he states, due to

[26] When Ah Lee comes from China and has the privilege of learning English in a Sunday School class he soon finds that a little knowledge of the new language will not carry him far in a conversation. Both Chinese and Americans have difficulty in understanding him when he says: "Long teem before (a long time ago) mi hab see one piece Melican joss pidgin man (missionary) Canton side. He talkee mi Melica side one man all same 'nother man, maskee (no matter if) he poor man, richee man, white man, black man, Chinaman, any fashion man, he can stop this side, mandalin (government) take care he alla same. Mi fear he talkee lie pidgin (told a lie) Melica side no p'loppa (proper) maskee (never mind). S'pose Ilishman no too muchee bobbery, mi can stop two, three year, catchee little chancee, takee that dollar, buy shilling billee (exchange), takee steamer, go back Canton side." C. C. Wu, *op. cit.*, p. 278.

Likewise experiences of an Italian immigrant show how ignorance of the language sets bars against participation in American life. "And now, just before we reached the station, I began to notice that there were signs at the corners of the streets with 'Ave.! Ave.! Ave.!' How religious a place this must be that expresses its devotion at every crossing, I mused. Still they did not put the 'Ave.' before the holy word, as in 'Ave Maria,' but rather after. How topsy-turvy. . . . . None of us, including myself, ever thought of a movement to broaden our knowledge of the English language. We soon learned a few words about the job, that was the preliminary creed; then came 'bread,' 'shirt,' 'gloves' (not kid gloves), 'milk.' And that is all. We formed our own little world—one of many in this country. And the other people around us who spoke in strange languages might have been phantoms for all the influence that they had upon us or for all we cared about them." From Pascal D'Angelo, *A Son of Italy* (New York, 1924), pp. 61, 70. D'Angelo also tells how he as a boy was sent out to buy a dozen eggs. He was instructed to buy "aches." He kept repeating the word on the way to the store when it had by imperceptible changes become "axe." The Polack storekeeper brought out an axe. The boy shook his head but could not make him understand. The wife of the storekeeper also showed the boy a number of wares but did not find the right one. Finally, Pascal began to illustrate his wish somewhat better by cackling like a hen and indicating an oval shape with his fingers. This they understood and brought the eggs after which he returned home in triumph. Cf. *Ibid.,* pp. 70–71.

At one time he got into a fight in which he received a black eye. He decided to tell everybody he had fallen down. He asked the foreman for the proper word which was "faw don." This he repeated several times. As he walked along the street he found two men quarreling. One of them shook his fist at him and said "You damn." Then he forgot the words "faw don" and began to say "You damn." He shocked several persons and made several others laugh. Presently he met a friend who asked "What happened to you?" D'Angelo then assumed an expression of sad innocence and said, "Me? You damn," and pointed to the ground. The friend laughed and D'Angelo was offended at the lack of sympathy. *Ibid.,* pp. 72–73. Above quotations are used by permission of The Macmillan Company, publishers.

inferior linguistic ability but the difference between the languages is an all but insurmountable obstacle.[27]

Another aspect of the language situation is prejudice against the tongue of the immigrant. His speech is considered barbarous because it is different—it should have been dropped at Ellis Island. Because the immigrant's first attempts in using English are colored by his mother tongue, he becomes the butt of jokes.[28] This has an unfavorable result. Rather than subject themselves to ridicule, "the more sensitive ones prefer to stay closely within their own group and forego contacts with the new cultural world." [29]

Religion. A common religion is an important aid to assimilation.[30] Adherents of the same faith, as it were, are dwellers in the same climatic zone. "A religion," wrote Ross, "which provides the entire intellectual background so knits together its followers that the toughest population lump begins to dissolve when it is no longer held together by a religion of its own." [31] According to Nels Anderson, the Protestant Bohemians in Virginia will in all probability break down the barriers in the way of their assimilation sooner than the Catholics, who studiously keep to themselves. The latter are more desirous of retaining their language and religion and have established schools for that purpose.[32] The fact that many Armenians have been accepted with some degree of readiness is probably due in part to the fact that a considerable number are Protestants, through the influence of the American missions.

Differences in religion are strictures on free assimilation.[33] Brun-

[27] *Op. cit.*

[28] The following jingle was directed at members of one immigrant group in a community in Minnesota:

Swedie, Swedie, stuck in the straw,
Can't say nuthin' but "Yaw, yaw, yaw."

[29] C. A. Dawson and W. E. Gettys, *op. cit.*, p. 535.

[30] On the other hand, religion can be one of the strongest forces against assimilation. W. Z. Ripley considers that difference in religion alone has kept the Armenians from being absorbed by the Turks. *Races of Europe* (New York, 1899), pp. 444–48.

[31] E. A. Ross, *Principles of Sociology* (New York, 1930), p. 258.

[32] E. deS. Brunner, *op. cit.*, p. 211.

[33] This has been evident from the very early days in our American history. "Religion, however, played a more conspicuous part in colonial immigration legislation than either economics or politics. The Massachusetts colonies opposed the coming of adherents of the established church and Virginia on the other hand, objected to non-conformists, but both were in complete accord as to the total undesirability

ner found in a Michigan community with a sizeable Polish population, that a Methodist minister, in coöperation with the school, had organized a Boy Scout troop. When the Polish boys asked to join, the scoutmaster and the troop welcomed them, and the priest voiced his approval. The Protestant parents, however, entered a strenuous protest.[34] Theodore Abel studied a New England farming community and learned that the chief objection to the Poles was due to their allegiance to the Catholic church which was considered an un-American institution. If the Poles had been Protestants, all would have been well.[35] It is evident that these are not empty words since the few Latvian families that attended the Protestant church have been accepted and no longer are considered foreigners.[36]

Since America is predominantly Protestant, Catholic immigrants receive a less cordial welcome and assimilate more slowly.[37] Judaism is still farther removed and Jewish immigrants are accepted even more reluctantly.[38] It is not, however, a one-sided matter. The Jews consider themselves the chosen people and deride the Gentiles as "pork-eaters." Dietary regulations, Sabbath observ-

of Quakers and Jesuits. Virginia imposed a fine of 100 pounds for bringing a Quaker into the colony, and Massachusetts Bay passed an act for the exclusion of Jesuits and other ecclesiastical persons ordained by the pope, the death penalty being provided in case any such person returned after banishment. The middle colonies were somewhat more liberal toward newcomers. Indeed Pennsylvania was so liberal in this respect that it was said toleration had made the colony a religious museum. However, Pennsylvania yielded for a time to the prevailing fear of the immigrant and in 1729 levied a duty on 'foreigners and Irish servants,' but several shiploads of settlers were thereby diverted to other colonies and the law was soon repealed." W. W. Husband in *National Conference of Social Work,* 1922, p. 458.

[34] E. deS. Brunner, *op. cit.,* p. 97.

[35] *Ibid.,* p. 234.

[36] *Ibid.,* p. 234.

[37] E. deS. Brunner concluded that the Protestant Bohemians would probably break down the barriers in a Protestant community more readily than the Catholics who persisted in keeping themselves apart. *Ibid.,* p. 211.

[38] According to Konrad Bercovici, "You can kill a Jew, ten, a hundred, a thousand, but you can't kill the Jews. They cannot even be absorbed. No sooner has the inevitable process of absorption begun in a country after two generations of tolerance have put their national or racial consciousness to sleep, than an anti-Semitic outbreak in that country or in another awakens the consciousness in the Jews and the reluctance to absorb them in the non-Jews." "The Greatest Jewish City in the World," *The Nation,* CXVII (September 12, 1923), 259. Cf. Heywood Broun and George Britt, *Christians Only: A Study in Prejudice* (New York, 1931), for anti-Semitism in the United States.

ance, and many ritualistic practices set the Jews off by themselves.[39] If we go farther afield and consider Japanese Buddhism we discover an even greater striction. When the Japanese in Pasadena and Los Angeles made plans for building Buddhist temples they encountered opposition.[40]

Many Americans expect immigrants to renounce their religion as soon as they disembark, but in the strangeness of exile in the new land the old religion becomes all the more precious and can be surrendered only with anguish. In religion are embedded the priceless values of the immigrant; it represents virtually all that is sacred in his heritage.[41] Soon after he arrives in America he must give up certain old practices that he may earn his daily bread. Religion then assumes greater importance as a bond linking him to his past. In his economic activities he must venture forth into the new and, to him, uncharted world. Here is uncertainty. In his old religion he finds security, despite the trials of adjustment to the new environment. Hence, in this sector of his life the immigrant tends to change most slowly. Nevertheless, where religious elements tends to interfere with the earning of a livelihood, modifications come. Millions of Jews are working in our industries today, despite the fact that the orthodox faith was a serious impediment to their industrialization. It has been, however, at the sacrificial price of their orthodoxy. The Jewish Sabbath stood in the way of employment. Furthermore, in his daily life the Jew has a series of prayers at certain periods of the day. If, in a factory, he closed down his machine from four to five times a day to pray or perform some other religious rite he would be a misfit in the industrial scheme. Because of this many of the older and more orthodox men have gone into the push-cart trades where they could regulate their own time schedules. Younger and more ambitious men, however, have sacrificed their religion. Phil Davis, a Russian Jew, came here in youth, began work in a sweatshop, and later graduated from

[39] Even though Judaism is more or less inflexible, it finally has to yield. According to Abraham Cahan, the adoption of new clothes in America had a fatal effect on his religious habits. He stated that the influence of a starched collar and necktie on a man brought up as an orthodox Jew was tremendous. *Op. cit.*, p. 210.

[40] Cf. *Survey of Race Relations*, 238–A, and 194–B.

[41] Cf. H. P. Fairchild, *Greek Immigration to the United States*, p. 46.

Harvard University. His story gives an example of what happens to the religion of the Jew when he becomes enmeshed in our workaday life.

For the first six months my religious convictions were unshaken. Somehow, I could find no work and therefore I had plenty of time to take in more than three divine services a day, if need be. But at last I got work in one of the old-time sweatshops of New York, first as a basting puller, then as a half-baster. From the moment I entered the shop my religious interest began to decline. In a year it was practically *nil.* My "four corners" wore out and were never replaced; my forelocks disappeared; my phylacteries and my prayer book were in exile. I ceased going to the synagogue, first only on week days, later on Saturdays as well. In after years I never entered it but twice a year, at the anniversary of my mother's death and on the Day of Atonement.[42]

Thus it is. If the Jew or any other immigrant is to function in our economic set-up much of his old culture must be discarded.

Ethnocentric attitudes in the immigrant are more likely to appear in this aspect than in any other. While he may admit the superiority of the machines of the American he will concede nothing with reference to his religion. According to a young woman of Swedish ancestry, "Some Swedish people have a very stubborn and persistent idea that no one can be quite as religious as a Swede." [43] Immigrants are often shocked by the seemingly irreverent behavior of the Americans while the natives, on the other hand, make light of the queer religious practices of the foreigners.[44] This situation, then, becomes a bar to mutual understanding.

Home life. Married persons with children have an avenue of communication with the new world which is absent in the case of a group of unmarried, childless adults.[45] To be sure, if girls marry

[42] Ray Stannard Baker, "Spiritual Unrest," *American Magazine,* LXVIII (October, 1909), 594.

According to Lewis Browne, in Poland Jew competed with Jew and Sabbath-keeping was no disadvantage. In America, however, he has to compete with Gentiles and piety becomes a luxury he cannot afford. *How Odd of God: An Introduction to the Jews* (New York, 1934), p. 72. Cf. pp. 71–93.

[43] Unpublished life history.

[44] According to Pauline V. Young, " 'Holy Jumping' affronts the city man's sense of personal dignity, but to the Molokan it is a demonstration of the immanent presence of God." *Op. cit.,* p. 147.

[45] See Chapter XXXII, "Assimilation of Parents through Their Children."

at an early age and begin the onerous task of housekeeping and child-bearing they have fewer opportunities for making contacts than single girls who work outside the home. Married persons tend to be interested in improving themselves and their condition for the sake of the children, and in this effort they learn about American life.[46] As they watch their children progress in school and see better economic opportunities open for them than they themselves had, they become more satisfied with America. Vicariously, in and through their children, they realize some of their own thwarted ambitions. They recognize that their children are Americans and could not be happy under the severe handicaps in the homeland. Thus one by one the ties that bind them to the old world are broken, their inhibitions against things American are dissolved, and the assimilative process moves quietly on.

Similarities in home life,[47] foods, and methods of cooking pave the way for closer relationships. "The mothers in Danish and Swedish homes," wrote a girl, "are genuine housekeepers and home-makers. They all know how to sew and cook to perfection. . . . . I had two lovely neighbors, a Danish and a Swedish family. . . . . I loved both homes and thought them ideal." [48] The significant factor here is that the household life and the cooking followed the pattern to which the girl was accustomed. Had some natives of Burma moved into the settlement and offered her their favorite condiment, *ngapi,* or pressed fish, it is highly probable that she would have been less fulsome in her praise.[49] "No Burman would think a dinner complete without his modicum of *ngapi.*" There is no great likelihood that she might consider either the women of southeastern Europe who would offer their dainty "ripe" cheeses or the women of Hawaii who would serve *poi* able to "cook to perfection." Furthermore, the Hindu's method of eating with his fingers or the use of chopsticks by Chinese are strictures upon social intercourse.

[46] The Japanese on the Pacific Coast have had a more normal family life than the Chinese and they have moved ahead more rapidly in the assimilative process.

[47] Peter Roberts enumerates a number of domestic customs that could raise barriers against assimilation. *Op. cit.,* pp. 139–55.

[48] E. S. Bogardus, *Immigration and Race Attitudes* (Boston, 1928), p. 81.

[49] From Shway Yoe, *The Burman: His Life and Notions* (London, 1910), p. 280. By permission of Macmillan & Co., Ltd., publishers.

C. The Rate of Entrance

Physiological and cultural differences, in and of themselves, are not entirely the determinative factors.

If the flow of immigrants into an area is slow and gradual they are more readily accepted. They can be absorbed without causing any serious disturbance in the existing order. Immigrants already adjusted assist their compatriots in sloughing peculiarities that might cause resentment. The old settlers of native stock are accustomed to members of this particular ethnic group and an additional arrival now and then causes no excitement. If, however, the aliens come in large numbers the natives become fearful; they fear competition and a lowering of their standard of living; they fear that their institutions cannot digest so much new material and will be destroyed in the attempt; and they fear that everything for which they have struggled and sacrificed will be trampled under foot by inferior peoples that do not know the ideals of Washington, Jefferson, and Lincoln. The fears, due to causes real or imagined, raise impassable barriers of prejudice against the newcomers and they are denied all wholesome contacts with the old residents. This attitude tends to solidify the immigrant group and they become more interested in continuing their old ways of life than they would be otherwise. The prejudicial attitude of the natives is no solvent that will tend to reduce the old-world customs of the immigrants. California has made this evident. The influx of large numbers of Chinese after 1849 aroused apprehension in the white population.[50] The white workers who had to compete with these quiet, unobtrusive, pig-tailed, *different* men objected vehemently to them. They attacked the Chinese [51] and drove them into a ghetto life in San Francisco from which they have never emerged and where they still maintain ways that are strange and queer.[52]

[50] According to E. A. Ross, a group of Sacramento business men "introduced Chinese coolies into California in order to avoid paying an American wage in the construction of the Central Pacific Railroad." *Seventy Years of It* (New York, 1936), p. 69.

[51] M. R. Coolidge, *op cit*. Cf. Charles H. Young and Helen R. Y. Reid, *The Japanese Canadians* (Toronto, 1938), pp. 19–84.

[52] Cf. A. M. Schlesinger, *op. cit.*, p. 34.

California continued to develop and the big employers desired cheap labor, but the Chinese had been excluded. The Japanese, then, came by thousands to fill the vacuum. Again the Californians went into action, and forced the Japanese off the land, into the segregation of "Little Tokyo" in Los Angeles. The Gentlemen's Agreement of 1907 and the Exclusion Act of 1924 put an end to Japanese immigration. This, however, was only a breathing spell. Melons, oranges, and peaches had to be picked cheaply and Filipinos began to swarm in from the Philippine Islands and Hawaii. Again for a third time the Californians were stirred into activity, and the Filipinos were excluded.

CHAPTER XII

FACTORS IN ASSIMILATION

(Continued)

Although many factors restrict freedom of contact, they do not necessarily beget hostilities. Americans of old native stock react to the stimuli presented by the immigrants—physiological and cultural differences—and make it easy or difficult for them to become assimilated. Through behavior ranging all the way from attitudes of aloofness to passage of discriminatory laws, the natives frequently arouse antagonisms that are prone to retard the assimilative process.

D. American Behavior and Assimilation

Exploitation by natives. The newly-arrived immigrant must bear many crosses. "Exploitation," says Panunzio,[1] "hangs upon him like a dark shadow, exploitation at the hands of so-called Americans." Advantage is taken of his greenness; he is a source of profit not to be ignored. The experience of an Italian immigrant presents a concrete case.

They bargained with a cabman standing at South Ferry to take Guiseppe and his baggage for $1.50 and Guiseppe got on. As soon as the cab was out of sight of the Battery and of the friends who had met him, Guiseppe was astounded by the cabman stopping and demanding a dollar more before he would drive on. After a futile argument in sign talk, and with a great waste of language which neither understood, Guiseppe suc-

[1] From C. M. Panunzio, *Immigration Crossroads,* p. 261. By permission of The Macmillan Company, publishers. Even immigrants, who have learned some of the ways of America, prey upon those who have just arrived from their own homelands. Because of the immigrants' knowledge of the ways of the "greenhorns," because of their own experiences, and because of the confidence the new arrivals place in those who can speak their own language, these immigrant exploiters are all the more reprehensible. Cf. Peter Roberts, *The New Immigration* (New Work, 1912), pp. 178–79.

cumbed and paid the dollar. In ten minutes more the cabman stopped and demanded another two dollars. Just about the time Guiseppe knew he was near the station, Guiseppe received another demand for $3. He did not have it and after a violent scene with the cabman, who threatened to beat him with the butt of his whip, Guiseppe burst into tears, overcome with his feeling of being alone in a strange world and the helpless victim of such a villain. He decided to climb out and try to find his way to the station, so he shouldered his baggage and trudged off, toward the north for he knew the station lay that way. Finally after asking scores of people where the station was, and being laughed at by some and pitied by others, he met a little girl who understood Italian and she pointed out the way. He was only two blocks distant.[2]

Peter A. Speek [3] exposes fraudulent practices in the sale of land to immigrants, as the following illustrates:

I have saved a small sum of money for the purpose of buying a piece of land. . . . . Last year a "Yankee" sold me some land but he did not give it to me; he wanted only my money. I had to take a lawyer, but he did not get the land that I had bought for me. Only my money was returned, half of which the lawyer kept for himself as a fee for his services. There is no help from lawyers or courts. I lost my savings of years. The land-selling business in this country is a big humbug. Too bad! [4]

The Russian Molokans also have been victimized.

The first few years were very trying for them. Strange, idealistic, tongue-tied, they were exploited by many real estate men who sold them dry, sandy desert land with no prospects for water or crops. They moved their families hundreds of miles away from the main Colony, only to come back penniless, and a few of them broken in health.[5]

[2] B. Brandenburg, *op. cit.*, pp. 223–24. Cf. S. C. Johnson, *op. cit.*, pp. 117–18. G. H. von Koch, *Emigranternas Land* (Stockholm, 1910), p. 33; W. Halich, *op. cit.*, pp. 26–27. The exploitation stops at nothing, as evidenced by Michael Pupin. Immediately on landing in New York he bought a piece of prune pie. The prune is a national sweetmeat which no true Serbian can resist. But this first purchase was a disappointment—the pie was filled with prune pits. This transaction made him realize that he was a "greenhorn" in America. *Op. cit.*, pp. 43–44.

[3] *Op. cit.*, pp. 26–29. Cf. E. deS. Brunner, *op. cit.*, pp. 32–33.

[4] P. A. Speek, *op. cit.*, p. 10. Cf. Hornell Hart, *The Science of Social Relations* (New York, 1927), pp. 476–77 [quoted from Lillian D. Wald, *House on Henry Street* (New York, 1915), pp. 287–88], for a case of exploitation. Also E. A. Steiner, *From Alien to Citizen*, pp. 165–66.

[5] P. V. Young, *op. cit.*, p. 156.

Swindlers have found spurious naturalization papers to be a source of profit.

To the Trouble Bureau of the Delaware Americanization Committee came an Italian who was "sent in by the Associated Charities to get a copy of his naturalization certificate," without which it was almost impossible for him to obtain employment. Investigations revealed that the Court had no record of his naturalization. Then it came out that he had not gotten his papers in court at all, but from a "boss" who had charged him $5 for his declaration and $10 for his final paper. "I guess maybe that boss, he fool me," he said simply. "No speak English—no understand." He had been under the impression all these years that this is the way the great American nation bestows the priceless gift of its suffrage upon newcomers.[6]

Quite commonly immigrant workers have been exploited. Theodore Abel encountered a situation in the Connecticut Valley of Massachusetts where newcomers passed through a period of virtual slavery—they were overworked, underfed, inadequately housed, and poorly paid. The period of humiliating apprenticeship, however, was comparatively short. Many quit the farms. Those who remained made demands of their employers for better treatment and increased pay.[7]

When Americans thus exploit the immigrants, resentment and distrust are aroused. The newcomers become suspicious and develop an aloofness which stands in the way of normal assimilation. If, however, the immigrant finds a fair degree of security in the ordering of his life he will be more favorably disposed toward America and the assimilative process will move forward more readily. If he receives a reasonable amount of assistance in finding a place in American industry [8] where he may earn a decent livelihood and is not subjected to wholesale exploitation because of his "greenhornhood," if he finds an industrial welfare commission or other official body to which he can appeal in the event of unfair treatment, if he finds that some provision has been made to protect him against frauds and abuses to which the immigrant is liable, if

[6] W. M. Leiserson, *op. cit.*, p. 253.

[7] E. deS. Brunner, *op. cit.*, p. 214. Cf. E. Abbott, *Immigration: Select Documents and Case Records,* p. 583; E. A. Steiner, *From Alien to Citizen,* pp. 106–07.

[8] Cf. W. M. Leiserson, *op. cit.*, pp. 28–64.

he finds some provision for legal aid to protect his rights, if he finds some agency for the protection of the health of himself and family,[9] if he finds that the police are his protectors and not his oppressors, he is duly grateful to America and will repay her by becoming a more useful citizen.

Unfriendly attitudes. Nels Anderson observed that a group of Czecho-Slovakian farmers were received with cynical indifference in Virginia. The real estate agents, to be sure, welcomed them. The marginal land they acquired was made productive by unremitting toil. At first they were ignorant of local agricultural methods and the victims of practical jokes on the part of the old settlers, but presently they outstripped the natives and were acknowledged the best farmers in the area. Through their diligence they gained economic status, but socially they were not accepted—even members of the third generation were considered foreigners.[10]

A colony of Italians who settled in Tontitown, Arkansas, in the late nineties encountered ill humor in the native farmers. A number of the Italians were sick when they arrived but neither sympathy nor aid was extended to them.[11] They secured a building and opened a school. Shortly after its opening a group of young men, determined to intimidate or drive away the "Dagoes," attempted to burn the schoolhouse.[12] Villagers from the nearest towns, who

[9] Cf. Michael Davis, *Immigrant Health and the Community* (New York, 1921).

[10] E. deS. Brunner, *op. cit.*, pp. 183–84. Cf. also pp. 208–12. Edith M. Miniter shows how a certain group "froze out" a Polish boy. "Wajeiceh Natupski ate sandwiches when he could reach them. No one passed him anything. Every one wondered what he wanted there anyway, at a 'get together' picnic. It was impossible to get together when fellows would push in whom it was desirable to keep out. He spoke twice. To the man at his left he said, 'Please pass the sardines.' He didn't hear him. Later he asked the girl on his right, 'What we going to do after supper?' She didn't hear him, either.

"Presently the young people grouped themselves under the trees by the side of of the pond and lifted their voices in song. Wajeiceh could sing as much as any one there, which wasn't much. When 'There's a Little Spark of Love Still Burning' was started, he joined in. Five seconds later he was singing alone. In a bitterness which he could feel, but not express, the boy hot-footed it to Mifflin Grove.

" 'What do you think?' buzzed the rural 'phones next day. 'Whatever do you think? That dreadful Natupski scalawag went right straight from the picnic to a barroom in Mifflin, and never came home till daylight. He looked dreadful peak-ed. He'll land in jail sure as fate.' " Edith M. Miniter, *Natupski Neighbors* (New York, 1916), p. 197.

[11] Newell L. Sims, *The Rural Community* (New York, 1920), p. 170.

[12] *Ibid.*, p. 179.

wanted no Italians and no Catholics, burned two of their churches.[13] It seems that no matter what the immigrant may do he encounters antagonistic attitudes on the part of the natives which constantly repel him.[14]

Coercion. Coercive measures, for the most part, have been retarding influences.[15] Where ardent Americanizers have attacked elements in the cultures of immigrants, these traits have become more precious than ever—they became focal points for their loyalties. The fight against the Chinese and Japanese language schools in Hawaii increased interest in the Oriental languages.[16]

Pressure has been brought to bear on the immigrant to discontinue use of his native tongue but he must, at all hazards, be prohibited from teaching the offensive speech to his children. This idea developed into a frenzy during the World War when several states enjoined the teaching of any foreign language in the schools. In some places telephone conversations in a foreign language were taboo. Churches were virtually compelled to discontinue the use of the mother tongue.[17]

If the immigrant is forbidden to use his own vernacular, his problems will be accentuated. Obviously English is a useful tool for participation in our life, but since the immigrant does not possess it he uses his own speech to make the necessary contacts. It is, therefore, through the instrumentality of his own language that he begins to take possession of America. The old medium of communication cannot be thrown away until another has been mastered.

In the political campaign of 1936, Governor Landon of Kansas,

[13] Cf. Bruno Rosselli, "An Arkansas Epic," *Century,* XCIX (January, 1920), 383. Cf. C. M. Panunzio, *The Soul of an Immigrant,* pp. 211–12, for the reaction of a congregation to a minister on account of his Italian origin.

[14] Cf. C. M. Panunzio, *Immigration Crossroads,* pp. 262–63; Peter Roberts, *op. cit.,* p. 295, for the effect of antagonistic attitudes on immigrant laborers.

[15] Several historical examples bear witness to this fact. Bismarck, notably, tried to Germanize Poland by suppressing the Polish language, with the result that the Poles idealized their vernacular and the German speech became a symbol of oppression.

[16] In the Territory of Hawaii there was a prolonged fight against the Japanese Language Schools. The law, which all but eliminated these schools, was declared unconstitutional by the United States Supreme Court. For the situation in California, cf. Y. Ichihashi, *op. cit.,* pp. 325–33; W. C. Smith, *op. cit.,* pp. 175–85, 328–29.

[17] Cf. *National Conference of Social Work,* 1924, pp. 581–83; Caroline F. Ware, *op. cit.,* pp. 169–70.

the republican nominee for the presidency, delivered his opening address at West Middlesex, Pennsylvania, his birthplace. The people of Kansas did not censure him for cherishing certain memories of his childhood home. To an immigrant, memories of the old home mean even more—they are stabilizing influences that help him at times when the going is hard. Preservation of certain symbols which are identified with the past should not only be tolerated but encouraged—they steady his life and may enrich ours. Since these sentimental memories do not interfere with our lives, we should not molest them. "We should know by this time," as Park and Miller put it, "that under tolerance, peculiar group values—such as language and religion—are only means to a fuller life; under oppression, they become objects of life." [18] Kutak indicated that Bohemian immigrants in a Nebraska community gradually absorbed a considerable amount of American culture because no pressure was exerted on them.[19]

The reaction of an immigrant to an intolerant attitude is illustrated by the following:

When I started to go to Grammar School, one of the teachers asked: "What is your name?"

I answered, "It's a hard name and I'll write it for you," which I did. She looked at it for a moment and then turned to me and said, "Oh, give that up and change your name to Smith, Jones, or a name like that and become Americanized. Give up everything you brought with you from the Old Country. You did not bring anything worth while anyway."

I was shocked by her idea of Americanization and thought to myself: "The Turkish sword did not succeed in making me become a Turk and now this hare-brained woman is trying to make an American out of me. I defy her to do it." After that I was more of an Armenian patriot than I had ever thought of being. Her remarks cut deep into me and I felt the pang, for I knew that without my childhood training to sustain me during my first two years in America, I would have gone under.[20]

[18] *Op. cit.*, pp. 286–87.

[19] *Op. cit.*, pp. 147–48.

[20] Bagdasar Krekor Baghdigian, *Americanism in Americanization* (Kansas City, 1921), pp. 17–19, 20. Cf. E. T. Hiller, Faye E. Corner, Wendell L. East, *Rural Community Types* (Urbana, 1928), pp. 40–43, for an interesting contrast between the effects of tolerance and coercion.

Adverse propaganda. Books,[21] magazines, pamphlets, "yellow" journals, and the platform have been used to level propaganda against immigrants as a whole and against particular groups.[22] We present samples from these writings.

Ominous statistics proclaim the persistent development of a parasite mass within our domain—our political system is clogged with foreign bodies which stubbornly refuse to be absorbed, and means must be found to meet the menace. We have taken unto ourselves a Trojan horse crowded with ignorance, illiteracy and envy.[23]

I ask you to call the roll of the armies of gunmen in our cities, of the worst criminals in our jails and penitentiaries, of the anarchists, communists, foreign-language newspapers, and other lists of disturbers containing unpronounceable or exchanged names. Then go back to the time when the foreign tides began to sweep into our country and measure the distance that we have retreated in those years from the moral and political standard which we then commonly recognized and accepted.[24]

Races cannot be cross-bred without mongrelization, any more than breeds of dogs can be cross-bred without mongrelization. The American nation was founded and developed by the Nordic race, but if a few million members of the Alpine, Mediterranean and Semitic races are poured among us, the result must inevitably be a hybrid race of people as worthless and futile as the good-for-nothing mongrels of Central America and Southeastern Europe.[25]

Such propaganda can and often does take advantage of the ignorance of large numbers in the population and through the misrepresentation of facts plays upon the prejudices of the different

[21] Out of a large number of books we may select the following samples: Madison Grant, *The Passing of the Great Race* (New York, 1918); Madison Grant and Chas. Stewart Davison, *op. cit.;* Wallace Irwin, *Seed of the Sun;* Peter B. Kyne, *The Pride of Palomar* (New York, 1921); Kenneth L. Roberts, *Why Europe Leaves Home* (Indianapolis, 1922); Lothrop Stoddard, *Re-Forging America* (New York, 1927).

[22] Cf. Will Irwin, "The Pleasures of Hate," *Survey Graphic,* XXV (June, 1936), 369.

[23] Dr. H. W. Evans, Imperial Wizard, *Americans Take Heed,* leaflet issued by Imperial Palace, Invisible Empire, Knights of the Ku Klux Klan. Cf. also *The Menace of Modern Immigration,* address delivered October 24, 1933; *The Obligation of American Citizens to the Free Public Schools* (leaflet).

[24] M. Grant and C. S. Davison, *op. cit.*, p. 6. Cf. *Ibid.*, pp. 39–40, 55, 231–32.

[25] From *Why Europe Leaves Home,* by Kenneth L. Roberts, copyright, 1922, p. 22. Used by special permission of the publishers, The Bobbs-Merrill Company.

ethnic groups. The result is unwholesome, so far as assimilation is concerned, for both native group and immigrants.[26]

Legal obstacles. Legal enactments of many kinds have been directed against aliens by federal, state, and municipal governments. These various restrictive measures were enacted to check the immigrant tide and to make America safe for those of old native stock.[27]

It has been a common practice to exclude aliens from employment on public works projects.[28] Furthermore, when aliens do secure employment, they usually have to face serious handicaps in that many compensation laws make no provision for their dependents or seriously limit the benefits.[29]

The professions have been open freely to aliens, with the exception of the practice of law. Since an attorney is an officer of the courts, it has been considered a wise policy to deny the privileges of this profession to non-citizens.[30]

[26] Cf. C. M. Panunzio, *Immigration Crossroads,* p. 261.

[27] Cf. W. M. Leiserson, *op. cit.,* p. 249–50. Cf. also E. G. Mears, *op. cit.,* pp. 284–88; Jerome Davis, *The Russians and Ruthenians in America* (New York, 1922), pp. 118–19. Max J. Kohler, *Immigration and Aliens in the United States* (New York, 1936), pp. 327–39. "Many forms of employment are at all times closed to the alien and there is not a state in the Union which does not exclude him by law from certain occupations. In most states, lawyers, doctors, architects, pharmacists, public school teachers, accountants, and state peace officers must be citizens. More serious to the average immigrant are the number of small trades and crafts from which he is barred—licensed occupations usually. . . . . New York State, with its large foreign population, bans at least twenty-two professions and occupations to aliens and requires citizenship or a declaration of intention for ten others.

"The most serious employment disability, however, is that in regard to 'pick and shovel' jobs, which since earliest times have fallen to the lot of newcomers. At the present time aliens are discriminated against to varying extent in employment on public works in all but seventeen of the states, most of which are located in the South, where the foreign farm population is negligible. In view of the important part public works play in the recovery program, this is a serious hardship. Twenty-five states exclude aliens from employment in public works and for public service or else give preference to citizens in such employment, tantamount—in times like these—to exclusion. In six others, there are no state laws discriminating against such employment, but some or all of their cities with a population of 100,000 or more have laws to that effect." *Social Work Year Book, 1937* (New York, 1937), pp. 213–14. Cf. Herman Feldman, *Racial Factors in American Industry* (New York, 1931), pp. 134–79; C. F. Ware, *op. cit.,* p. 169.

[28] Cf. W. M. Leiserson, *op. cit.,* pp. 251–52; E. G. Mears, *op. cit.,* pp. 333–38.

[29] W. M. Leiserson, *op. cit.,* pp. 252–53.

[30] Cf. E. G. Mears, *op. cit.,* pp. 318–19.

Restrictions on the ownership of land by aliens in the United States are so widespread that, in general, an alien may hold realty only when guaranteed by treaty provisions. The alien land laws of California have received more publicity than any others because of the distinction between aliens eligible and those not eligible to citizenship which was directed at the Japanese when the anti-Japanese agitation was developing on the Coast.[31]

The quota law for limiting the volume of immigration which was enacted in 1921 brought many hardships.[32] Cecilia Razovsky reports a case.

> Here a husband is torn apart from his wife and children. What is there to be said about this? Nothing remains but to hang a stone about one's neck and jump in the river, for this is not life but torture. I want to get citizenship papers and am told that I must bring my wife to America. How can I bring her over when the steamship company notified her that since her husband is not a citizen she cannot go to America. I have tried every means but nothing helps. . . . . I am in America 13 years. The papers say that you cannot bring your family here unless you are a citizen. I want to become one but am not allowed to do so. . . . . It is impossible to get naturalization papers when the family is not here. . . . . Please explain the situation to me as I am losing my head. It seems impossible to refuse me citizenship because my wife is not here and to refuse to let my wife come here, because I am not a citizen. It is unreasonable and I cannot understand it. Please explain to me and advise me what to do.[33]

A number of Japanese came to America in infancy or early childhood and have become more fully assimilated to the life about them than have many of North-European ancestry, yet their participation in our life is restricted because they cannot be naturalized. Al-

[31] Cf. E. G. Mears, *op. cit.*, pp. 158–87; Y. Ichihashi, *op. cit.*, pp. 261–82.

[32] The Cable Act of 1922 complicated the situation. According to this law the wife can no longer assume the citizenship of her husband when he receives his certificate of naturalization. Under the provisions of the old law, when the husband received his certificate, the wife could enter as a citizen. Under the Cable Act, wives and children are admissible only if they are within the quotas. The quotas of some countries are filled for years in advance and it may be years before the families can be reunited.

[33] Cecilia Razovsky, "Americanizing Husbands," *The Survey*, LIV (August 15, 1925), 515–16. Cf. *Ibid.*, p. 516. Cf. R. D. McKenzie, *Oriental Exclusion* (Chicago, 1928), pp. 79–97 for the problem among the Orientals in America.

though the process of assimilation has proceeded naturally, such persons, owing to legal proscriptions, are not permitted to enjoy a status which is satisfying. Because of this situation a number of them have developed cynical attitudes which restrict their contacts with Americans.[34]

Illegal practices. Over and above the legal discriminations, the immigrants have suffered grievously from illegal practices. Jerome Davis cites an instance where the police went into the home of a Russian and arrested him without a warrant after a refusal to return to work when requested to do so by his foreman.[35] Edith Abbott presents cases of fraudulent practices on the part of sworn officers of the courts.[36] Kate Halladay Claghorn recites a number of infringements on legal rights.[37]

> In a Pennsylvania town where large numbers of immigrants are employed in a great basic industry, the field agent found the justices inclined to take advantage of the foreign born and anyone else where possible. One in particular resorted to all the common methods of extortion, and would even issue separation papers for $50 each, and other papers which he had no legal right to issue for correspondingly large amounts.[38]

A report of the Carnegie Foundation tellingly portrays the injustices of our legal machinery and in making a plea for equality before the law concludes:

> For no group in the citizenship of the country is this more needed than in the case of the great mass of citizens of foreign birth, ignorant of the language, and helpless to secure their rights unless met by an administration of the machinery of justice that shall be simple, sympathetic, and patient. To such the apparent denial of justice forms the path to disloyalty and bitterness.[39]

[34] Cf. Kazuo Kawai, "Three Roads, and None Easy," *Survey Graphic,* IX (May, 1926), 164–66.

[35] *Op. cit.,* p. 121.

[36] *Immigration: Select Documents and Case Records* (Chicago, 1924), p. 592.

[37] *The Immigrant's Day in Court* (New York, 1923), pp. 168–73.

[38] *Ibid.,* p. 171. Cf. Peter Roberts, *op. cit.,* p. 244.

[39] Reginald Heber Smith, *Justice and the Poor* (New York, 1919), p. xiv. Cf. Thorsten Sellin, "Race Prejudice in the Administration of Justice," *American Journal of Sociology,* XLI (September, 1935), 212–17.

The illegal tactics reached their highest peak in connection with the wholesale raids on the "reds" which began under U. S. Attorney General Palmer in the Wilson administration. A committee of twelve eminent lawyers, headed by Dean Roscoe Pound of the Harvard Law School, issued a stinging report on these practices in May, 1920.

Under the guise of a campaign for the suppression of radical activities,[40] the office of the Attorney General, acting by its local agents throughout the country, and giving express instructions from Washington, has committed illegal acts. Wholesale arrests both of aliens and citizens have been made without warrant or any process of law; men and women have been jailed and held *incommunicado* without access of friends or counsel; homes have been entered without search-warrant and property seized and removed; other property has been wantonly destroyed; workingmen and workingwomen suspected of radical views have been shamefully abused and maltreated.[41]

Such practices, according to John A. Lapp, have stood in the way of assimilation.

We cannot make good citizens by intimidation through espionage systems of private and public detectives. After the Palmer, Daugherty, and Burns régime of the last five years, it is a wonder that any immigrant trusts us. The "deportation deliriums" of 1919 and 1920, so well pictured in Louis F. Post's book by that name, were enough to destroy all of the good work of those who had been preaching that this was the land of freedom and opportunity, where the oppressor's hand was not seen. No act of a Prussian kaiser was ever more flagrant than those committed in the United States in the name of "law and order" against harm-

[40] H. P. Fairchild comments on this: "Suffice it to say that under the guise of protecting American institutions a pursuit of unorthodoxy was inaugurated which enlisted a fanatical zeal and relentless intolerance worthy of the most devoted agent of the Holy Office during the Inquisition or the most infallible witch hunter of the palmy days of Salem, and which resulted in the deportation of hundreds of hapless individuals and the imprisonment and detention under intolerable conditions of many more." From *Immigration* (New York, 1928), p. 427. By permission of The Macmillan Company, publishers. Cf. also Jerome Davis, *op. cit.*, pp. 121–26; C. M. Panunzio, *The Deportation Cases of 1919–20* (New York, 1921); L. F. Post, *Deportations Delirium of 1920* (Chicago, 1923); and K. H. Claghorn, *op. cit.*, pp. 335–467.

[41] *Illegal Practices of the United States Department of Justice.* Quoted in *The Russians and Ruthenians in America* by Jerome Davis, copyright, 1922, by Doubleday, Doran and Company, Inc., New York, p. 122.

less immigrants who took literally the declarations of civil liberty contained in the Constitution. Until we make retribution for those acts and make good our belief in liberty by really guaranteeing free speech, free press, freedom of assemblage, religious freedom, freedom from false or arbitrary arrest, habeas corpus, trial by jury, and the right of all, not some, to be protected in life, liberty, and property, we cannot truly assimilate immigrants nor even hold our citizenship in high respect.[42]

Reginald Heber Smith says of those who suffer injustices through our legal mechinery,

The consequence is that they become bitter, not only against the particular person who has wronged them but against society in general, against the country which permits society to be organized on so unjust a basis. Such persons—and they need not be confined to persons of foreign birth by any means—are ripe to listen to those social agitators and disturbers who are only too prevalent. They are ripe for enlistment in the ranks of those who are regarded as dangerous to the security of law and order.[43]

[42] *Proceedings of the National Conference of Social Work, 1924,* p. 585.
[43] *Op. cit.*, p. 218. For the attitude of many Italians, see John H. Mariano, *The Italian Immigrant and Our Courts* (Boston, 1925), pp. 36–45, 77–78.

CHAPTER XIII

FACTORS IN ASSIMILATION
(*Concluded*)

Satisfactory economic adjustments. The majority of immigrants have come because of a desire for a better livelihood. A modicum of economic success, then, will do more to assimilate an alien than any amount of formalistic patriotic training. "If he gets on," writes Robert E. Park, "if he is able to realize here in America some of the fundamental wishes that were denied him in his mother country, he will eventually become an American in every sense that we desire to give to that title." [1] "Where bread is, there is my country" explains the readiness with which immigrants in the eighteenth century as well as in the twentieth became Americans.[2]

Hans Mattson said of the Scandinavians that they had been received cordially by the pioneers in the West and that they had become both prosperous and happy. As a consequence they learned to love this country of freedom and wished to become and remain Americans.[3] On the whole it may be said that the Scandinavian immigrants have been at least moderately prosperous and this no doubt has been a factor in making them patriotic American citizens. Bercovici tells of some Poles in Wisconsin who had cleared land and were enjoying good returns from the soil—and they loved America.[4] When the Ukrainian immigrant from poverty-stricken

[1] *National Conference of Social Work,* 1921, p. 497.

[2] As the Lettish immigrants gained economic security they began to participate in the political and social life of America and assumed a conservative attitude toward things as they are. C. J. Bittner, *op. cit.*

[3] *Op. cit.,* p. 116. S. M. Swenson came to Texas from Sweden with practically nothing. He became a successful business man and a loyal, enthusiastic American. August Anderson, *Hyphenated, or the Life Story of S. M. Swenson* (Austin, Texas, 1916). A man from Sweden, who visited several Swedish communities in the United States, observed that where the settlers were making good economically, they tended to forget Sweden. G. H. von Koch, *op. cit.,* p. 351.

[4] K. Bercovici, *On New Shores,* pp. 128–31.

surroundings began to rise to a more comfortable station in life he, too, experienced a change in attitude. "Where formerly his primary thought was to return to the old country as soon as he had made his so-called 'pile,' now, on the contrary, he began to send for his family back home, with the intention of making America his permanent home." [5] Says Brunner of an immigrant colony in North Carolina that worked hard in its truck gardens and found a ready market for the produce:

Prosperity came with amazing rapidity. Negroes were employed. Cars were purchased, ending isolation. The foreign-born visited the city and near-by coast resorts, weakening thereby social organization within their own community but hastening their own adjustment to their new environment. . . . . So great has been their success that some of the native-born are now cautiously adopting the practices of the recent immigrants. Ridicule has stopped and the resentment caused by the arrival of these Catholic settlers in an intensely Protestant community is slowly dying away. Economic success and the common use of English have carried this group of foreign-born farmers far toward complete adjustment to American conditions.[6]

Dr. Galitzi tells of a family of Roumanians which planned to remain only a few years in America and then return to their native village. But a greatly improved economic status made them feel so at home in this environment that they became American citizens. They were able to live in a comfortable home in a newly developed residential section for the better-class working people. The daughter had moved higher in the occupational ladder than her mother, who was an expert button-hole maker. The mother said, "America is a nice place to live in," and "it is far better to stay here." [7] In another family the husband earned $120 a week as a carpenter contractor. Both man and wife became citizens and definitely settled in the United States. The wife was not even interested in a visit to the Old Country. She said:

Here I live like a "boereasa" (noblewoman). I go to the movies whenever I like, I listen to the radio, I go to the parks. On Sundays my hus-

[5] *The Ukrainian Weekly,* English Supplement to *Svoboda,* October 13, 1933.
[6] E. deS. Brunner, *op. cit.,* p. 95.
[7] *Op. cit.,* pp. 175–76.

band always drives us out of the city. He has two cars and he earns more money than a general in the Roumanian army. Why give up my luxuries and return to a less comfortable life? I do not speak good Roumanian and nice people over there would make fun of me. Here I am free to do as I please.[8]

An Italian immigrant appreciated America for what she had done for him. He became more prosperous than he could possibly have been in Italy. He came to accumulate a competence and return home, but decided to remain because America was good to him. He was admitted to the bar within six years after his arrival and met with success far beyond anything he had even dreamed. To him America had proved herself to be the land of opportunity and gave promise of continuing to be. With confidence he looked forward to still greater successes.[9]

Very often a taste of economic success spurs the immigrant on to greater efforts. Old-world culture traits which hamper him in satisfying his desire for economic success must yield, and gradually he comes to be a more or less standardized American.

Opportunities for acquiring status. Human beings everywhere have a tendency to be interested in improving their status, and that factor has lured many immigrants to our shores. In older European countries social distinctions are drawn rather sharply and there is comparatively little chance for the peasant to cross class lines. In certain places land ownership is the magic key to an improved status, but not all find it possible to acquire realty titles. Many aliens endure great hardships in order to accumulate savings for the purchase of land near the native village. They come with the intention of remaining only long enough to save sufficient funds to buy the desired acreage. However, many find that the more or less open class system in America makes it comparatively easy to rise and gradually the wish to return loses strength. A Roumanian woman in Chicago seemed to enjoy the new life in the city.

No one troubles you if you mind your own business. You can become rich quickly and nobody questions who you are, so long as you lead a peace-

[8] *Ibid.*, pp. 182–83.

[9] Cf. H. G. Duncan, *op. cit.*, p. 564. (The millions, however, who failed left no "success stories." Editorial comment by E. A. Ross.)

ful life and the police do not come after you. If you follow the rules everything goes all right. And think of the abundant hot water, the heating system, the cars. If we were to have those things in our village, the people would make fun of us saying we had become the *Ciocoi* (self-made land-owning aristocracy). It is far better to stay here, where every one shakes hands with you, from the mayor of the city to the judge, without any class feeling. This is the country of the people.[10]

The immigrant soon learns that money gives recognition in America.[11] In the old country birth confers standing and the person of lowly origin finds it hard to rise even if he has ability. In America a man has a better chance. Artificial distinctions vanish and the real man comes to the front. When a person sees that he can rise, he gets a stimulus—he becomes enthusiastic.[12] He works hard to acquire the prestige-giving dollars. The Japanese who came to Hawaii to work on the sugar plantations were assigned a status of inferiority. This did not appeal to them and large numbers left the plantations in quest of dignity-conferring occupations. Those who are able to make headway become ardent supporters of America and gradually take on American ways. A Roumanian

[10] C. A. Galitzi, *op. cit.*, pp. 175–76.

[11] Cf. Harvey W. Zorbaugh, *The Gold Coast and the Slum* (Chicago, 1928), pp. 47–57, for the importance of wealth in gaining social recognition. Wealth is undoubtedly the first qualification for inclusion in the *Social Register*.

[12] The struggle for recognition in one group is presented in the following excerpt: "Although the 'successful' Hungarian is able to pass over easily into the American group, he is not satisfied with any lesser goal than acceptance by the socially élite. Life for him has become a struggle to gain social status. Every other value appears inferior to this. He wants to have his name listed in the *Social Secretary* and know that he has 'arrived.' In spite of their ambitious efforts, however, well-to-do Hungarians in Detroit have not yet achieved marked success in their 'social climbing.' There is a wide margin between the status they seek and the status which is granted to them by consent of Detroit's society leaders. A 'successful' Hungarian frequently boasts: 'I know practically everyone who matters in Grosse Pointe.' Yet closer questioning reveals that only a few persons of actual social status, and those only who are noted for their Bohemian tendencies, are willing to accept the hospitality of the ambitious Hungarian. A Hungarian woman of this group remarked, naming a well-known post-debutante: 'She is my warmest friend. We are always together.' The post-debutante, however, said icily: 'Yes, I *have* met this woman you speak of.' Acquaintances of a noted Hungarian painter spoke thus of his struggles: 'At last he has been accepted by Bloomfield Hills society, but he has not yet made the grade of Grosse Pointe society.' In their eagerness to gain social status, some of the Hungarian intellectuals adopt methods which actually bar them from acceptance by socially prominent American families." E. D. Beynon, *American Journal of Sociology* XLI (January, 1936), 432–33.

woman who had risen far above her old-country position lost interest in the homeland.

> I enjoy the democratic freedom that America gives. Everyone is equal here, and you can make a fortune or lose it, it matters not. You can start all over again with no feeling of failure or of shame. . . . . One day you are a street cleaner and the next you awake to find yourself a millionaire.[13]

Immigrant autobiographies make it evident that when a person has the opportunity to enhance his status he becomes more favorably disposed toward America and inhibitions against taking over her culture gradually vanish. George Linhart, a poor orphan boy from Austria, received a certain amount of recognition in scientific circles through the articles which he published in several journals. He is grateful to America.[14] T. M. Nielsen came from a humble peasant cottage in Denmark and became an English-speaking minister in America. "I am thankful," he writes, "to the Church who took me in, to the United States who adopted me as a son." [15] Andreas Ueland was admitted to the bar in Minnesota six years after his arrival from a small rocky farm in Norway and four years later, at the age of twenty-eight, was elected probate judge in Minneapolis—an honorable position. He became an ardent American and criticized severely the attempts of some of his country-men to preserve the Norwegian culture in America.[16] Edward A. Steiner, an immigrant from south-eastern Europe, labored in sweat shops, in harvest fields, and in mines in America. Gradually, however, he worked up and for more than thirty years has held a professorship in one of our colleges. He has received considerable recognition as a writer and lecturer. He, too, has become quite thoroughly Americanized and could say, "Thank God for America." [17] Mary Antin, a Jewish girl from the ghetto in Russia, moved out of her home in the slum and mingled freely with the better class of

[13] C. A. Galitzi, *op. cit.*, p. 183.

[14] Cf. G. A. Linhart, *op. cit.*

[15] T. M. Nielsen, *How a Dane Became an American* (Cedar Rapids, Iowa, 1935), p. 305.

[16] Andreas Ueland, *Recollections of an Immigrant* (New York, 1929).

[17] E. A. Steiner, *From Alien to Citizen*, p. 332.

Americans in Boston. In her own estimate she won for herself a status as enviable as that held by any native child.[18] Rose Cohen's father, an immigrant from Russia, struggled to make a living here. Her brother went to Columbia University where he won second prize in an essay contest. This is the sister's comment:

> But far greater than the value of this money was the honour, for so we felt it to be. Mother had tears in her eyes. Her boy was at the great University! Her boy's article was valued second to that of a superintendent of Industrial Schools! And father looked on at us silently unbelieving; then he said, "Oh! After all this is America." [19]

While the parents in this instance had not received any recognition themselves, yet vicariously, in and through their son, their status was enhanced—and they were grateful.

The autobiography of Ludwig Lewisohn reveals something different. He had prepared himself to teach English literature but was unable to find a position for which he considered himself qualified. Finally he was appointed to an instructorship in German. Not receiving the recognition he desired, he became critical and even cynical.[20]

Denied status, Chinese immigrants have not been greatly interested in American life; they retreated to their Chinatowns and comparatively few have become Americanized in any measure.

Primary contacts. Contact is the first essential to success in assimilation. Moreover, the rapidity and completeness of assimilation, other things being equal, are directly dependent on the number and intimacy of these social impacts.[21] This may be qualified in some measure, to be sure, because not all persons are equally responsive to stimuli offered. "Theoretically," writes Taft, "each of us may be said to have a *contact index*—a capacity to learn from others with a minimum of friction. Similarly, national and local

[18] Cf. Mary Antin, *op. cit.*, p. 360.

[19] From *Out of the Shadow,* by Rose Cohen, copyright, 1918, by Doubleday, Doran and Company, Inc., New York, p. 313.

[20] Ludwig Lewisohn, *Up Stream* (New York, 1922).

[21] Carl Christian Jensen, a Danish immigrant, wrote that while attending the university he was admitted to good American homes. "That," he said, "was the greatest thing I found at college. . . . . They made me American." *An American Saga* (Boston, 1927), p. 175.

groups have varying contact indices." [22] A person or group with a high contact index tends to profit most from the significant interactions. It is possible for persons and groups to be immersed in another group and have business relationships extending over long periods, yet remain comparatively untouched. Where, however, the associations are intimate and personal, as with children on the playground, the change is both rapid and profound.[23] Immigrant women usually are more restricted and assimilate more slowly than men.[24] Some, however, who work as domestics under favorable circumstances make intimate contacts in households and become Americanized quite readily. Park and Burgess support this position. "By a curious paradox," they write, "slavery, and particularly household slavery, has probably been, aside from intermarriage, the most efficient device for promoting assimilation." [25]

Many immigrants are desirous of becoming acquainted with the better element in the American group; they are hungry for sympathy and understanding. They feel certain that even in this cold and forbidding outside world there must be some one, somewhere who exemplifies the better things in life. Rihbany concluded that it was well-nigh impossible for a foreigner like himself to come into helpful contact with real American families in the cosmopolitan city of New York. He had seen large numbers of Irish, Poles, Italians, Chinese, Russians and others in the area where he moved about, but he was eager to know where and how the Americans lived.[26]

Progress comes slowly. Some have ventured out and tried to make desirable friendships only to be rebuffed. At times fortunate

[22] Donald R. Taft, *Human Migration* (New York, 1936), pp. 16–17.

[23] Cf. M. E. Ravage, *An American in the Making* (New York, 1917), pp. 227–53; Elias Tobenkin, *House of Conrad* (New York, 1918), pp. 18–22.

[24] The Immigration Commission study bears this out. Vol. XXVI, *passim*. Mary Antin, *The Promised Land,* shows that the mother clung more tenaciously to the old-world traditions than did the father.

[25] R. E. Park and E. W. Burgess, *Introduction to the Science of Sociology*, p. 739. Cf. also E. B. Reuter, *The American Race Problem* (New York, 1927), pp. 108–15. The value of living within a household is illustrated by Bercovici. A cultured Japanese desiring to improve his English before entering Columbia University worked as a servant in a New York home. Here he had six fellow servants from whom he learned English rapidly. *Op. cit.*, pp. 267–68.

[26] Cf. A. M. Rihbany, *op. cit.*, pp. 245–46.

relationships have come by accident, as it were.[27] Illness, with a period of hospitalization, was the instrumentality which brought Rose Cohen in touch with the better class of Americans.[28]

Segregation. Contact promotes assimilation while segregation, be it voluntary or enforced, isolates and consequently retards. Immigrants tend to gravitate toward the areas where their fellow countrymen reside. In these colonies, which are fragments of the old world transplanted to American soil, they understand and are understood. Here is a warmth of fellowship which cannot be found elsewhere in the strange land. Because of the satisfactions derived from this transplanted old-world life, many immigrants are content to remain in the colonies and not explore the new world outside. Brunner shows the effect on a colony of Swedes in Minnesota.

> Trained in the hard school of the agricultural depression then gripping their native country, they built a bit of old Sweden in a new land. With no neighbors, they continued to speak their mother tongue. Their church, too, was Swedish to the core. Lacking contact with the native-born, the customs and ways of old Sweden were perpetuated in social life, in religion, even for some time in education through the parochial school. The community became a part of that great unassimilated northern European immigration that in the quarter century from 1850 to 1875 caused much concern to the older Americans of the seaboard states who feared that it threatened to build a foreign state on the western frontier.
>
> The effect of this obstacle of isolation to complete adjustment to American life is still seen in this community and in many like it. Thoroughly modern and indeed progressive as Litchfield is to-day, Swedish is still heard on its streets and in some of its church services. There are few who do not speak English with an accent.[29]

The problem of assimilation is accentuated where the segregation is enforced and is not approved by the segregated group. Wholesome social contact and interaction of culture is precluded

[27] Cf. E. G. Stern, *My Mother and I*, pp. 113–14.
[28] *Out of the Shadow* (New York, 1918), p. 246. Cf. also pp. 229–50.
[29] E. deS. Brunner, *op. cit.*, p. 94. Cf. W. M. Leiserson, *op. cit.*, p. 14.

thereby and the immigrants cling the more tenaciously to their old-world traditions. Panunzio discusses enforced segregation.[30]

> The treatment he receives in his work—these and other influences hold the immigrant to the "colony" or drive him back whenever he attempts to emerge.
>
> The immigrant community [31] becomes a city within a city, separated by virtual walls from the larger community of which it is a part. In that city not only the better elements of the immigrant's native culture are absent but also he is practically shut off completely from the better aspects of American life. Beyond those narrow, stifling walls the immigrant rarely goes, rarely can go, save as he goes in and out in search of daily bread. The daily round takes him over the same tracked ways, cutting the confines of his little world at one and the same point day in and day out, week in and week out, often life in and life out. Out in that workaday world, moreover, he frequently meets with crude misunderstanding, drab discourtesy, subtle or blunt abuse.

Intermarriage. Intermarriage, because it provides a setting favorable to intimate understanding is conducive to assimilation.[32] Carpenter concludes that intermarriage "provides the most direct and powerful force by which the present and the next generations may be welded together into a unified social and cultural amalgam, in short, be truly 'Americanized'!" [33] If a Roumanian marries a woman of Pilgrim ancestry, New England traditions and practices will inevitably set the pattern for the new home, and this immigrant will be more favorably situated for Americanization [34] than if he

[30] From C. M. Panunzio, *Immigration Crossroads,* pp. 260–61. By permission of The Macmillan Company, publishers.

[31] Cf. C. M. Panunzio, *The Soul of an Immigrant,* pp. 205–06, for opposition to an Italian vice-consul who wished to live in a desirable section of Portland, Maine.

[32] Cf. M. T. F., *My Chinese Marriage* (New York, 1927), for an interesting autobiographical document by an American woman who married a Chinese student in one of our universities. They went to China where they resided for several years. The American wife lived for a time in her husband's parental home. She adjusted herself to the situation and left China with some regrets when her husband was sent back to the United States as a consul. Her marriage was a distinct aid to her assimilation. The Chinese husband also made changes.

[33] Niles Carpenter, *Immigrants and Their Children, 1920* (Washington, D.C., 1927), p. 232.

[34] A German visitor reported of Louis Eversmann, an immigrant to Missouri who had married an American woman: "Eversmann has become much Americanized.

had brought a mate from his homeland. Obviously in the latter home old-world customs and the language would tend to persist for some time.

The number of foreign-born men married to native women is particularly impressive.[35] Not all of these American women, however, are "pure" descendants of the old colonial stock. Carpenter's researches indicate that many of the German-American marriages represented unions with Americans who were only one generation removed from Germany. Many second, third or fourth generation immigrants enter into these mixed native and foreign marriages. For the most part, however, marriages with these natives of the same ethnic stock are as favorable to assimilation as unions with members of the old stock. Natives of foreign parentage reared in our culture usually become American in manners, ideas, attitudes, and speech.[36] In some places, to be sure, they have been isolated and almost completely under the influence of the transplanted parental culture.

It may be assumed without much question that the assimilation of an immigrant is accelerated if he marries a woman of native parentage.[37] His assimilation may be hastened also if he marries an immigrant woman from another ethnic group. If a Greek marries a Bohemian, the wide divergence in their cultures may lead to a more rapid assimilation than if both had come from the same village in Europe. Since they have no common language, they will probably find it mutually advantageous to learn English. Instead

His children speak English and do not understand any German, because their father, as well as their mother, speaks only English with them. But the big German pipe has been preserved after all." *Missouri Historical Review,* XII (October, 1917), 7.

[35] Cf. N. Carpenter, *op. cit.,* pp. 232–43.

[36] Cf. *Ibid.,* p. 242.

[37] Intermarriage may also have an assimilative effect on others beside the two persons concerned. "The proportion of mixed to homogeneous marriages rose after 1926. More important than this increase was the tendency of the contractants to remain in Conneaut and to share, temporarily or permanently, the homes of the foreign-born. The effect of this very close relationship between immigrants and mixed-marriage contractants was that within the family of each foreign-born there was now set up a process of assimilation, contributing to that of the whole group. The gap between foreign-born Finns and non-Finns was spanned by the action of a great number of these rapidly Americanizing family units." John I. Kolehmainen, "A Study of Marriage in a Finnish Community," *American Journal of Sociology,* XLII (November, 1936), 375.

of adopting the customs of one or the other, it may be easier to compromise on American ways of living.

Available statistical data make it evident that considerable intermarriage is taking place and is thus hastening the process of cultural fusion. Contrariwise, intermarriage may be considered one of the measures of assimilation. When intermarriages between different cultural groups take place freely it indicates a relatively complete assimilation.[38]

[38] For statistical data see the following: Romanzo Adams, *Interracial Marriage in Hawaii: A Study of the Mutually Conditioned Process of Acculturation and Amalgamation* (New York, 1937); E. deS. Brunner, *op. cit.*, pp. 75–91; N. Carpenter, *op. cit.*, pp. 232–49; Paul G. Cressey, *The Taxi-Dance Hall* (Chicago, 1932), pp. 167–74; Julius Drachsler, *Democracy and Assimilation* (New York, 1920); Julius Drachsler, *Intermarriage in New York City* (New York, 1921); J. V. De Porte, *Marriage Statistics, New York State,* 1921–1924; Bessie Bloom Wessel, *An Ethnic Survey of Woonsocket, Rhode Island* (Chicago, 1931); D. J. Williams, *op. cit.*, pp. 83–85; John I. Kolehmainen, "A Study of Marriage in a Finnish Community," *American Journal of Sociology,* XLII (November, 1936), 372–81. For a brief summary of the data see D. R. Taft, *Human Migration,* pp. 252–56.

CHAPTER XIV

AGENCIES OF ASSIMILATION

A. The Ethnic Colony

All immigrant peoples tend to form settlements of their own for mutual protection and coöperation, and subsequent arrivals gravitate toward these colonies. The most peculiar and undoubtedly the most efficiently organized are the Jewish ghettos in our large cities, the Chinatowns, and Japanese communities on the Pacific Coast. The various immigrant groups do not speak our language, they follow different traditions, eat different foods, even sleep on different beds. Without a colony with, at least, some partially transplanted institutions, the immigrants would be completely lost in the New World. The colony enables strangers to live in the midst of an alien and more or less intolerant group with a certain sense of security and freedom.[1] The value and meaning of Chinatown to the newly arrived Chinese immigrant is indicated by the following quotation:

My father gave me $100, and I went to Hong Kong with five other boys from our place and we got steerage passage on a steamer, paying $50 each. Everything was new to me. All my life I had been used to sleeping on a board bed with a wooden pillow, and I found the steamer's bunk very uncomfortable, because it was so soft. The food was different from that which I had been used to, and I did not like it at all. I was afraid of the stews, for the thought of what they might be made of by the wicked wizards of the ship made me ill. Of the great power of these people I saw many signs. . . . . When I got to San Francisco, which was before the passage of the Exclusion Act, I was half starved, because I was afraid to eat the provisions of the barbarians, but a few days' living in the Chinese quarter made me happy again.[2]

[1] Cf. Edward Corsi, "The Voice of the Immigrant," *Outlook,* CXLVII (September 21, 1927), 89–90.

[2] Hamilton Holt, *op. cit.,* p. 289.

In the words of C. C. Wu,

> Chinatown, therefore, affords a *milieu* where the Chinese feels comfortable and safe. No one will stare at him, make fun of him, nor mistreat him there. Here he may eat with chopsticks instead of knife and fork, drink tea instead of cold water, wear comfortable dress instead of stiff collar and unmanageable tie, talk and swear in Cantonese dialect and indulge in a cup of *Wu Chah Pi* or a game of *Fan Tan.*[3]

Wirth states the case for the Jews.

> While the Jew's contacts with the outside world were categorical and abstract, within his own community he was at home. Here he could relax from etiquette and formalism. His contacts with his fellow-Jews were warm, intimate, and free. Especially was this true of his family life, within the inner circle of which he received that appreciation and sympathetic understanding which the larger world could not offer. In his own community, which was based upon the solidarity of the families that composed it, he was a person with status. Whenever he returned from a journey to a distant market, or from his daily work, he came back to the family fold, there to be recreated and reaffirmed as a man and as a Jew. Even when he was far removed from his kin, he lived his real inner life in his dreams and hopes with them. He could converse with his own kind in that familiar tongue which the rest of the world could not understand. He was bound by common troubles, by numerous ceremonies and sentiments to his small group that lived its own life oblivious of the world beyond the confines of the ghetto. Without the backing of his group, without the security that he enjoyed in his inner circle of friends and countrymen, life would have been intolerable.[4]

Fundamentally the immigrant colony develops to make it possible for the newcomer to live—not merely to exist. Without this community, the immigrant would only vegetate or lead an animal-like existence, but in it he can actually live and become a person with status.[5] Even with its many disadvantages the immigrant

[3] *Op. cit.*

[4] Louis Wirth, "The Ghetto," *American Journal of Sociology,* XXXIII (July, 1927), 61.

[5] According to E. D. Beynon, a number of Hungarian immigrants have been able to preserve their occupational status through the protection of the foreign-language colony as they have entered symbiotic relationships with the laborers and tradesmen of their own ethnic group. "Some of these intellectuals, especially physicians, have been able to continue in America the occupation which was theirs prior to mi-

settlement is a rather desirable place of residence. The reason is plain: Most of us live a more free, comfortable, and even human life among friends and kinfolks than among strangers.[6] As Park has pointed out, "Man is a creature such that when he lives at all he lives in society, lives in his hopes, in his dreams, and in the minds of other men." [7] The colony is an area where the immigrant may enjoy life on the basis of primary relationships. It is, in fact, a home away from the old home, where the immigrant may feel the warmth and glow of intimate fellowship which is denied him in the cold outside world. It is only in the colony that the immigrant has relatives, friends, and fellow countrymen who can share his hopes and his dreams, his hardships and his disappointments.[8] Here he may tell a joke that will bring laughter and not ridicule; here he may hear the tales of the homeland told and retold until the illusion is created that Boston is Naples, Cleveland is Prague, or Chicago is Warsaw.

According to many observers, this very congeniality of the racial colony is a hindrance to assimilation; the immigrants prefer to associate with members of their own group and avoid contacts with Americans. This aloofness is conducive to a continuance of "the village traditions of the mother country." [9] "The process of becoming an American," concluded the Immigration Commission,

gration, but for some reason have not been able to enter into competition with American professional men in American neighborhoods." Most of the intellectuals, however, have maintained their status through other agencies such as newspapers, steamship offices, private banks, real estate and insurance agencies. Others, who cannot find places in legitimate occupations turn to the direct exploitation of the "dumb laborers." "Social Mobility and Social Distance among Hungarian Immigrants in Detroit," *American Journal of Sociology,* XLI (January, 1936), 427–28.

[6] M. E. Ravage had to endure much at first. Friends in a colony would have helped by pointing out certain things to him. Cf. *op. cit.,* pp. 206–09; 237–40; 252–53; 258–59.

[7] R. E. Park and E. W. Burgess, *The City* (Chicago, 1925), pp. 118–19.

[8] Harvey W. Zorbaugh writes: "The immigrant finds in it [the colony] a social world. In the colony he meets with sympathy, understanding, and encouragement. There he finds his fellow-countrymen who understand his habits and standards and share his life experience and view point. In the colony he has status, plays a rôle in a group. In the life of the colony's streets and cafés, in its church and benevolent societies, he finds response and security. In the colony he finds that he can live, be somebody, satisfy his wishes—all of which is impossible in the strange world outside." *Op. cit.,* p. 141.

[9] From Angelo Patri, *A Schoolmaster of the Great City* (New York, 1917), p. 3. By permission of The Macmillan Company, publishers.

"is dependent upon acquaintance with America. Such acquaintance proceeds most slowly in racial colonies, where the individual is surrounded by others like himself in language, thought, customs, and attachment to things of the past." [10] In the words of Van der Zee,

When he [the Dutch immigrant] prefers to throw in his lot with a community of his fellow-countrymen, he conforms to a well-preserved social order based on Dutch stability and stolidity. He finds that his Dutch neighbors have lived and worked within the confines of their settlement, whether in town or in the country; that nearly all are engaged and interested in the same occupations; and that their whole life is centered about their churches. And so with the retention of old Dutch national traits intensified by constant accessions of fresh blood from the Netherlands, despite their patriotism and partial adoption of the English language, American inventions, and a few American ways, the Hollanders of Iowa form a lump which cannot truthfully be said to have entered the American "melting pot." They are still for the most part an unassimilated, clannish, though not entirely isolated, mass of foreigners who have necessarily acquired an American veneer from the environment created by the political and social ideas of America.[11]

Without doubt the colony life, Wirth found, exerted a retarding influence on the Jews.

Through the instrumentality of the ghetto there gradually developed that social distance which effectually isolated the Jew from the remainder of the population. These barriers did not completely inhibit contact, but they reduced it to the type of relationships which were of a secondary and formal nature. As these barriers crystallized and his life was lived more and more removed from the rest of the world, the solidarity of his own little community was enhanced until it became strictly divorced from the larger world without.[12]

Ray Stannard Baker sketches a picture of a certain type of ghetto Jew in New York City.

His black coat, his long black beard, his rounded shoulders, the Hebrew curls at his temples, indelibly mark his place in the heterogeneous life

[10] *Reports*, Vol. XXVI, p. 667. Cf. also pp. 593, 749.

[11] Jacob Van der Zee, *The Hollanders of Iowa* (Iowa City, 1912), p. 319.

[12] L. Wirth, "The Ghetto," *American Journal of Sociology*, XXXIII (July, 1927), 61–62.

of the streets. He can be seen walking with serene countenance in the midst of this seething cauldron of modern life as unscathed as Shadrach, Meshach, and Abednego in the fiery furnace of King Nebuchadnezzar.[13]

Konrad Bercovici is emphatic on this point.

I have in mind certain sections of New York, Boston, Chicago, and San Francisco where only Italians can live and do business; certain sections of Detroit, Boston, and some rural sections in upper Michigan where only Poles can live and do business; Yorkville in New York City, and the German sections in Cincinnati and Milwaukee; and ghettos all over the country from the Atlantic to the Pacific. In those sections one is in America theoretically only; actually one is in a foreign country ruled really by its own laws, its own national hatreds and prejudices brought here by immigrants. . . . . The breaking up of the solid foreign settlements would start the great melting pot a-boiling. Until this is done, most of the large cities will be foreign cities in the United States.[14]

Without doubt, colony life has a retarding influence under certain conditions. Generally speaking, the rate of assimilation of an immigrant group is inversely proportional to its numbers and its compactness. A large settlement with a high ratio of cultural and racial homogeneity will tend to continue its traditional life for a comparatively long time.[15] But resist as they may, the different immigrant colonies, as illustrated by the attempts of the Russian Molokans [16] of Los Angeles to isolate themselves, will succumb to Americanizing influences.[17] Jews have been highly organized.

[13] "Spiritual Unrest," *American Magazine,* LXVIII (October, 1909), 592.

[14] "The Land of the Too Free," *Good Housekeeping,* CI (August, 1935), 44–45. On the other hand, while some of these colonies lack certain externals of Americanization, they may be making valuable contributions. We may refer to Askov, a Danish community in Minnesota. Some years ago certain specialists were sent there in connection with a nation-wide program of Americanization. They returned to Washington and reported that we should take lessons from these Danes. They had no jails, no crime, no poverty. They had coöperatives, community theaters, schools for farming, cooking and singing. Cf. William Seabrook, "Imported Americans," *American Magazine,* CXXIII (March, 1937), 91. For the effect of the Hungarian colony of Detroit on the delinquency rate of the second generation, cf. *Journal of Criminal Law and Criminology,* XXV (January, 1935), 762.

[15] Cf. K. Bercovici, *On New Shores,* pp. 190–91.

[16] Cf. *American Journal of Sociology,* XXXV (November, 1929), 400–01. Cf. C. F. Ware, *op. cit.,* pp. 152–202, for an Italian colony.

[17] The Doukhobors and Mennonites segregated themselves in certain areas in Canada, but even the most rigid attempts of these sectarians have not been able to withstand the subtle influences of Canadian life. The process of secularization has

Furthermore, it may be said that they brought more of their culture with them than have many other groups; they came by village units and organized their life about the synagogue. Yet dissension and discord weakened their defenses against the alien culture. Moreover the secondary contacts in their commercial life exerted an assimilative influence.

Many of these condemnations of the immigrant colony, we must conclude, are based on prejudice, on superficial and hasty judgments, rather than on a careful and thorough consideration of the facts. It may be paradoxical, but while the colony isolates the immigrant and keeps him out of touch with the American culture it is at the same time interpreting that culture to him and is preparing him to participate in it. Sufficient evidence is at hand to show that too rapid change may result in serious disorganization and attendant loss in social values. On the basis of his studies in Honolulu, Lind concluded that "One of the most important functions of the racial colony in any city is that of providing during the trying period of readjustment to a new culture and civilization, a haven where the habitual and customary patterns of life are unquestioned and absolute." [18] Immigrant communities facilitate the adjustment of the newcomers to American attitudes and standards. Instead of preventing assimilation, the immigrant quarter affords an accommodation which is favorable to the progress of assimilation. It makes possible the participation of the immigrant in American life without the loss of memories and ideals which are essential elements in his personality make-up. The immigrant, like other men, makes adjustments to new situations in terms of his past experience. Under the protection of the colony he may experiment and gradually habituate himself to the new life while steadying himself by leaning upon the past. The founder of the Dutch colony in Michigan desired to retain the purity and fervor of the old religious faith and to keep the members from endanger-

been slow but nevertheless sure. The German Catholics likewise have isolated themselves and have tried to live their old life, but gradually they are being transformed into Canadian communities. C. A. Dawson, *Group Settlement: Ethnic Communities in Western Canada* (Toronto, 1936).

[18] A. W. Lind, "The Ghetto and the Slum," *Social Forces,* IX (December, 1930), 208.

ing contact with unbelieving strangers. He realized, however, that they could not maintain a "Little Holland" in this country. As the Hollanders came in large numbers and lived together in the settlement, the process of assimilation was slow. Nevertheless changes came, and, together with their children, the immigrants have become loyal sons and daughters of their adopted country.[19]

To the newly-arrived immigrant everything is strange; he has no guideposts to direct him through the tangled maze into which he has come. If he can go to an area in which a number of his own countrymen are congregated, he will find both protection [20] and guidance as he ventures out into the bewildering world. The Syrian colony in New York protected Rihbany from the dangers of an abrupt transition. Here he found a habitat with enough of the familiar oriental atmosphere to brace him in the face of difficulties that confronted him those first months. Yet, there was an occidental tinge which aroused in him a desire to know more about the enveloping American life.[21]

Oftentimes the immigrant receives a certain amount of attention because he is different; the Americans stare at him and make him self-conscious. This makes him all the more hesitant about trying to make contacts with Americans, and it is then that the colony is a welcome refuge. Abraham Cahan felt the sting of the word "greenhorn" which he heard frequently in tones of blighting gaiety. Even those who tried to help him manifested a spirit of self-complacent condescension—and that, too, cut deeply.[22]

The immigrant becomes eager to efface his "greenhornhood." His fellow countrymen, too, are desirous of removing the evidences

[19] Cf. A. J. Pieters, *op. cit.*, pp. 7-8, 46–49.

[20] Lawrence M. Larson writes of the immigrant, "He discovered quite early in his sojourn in the West that he was being exploited by the native element. Too often the banker, the lawyer, the wheat buyer, and other 'smart' business men coined good money from his ignorance of American ways. For his economic protection, therefore, he realized that he must settle among men of his own race; he felt that he was safer among his own countrymen, and in this he was usually correct." *American Historical Review,* XL (October, 1934), 74. On the other hand the colony has afforded a place for the maladjusted to live as parasites by exploiting their fellow countrymen. Cf. E. D. Beynon, *American Journal of Sociology,* XXXIX (March, 1934), 605–07.

[21] Cf. A. M. Rihbany, *op. cit.*, pp. 243–44.

[22] Cf. A. Cahan, *op. cit.*, p. 94.

that brand him as a new arrival, because his queerness reflects upon them. Abraham Cahan went to a Jewish colony on his arrival in New York City and there found a man who took him in hand and set the Americanization process in operation at once. He took Cahan from store to store and outfitted him from head to foot. With each addition to the wardrobe he made comments that the "green one" was gradually beginning to look like an American. When all the necessary purchases had been made a barber shop was visited and a hair-cut and bath were ordered. As a finishing touch the side-locks had to go, since it was possible to be a good Jew even without a beard.[23]

E. A. Steiner was helped in Boston. He offered to carry a large satchel from the railway station for a woman and walked on the inside of the sidewalk. Presently a Russian Jew, in English with a decided Yiddish flavor, called from his shop that men should walk on the outside. That Jew had responded to the folkways of the American city and did not want the "greenhorn" to disgrace him.[24] A transformation of Natalie De Bogory was effected soon after her arrival.

> Mrs. Zielinski turned her critical eye on me. "You're in America now," were her first words as she surveyed my pale-green dress with its three pathetic frills around the bottom; "You must be properly dressed. We'll get you a suit." . . . .
> "That coat of yours won't do," and she glanced at my good woolen coat with its thick cotton padding, "and we'll get you some nice American shoes." . . . . My coat was apparently so disgraceful that to prevent its being seen in the street she lent me her big shawl. . . . . It was my first step towards becoming an American.[25]

In the rural immigrant communities there are fewer disorganizing contacts than in the city and the assimilative process goes on more slowly but nevertheless surely.[26]

[23] Cf. *Ibid.*, p. 101.

[24] Cf. E. A. Steiner, *On the Trail of the Immigrant* (New York, 1906), pp. 329–30.

[25] "The Greenhorn within Our Gates," *The Outlook*, CXXXI (May 17, 1922), 114–15.

[26] Cf. J. A. Saathoff, "Function of Rural Immigrant Communities," *Sociology and Social Research*, XVI (September-October, 1931), 58–59. *Proceedings of the State Historical Society of Wisconsin*, 1907, p. 281, for a rural colony of Poles.

As a conclusion we may turn to the words of Robert E. Park:

It is reasonably clear, then, that the immigrant lives in America where he can, and there learns of America. He lives in a colony of his own people because, under ordinary circumstances, that is the only place he can live at all. He learns about America what the experiences of those who preceded him have taught them. He makes the accommodations that others have made. For a long time the immigrant community is almost the only source of information about American life that is accessible to the newly arrived immigrant. *For a long time, as far as he is concerned, the immigrant community is America.* If this community is well organized, if it is directed by leaders of intelligence and understanding, if the average of intelligence and culture in the community is high, as is the case with the Jews and the Japanese, then the difficult, painful, and often heart-breaking process of accommodation to American life will proceed, relatively speaking, rapidly and easily. If the situation is, as frequently happens, just the opposite, then Americanization will lag, and the natural animosities or indifference to American institutions and life will obstruct where it does not altogether inhibit the process of assimilation. The fact is, however, that the immigrant community, which is itself an accommodation to American life, is almost the only institution outside of the public school that has actually helped the immigrant to find his place and make his way in America.

Looked at disinterestedly it is, consciously and unconsciously, an institution for Americanization. It is at any rate so necessary and inevitable a part of the life of the immigrant in this country that, rather than destroy it, as has been so frequently proposed, we should seek to coöperate with and use it.[27]

B. Immigrant Institutions

Immigrant institutions develop to satisfy the needs of newcomers in an alien environment. They are not outright transplantations from the homeland but grow up in response to the needs in a new situation. A number of the organizations have come into being to help the immigrant through the difficulties of adjustment to unfamiliar conditions, and as these agencies carry on their activities they do much to forward the assimilative process. The Pan-Hellenic Union aids Greek immigrants in many ways and at

[27] *National Conference of Social Work, 1921,* pp. 496–97.

the same time instills in them "veneration and affection for the laws and institutions of America." [28] The Polish Young Men's Alliance, among its several activities, conducts evening classes in English and civics.[29] A Syrian society planned to have some of their number who had been here for some time to "assist the recent arrivals by lectures and informal talks, and so prevent the mistakes and failures which might bring the Syrian into disrepute." [30] Some groups also have naturalization clubs to attempt to prepare each other for citizenship.[31] Schiavo maintains that organizations, such as the Italian-American Citizens' Club in Chicago, are important media in the political education and Americanization of aliens.[32]

These organizations ease the transition of the immigrant and tend to accelerate his assimilation. He can discard his foreign clothes and can change some of the externalities quite readily, but attitudes and habits are more deep-seated, hence less easily modified. In the new environment the traditional behavior patterns do not bring the customary results. Furthermore, even if the old results were readily available they would not function efficiently in the new situation. If each individual immigrant had to solve his own problems, there would be much disorganization and demoralization, but when he can use institutions that have developed out of the conditions in America the transition is made with greater ease. These agencies guide him in his relations with the new environment. In the words of Kallen, they "speak his language and convey his ideas; they speak the language of the land and communicate its moods. They are the intermediaries between him and it. They carry him over and ultimately they adjust him." [33]

The immigrant press. According to some, the foreign-language press retards assimilation. By its very nature it tends to preserve the foreign language and sustain those feelings which bind the im-

[28] *Report of the Massachusetts Commission on Immigration,* 1914, p. 203.
[29] *Ibid.,* p. 205.
[30] *Ibid.,* p. 206.
[31] *Ibid.,* p. 159.
[32] G. E. Schiavo, *The Italians in Chicago,* p. 104.
[33] Horace M. Kallen, *Culture and Democracy in the United States* (New York, 1924), pp. 161–62.

migrant to his home country; it keeps him in touch with the events at home and thus evokes nationalistic tendencies. As the press directs the interest of the immigrant toward the home country, it may create an antipathy against American life. Immigrants in America use the newspaper more than they did at home. It serves as a medium for maintaining contacts with nationals in different parts of America with whom the immigrant can no longer exchange the gossip of the day in his home village. The immigrant press has catered to the masses in America through the use of the folk speech. After an editor has developed a public he tends to monopolize it and seeks to focus the attention of his readers upon the homeland. It is to his advantage to have the foreign language continued and some editors have done everything possible to discourage the immigrant from becoming Americanized. In the words of Sartorio,

> Usually either the articles concerning America are written by people who have lived all their life among Italians and, being prejudiced through their lack of understanding of the new country in which they live, are ready to misrepresent it; or they are written by unscrupulous men who play upon popular feeling and endeavor to get into the good graces of the subscribers by exalting everything Italian and decrying everything American. I have read articles written by men who knew the American institutions of learning only through the study of a few specimens of their profession graduated from a fourth-rate professional school, describe America as the land of quacks and bluffers. The writer could not have passed an entrance examination to Harvard or any other great university to save his life. I have seen the articles denouncing with fiery words the political corruption of this land, and I have noticed at the same time that the paper was advising its readers simultaneously to vote for three different parties, and on the fourth page advertising whiskey concerns and public houses of bad fame. I have read descriptions of American life calling it artificial, unscrupulous, money-crazed, hypocritical, only to discover that the writer did not know a word of English or that he had no American friends except a few doubtful characters of the sporting set whose accent was anything but American.[34]

[34] Enrico C. Sartorio, *Social and Religious Life of Italians in America* (Boston, 1918), pp. 41–43.

The Immigration Commission found that many immigrant bankers conducted newspapers, not always for the benefit of their fellow nationals. The Commission wrote:

> The most serious charge that is brought against such a coalition of bankers and newspapers is that by constant appeal to the prejudice and patriotism of the immigrant, his Americanization is not only retarded, but deliberately combated in order that he may be held as a source of income to those whom he trusts. An instance in point is the case of a certain Slovak banker, an ex-student of theology, who operates a large handsomely furnished establishment, with two branch houses. This banker is a national and religious leader among his people, having organized and headed a national Slovak society in this country. He issues a daily, a weekly, a humanistic monthly, a yearly almanac, and from time to time other publications. Although he has renounced allegiance to Hungary, severed all political ties with that country, and become an American citizen, he does not advise his Slovak countrymen to do the same, but instead preaches in all his publications a militant and enthusiastic "Pan Slovakism." So long as the Slovaks remain Slovaks and can be filled with Slovak patriotism and enthusiasm by such agitation, just so long will they remain a source of profit to the banker. Prior to the recent industrial depression this man was accustomed to transmit abroad, on behalf of his patrons, from $2,000,000 to $2,500,000 annually and to sell 6,000 steamship tickets per year.[35]

While it is true that certain nationalist newspapers have not favored the Americanization of their readers, yet by encouraging the immigrants to read they have become more intelligent. By printing the news about America, which they must do in order to circulate at all, they have prepared the readers for American citizenship. Even the advertisement of American goods is an Americanizing influence.[36] Bojer shows how the foreign-language papers Americanized the Norwegians.

[35] *Op. cit.,* Vol. XXXVII, pp. 229–30.

[36] Closely related to this is the influence of the mail-order catalogue in an East Frisian community in Illinois. "Advertisements are found to be a significant means of acculturation, especially with reference to material elements. One common source of reading for all is the mail order catalogue, of which every household has one or more. From the illustrations in these the women make clothing for themselves and their children. Any little innovation in furnishing comes from the catalogue. 'I saw it in the catalogue,' or 'it is in the catalogue' stamps a style as authentic. Among the younger people the catalogue furnishes a guide for the arrangement of furniture and

Now that the post-office was so near, the settlers began to take newspapers. As a rule they preferred the Norwegian-American papers, with all the news from the old country; they read them aloud on Sunday evening, and every number was as good as a budget of letters from home. There was a lot about America as well, from every part of the country, and that interested the settlers, too, for, after all, it was in America that they lived. It seemed that there were politics and parties and controversies even here; who would have thought it? These colonists had been so isolated up to now; their hearts had remained in the old country; they had felt that they were staying in a foreign land merely to till the soil and grow rich. But the newspapers were teaching them to think of the country which had given them the soil and the opportunity to become rich if only they had the will.[37]

The millions of immigrants could be reached far more effectively through their own languages than through the English. They could not wait until they mastered the English language before learning anything about America. They must acquire information about the customs, traditions, and institutions of their adopted country, and about the political, economic, and industrial organization of America through the medium of their own native languages.[38] The foreign-language press, then, in spite of many shortcomings, has been an educational agency without equal among our immigrant population.

In addition to the incidental Americanization which resulted, despite the fact that certain nationalist editors actually tried to prevent assimilation, other editors have endeavored in all earnestness to orient the immigrants in the American environment and to help them share in the political, intellectual, and social life of the

trimmings in the home. When they go to town and see some article that is new, they come home and look at the catalogue and see if they can find it there. If it is not there it is seldom adopted; but if it is, it is soon imitated or purchased." E. T. Hiller, F. E. Corner, W. L. East, *op. cit.*, p. 57.

[37] J. Bojer, *op. cit.*, pp. 291–92.

[38] According to Johannes B. Wist, the greatest service of the Norwegian-American press has been that of acquainting the immigrants with American institutions and of awakening their loyalty to the land of their adoption. *Norsk-Amerikanernes Festskrift*, p. 39. Cf. Lucy M. Salmon, *The Newspaper and Authority* (New York, 1925), p. 215; O. A. Benson, *op. cit.;* E. Corsi, "The Voice of the Immigrant," *Outlook*, CXLVII (September 21, 1927), 90; *Proceedings of the State Historical Society of Wisconsin*, 1901, p. 160; F. J. Brown and J. S. Roucek, *op. cit.*, pp. 573–94.

New World. Hans Mattson published two Swedish weeklies, one in Minneapolis and one in Chicago, of which he wrote:

My aim in this journalistic work was mainly to instruct and educate my countrymen in such matters as might promote their well-being and make them good American citizens. The *Stats Tidning,* or at least a part of it, gradually became a kind of catechism on law and political economy, containing information under the heading "Questions and Answers." This was intended especially for the Swedish farmers in the state. If a farmer was in doubt as to his legal rights in the case of a road, a fence, the draining of a marsh, or wished to know how to cure a sick horse or other animal, or how he could get money sent from Sweden, or if he wished advice or information on any other question relating to everyday life, especially if he got into trouble of some kind, he would write to the *Stats Tidning* for the desired information. Such letters were then printed in condensed form and followed by short, clear, pointed answers, and, so far, I have not heard of a single person being misled by those answers. On the other hand, I know that the public, and more especially the newcomers, reaped very great benefits from them. Few persons have any idea of how irksome and laborious this kind of journalism is, and at times I was on the point of giving it up in despair.[39]

Soltes points out that the Yiddish press prints special articles on American history, geography, government, education, and naturalization. He writes:

A consideration of the nature of the subjects which it treats editorially, as well as the attitudes and sentiments which it expresses, warrants the conclusion that the influence which the Yiddish press radiates through its editorial columns is wholesome civically, and that it is a vital factor in the Americanization of its immigrant readers. It consciously attempts to bring them nearer to America in sentiment, thought, and action, by the constant discussion of American events and problems—political, economic, and cultural; by taking advantage of every opportunity to educate its readers up to the American point of view in matters which have been generally accepted and which are beyond the realm of controversy. It endeavors to inculcate an understanding and respect for American institutions; to explain to its readers the significance of American festivals and customs and to urge their observance; to stimulate

[39] H. Mattson, *op. cit.*, p. 140.

national pride in their adopted country by pointing out the advantages of the American government and institutions in both form and spirit, by comparison and in contrast with those of other countries; to imbue its readers with American ideals and with reverence for the principles of American democracy; to give them a proper conception of the duties and opportunities of American citizenship and to quicken their sense of responsibility.[40]

Mark Villchur indicates changes in the Russian immigrant press. In recent years many of the newspapers have carried special articles on American life, thereby reducing the space usually allotted to homeland news.[41] Galitzi states that the Roumanian press has publicized night schools and classes in English in an effort to stimulate interest in adult education and in the English language.[42] The *Novy Swiat,* a Polish weekly in Chicago, carried lessons in English and several columns of United States history. The issue of January 4, 1919, contained an editorial in English entitled, "Learn English —It is Easy," from which we quote the last paragraph.

Knowledge of the language of the country in which you reside is so useful, almost indispensable, that every man and woman, irrespective of age, ought to avail himself and herself of the opportunity afforded by the free schools and make up their minds to attend regularly till they acquire a practical working knowledge of the English language.

Norwegian immigrants brought two heritages which colored practically all their activities: class distinction and the state church. Class distinctions, enforced by certain formalities of the church and officialdom, were so deeply rooted in the attitudes of the people that the conscientious adherence to one fulfilled the precepts of the other. A good citizen in Norway was one who kept his aspirations rigidly within the bounds of his social class and even under American conditions there is no complete leveling out of these differences. The church, transplanted both as to concepts and outward organization, exerted a powerful control over the immigrant. The ministers came from Norway and interpreted the Bible in the light of

[40] Mordecai Soltes, *The Yiddish Press—An Americanization Agency* (New York, 1924), p. 177.

[41] *The Interpreter,* IV (November, 1925), 7.

[42] *Op. cit.*, p. 123.

their past lives in the state church. Thus, this institution became a retarding medium with a linkage to the past. The influence of the frontier, however, developed a spirit of revolt. The early Norwegian press in Minnesota was strong in its opposition to the traditional policies. It opposed the continuation of the old-world social distinctions on the part of the clergy who were offshoots of the Norwegian aristocracy. The editor of *Budstikken* in Minneapolis severely rebuked the domineering sway of the church. A number of the clergy argued for parochial schools. The same editor opposed this and favored the public schools as being better suited to the needs of a free people.[43]

The foreign-language press can be used as a barometer of Americanization. A daily paper indicates that there is a large, isolated group which depends upon the mother tongue for all the news, both of America and of the homeland. When a group has weeklies only, it indicates that most of the news is read in the American dailies while they turn to their own weeklies for news of their fellow nationals in America and from the home country. When a group has only a monthly paper or magazine that is an indication of long residence here and assimilation to the extent that all the news in which they are interested is found in the English papers. Then as a group becomes completely assimilated, the foreign-language publications entirely disappear: they have then fulfilled their function of graduating the immigrants into American life.

The immigrant church. Immigrants do not throw their cultural baggage overboard as they enter American ports; they bring their religion and keep it. A quotation from Roberts shows what certain groups will do for the church.[44]

> Religion forms an essential part of the life of the southeastern European, and much money is spent on church edifices where the faithful may worship. In Shenandoah, Pa., the foreigners have invested no less than $100,000 in church property and the total population is a little over 30,000, of whom 80 per cent are either foreign-born or descendants of foreign-born parents. In Buffalo the most imposing church building is

[43] Cf. J. A. Fagereng, *op. cit.*

[44] From Peter Roberts, *The New Immigration* (New York, 1912), pp. 200–01. By permission of The Macmillan Company, publishers.

that of St. Stanislaus, built by the Poles. The churches built by the foreigners on the South Side of Pittsburgh are far more magnificent than any built by their predecessors—the men of the old immigration. The same is true of towns and cities in New Jersey and New England. A church in Pawtucket, R. I., has mural decorations that are superb. It is impossible to state how much money the peoples of southeastern Europe have put into stone and wood, in window and altar, in art and music, for the purpose of worshiping God, but it is safe to put it at $10 per capita, which would make a sum of not less than $75,000,000. When they come, they are poor, having less than $16 each; they get the lowest wages in the industries of America, but when the appeal for funds is made to put up a church to worship God, these people respond. And it is absurd to say that all this wealth molded into sacred structure is forced out of the people by ecclesiastical terror. The foreigner is not long in America before he knows that there is no connection between the government and the church and that the faith of his fathers and the service of God must be preserved and propagated by voluntary contributions, and no priest could compel the people to give freely of their substance to this purpose if their religious faith and love of sacred ideals did not impel them.

The foreign-language church tends to be slower in breaking away from the loyalties, customs, and traditions of the Old World than any other institution. C. M. Rosenquist regards the immigrant churches in Texas as "more foreign in character than any other activity found in the Swedish community." [45] A. Kaupas wrote of the immigrant church:

> The most powerful bond which unites immigrants of the same nationality in a foreign country is that represented by religion and the church. Pious people, like the Poles, Slovaks, Lithuanians, and others, carry with them to the land across the sea their own profound religious sentiment. In their churches they feel at home. The church is a little corner of the distant fatherland. It is thus in America that religion has become the most powerful source of resistance against Americanization (assimilation).[46]

While the church may be conservative and stand in the way of assimilation in some measure by clinging to the old language and

[45] *Op. cit.*

[46] Quoted by R. E. Park, *The Immigrant Press and Its Control* (New York, 1922), p. 53. Cf. A. Ueland, *op. cit.*, pp. 150–51, for the retarding influence of the Norwegian Lutheran Church in America.

traditions, it serves as a stabilizer and thus tempers the disorganizing forces.[47] Under its influence the assimilative process has proceeded slowly but on a firm basis. Wirth says of the Jewish immigrant and the synagogue: "There he becomes oriented to the new surroundings and finds the familiar scenes and experiences that bridge the gap between the Old World and the New." [48] The church thus enables the immigrant to make the transition by easy gradients. "Throughout this transition period," writes Hiller, "the group maintains cohesion and mutual aid; it reorganizes its internal structure and consensus at the same time that it adjusts itself to a new external world consisting of other groups and alien practices." [49]

Mutual aid organizations. While the societies for mutual aid were organized largely to function in connection with the dangers and uncertainties attendant upon the industrial activities of the immigrants, they provided opportunities for the discussion of questions arising out of their life in a strange environment. This deliberation upon their new problems inevitably forced them to pay attention to their adjustments to American conditions. Furthermore these organizations regulated the lives of the members and kept them from disorganization in the midst of painful experiences and sickening disillusionments. This steadying influence was an important factor in promoting assimilation.[50]

[47] Cf. M. Zelditch, *op. cit.,* and J. A. Saathoff, *op. cit.,* for the steadying influence of the church in two immigrant groups. *Proceedings of the State Historical Society of Wisconsin,* 1907, p. 287 for the Poles.

[48] Louis Wirth, *The Ghetto* (Chicago, 1928), p. 207.

[49] E. T. Hiller, *Principles of Sociology* (New York, 1933), p. 393. Cf. H. P. Fairchild, *Immigration* (New York, 1925), pp. 292–93.

[50] See chapters on "Reorganization of the Immigrant."

CHAPTER XV

AGENCIES OF ASSIMILATION
(*Concluded*)

C. American Institutions

In addition to the institutions which the immigrants developed to aid their adjustment to American life, the receiving group set up certain organizations for the specific purpose of assisting the newcomers. Furthermore, certain distinctively American institutions functioned in the period of transition, and some of these, like the Y.M.C.A. and the Y.W.C.A., developed special departments for work among the immigrants. In this discussion we shall select only some of the more outstanding agencies.[1]

Foreign Language Information Service. The Foreign Language Information Service (F.L.I.S.) [2] grew out of a governmental activity which had for its purpose the creation of morale needed to win the World War. It was at first a news service for releasing official information to the foreign-language press. Through this medium the Service sought to acquaint the immigrant in his own language with the traditions, customs, laws, and opportunities of his adopted country, so that he might begin his readjustment with the least delay, and before he would have time to learn English.[3]

With the passage of years the Service has extended its activities in considerable measure. After the close of the World War much information was given out on war-risk allotments, citizenship, passport regulations, income tax, health, land regulations, agricultural opportunities, and employment.[4] The organization provided in-

[1] For a fuller discussion, cf. D. R. Taft, *Human Migration,* pp. 269–70; 527–54.

[2] Cf. R. E. Park, *The Immigrant Press,* pp. 458–63; D. R. Taft, *Human Migration,* pp. 539–49; and publications of the F.L.I.S.

[3] Cf. *The Interpreter,* VIII (May, 1929), 66; also *National Conference of Social Work,* 1921, p. 482.

[4] The following quotation gives an idea of the inquiries addressed to the F.L.I.S. "A Jugoslav admitted as a preference farmer writes from Chicago to find out

formation for individuals and agencies engaged in Americanization work. It has endeavored to stimulate immigrant agencies to carry on activities that would bring the foreign born into more vital contacts with American life. It has sought to encourage the preservation and interpretation of the best group traditions and the establishment of wholesome relationships between the two generations.[5] The Service has also coöperated with the American press by furnishing copy to interpret the immigrants and their culture to Americans. This has been done on the theory that "sympathetic appreciation of the immigrant's problems and contributions will do more than anything else to encourage him to participate in our national life." [6]

Quite recently the Service began to focus attention on the American-born generation of immigrant parentage. It publishes and circulates material designed to make the second generation young people familiar with and proud of their double cultural inheritance. Doubtless the activities of the organization will gravitate increasingly toward this group and its problems.

The F.L.I.S. has taken a liberal point of view relative to assimilation; it recognizes the Americanization process as a mutual give-and-take and has even advocated the inclusion of cultural values from many sources into our American life. It has endeavored through its various activities to interpret America to the alien and equally well to interpret the immigrant to America. According to Read Lewis, the director of the Service, the organization has been endeavoring "by means of accurate information and sympathetic understanding to work out among the many different elements in our population a more tolerant and effective unity, and to

whether, having given up farming, he can become a citizen. . . . . An Italian in Kansas City whose sister was killed in the recent earthquakes in Italy wants to know how she can bring her orphan niece to this country. . . . . A Danish woman in California inquires about obtaining a homestead for herself and her children in Oregon. . . . . An Armenian in Constantinople hears that his lost children have found their way to the United States and asks us to advertise for them. . . . . A Finn writing from Alaska wants to know about wages and chances for employment in deep sea fishing on the Atlantic coast. . . . . A young Norwegian from up-state New York asks for books on American history." *The Interpreter,* IX (September-October, 1930), 98.

[5] Cf. *Ibid.,* VIII (November, 1929), 130.

[6] F.L.I.S. folder.

replace prejudice and suspicion with a sense of common humanity shared alike by native and foreign born." [7]

The Immigrant's Protective League. The Immigrant's Protective League, with headquarters in Chicago, has carried on a notable work for immigrants since its establishment in 1908. The activities of the League have included: (1) the protection of immigrants against exploitation on their arrival in Chicago; [8] (2) visitation of immigrant girls; (3) placing women inspectors on immigrant trains; (4) employment direction; (5) coöperation with the schools in the adjustment of immigrant children; (6) education of the adult immigrant and the promotion of his assimilation; (7) coöperation with other agencies that make contacts with immigrants; (8) the fostering of intelligent public opinion with reference to treatment of the immigrant; (9) the investigation of "detention" and "exclusion" cases at ports of entry; (10) support of progressive and humanitarian legislation; and (11) research.

The functions of the League have shifted considerably in recent years.[9] The character of the immigration has changed, and the volume has been reduced greatly. "In the place of the old difficulties attendant upon mass arrival in Chicago, and the old types of exploitation during the various stages of unprotected travel, have come those attendant upon the stricter tests of admissibility and upon the inflexibility of fixed quotas." [10]

While the League is a local organization, its activities have extended far beyond the confines of Chicago. Oftentimes assistance to prospective immigrants has been given in peasant communities of Europe. It is at such far-away points and with the relatives in Chicago that much of the work is now being done. Complicated documents and procedure are explained to the interested person in the remote Carpathian village and to the relatives or friends in Chicago. Since the new Immigration Policy went into

[7] F.L.I.S., *Report for 1927*.

[8] A sample of this activity may be taken from the Report for the year 1912 (p. 10): "The suspension of sixteen cab and expressmen during the past year because of complaints from our office has also helped to convince them that exploitation is not as profitable as formerly."

[9] Cf. *The Immigrants Protective League in 1930*, p. 11.

[10] *Ibid.*, p. 26.

effect, the League has acted increasingly as a Bureau of Information both at home and abroad.[11]

The League has promoted an educational campaign through press releases, lectures, exhibits, publication of pamphlets, and through contacts with other agencies. This has done much to develop a favorable attitude toward the foreign born. The fairness and the liberal attitude of the League has appealed to the immigrants. In this way the organization has served as an assimilative agency.

The Young Women's Christian Association. The Y.W.C.A., through the International Institutes [12] and Foreign Communities Departments, has contributed a noteworthy service to foreign-born women and girls while they were making their transition from the Old World to the New. Port service has been carried on in New York and San Francisco and there has been a nation-wide follow-up of port cases. The organization has studied questions affecting aliens, such as the effect of deportation laws, and has given advice on immigration and naturalization laws. Various festive occasions have been utilized for bringing the different ethnic groups together in an endeavor to help the immigrants win recognition and thus make their adjustments more satisfying. The goal of the National Board of the Y.W.C.A. has been that of "helping every Association to reflect by its cosmopolitan attitudes an appreciation of, and delight in, cultural differences and to evidence in all phases of its fellowship, the richness which comes from having in its membership and constituency women and girls who bring the contribution of other countries to American life." [13]

Changing conditions with reference to immigration and the growing up in large numbers of the second-generation girls led the National Board of the Y.W.C.A. to take the initiative in the establishment of a new national agency, The National Institute of Immigrant Welfare, which was organized December 13, 1933. The Institute has taken over a portion of the work formerly carried by the Y.W.C.A.

[11] Cf. *Ibid.*, p. 15.

[12] Cf. *Record of Proceedings, Twelfth National Conference of International Institutes,* 1932.

[13] *Our New Americans,* folder by National Board Y.W.C.A., 1935.

The National Institute's program includes protection and guidance for the newest as well as for the old-time immigrant. The local Institutes in the different communities offer programs of adult education to groups of foreign-born, render service on immigrant or deportation problems, and aid naturalization. They set up civic projects which bring together native-born and foreign-born on a basis of mutual appreciation. They stress folk arts and the riches and skills of hand and mind that have come to America from the various lands.

Social settlements. Social settlements, like Hull House in Chicago, the South End House in Boston, and the "House on Henry Street" in New York, have rendered signal services to the immigrants in our large cities. The early settlements were pioneers in promoting classes in English and citizenship for foreigners. Furthermore they experimented with the education of adult immigrants in other branches. The settlements also made a valuable contribution through their efforts to encourage and conserve the folk arts of the various ethnic groups. Doubtless a large measure of the success enjoyed by the settlements in dealing with immigrants has been due to the fact that they have respected the cultural backgrounds of the different ethnic groups.

Immigration commissions. In 1913 the state of California created a Commission of Immigration and Housing.[14] The motive underlying this provision was a desire to aid the immigrant in overcoming the serious handicaps that surround him from the moment he sets foot on our soil. In the words of the Commission:

> Unprotected, the immigrant falls a ready victim to fraud. He, himself, suffers. But his community suffers also, for every dishonest trick played within its confines necessarily undermines its traditions of law and order.
>
> Unaided, the immigrant usually settled in the least desirable section of town or city, crowding close to his own people, fearful of spending an extra dollar for rent because of the uncertainty of his immediate future. He pays dearly for this congestion, but his city also pays, with all the evils which follow upon wretched housing conditions.

[14] In the same year the state of Massachusetts provided for a Commission on Immigration which has carried on a program much like that of California. See "The Problem of Immigration in Massachusetts," *Report of the Commission on Immigration, 1914.* The Illinois Immigrant's Commission was created in 1919.

Having come here to work the immigrant is usually over-anxious to secure his first job. Here the operators of labor camps have an opportunity to profit, for the "foreigner," knowing little or nothing of America's living standards, is more likely to accept filthy surroundings than is his American neighbor. And here again, although the immigrant is badly treated, the injury extends to the native-born camp laborer as well and, moreover, insanitary labor camps become breeding holes of disease which endanger the entire State.

Unable to fight his own battles successfully, bitterly disappointed in the hopes which prompted his coming from his own land, the immigrant often grows sullen and discontented. In his own misfortune he begins to see the results of an imaginary class oppression. The next step is anarchy. It may destroy him, but it also works inestimable injury to all who come in contact with him in his community.[15]

The Commission has been interested in helping immigrants become worthy Americans. Assimilation of a sane and rational type has been stressed.

From the first the Commission took its stand against that form of assimilation which hands to the immigrant some things which he is supposed to swallow. So, while emphasizing the things we must give the alien, it has placed equal emphasis upon the things he can give us. This conception makes a natural place for the immigrant in America, by making him welcome, by giving him a share in the common tasks, and by educating him properly, basing that education upon things already known to him.[16]

The liberal point of view is made evident in the attitude toward the national heritages of the immigrants.

The Commission has sought to encourage the preservation and development of the best national cultural elements, in art, literature, music, science, the crafts, and in things spiritual. Only by preserving and developing these heritages and combining them with the cultural elements which are distinctly American can the foreign-born be given their rightful place in the tasks of our nation.[17]

[15] Commission of Immigration and Housing of California, *Ninth Annual Report,* 1923, p. 13.

[16] *Ibid.,* pp. 10–11.

[17] *Ibid.,* p. 10.

This point of view is further exemplified in the attitude toward Americanization.

> The Commission found that Americanization was not flag raising and "patriotic" howling; that it was not suppression of speech and honest opinion; that it was more than teaching English to foreigners. Americanization, it found, is the encouragement to decent living, and making possible the attainment of decent standards. It involves the development of national ideals and standards and the schooling of all residents, foreign-born as well as native-born, in those ideals and standards.[18]

The activities of the Commission fall into three main divisions: the bureau of complaints, housing, and labor camp inspection. The work of the bureau of complaints was the first activity of the Commission, and has remained the most important. This bureau has done much to protect the immigrant against fraud, has adjusted many misunderstandings, and has carried on investigations which have resulted in improved legislation. After the Commission had investigated several hundred complaints against land companies that had defrauded immigrants, a section was added to the Penal Code making it a misdemeanor to publish or disseminate any untrue or misleading statement concerning real estate in California or elsewhere. The Commission also aided the passage of another amendment which made the father of an illegitimate child responsible for its support. This law came as the direct result of the many pathetic stories brought to the bureau by wronged immigrant girls. These, together with several other laws, gave relief both to the foreign born and to those of native birth.

Not only does this bureau act on complaints but it gives advice and information to immigrants. Numerous questions concerning our laws relative to land, labor, wages, citizenship, military service, housing, etc., are asked. Newcomers look to the Commission for advice relative to the safety of investments, on farm lands, the most profitable crops, and on the best way to educate children.

> And, sometimes, a bewildered immigrant woman slips in to ask how her half-grown boy, who has learned the language which is still dark to her

[18] *Ibid.*, p. 11.

and has made friends whom she has never seen, can be made to stay at home again in the evenings and be "as he was before." [19]

Labor unions. For the most part organizations open to the immigrant are those restricted to his own nationality group. The trade union, however, organizes men by occupations and cuts across ethnic lines. In the union the Bulgarian mingles with the Sicilian, the Dalmatian with the Norwegian, and this is the only place they mix at first. When, however, they have rubbed shoulders in the union for some time the characteristic clannishness is gradually dissipated and a social commingling along other lines can come into play quite naturally. Labor organizations meet regularly in shop meetings, local unions, district councils, and national conventions to discuss their problems. They send delegates to the various gatherings where they consider not only their relations with their employers but to the state and nation as well. They study matters relative to unemployment, old age, sickness, education of children and adults, and a wide range of problems that vitally affect their lives. Leiserson says of this activity:

> Obviously the immigrant who participates in organizations, institutions, and activities of this kind learns in a most practical way to co-operate with his American fellow workers for mutual benefit, and through such participation, unity of mind is developed between the native and the foreign born. Through parliamentary practice made necessary by the organizations, through election of representatives, officials, and delegates, through voting on agreements with employers and on other policies, through the business dealings of his union, through discussions of men and measures, and through the public activities of his organization and its officers, the immigrant learns American methods, traditions, governmental practices, and problems in the best school the adult can have, the daily experiences surrounding his work.[20]

Through participation in the activities of the labor union the immigrant becomes acquainted with the standard of living characteristic of American workers and learns how this may be attained. In the words of Leiserson,

[19] Commission of Immigration and Housing of California, *Ninth Annual Report,* 1923, p. 56.

[20] W. M. Leiserson, *op. cit.,* pp. 234–35. Cf. also pp. 169–245.

Thus has the union not only assured him an American standard of living, so he can bring over his family and educate his children American fashion, but it has also furnished him a practical school in citizenship, giving him practice in voting, elections, and lawmaking, teaching parliamentary practices, methods of lawmaking, obedience to the agreements of the union and the employers, which are the laws of his industry, and introducing him to judicial processes and methods through the arbitration procedure which the agreement has established. The union is a miniature republic, training him for American citizenship by teaching him American democratic methods of dealing with the problems of his work and wages, the things of most vital interest to him. . . . . A trade union needs to engage in no Americanizing or proselytizing campaigns to make Americans of immigrant workmen. If it is efficient and successful as a union, it unites all the workers in the industry and imperceptibly fuses native and foreign born into a common folk.[21]

William Z. Ripley has pointed out the influence of the labor union on the immigrant in these words:

Whatever our judgment as to the legality or expediency of the industrial policy of our American unions, no student of contemporary conditions can deny that they are a mighty factor in effecting the assimilation of our foreign-born population. Schooling is primarily of importance, of course, but many of our immigrants come here as adults. Education can affect only the second generation. The churches, particularly the Catholic hierarchy, may do much. Protestants seem to have little influence in the industrial centers. On the other hand, the newspapers, at least such as the masses see and read, and the ballot under present conditions in American cities, have no uplifting or educative power at all. The great source of intellectual inspiration to a large percentage of our inchoate Americans, in the industrial classes, remains in the trade union. It is a vast power for good or evil, according as its affairs are administered. It cannot fail to teach the English language; that in itself is much. Its benefit system, as among the cigar makers and printers, may inculcate thrift. Its journals, the best of them, give a general knowledge of trade conditions, impossible to the isolated workman. Its democratic constitution and its assemblies and conventions partake of the primitive character of the Anglo-Saxon folkmoot, so much lauded by Freeman, the historian, as a factor in English political education and constitutional development. Not the

[21] *Ibid.*, pp. 244–45.

next gubernatorial or presidential candidate, not the expansion of the currency, nor the reform of the general staff of the army; not free-trade or protection, or anti-imperialism, is the real living thing of interest to the trade-union workman. His thoughts, interests, and hopes are centered in the politics of his organization. It is the forum and arena of his social and industrial world.[22]

The school. The American school has been one of the most important agencies promoting assimilation. The schools through their "steamer classes" have made contacts with the children immediately upon arrival in this country and thus the acquisition of English has been hastened. The influence of the school on the adult immigrants, however, has been largely an indirect one through the children. Galitzi says of the Roumanians:

The children learning the English language become the carriers of the new language and new ideas into the Roumanian home. They interpret to their parents the American standards of health, economic efficiency, civic duties and fair play. They explain to them the history of the American people and the formation of the American nation.[23]

A Swedish immigrant told how he was influenced by the school.

I learned to speak correct English from my son Christian. He taught my wife and me. I learned from him of George Washington, of Abraham Lincoln, of Nathan Hale, of Grant, of a thousand others. He got it at school, got it from the principal who didn't care whether I was a janitor or barrister, and whose only duty it was to teach boys to be good citizens.[24]

Furthermore, the immigrant homes are influenced by the more informal and intimate contacts of the home teacher, the school nurse, and the activities of the parent-teacher association in which the immigrant mothers in some measure mingle with women who are exemplars of American culture patterns.

The night school has become an important instrumentality for the instruction of adult immigrants.[25] In Cleveland the night

[22] "Race Factors in Labor Unions," *Atlantic Monthly,* XCIII (March, 1904), 307.

[23] C. A. Galitzi, *op. cit.,* p. 121.

[24] James F. Dwyer, "The Little Man in the Smoker," *Ladies' Home Journal,* XXXV, Part I (April, 1918), 18.

[25] Cf. E. Abbott, *Immigration: Select Documents and Case Records,* pp. 549–80, and Frank V. Thompson, *Schooling of the Immigrant* (New York, 1920), for data on immigrant education.

schools gradually became a large educational enterprise with an enrollment beyond 11,000 in 1914–1915.[26] The evening schools have usually stressed English and civics in an effort to prepare for naturalization. The immigrant inevitably learns a few English words through his work contacts, but this process is a slow one. Efficient instruction in the night school can accelerate his progress and give him a most important tool for the acquisition of American culture. Obviously the man or woman who cannot converse with and understand Americans will be retarded in his assimilation. By way of contrast,

> It is also necessary for another reason, less obvious but no less important —that without the knowledge of English, the immigrant can not make himself known to America, and his potential contributions to the community in which he finds himself must remain locked away because he can not speak English. Thousands of immigrants who live in our midst today are looked down upon as "ignorant" while in reality their cultural attainments in their own tongue are at least equal to those of the native-born neighbors around them.[27]

[26] Herbert A. Miller, *The School and the Immigrant* (Cleveland, 1916), pp. 85–86.

[27] Commission of Immigration and Housing of California, *Ninth Annual Report,* 1923, p. 87.

CHAPTER XVI

IMMIGRANT HERITAGES AND THE ADJUSTMENT PROCESS

Every human group, no matter what its situation, has developed through its own experience certain distinctive values and a set of attitudes toward these values. The fund of values and attitudes which any immigrant group brings to America—the totality of its sentiments, memories, traditions, and habits which are peculiar to itself and different from our own—is its heritage.[1]

Memories. When immigrants come to America they cannot divest themselves of the things that have grown into their lives in the homeland. There are innumerable ties which bind the immigrant to a social group and to a traditional background. The strength of these bonds was made evident by Panunzio when he wrote about his hesitation in becoming naturalized in America. It was not because of any deep attachment to the political life of his native country, but the memories which clustered around the scenes of his childhood were the cords which held him.[2]

Even those who have suffered hardships in the homeland tend to forget those soul-sickening events. With the passing of years memory becomes selective, eliminating the unpleasant experiences and retaining the pleasant and satisfying ones. While appreciating what America has done for them, the immigrants still cherish the old home with its customs and traditions.[3] "It is wonderful here

[1] Robert E. Park and Herbert A. Miller, *Old World Traits Transplanted,* pp. 2–4.

[2] Cf. C. M. Panunzio, *The Soul of an Immigrant,* pp. 193–200. Also M. E. Ravage, *op. cit.,* pp. 199–200.

[3] Cf. J. A. Saathoff, *op. cit.*

Memories become particularly sweet when life in America has been filled with disappointments. An old man, broken by years of toil in the blast furnaces of Pennsylvania, whose wife had died many years ago and whose American-reared children had grown away from him, found his only consolation in memories of his childhood days as he spent them in the great green forests of Lithuania where there was no coal dust to coat his lungs. F. J. Brown and J. S. Roucek, *op. cit.,* pp. 278–79.

in America," observes an Armenian, "but in my heart I can never forget Smyrna." [4] George M. Day has written of the Russians in Hollywood, many of whom are refugees from their native land.

One prominent Russian . . . . said that he never answered any letters from Russia, and that for many years purposely never read a Russian book because, as he said, "I knew that I would suffer too deeply." He avoided Russian shows, did not attend the Russian Church. It was a matter of exposing the intimate nerves.[5]

Deep-rooted quality of memories. These heritages—these traditions and memories—are very real and tenacious, and cannot be brushed aside lightly [6] without sad results. Americanization movements have been inclined to set the heritages aside [7] and make abrupt breaks with the past. This has brought disorganization. "To require that he [the immigrant] forget the home of his birth is neither necessary nor desirable. Memory may enrich the present while it sanctifies the past. Destroy it, and we have by that much

[4] Unpublished life history.

[5] George M. Day, *The Russians in Hollywood* (Los Angeles, 1934), p. 82.

[6] See note 47, p. 57.

Thomas Čapek recounts a situation which shows how memories affect the Bohemian immigrant in America. A noted Bohemian violinist, who had come to New York City, played at a reception given by his fellow countrymen. "On the great day the Bohemian Hall was crowded with people eager to do homage to the artist who contributed to the fame of his country's music. Every one was pleasurably expectant when the artist arrived in company with his manager, carrying the magic violin under his arm. The violinist played a bar or two of the national anthem *Kde domov muj,* putting into the simple air all the feeling of which a Čech musician away from home is capable. At that moment, tense with emotion, women were seen to press handkerchiefs to their eyes. But it was interesting to note the unequal effect of the anthem on the hearers. While the old folks were visibly moved by the appealing tones that reminded them of the Fatherland, the young people listened coldly, critically.

"In the orchestra sat an elderly man, a staid citizen, father of several children, all of whom had been born in the metropolis. As the violinist struck the first bar of the *Kde domov muj,* the old gentleman's powerful frame was seen to shake and his eyes grow moist. His son of about sixteen, who sat next to him, was also aroused by the music, but in a different way. He turned to his father and remonstrated: 'Father, why do you weep? Why do you make such a show of yourself?' " *Op. cit.*, pp. 100–01. Cf. Hamilton Holt, *op. cit.*, p. 85, for a Swedish immigrant.

[7] "Instead of conceiving the immigrant as he really is," said Julius Drachsler, "an individual with innumerable ties binding him to a social group and a traditional background, we think of him as a detached, atomized labor unit, as a pair of hands, as a bunch of muscles. But not only is he conceived as arriving from a sort of cultural vacuum across the seas; when he settles here he is still thought of as a solitary individualist." *National Conference of Social Work,* 1919, p. 486.

less a man." [8] In 1917 W. I. Thomas said of the Czechs that they were the best immigrants in Chicago because they retained their values.[9]

Immigrants have taken on their heritages in primary groups in the homeland—in the family, in the neighborhood, in the village. Having acquired most of these practices unconsciously, they are deeply rooted in their lives. Many are not even aware of the memories until they are brought into consciousness in a crisis. In the primary group every member is expected to conform—the rules are sacred and variations are not tolerated. It is not necessary to tell a person who is growing up in such a situation what is right or wrong. When he goes into another group with new standards, however, it becomes a matter of conscience, whether or not he will cling to the old code or adopt a new one. Often conflicts arise. A young Japanese woman came to the United States and married, and after the marriage the young couple stayed in the home of an American woman. The Japanese husband worked at night and the young wife was greatly disturbed as to what course she should pursue.

Mother [the American woman] objected to my sitting up to await his [husband's] return. This troubled me greatly; for in Japan it is considered lazy and disgraceful for a wife to sleep while her husband is working. Night after night I lay with wide-open eyes, wondering whom it was my duty to obey—my far-away mother who knew Japanese customs, or the honoured new mother, who was teaching me the ways of America.[10]

[8] A. E. Wood, *op. cit.*, p. 430.

[9] Jakub Horak, *op. cit.*

Memories have had a steadying influence. Life was hard and lonely for the Scotch settlers in Michigan. A family would strike out through the woods a distance of two or three miles to find companionship at a neighbor's cabin. It would take only a few minutes to tell all they had done on their clearings and then they would drift back to Scotland. "Finally they would change off into song when all their troubles would vanish and they were back again amid the scenes of their childhood. When they went back to their humble homes, thanks to the songs of Burns and the Ettrick Shepherd, they were again ready to face any hardships." *Michigan Historical Collections,* XXXIX (1915), p. 367.

[10] From *A Daughter of the Samurai,* by Etsu I. Sugimoto, copyright, 1925, by Doubleday, Doran and Company, Inc., New York, p. 163.

Persistence of heritages. In colonies where large numbers of immigrants settle, conditions are favorable to the persistence of heritages. Festivals and holidays, in many instances, continue for long periods. "The Norwegians of America," according to Norlie, "delight in celebrating the Seventeenth of May by speech and song, in athletic contests and games. It is Norway's 'Fourth of July,' her Independence Day." [11] Among the Swedes,

> Christmas was the greatest season of all. In the country it lasted twenty days, as in Sweden. In fact, it was a Swedish festival transferred to America. For weeks the busy housewife had made preparations. Then, if ever, the home should be spotless. On Christmas Eve the presents were distributed, and Santa Claus was as familiar to the Swedish child as to his American cousin. The family retired early for matins (*Julotta*) began at four o'clock on Christmas morning in the early years, although more recently the time has been advanced to five or more often to six o'clock. Everybody in the community, religious or irreligious, attended the service. The church was crowded to suffocation. To have missed *Julotta* would have spoiled the entire season for many persons. Some came because it was a custom, and did not appear at church again until the next Christmas.[12]

Food habits are closely linked to memories and tend to persist, particularly in colonies.[13] A Norwegian girl in Nebraska said that her mother had been less homesick since her father raised rye and had it ground into flour for bread.[14]

[11] O. M. Norlie, *op. cit.*, pp. 501–02.

[12] G. M. Stephenson, *The Religious Aspects of Swedish Immigration*, p. 408. By permission of the publisher, The University of Minnesota Press, Minneapolis, Minn. Cf. also Dorothy G. Spicer, *Folk Festivals and the Foreign Community* (New York, 1923); Alfred Bergin, *Lindsborg efter Femtio År* (Rock Island, 1919), p. 148.

[13] "American people," writes E. A. Steiner, "wonder at the tenacity with which the immigrant clings to the foods of his Fatherland. It is not strange, for the nostrils, the lips, and the whole body retain precious memories of odours and tastes which are seldom forgotten. I am inclined to believe that noodle soup, with the right kind of seasoning, touches more channels of memory than—say, a lullaby or even a picture of the homeland." *From Alien to Citizen* (New York, 1914), p. 68. Cf. also p. 67; Nels Anderson and Eduard C. Lindeman, *Urban Sociology* (New York, 1928), p. 104.

[14] Cf. Willa Cather, *op. cit.*, pp. 272–73. Rye flour was used for bread in Norway and Sweden. Cf. also R. I. Kutak, *op. cit.*, p. 67.

Wherever a number of Swedish immigrants congregate, a coffee-culture complex of a certain kind inevitably appears.

> The emigrant had a taste for coffee before he purchased his steamship ticket. In the forties and fifties the consumption of sugar and coffee almost doubled. So excessive was the indulgence that coffee temperance societies were organized. Coffee was drunk in the poorest homes and small beer in all but the poorest. Servants demanded coffee as their daily ration. It was served not only at regular meals but several times a day and always to callers. This custom was continued in Swedish-American homes, and the farm hands at eleven o'clock in the forenoon scanned the horizon for sight of the housewife or her daughter carrying a steaming coffeepot, with toast (*skorpor*) and fancy pastries to make the interruption of work even more welcome. Coffee was given to children as freely as milk was given to American children. Perhaps the popularity of coffee among the Swedes in both countries is due partly to its excellent quality and to the cream and pastry that invariably accompany it. Their skill in preparing these delicacies may help to explain the demand for Swedish housemaids. . . . . Finally, coffee socials have certainly enriched the treasuries of church organizations and have sustained foreign missionaries for many days and months in the aggregate.[15]

Memories persist long and exert much influence.[16] The majority of the Irish in the United States are native-born, yet in important elections the Irish vote is at times more largely determined by the situation in Ireland than by that in the United States. Succeeding generations of Irish react on the basis of memory and tradition.[17]

Certain social possessions are more lasting than others. "Of all the items in the social heritage of the Texas Swedes," states

[15] G. M. Stephenson, *The Religious Aspects of Swedish Immigration,* pp. 404–05. By permission of the publisher, The University of Minnesota Press, Minneapolis, Minn. Many families that have adopted an American diet consider certain Swedish dishes indispensable to a proper celebration of Christmas. Cf. O. A. Benson, *op. cit.*

[16] Cf. H. A. Miller, "The Treatment of Immigrant Heritages," *Proceedings of the National Conference of Social Work,* 1919, pp. 731–36.

[17] In a crisis there is a tendency to react on the basis of customary practice and not on reason. The South is solidly Democratic, and the vote of the white electorate depends on the basis of habit determined by the race problem. This was made evident in the election of 1928 when the states with a high percentage of Negroes remained Democratic while others turned Republican. There were a few exceptions to this rule, and there were good reasons for those. Such behavior on the part of the voters cannot be explained apart from the traditions involved.

Rosenquist, "the church is undoubtedly the most deeply rooted."[18] It appears that the Italians cling more tenaciously to their music and art than to anything else in their cultural inheritance. According to Bruno Rosselli,

> The Italian immigrant, when he has acquired a slight financial competence, invests in a piano the savings which his fellow-immigrant invests in an automobile, and sees to it that his daughter learns how to play it. . . . . They crowd America's museums on Sunday, poring over the masterpieces of their ancestors, instead of wasting their time in the movie houses.[19]

Perpetuation of heritages. Many immigrant groups make special efforts to perpetuate their heritages and hand them on to their children in America. Foreign language newspapers, language schools,[20] and various nationalistic and cultural organizations endeavor to carry on the heritages. *The American-Scandinavian Review* is a journal, printed in English, which seeks to preserve the memories of the Old World. The Scandinavians pay considerable attention to music. They take pride in this heritage and seek to perpetuate it. They have several famous choirs and musical organizations. The annual rendition of the "Messiah" at Bethany College, Lindsborg, Kansas, has become traditional.[21] The choir of St. Olaf College (Norwegian), Northfield, Minnesota, is widely known. According to Rosenquist, the Swedes of Texas have made an endeavor to preserve their culture through the "Svenska Klub-

[18] *Op. cit.*

[19] H. P. Fairchild, *Immigrant Backgrounds* (New York, 1927), pp. 98–99. Cf. K. Bercovici, *On New Shores,* pp. 98–99.

[20] In the Greek church in Lowell, Mass., is a school room fitted with desks. "This is maintained at the expense of the church, with the main purpose of cherishing the national feeling for Greece in the hearts of the rising generation." H. P. Fairchild, *Greek Immigration to the United States* (New Haven, 1911), p. 142. "The Roumanians in Chicago have developed a great number of institutions around which centers their group life. Beneficial and cultural organizations, churches, parochial schools, and newspapers have contributed in strengthening their ethnic allegiance to the Old Culture and in helping them at the same time to understand their environment better." C. A. Galitzi, *op. cit.,* p. 239. Cf. also pp. 87–117; E. deS. Brunner, *op. cit.,* pp. 172–74, for the Danish immigrants; A. Ueland, *op. cit.,* pp. 150–51, for the Norwegians; A. Bergin, *Lindsborg efter Femtio År,* pp. 146–49, for the Swedes of Kansas.

[21] Cf. K. Bercovici, *On New Shores,* pp. 248–49; A. O. Fonkalsrud, *The Scandinavian-American* (Minneapolis, 1915), p. 58.

ben" (The Swedish Club) which has its headquarters in Austin, Texas.

Preservation of the Swedish language is the sole aim of this club. The rapid decline in the use of Swedish resulting in part from the cessation of immigration following the World War aroused the community and led to the formation of the organization. Its constitution provides that Swedish shall be the official language of the club and that programs and deliberations shall be in Swedish. . . . . The programs consist of Swedish music, readings of Swedish literature and speeches of a mildly propagandistic nature in praise of all things Swedish. Some of the programs are purely entertaining and are utilized for the purpose of raising funds to support a Swedish summer school for children. Practically all the dues collected from members are also utilized for this purpose. Swedish parents are urged through the *Texas Posten* to send their children to the school.[22]

Rural life usually tends to conserve and continue immigrant heritages in America.[23] Under the impact of the frequent and varied contacts in urban life, traditions are weakened more rapidly.

[22] *Op. cit.*

[23] Cf. *Proceedings of the National Conference of Social Work,* 1921, p. 494.

CHAPTER XVII

IMMIGRANT HERITAGES AND BEHAVIOR

The old-world heritages of immigrants have a marked influence upon behavior.[1] In fact, much of the behavior of any immigrant group in America can be explained only on that basis. "The naturalist," writes Emily G. Balch, "might as well study the habits of a lion in a menagerie or of a wild bird in a cage. To understand the immigrant we should know him in conditions which have shaped him, and which he has shaped in his own village and among his own people." [2]

Much has been said about the Jew in his business dealings in America. This is to be explained almost wholly in terms of his old-world traits which have been transplanted. In the old country the Jew lived under a double system—he lived in a primary group about the synagogue where his real standards were formed. He lived in a secondary group in his trade relations where he made contacts with the Gentiles. In his dealings with those of the secondary group he did not follow the primary group standards—he developed a dual conscience. Mary Antin tells of her cousin cheating the railway out of a ticket. But the railway was not

[1] Willa Cather shows how heritages influence behavior. She tells of an immigrant woman in Nebraska who had done much to retain the old-country habits in a new environment. She would not live in the customary prairie sod house, but demanded a dwelling built of logs. She missed the traditional fish diet and would send her boys a distance of twenty miles to the river to catch channel cat. When the children were small she would take them in a wagon and go fishing herself. She had never forgiven her husband for taking her to this desolate place, but since she was there she would reconstruct the old life as fully as possible. *O Pioneers* (Boston, 1913), pp. 28–29, 30. Piles of soiled clothing heaped in a corner or even in a cupboard do not necessarily reflect a slovenly attitude but rather the persistence of old-country customs among some Italians. A shortage of water in several areas developed certain practices which have been transplanted to America. Phyllis H. Williams, *South Italian Folkways in Europe and America* (New Haven, 1938), pp. 3–4. Peter Roberts gives an interesting insight into differences in behavior due to old-world backgrounds. *Op. cit.*, p. 139.

[2] E. G. Balch, *op. cit.*, p. v.

Jewish and did not belong to her primary group; hence it was not wrong—it was rather to be commended. She would have been horrified, however, at such an attempt to cheat a Jew.[3]

Jewish immigrants come to America with a high regard—an almost fanatical reverence—for learning.[4] Abraham Cahan tells of the struggle and determination of his mother, a poor widow, to give him a Rabbinical education. In this, however, she was no exception, for it was not unusual to find families that would literally starve themselves in order to make it possible for their sons to study the Word of God in some Talmudic seminary.[5]

This heritage colors the lives of the Jewish immigrants. Russian and Polish Jews in particular are eager to take advantage of educational opportunities and many families make sacrifices that their children, particularly the most promising boys, may go to school.[6]

In the European ghettos, with all the discriminations against them, learning did give a certain status and made life more tolerable for some. According to Mary Antin,

[3] Cf. Mary Antin, *op. cit.*, p. 150. Thorsten Sellin reports an interesting situation from a small Hungarian community in the Middle West where it was considered proper to take coal from the railroad. They would not steal from an individual, but from the impersonal railway—that was different. *Interpreter Releases,* XIII (May 23, 1936), 147–48.

[4] Among the Syrians we find a somewhat different heritage. According to P. K. Hitti, "On analysis it will be found that on the part of the reader what provides the basis for this leadership is respect for the written word. 'Didn't you see it in print?' is enough assurance to a skeptic in a debate that the thing is true. Coming from a country where the Muhammadan would stoop in the street to pick up a paper and deposit it in a hole in the wall lest there be on it the name of Allah that might be defiled by the feet of the passers-by, the Syrian holds the printed page in special reverence and esteem." From *Racial Studies of the New American Series,* by P. K. Hitti, copyright, 1924, by Doubleday, Doran and Company, Inc., New York, pp. 96–97.

[5] A. Cahan, *op. cit.*, pp. 16, 23. Cf. C. F. Ware, *op. cit.*, p. 222.

[6] Anzia Yezierska tells of a Jewish woman who was very proud of her son, soon to receive the Ph.D. degree from Columbia University. She slaved and supported him while he worked over his books. Her husband was a Hebrew scholar and she had also slaved to support him. But she did not murmur: that was a great honor for her to be able to support these scholars. "I'm glad," she said, "when I drank in pleasure from my Shlomoh. Soon he'll finish Doctor of Philosophy. What greater honor can I have in this world than to have a son, a learned man, a Doctor of Philosophy!" From *Arrogant Beggar,* by Anzia Yezierska, copyright, 1927, by Doubleday, Doran and Company, Inc., New York, pp. 14–20. Mary Antin wrote of her father as he took his three children to school shortly after their arrival in Boston. Cf. *The Promised Land,* p. 205.

One qualification only could raise a man above his social level, and that was scholarship. A boy born in the gutter need not despair of entering the houses of the rich, if he had a good mind and a great appetite for sacred learning. A poor scholar would be preferred in the marriage market to a rich ignoramus. In the phrase of our grandmothers, a boy stuffed with learning was worth more than a girl stuffed with bank notes.[7]

This heritage is undoubtedly a big factor in spurring many Jewish students on to outstanding scholastic records in our schools and colleges. Restricted in opportunities to distinguish themselves, they turn to scholarship where they may excel.

Jan Amos Komensky,[8] born in a small Moravian village, published a book in 1631 which won him the plaudits of the educational world. This Komensky tradition inspired the Czech immigrants of Texas to establish schools in their pioneer settlements.[9] The sentiment for giving their children educational opportunities is also conspicuous among the Bohemians of Nebraska. According to Robert I. Kutak, Milligan, a small town in that state, sends an unusually large quota of young people to the State University.[10]

Heritages and status. Heritages related to status and class distinction exercise considerable influence on behavior. According to Brandenburg,

The lower class of Italians in this country continue to pay the respect and homage to those of their race who have been born to position, without regard to the changed and democratic conditions under which both gentleman and peasant are now living. An Italian of humble birth who may have prospered in this country and have risen to a high position of commercial and political eminence among New Yorkers will cringe unhesitatingly to some worthless scamp who chances to be well born. . . . . Twenty years of residence and fifteen of citizenship in the United States will change the average Italian into a very American sort of a person, but I know to a certainty that he will suffer silently at the hands

7 *The Promised Land* (Boston, Houghton Mifflin Company, 1912), p. 37.

8 Known in much educational literature as Comenius.

9 Cf. E. Hudson and H. R. Maresh, *op. cit.*, pp. 171–79. In Czecho-Slovakia, and particularly among the Czechs, education is virtually a passion. Cf. *Survey*, LXIII (March 1, 1930), 637.

10 *Op. cit.*, p. 66. Cf. W. C. Smith, *op. cit.*, pp. 159–74, for the oriental attitude toward learning in Hawaii and on the Pacific Coast.

of a countryman of superior birth what he would not submit to for one minute from an American, no matter what might be the latter's station in life.[11]

The whole stratificational system of Hungary was conducive to land worship. Being an agrarian country in which most political rights and prestige were vested in property holders, a deep respect for land had developed through the centuries. This persistent desire for land as the symbol of attainment was transplanted to America.[12]

"The Norwegian immigrant," wrote Lawrence M. Larson, "came with a strong attachment to the soil. He hungered for land; he felt the need of a home."[13] When one considers the honorable position the *bonde* (independent landowner) held in Norwegian life, he can appreciate Per Hansa's behavior, as depicted by the novelist.[14] By becoming owners of their acres over here, the emigrants made themselves the equals of the aristocratic set in Norway. This explains the love for the soil which in many becomes an absorbing passion.[15] When they sow their fields with grain, they do not go about the task perfunctorily—it is a profound experience. Unless we recognize this attitude, we might consider Rolvaag's description of Per Hansa's mood an exaggeration. When he examined the seed wheat, he lifted up the handfuls of it with reverence. Undoubtedly this was the greatest moment of his life—he was now ready to sow wheat on his own land.[16]

[11] B. Brandenburg, *op. cit.*, p. 16.

[12] S. C. Newman, *op. cit.* Newman reports a case. A single man, aged fifty-five, who had worked for the National Tube Co. twenty-three years, quit and lost his pension rights. He had come to earn money to buy land in the home district. He gave up the idea of a return and decided to buy land here. He had saved about $6000 and planned to "buy much land cheap, land values will rise, will be rich man." He envisaged himself owning much land which is the old Hungarian measure of success. He had no conception of the sorry state of agriculture in recent years, and he refused to face the fact that farming operations here differed from those in the old country. *Ibid.*

[13] *American Historical Review,* XL (October, 1934), 74.

[14] Cf. O. E. Rölvaag, *op. cit.*, pp. 298–338.

[15] A little Norwegian boy, whose father happened to be too poor to own land, was asked where they lived. He replied: "Oh, we don't live nowhere; we hain't got no land." Like all Norwegians, his father did not feel that he had a home until he could call the soil his own. Sigrid Moe, *The Norwegian-American Novel,* unpublished dissertation, University of Chicago.

[16] O. E. Rölvaag, *op. cit.*, p. 298.

Furthermore, when the harvest began Per Hansa was in a rare frame of mind. After the long struggle he was harvesting his own wheat. He was deeply moved. Every bundle he tied gave him a sensuous pleasure. He walked lightly as if on cushions of air.[17]

The attitude of the East Frisians to a proprietary control of the soil is made evident by a letter of an Illinois farmer to his parents in Europe. "When I am plowing," he wrote, "I can shut my eyes and smell the dear land under me and say it is mine, mine, all mine. No one can take it away. I am king as you said." [18] The traditional attitude is revealed in a letter from his parents.

> You say that you have all the papers for the land now? Please put them where they will not take them back. When they try to take your land, you can show them the papers. Be sure to take care of them. If you have land you are as a king. Land is everything. One cannot move land away from you. If one has the land by a paper one cannot be made to leave the land.[19]

The Czech immigrant brought to Texas the desire to own land and cultivate it. "The sight of the vast expanse of untilled acres . . . . was indeed an inspiration. . . . . Always as the story of the Czech pioneer unfolds there is the mention that he bought land, and that after a time he bought more land, and so on until he was a substantial land-owner." [20]

Heritages and occupations. In the older countries occupations are rigidly graded. Against this old-world background some have refused to accept certain kinds of work. Members of the intelli-

[17] *Ibid.*, p. 338.

[18] E. T. Hiller, F. E. Corner, W. L. East, *op. cit.*, p. 27.

[19] *Ibid.*, p. 25.

[20] E. Hudson, and H. R. Maresh, *op. cit.*, p. 4. A letter of July 5, 1938, from Dr. Maresh states that at the Texas Centennial Exposition in 1936, a topographical map of Texas showed that the Czechs occupy the richest soil belt in the state. The desire to own great expanses was carried to an extreme by the Poles in New England. "He prefers a hundred acres of infertile land, producing what fifty fertile acres would produce, because of the vastness of the possession." K. Bercovici, *On New Shores,* p. 10. Cf. also pp. 9, 120, 132–33 for other immigrant groups. On the contrary, "Although the majority of the Lithuanians have farming for their background, only a minority of them have pursued that occupation in America. . . . . Most Lithuanian immigrants associate farming with the ruinous taxes and unprofitable drudgery experienced by them in Lithuania, so they have turned to industrial work." J. S. Roucek, "Lithuanian Immigrants in America," *American Journal of Sociology,* XLI (January, 1936), 449.

gentsia among the Hungarian immigrants of Detroit have sought in every way to avoid manual labor. One man, working in an office, explained why he declined employment in the factory where his pay would have been higher. "In Hungary I was a lawyer," he said. "Would you expect me to work beside former peasants in . . . . an automobile factory? Every peasant who knew me would ridicule me. I may not receive as much money a week as they do. At any rate I keep my self respect." [21] Others have been greatly disturbed because they had to accept certain kinds of employment. Park and Miller [22] report the experience of an immigrant from Austrian Poland. He worked in a factory where typewriter ribbons were inked, and one by one the ten suits of clothes he brought with him were ruined. The last suit was a Prince Albert and he went to work in that; he would not wear overalls. "I was ashamed," he said, "to wear overalls." He belonged to the class in the homeland which was superior to the wearers of overalls, and he could not bear to have his status endangered.[23]

Certain American women who are more tender-hearted than wise talk about the ingratitude and utter inefficiency of the Sicilian women because they do not know how to make over for their children the thread-bare clothes that are given to them from the missionary barrel. According to Celena A. Baxter, cast-off clothes are very much in disrepute among Sicilians; they indicate that one belongs to the lowest class.[24] Mere contact with American soil will not uproot that heritage and its attendant behavior; they are still conscious of class distinctions.

Ethel Bird comments on the greater success in adjustment to

[21] E. D. Beynon, "Occupational Succession of Hungarians in Detroit," *American Journal of Sociology,* XXXIX (March, 1934), 605.

An employment bureau offered a job to Michael Pupin. When he learned that he would have to milk a cow, he refused. Milking a cow was unequivocally a feminine task, according to Serb tradition. *Op. cit.,* p. 45.

A. M. Rihbany would not carry the peddler's pack under any conditions—that was a degrading occupation. *Op. cit.,* p. 199.

[22] *Op. cit.,* p. 49.

[23] Miss Sophonisba Breckenridge has stated the philosophy of clothes in these meaningful words: "In Europe clothes were to indicate 'where one came from' while here the whole effort is to conceal that fact by an almost abject imitation and deadly sameness." *National Conference of Social Work,* 1923, p. 305.

[24] "Sicilian Family Life," *The Family,* XIV (May, 1933), 84.

American life on the part of immigrants from so-called "yeasty" countries, which permit individuals to rise from the bottom to the top both socially and economically. Heritages transplanted from the "yeasty" countries of Scandinavia, Germany and, in less measure, England have been generally favorable to assimilation.[25]

Heritages and American government. What H. A. Miller calls the "oppression psychosis" [26] is the key to much immigrant behavior. The Finns in the homeland were oppressed first by the Swedes and then by the Russians. This undoubtedly influenced the growth of coöperatives [27] which was a revolt against the capitalist class. Living in memories of the old world, many Finnish immigrants became socialistic—almost violently so. The Swedes, however, who were the rulers in Finland, have usually become capitalistically-minded Republicans.[28]

The Letts went through a baptism of fire under the oppression of Russia. They could not forget that experience at once on arrival in the United States, and, on the basis of those memories, they became radicals in the labor movement. They formed a nationalistic organization which affiliated with the American Socialist Party in 1909.[29]

The Irish afford a fine example of oppression psychosis.[30] The wrongs of Ireland formed a bond of allegiance that has kept even the children's children in America interested in Irish affairs [31]

[25] Cf. *National Conference of Social Work,* 1923, p. 305.

[26] By that he means "those persistent and exaggerated mental states which are characteristically produced under conditions where one group dominates another." H. A. Miller, *Races, Nations and Classes* (Chicago, 1924), p. 32. Cf. *ibid.*, pp. 32–38, for a discussion of this subject.

[27] Cf. K. Bercovici, *On New Shores,* pp. 31–32; E. deS. Brunner, *op. cit.*, pp. 178–82, for the Danes.

[28] The "oppression psychosis" is a most powerful instrumentality in the creation of group solidarity. Cf. H. A. Miller, *Races, Nations and Classes,* p. 36. Sweden has been a free country for a long time. As a consequence, Swedish immigrants assimilate readily. Norway was under the control of Sweden until recently and Norwegian immigrants assimilate more slowly—they cling together with greater solidity and retain their old-world culture longer.

[29] C. J. Bittner, *op. cit.*

[30] Cf. H. A. Miller, *Races, Nations and Classes,* pp. 105–12. Cf. *ibid.*, pp. 91–104, for the Jews.

[31] An Irishman who visited the United States wrote: "If a question ever arose in which American interests clashed with Irish interests, there might be a solid Irish vote in favor of sacrificing America to Ireland." From *From Dublin to Chicago,* by

and made them willing to strive for the independence of the Emerald Isle. Denied an opportunity for participation in political affairs in Great Britain, they probably overestimated its importance. Hence they turned to that field of activity in America with all but religious fervor. Furthermore, the demands of the Irish voters have influenced international policies when they touched Ireland.[32]

Many foreigners come with a fear and distrust of government officials by whom they have been abused and oppressed. For a long time authority to the Syrian had been identified with confiscation and ruin. Furthermore, the governmental agents were notoriously subject to bribery.[33] When immigrants find that officials in America also are subject to bribery, it does not create in them respect for government.

At times the attitudes toward officials and the owning class, when transplanted to America, bring deplorable results. An heritage from Ireland was in considerable measure responsible for a reprehensible situation in the anthracite coal districts of Pennsylvania. In 1854 an organization known as the Molly Maguires appeared among the Irish miners and inaugurated a reign of terror in which threats, beatings, arson, and murder were the order of the day. Murder after murder was committed and without a conviction. Fairchild comments: [34]

Geo. A. Birmingham, copyright, 1914, by Doubleday, Doran and Company, Inc., New York, p. 304.

[32] Cf. H. A. Miller, *Races, Nations and Classes,* p. 112, for the Irish vote in Massachusetts and the League of Nation's Covenant.

[33] Morris Zelditch reports an incident: "On the annual visit of the tax collector to my home village, my uncle was greatly perturbed by our Turkish rulers who were afraid that Syrian tobacco might be a successful competitor to Turkish tobacco. When the collector came, my uncle, armed with a loaded gun, met him at the gate of his farm. The collector demanded entrance to the farm, but my uncle refused to let him in, afraid he would see the tobacco field. I thought a fight would ensue, but after they had talked a short time my uncle bribed the collector with a little extra money and the collector went on to his next visit without entering the farm at all." *Op. cit.*

[34] From H. P. Fairchild, *Immigration,* p. 106. By permission of The Macmillan Company, publishers. Cf. E. Abbott, *Historical Aspects of the Immigration Problem,* pp. 671–82; *American Historical Review,* XV (April, 1910), 547–61.

Edward F. Roberts gives the Irish heritage of hatred of England credit for a large share in fomenting the American Revolution. Because of drastic laws enacted against Ireland in 1695, a large number of Irish schoolmasters came to the American colonies.

This series of events is a remarkable illustration of the way in which customs and habits of thought, and standards of conduct, which have grown up by a natural process, and are comprehensible if not excusable in one land, may develop more alarming and disgraceful features when transplanted to a new environment.[35] The essential strength of the Molly Maguires lay in that deep-seated hatred of an informer which has become a pronounced feature of the Irish character, as a result of the conditions to which they have been subjected at home. Thus, while the great mass of the Irish settlers of the anthracite region abhorred the principles and deeds of the Molly Maguires, it was almost impossible to secure witnesses against criminals whose identity was a matter of general knowledge because of the greater repugnance to the character of an informer. The traditional hatred of the Irish peasant toward the landlord was, in this country, diverted to the capitalist class in a wholly unreasonable but efficient manner.

Heritages and crime. The criminality among immigrants in America can be explained largely in terms of heritages. According to E. H. Sutherland,

> These national groups differ in their crimes, not because of differential selection by immigration officials, but because of differences in habits formed in their home countries. They commit fewer crimes than native born as a whole because of the strength and consistency of the traditions which they assimilated in their home communities. . . . .
>
> Similarly, the persistence of habits, codes, and ideals is the explanation of the differences in the criminality of different groups. It is not because the Italians or Greeks are hot-blooded, innately incapable of inhibiting rage or lust in provocative situations, that they commit crimes of heinous nature more frequently than the native born do. . . . Furthermore,

These exiled pedagogues continued in their chosen profession and lost no opportunity to fan the already-smoldering fires of resentment against the British. *Ireland in America* (New York, 1931), pp. 95–100.

Certain heritages are used by immigrants in the exploitation of the more recent arrivals of their own groups. Cf. E. Abbott, *Immigration: Select Documents and Case Records,* p. 54.

The food habits, together with other usages, of national, racial, and religious groups are commercially exploited—a number of them quite legitimately, to be sure. Cf. N. Anderson and E. C. Lindeman, *op. cit.,* pp. 104–05.

[35] E. H. Sutherland writes: "The parents frequently bring with them heritages regarding behavior, law, and punishment which even when not resulting in lawlessness in their native countries, easily lead to lawlessness in America." In E. S. Bogardus, *Social Problems and Social Processes* (Chicago, 1933), p. 55.

their particular national crimes appear to be abandoned in one generation.[36]

Heritages and assimilation. Immigrant heritages are an important factor in assimilation.[37] Many of them are of such a character as to raise barriers which prevent the immigrant from making contacts and from participating in American life. Rihbany lost opportunities to learn American ways because of an Oriental trait. He received invitations to American homes, but, according to Syrian custom, declined when he would have gladly accepted. He expected to be urged and was greatly disappointed when he was taken at his word.[38]

Certain heritages keep the immigrant from making use of our institutions so that participation in our life is restricted.[39] Because of old-world superstitions, some immigrant parents refuse to permit proper medical treatment for their families. They are particularly obdurate when hospital treatment is necessary.[40] Mary Richmond gives an instance.

> One case worker found her ingenuity taxed to reconcile an Italian father's social conventions with American ways of restoring a dangerously ill girl to health. An operation was needed and the hospital in which it could be performed had been found. But no entreaties moved the father, determined that his child should not leave her home. At last the case worker discovered that he regarded a young unmarried

[36] *National Conference of Social Work,* 1927, p. 577. Cf. also E. H. Sutherland, *Principles of Criminology,* pp. 114–15; H. P. Fairchild, *Immigrant Backgrounds,* pp. 105–06; J. H. Mariano says of the Italian immigrant: "Where he witnesses repeated examples of unfairness, the natural tendency in such cases is to take justice in his own hands, because to him everything is terribly personal. His outlook on these questions is determined for him beforehand by his tradition and social background and it requires a long time of direction and reflection before he can understand our methods which in many ways are so different from those to which he has been accustomed." *Op. cit.,* p. 38. Cf. *National Conference of Social Work,* 1923, p. 312, for the attitude of the Armenian immigrant toward law which has grown out of his experiences under Turkish rule.

[37] Cf. C. A. Galitzi, *op. cit.,* pp. 168–69.

[38] A. M. Rihbany, *op. cit.,* pp. 258–59. Cf. H. P. Fairchild, *Immigrant Backgrounds* (New York, 1927), pp. 114–15; *National Conference of Social Work,* 1924, pp. 290–91.

[39] Cf. E. G. Stern, *op. cit.,* pp. 113–14.

[40] Cf. Joseph P. Murphy, *National Conference of Social Work,* 1925, p. 597; Rose Cohen, *op. cit.,* pp. 230–31.

woman as permanently disgraced who spent a night away from the parental roof. The adaptation made was an arrangement by which the father could accompany his daughter to the hospital and stay there long enough to assure her restoration to health without blasting her reputation! [41]

Immigrants from the ghettos of Europe bring many culture traits that are separatistic. Ritual regulates much of their home life and this stands in the way of domestic service in Gentile homes. Orthodox Jews do not like to go to American hospitals because proper provisions are not made for them. They are not served *kosher* food. For the proper observance of the rites the Jew wants sacred candles—Standard Oil products are not acceptable. These elements together with many others, hinder the assimilation of the Jewish immigrants.

Heritages and the treatment of immigrants. The recognition of the heritages of immigrants has a practical aspect. The American teacher, politician, employer, store-keeper, religious worker, and social worker [42] need to know the background of the immigrants and their children if they are to deal successfully with them.[43]

According to Bruno Rosselli, Austin Corbin, a New York

[41] Mary Richmond, *What is Social Case Work?* (New York, 1922), pp. 185–86.

[42] Mary E. Hurlbutt said of social workers: "But once we admit that mere physical vicinity in time or place is not the factor determining which of all the multitude of things our client is surrounded with shall have significance for him, but that things far away and long ago may truly be part of his environment, then we have committed ourselves to a very far-reaching proposition, which, if it can be made as urgent as it ought to be, would startle us into a realization of our present clumsiness and into demanding more and more help in equipping ourselves for our work with our foreign-born clients." *National Conference of Social Work,* 1923, p. 310. The entire paper, pp. 309–13, is excellent on this subject. Cf. also W. C. Smith, "Contributions of Cultural Sociology to Pre-Social Work Students," *Social Forces,* XII (May, 1934), 477–83.

[43] Failure to consider heritages may result in unfortunate situations. Y. B. Mirza reported an experience: "As I sat on the steps of the school one afternoon with a merry group of boys, one of them playfully knocked my hat off upon the ground. He could not have known that in Persia a hat is regarded as the most sacred part of one's apparel. To knock off a hat was to convey the most deadly insult. 'Pick up my hat!' I commanded threateningly, whereat the boy only laughed.

"I leaped upon him. He was so surprised that he could not defend himself from my first furious blows, but suddenly he hit back and we fought in grim earnest." From *Myself When Young,* by Y. B. Mirza, copyright, 1929, by Doubleday, Doran and Company, Inc., New York, p. 246.

financier, planned to establish an Italian colony on the Mississippi River. He thought that it was merely a matter of organization. He failed to see that the Italians being born individualists cannot be reckoned with as numbered human units. . . . . Although they were all farmers, the Venetians and Calabrians were accustomed to different crops and to different methods of cultivation, while the tools provided for all were utterly different from those with which they were familiar. Cotton, the main crop to be raised by the colony, does not grow in Italy, and the Italian peasant, accustomed to grow what he consumes and to consume what he grows, grumbled at the idea of raising a crop which the problematic river boat carried away bringing in return strange foodstuffs from elsewhere.[44]

Miss Balch shows the importance of considering the heritages.

As a matter of fact, it is often impossible in America to distinguish these national groups, the Slovaks, the Slovenians, and so on, especially as the men themselves, ignorant of English, can give little help. Yet the differences are there. The various Slavic nationalities are separated by distinctions of speech, historical experience, national self-consciousness, political aims, and often a religion. In American communities they have different churches, societies, newspapers, and a separate social life. Too often the lines of cleavage are marked by antipathies and old animosities. The Pole wastes no love on the Russian, nor the Ruthenian on the Pole, and a person who acts in ignorance of these facts, a missionary for instance, or a political boss, or a trade union organizer, may find himself in the position of a host who should innocently invite a Fenian from County Cork to hobnob with an Ulster Orangeman on the ground that both were Irish! [45]

According to one report, an employing group encountered difficulty with a number of workers because of the disregard of a heritage.

[44] Bruno Rosselli, "An Arkansas Epic," *The Century Magazine,* XCIX (January, 1920), 378.

[45] E. G. Balch, *op. cit.*, pp. 8–9. "The Italians' patriotism has its geographical limitations. With him *patria* means province. . . . . United Italy is a matter of too recent date to have taken deep root in her peasant class. And while they are most catholic in their attitude towards the world in general, for an Italian belonging to another province they evince an antipathy amounting almost to aversion." Alice Bennett, in *Survey,* XXII (1909), 173. Cf. P. H. Williams, *op. cit., passim.*

In the early days of the sugar industry in Hawaii, a number of Norwegians were recruited to work on the plantations. These workers annoyed the planters with their complaints about the food; they even reported the matter to the Norwegian government. An investigation was ordered and, according to its findings, the food was satisfactory both in quantity and quality. The investigators, however, overlooked the most important factor —*it was not Norwegian food.*[46]

Our recent experience with national prohibition has made it evident that it is not well to spurn the heritages of considerable blocs of people.

The century-old mores of a large section of the population of a country cannot be lightly overlooked by reformers. Three million Italians in this country belonging to a racial group accustomed since time immemorial to the consumption of some commodity should not have been ignored by the sponsors of so drastic an experiment, honestly designed to meet the scandalous craving for strong liquors on the part of early American elements.[47]

This shows the peculiar inclination on the part of the early American element in our population "to make light of the mores of large sections of its immigrants on the historically fallacious pretext that their 'Americanization' should change habits and traditions as rapidly as a new oath of allegiance changes their citizenship." [48]

To be sure, certain immigrant heritages pained and distressed those of old American stock who lived in the Puritan tradition. German immigrants "brought to rural life a *Gemüthlichkeit*, a

[46] W. C. Smith, "Contributions of Cultural Sociology to Pre-Social Work Students," *Social Forces,* XII (May, 1934), 481.

[47] B. Rosselli, in H. P. Fairchild, *Immigrant Backgrounds,* p. 121. J. H. Mariano says of this: "The prohibition amendment, for instance, has met with a scant number of enthusiasts among Italians. This is not difficult to understand. In fact the reason is perfectly obvious. Few Italians abuse liquor. The majority drink only light wines and cordials and this they take as a food usually at meals. The Italian has as much scorn for the individual who debases himself by abusing liquor as he has for the fanatic dry. As much as any group within our population the Italian is anxious to see real law enforcement." *Op. cit.,* p. 35. Cf. also C. M. Panunzio, "The Foreign Born's Reaction to Prohibition," *Sociology and Social Research,* XVIII (January-February, 1934), 223–28; E. Hudson and H. R. Maresh, *op. cit.,* pp. 36, 39.

[48] H. P. Fairchild, *Immigrant Backgrounds,* p. 121.

sociability, which set them apart from all other racial elements."[49] They attended the *Turnvereine* and held picnics on Sunday. They declared that the Puritanical Sabbath was an infringement on personal liberty and radicals in the group even scoffed at some of our institutions. The Germans, fond of their beer, joined the Irish in opposing prohibition.[50]

According to Dr. Jakub Horak, the saloon-keeper has been a prominent figure in many immigrant groups. He has played an important rôle in the benefit societies. Business motives, to be sure, have been a factor, but he has naturally gravitated into a position of prominence in community affairs because the saloon, in some measure, inherited the place which the inn and the *Gast Haus* occupied in the life of the home countries.[51]

Derogatory things have been said about the immigrant and his behavior. Many, to be sure, have not made the best adjustments. They have clung to their old-world heritages with bull-dog tenacity. But our intolerance of their group values and our disrespect for their sentimental memories have been barriers to them. According to Park and Miller,

> If we wish to help the immigrant to get a grip on American life, to understand its conditions, and find his own rôle in it, we must seize on everything in his old life which will serve either to interpret the new or to hold him steady while he is getting adjusted. The language through which his compatriots can give him their garnered experience, the "societies" which make him feel "at home," the symbols of his home land, reminding him of the moral standards under which he grew up. Common courtesy and kindness exact tolerance for these things, and common sense indicates that they are the foundation of the readjustment we seek.[52]

[49] From A. M. Schlesinger, *The Rise of the City* (New York, 1933), p. 56. By permission of The Macmillan Company, publishers.

[50] Cf. G. M. Stephenson, *A History of American Immigration*, p. 102. According to one German immigrant, "They have used liberty as a club with which to kill liberty. Certainly, to prohibit something which involves no moral turpitude, contravenes every sound theory of government and even despots have shrunk from it." R. Bartholdt, *op. cit.*, p. 17. Cf. pp. 422–31.

[51] Cf. *Report of the Health Insurance Commission of the State of Illinois*, 1919, p. 530.

[52] *Op. cit.*, pp. 395–96.

CHAPTER XVIII

THE IMMIGRANT AS A MARGINAL MAN

Divided loyalties of immigrant. The immigrant may, and very often does, spend all his time and energy in making a living. He learns a smattering of English, enough to carry on the ordinary, everyday transactions with his neighbors but not enough to conceal his foreign origin. Usually he remains rather closely within the bounds of the ethnic community. Thus he may pass his days, in ignorance of the real American life in which he is immersed. In such a situation there is practically no assimilation although there is some accommodation.

If, however, the immigrant does not settle in a colony of his own nationals but plunges into the whirlpool of American life, he must of necessity make more changes; he goes farther along in the process of Americanization. But no matter how favorable the situation, even though he may come in contact with the "melting-pot" at white heat, even though he may adjust himself so well to American life that the ear-marks of his foreign origin are obliterated so far as the casual observer is concerned, he can never be completely assimilated; [1] he feels the tug of two loyalties—on the one hand, there are old memories and sentimental attachments, and on the other, the satisfactions and associations of the new life.[2] Bi-cultural fealty is shown in this selection:

[1] Cf. C. A. Galitzi, *op. cit.*, pp. 168–69.

[2] Cf. S. Villa, *op. cit.*, pp. 1–6, 139–44. This dichotomy of loyalties is made to live for us through one of Bojer's characters, an aged, blind man who had returned for a visit to his ancestral home in Norway after a long struggle in North Dakota. He lay awake at night in the old house and meditated: "If you came back, you wanted to leave again; if you went away, you longed to come back. Wherever you were, you could hear the call of the home-land, like the note of a herdsman's horn far away in the hills. You had one home out there, and one over here, and yet you were an alien in both places. Your true abiding-place was the vision of something very far off, and your soul was like the waves, always restless, forever in motion. Was he not longing already to get back to his big farm . . . . with his children and

The fathers came to America and became Americans by choice. Though good Americans in every sense, yet they remained Norwegians to the end. They could not change their nature any more than the Ethiopian can change his skin, or the leopard his spots. They were more at home with the Norwegian language than the English. The Norwegian land and its scenery, the home in which they had lived and its surroundings, the laws and their lawmakers over there, the customs, ideals, culture, all had a peculiarly sweet and sacred charm altogether different from the things here in America. . . . . . Through their work and their achievements they are united to America by the strongest ties. But through their memories they are united to Norway. This is the peculiar position of the immigrant, his "tragedy." Parting is sweet sorrow, bitter sweet. The building of the new home was tragic. It must have something about it to remind him of the old home over there; it was the holy of holies. The estrangement from the children was tragic. They did not seem to understand when he spoke about the land of his birth. The death of the wife was tragic. She and he had sprung from the same root, had breathed the same national atmosphere, had roamed about the same surroundings, had sung the same songs, and had cherished the same thoughts; she alone could understand when he said, "Do you remember?" Her death brought him only sadness and an increased feeling of loneliness. His visit to the homeland was tragic. He did not find what he sought. "And what did he seek?" Without knowing it, he was in reality seeking his own youth. He found nothing of what he sought. Most of his old friends were resting in the churchyard where he could read their names on the tombstones. The people he met were strangers to him. Everything was changed. But he did not realize that he himself had changed most of all. The picture of the old home district which he had carried in his soul for forty years did not seem real. It was false. This was not his home district, his home, his people—poor, stripped of every illusion, he hastened back to Christiania where he took passage on the first steamer going to America. Neither steamer nor railway train could carry him back fast enough.[3]

Mere mention of the Czar's name may arouse bitter hatred in the Jew who left Russia, but relatives, friends, hallowed land-

relations close by? Well, he would soon be back now, he and little Morten would pack up to-morrow." J. Bojer, *op. cit.*, p. 351. Shortly before this the same man had said: "Well, you see, we who come out here have two souls, and two countries." *Ibid.*, p. 341.

[3] O. M. Norlie, *op. cit.*, pp. 254–55. Cf. also C. M. Panunzio, *The Soul of an Immigrant* (New York, 1921), pp. 299–329.

marks, and childhood associations release tender sentiments.[4] The new land may be idealized but it is never found to be exactly as imagined.

Between two worlds. Because of this condition the immigrant occupies a position more or less intermediate between the Old and the New Worlds. He has left the old behind—but not completely; he has taken on the new—but not whole-heartedly. An immigrant from Bulgaria brings out the dualism most vividly:

> Years have passed since then. And I am now a different person. Still I often ask myself these questions: What has been the result of this long and blind gestation in the womb of America? Have I become an American? Has the storm in my being lulled now that I have spent two-thirds of my life in a struggle for readjustment and adaptation? The one answer that pounds in my mind is this: Despite the readiness and zeal with which I tossed myself in the melting pot I still am not wholly American, and never will be.
>
> It is not my fault. I have done all I could. America will not accept me. I shall always be the adopted child, not the real son, of a mother that I love more than the one that gave me birth. It is hard for a man with ingrained native traits and characteristics to remake himself in the course of one generation. There is still something outlandish about me; mannerisms and gestures that must strike as odd one born and bred here; tints and nuances in my speech that must betray my foreign birth soon after I open my mouth to speak.
>
> I once believed that America demanded complete surrender from those who adopted it as their mother. I surrendered completely. Then I discovered that America wanted more—it wanted complete transformation, inward and outward. That is impossible in one generation. Then what is my fate, and the fates of the thousands who fall into my category, or, should I say, into whose category I fall? What are we? Are we still what we were before we came to America, or are we half Americans and half something else? To me, precisely there lies our tragedy. We are neither one nor the other; we are orphans. Having forsaken our own mothers to become the foster children of another, we find ourselves orphaned. Spiritually, physically, linguistically, we have not been wholly domesticated. And at the

[4] An Italian immigrant said that, even though he was forty years old, whenever Christmas and Easter came he wanted to return to the little village in Italy. At such times he would live in his childhood memories. Cf. H. G. Duncan, *op. cit.*, p. 564.

same time we have rendered ourselves incapable of resuming life in the old country.

While I am not a whole American, neither am I what I was when I first landed here; that is, a Bulgarian. Still retaining some inherited native traits, enough to bar me forever from complete assimilation, I have outwardly and inwardly deviated so much from a Bulgarian that when recently visiting in that country I felt like a foreigner and was so regarded. My Bulgarian speech is now cramped and rusty, clumsy and inadequate for my thoughts. I cannot now speak that language half so fluently as I speak English; nor can I write it with half the facility with which I string English words upon this page. In my audience with King Boris during my visit there I found myself compelled to ask permission from the King to speak to him in English. In Bulgarian I stammered and was hopelessly inarticulate. . . . .

In Bulgaria I am not wholly a Bulgarian; in the United States not wholly an American— I have to go through life with a dual nationality. When in the United States I long for the sleepy villages and the intimate life of the Balkans. When I am in the Balkans I dream of America day and night. An American-made motor car seen on the street, an advertising poster announcing the showing of a motion picture made in the United States, anything closely or remotely connected with America is enough to send thrills through my spine. I was taking an afternoon nap in the house of a friend in Sofia and upon waking was told that I had been talking in my sleep. "What did I say?" I inquired, afraid of having revealed some secrets, with which one's head is always filled in the Balkans. "Nothing much," they comforted me, "You just kept blabbering about America!"

And shall I forget my joy upon my return to America! I was downright foolish. I felt like a child at the sight of his mother from whom it had been separated for months. Without unpacking my things, I left my room at the hotel and for nearly two hours walked up and down Broadway like a man possessed. Everything that my eyes beheld, I felt like embracing within my arms.

But here I am. A year has barely gone by and I am ready to embrace a Balkan donkey with fraternal affection. Yet I cannot leave America, though I am but half American.[5]

An immigrant, even though reasonably well accommodated, may be unhappy here when he is not accepted because a slight accent

[5] Stoyan Christowe, "Half an American," *Outlook and Independent*, CLIII (December, 1929), 531, 557.

or other feature may brand him as foreign-born. He may consider a return to his native heath—many have tried it—but it has not worked successfully. Joseph S. Roucek expressed himself thus:

> I am living in a sort of spiritual vacuum, which provides no background, and which makes me feel that I am lacking that great feeling of belonging —something which every human being has to lean on for support. Or, to be more concrete, the more I try to become Americanized to the satisfaction of the 100 per cent Americans, the more I am reminded intentionally and even maliciously by various persons and circumstances that I might be legally a citizen of this country, but in heredity I still remain and always will be considered a foreigner. . . . .
>
> I have revisited my native country from time to time, and even considered remaining there to pursue my career. But not many days passed by in Prague when I became keenly aware of the reactions of the good Czechoslovaks who felt that I did not belong to their group either. The fact is I do not understand some of their psychological processes and much of their behavior—nor do they mine. For I have become Americanized to the extent of being somewhat unable to understand the viewpoint of my former compatriots. In addition, it is quite plainly indicated that I am not wanted any more.[6]

Marginal man defined. Robert E. Park coined the apt expression "the marginal man" for the one who must live in two worlds at the same time.[7] The marginal man may be defined as a person who occupies an intermediate position between two cultural groups; he is on the margin between two cultures or societies that are in conflict and never completely interpenetrate and fuse. He is, in the words of Dr. Park,

> a cultural hybrid, a man living and sharing intimately in the cultural life and traditions of two distinct peoples; never quite willing to break, even if he were permitted to do so, with his past and his traditions, and not

[6] J. S. Roucek, "The Problem of Becoming Americanized," *Sociology and Social Research,* XVII (January–February, 1933), 243–44.

[7] "Human Migration and the Marginal Man," *American Journal of Sociology,* XXXIII (May, 1928), 881–93. The idea has been carried farther by Everett V. Stonequist, *The Marginal Man: A Study in Personality and Culture Conflict* (New York, 1937), and "The Problem of the Marginal Man," *American Journal of Sociology,* XLI (July, 1935), 1–12.

quite accepted[8] . . . . in the new society in which he now sought to find a place.[9]

As Wirth puts it, "He stands on the map of two worlds, not at home in either. His self is divided between the world that he has deserted and the world that will have none of him."[10]

Everett V. Stonequist defines the marginal man as

> one who is poised in psychological uncertainty between two (or more) social worlds; reflecting in his soul the discords and harmonies, repulsions and attractions of these worlds, one of which is often "dominant" over the other; within which membership is implicitly if not explicitly based upon birth or ancestry (race or nationality); and where exclusion removes the individual from a system of group relations.[11]

"He is called on by the situation," says Kimball Young, "to participate in two divergent sets of ideas, attitudes, and habits."[12] But these can no more live together peaceably in any one man's mind than the two cultural groups can live in the same neighborhood without friction. Cultural conflict thus splits the individual's self. So far as it is possible the marginal man must identify himself with both cultures. He must participate in and must make himself so much a part of each that he is able to take the point of view of either culture toward the other.

Inner conflict felt. Since there are divergences in these two points of view the marginal man feels the conflict of the two cultures within himself. According to Stonequist,

> By conflict is meant a relationship between two groups which involves attitudes of superiority, contempt, prejudice, etc., on the part of the more

[8] W. O. Brown makes a slightly stronger statement. He puts it: "If he is accepted in the dominant group he does not become marginal. But, if, as is usually the case, he is refused admittance into the social order of the dominant group, he does become a marginal type. His marginality is a function, on the one hand, of his assimilation to the culture of the dominant group and, on the other hand, of the refusal of this same group to accept him as an equal." In E. B. Reuter (editor), *Race and Culture Contacts* (New York, 1934), p. 44. By permission of McGraw-Hill Book Company, publishers.

[9] *American Journal of Sociology,* XXXIII (May, 1928), 892.

[10] L. Wirth, *op. cit.,* p. 265.

[11] E. V. Stonequist, *op. cit.,* p. 8.

[12] From Young's *An Introductory Sociology* (New York, 1934), p. 512. Copyright. Used by permission of American Book Company, publishers.

powerful group toward the weaker group. These attitudes may find open and blatant expression or they may be subtly expressed by a reserve. The marginal individual is one who has ties of origin, either through one or both parents, with the weaker or minority group, and who has also come to identify himself in some way with the dominant group. Because he has this double identification with the two groups in conflict he experiences in his own mind the external cultural conflict.[13]

The marginal man feels the struggle within himself and often the conflict is a bitter one. Anzia Yezierska makes vivid the tragedy of living a dual life in her own immigrant home and in the American community. "My greatest tragedy in life is that I always see the two opposite sides at the same time. What seems to me right one day seems all wrong the next. Not only that, but many things seem right and wrong at the same time." [14]

The conflict became increasingly acute until she decided to break away from the old life. But this did not settle all and bring happiness. Said she:

I can't live with the old world, and I'm yet too green for the new. I don't belong to those who gave me birth or to those with whom I was educated. . . . . I'm one of the millions of immigrant children, children of loneliness, wandering between worlds that are at once too old and too new to live in.[15]

Jewish immigrants in particular have lived on the fringe of two inconsistent worlds where they have been torn by inner conflicts. Some who have felt cramped by the seemingly narrow life within the ghetto walls have tried to escape. Certain ones, in order to make the break complete have become converts to other faiths, but disillusioned and broken by coldness and unresponsiveness outside, they have returned to the warmth and intimacy of the ghetto.[16] They belonged to two worlds, but found satisfaction in neither. A

[13] *The Marginal Man: A Study in the Subjective Aspects of Cultural Conflict*, unpublished dissertation, University of Chicago, 1930, p. 307.

[14] Anzia Yezierska, *Children of Loneliness* (New York, 1923), p. 114. Cf. also pp. 114–16.

[15] *Ibid.*, pp. 122–23.

[16] Cf. *American Journal of Sociology*, XXXIII (July, 1927), 62, 70.

person in this situation is "a man with two souls, a man without a country." [17] Park says of these Jews:

> It is not easy, in the long run it is impossible, for those who have once gone out, ever to return. . . . . The result is, however, that they are obsessed with a sense of moral isolation; they feel themselves not quite at home either in the Gentile or the Jewish world. Life goes on outwardly as it did before, but they are possessed by insatiable restlessness, and a "secret anguish" gnaws at the core of their existence.[18]

At times, to be sure, the immigrant is not conscious of the "double life" he is living. He is unaware of his assimilation and, when the course of his life runs smoothly, there is no difficulty. But a crisis situation arises and the conflict becomes painfully evident. He has been gradually moving closer to America, but this shock startles him and he finds that he has not uprooted the old loyalties even though, for the time being, they have been dormant. The conflict comes to the surface.

Oftentimes these ambivalent attitudes result in a swinging back and forth between the two loyalties. Ravage reveals the alternating currents of enthusiasm and depression in his fellow countrymen. So long as they could display rolls of dollar bills, they would indulge in big talk at the coffee houses and boast of their prosperity. But a slight reverse in their economic fortunes changed the tune—America would be cursed while a longing for the fleshpots of the native village would become overpowering. One moment they would sing the praises of the "all-right country" and the next swear that it was the worst stronghold of fakes in all the world.[19]

Many, perhaps most, immigrants do not go beyond this stage in the assimilative process. They do not understand in any thorough

[17] L. Wirth, *op. cit.*, p. 267.

[18] R. E. Park, "Behind Our Masks," *Survey Graphic* LVI (May 1, 1926), 136. Some Jews, however, avoid such unpleasant experiences; they live in the ghetto for years and do not know it. They are so circumscribed and are so much an integral part of the ghetto life that they are unaware of its existence. It is through some chance contact that they discover the outside world, and in that same discovery they become aware of the ghetto. Then they are shocked and flee. Cf. L. Wirth, *op. cit.*, pp. 241–43.

[19] M. E. Ravage, *op. cit.*, pp. 83–85. For a case of vacillation, see life history of an Italian immigrant in H. G. Duncan, *op. cit.*, pp. 565–73.

way the life of America; they live in two conflicting worlds, but belong to neither.

Marginality and maladjustment. The marginal man in his unstable position between two conflicting cultures is under a great strain and he is in grave danger of becoming maladjusted.[20] The maladjustment may be an inner one and so well concealed that others do not notice it. Ravage gives an insight into his malaise and despondency. For a long time, while at the University, he was in the depths of the blues and contemplated suicide. The only step he took toward committing the act, however, was the writing of a vivid portrayal of the procedure and of the regrets of his fellow students for the uncharitable treatment they had accorded him.[21]

On the other hand, the terrific struggle often eventuates in overt behavior and brings tragedy in its wake; it may demoralize the person resulting in bitterness,[22] unrestrained dissipation, crime, suicide, or mental breakdown.

The intensity of the mental conflict and the degree of disorganization varies with the situation and with the individual. Where the cultural divergence is comparatively slight usually the disturbance is not serious. There are, to be sure, acute cases even in groups of close cultural kinship, but they are exceptional. Immigrants from southeastern Europe as a rule have more intense inner struggles.[23]

[20] Cf. E. V. Stonequist, *The Marginal Man: A Study in Personality and Culture Conflict,* pp. 201–09.

[21] M. E. Ravage, *op. cit.,* p. 210.

[22] Ludwig Lewisohn's autobiography *Up Stream* depicts a divided self that wavered between the warm security of the ghetto and the cold freedom of the outside world. He could not completely abandon the former, even though he tried to do so, and he was ill at ease in the latter. When this conflict did not resolve in a satisfying way, he became bitter and cynical. Cf. also *Mid-Channel* (New York, 1929), *Israel* (New York, 1925), and *The Island Within* (New York, 1928).

Heinrich Heine, while not an immigrant to America, is an excellent example of a person in "spiritual distress." He was torn by conflicting loyalties as he struggled to be a German and a Jew at the same time. The tragedy of living in these two conflicting worlds made his writings reek with bitterness and revolt. There was evidence of spiritual conflict and instability. His biographer says of him: "His arms were weak because his mind was divided; his hands were nerveless because his soul was in turmoil." Lewis Browne, *That Man Heine* (New York, 1927), p. 252. Cf. also pp. 251–56 on the inner conflict.

[23] Edward Bok (*The Americanization of Edward Bok*) and Michael Pupin (*From Immigrant to Inventor*) are examples of these groups. The Jew usually encounters conflict-generating difficulties. Cf. Abraham Myerson, "The Nervousness of the Jew," *Mental Hygiene,* IV (January, 1920), 65–72.

The Oriental brings a culture which differs more markedly than that of any of the European groups, in addition to which his physical traits set him apart and restrict his participation in American life. The presence and intensity of the prejudice encountered will have a marked affect upon conflict and may tend to prolong the stage of marginality.

The immigrant differs strikingly from a child in a native American home. The child takes over the culture with the very air he breathes, as it were, and knows no difficulty until he is exposed to outside influences. The immigrant, however, has grown up in one culture and is now called upon to take over a different one, but he can never become a 100 per cent American.[24] He remains on the margin between the two cultures. The native child knows what is right—he follows the conventional behavior without effort. The immigrant, however, who is pulled in two directions often, as a Russian found, has no clear idea of what to do.

> There is ever that impelling thought: Did I do right to take out the papers? Then I argue with myself that by renouncing Bolshevism I am not giving up my Russian culture. Shall I like this country? Only time can tell. Now I know only the contradictory feelings that constantly occupy me and cry out: "So help me God" and "Russia, will you forgive me?"[25]

The immigrant's behavior may be highly individualized, and individualized behavior in contrast to conventionalized behavior, may be immoral or anti-social.[26]

[24] This is illustrated frequently by the partiality shown to persons belonging to the same ethnic group. A second-generation Jew wrote: "My parents take keen pride in any Jewish person who succeeds in attracting the attention of the world. Eugene Debs is my father's ideal. My father wouldn't be paid to attend one of the modern football games, but yet, when the famous Hakaoh Soccer Team of Vienna, composed of all-Jewish players, came to America and won game after game from all-star combinations, he paid a good price to see them play in Philadelphia, even though he knew nothing of the game. He took a personal pride in the conquests of Benny Leonard, the undefeated, retired lightweight boxing champion of the world, who is Jewish." Unpublished life history. *The Jewish Daily Forward* of February 25, 1925, gives a long list of Jews who made records in the pugilistic arena. This is quoted in L. Wirth, *The Ghetto,* pp. 252–53.

[25] H. G. Duncan, *op. cit.,* p. 600.

[26] Individualized behavior is characteristic of the marginal man wherever he may be found. Cf. Felix M. Keesing, *Modern Samoa* (Stanford University, 1934), p. 439, for the marginal man in Samoa.

The marginal man is often hypersensitive—his self-consciousness develops raw edges. As Kimball Young puts it, "He grows suspicious, sometimes almost to the point of paranoia. He broods over slights to himself and to his race or nationality group." [27] He does not fully understand American behavior and oftentimes imputes wrong meanings to actions. He interprets some act, common in American life, as a snub or insult. The immigrant who has to step down in the social and economic scale is particularly sensitive as he idealizes the old situation and compares it with his present condition.

Contributions of the marginal man. While the marginal man creates problems, particularly when he becomes disorganized and demoralized, yet, on the other hand, he makes valuable contributions. His very hypersensitiveness makes him a keener observer than the complacent and self-satisfied native. He often becomes an effective critic [28] of the shallowness,[29] hypocrisy, and inconsistencies in American life.[30] An immigrant from England gave us this:

> Money is slavery. . . . . At any rate, it is not the kind of power I want. Most of you industrial Americans overrate the value of money or of the material things which it buys. Your higher standard of living as you proudly call it, does not seem so all-satisfying to me. Life has to yield me more than a competence or even an abundance of things necessary or desirable. But I suppose it is useless to discuss it.[31]

An immigrant from Mexico indicates his reaction:

> One of my greatest disappointments while in the United States has been these "Christians." There are many people in America who claim that

[27] From Young's *Introductory Sociology* (New York, 1934), p. 513. Copyright. Used by permission of American Book Company, publishers.

[28] Cf. E. V. Stonequist, *The Marginal Man: A Study in Personality and Culture Conflict*, pp. 154–55.

[29] A Dutch immigrant said: "There is one way in which I want my children to differ from the general run of Americans: I want them to be deeper individual thinkers than the average American is. I believe most Americans leave the deep thinking to a few leaders and are governed by mob psychology." Unpublished life history.

[30] In reading the autobiographies by immigrants, such as Ravage, Lewisohn, Panunzio, Hasanovitz, Steiner, etc., one finds much wholesome and well-founded criticism of American life.

[31] Frederick Philip Grove, *A Search for America* (New York, 1928), p. 299. Reprinted by permission of The Ryerson Press, present publishers. Cf. Anzia Yezierska, *Children of Loneliness*, pp. 25–28.

they are "Christians." The larger per cent are business men. They claim God blessed them and made them wealthy. They go to church to pray for pardon for their sins and the opportunity to deceive more people during the week. Or they starve healthy girls in their stores, paying them a meager salary of eight dollars a week and later they build homes and schools for these same girls. Sometimes these girls contract some disease and are unable to care for themselves. They are sent to these institutions built by these "Christians" who robbed them of their health. This is an inconsistency that I cannot understand. I have no use for such "Christians." [32]

From his marginal position the immigrant is in a situation to compare and evaluate. In the new country he had to develop a different set of habits and in that process deliberation was necessary.[33] The native, on the other hand, accepts the enveloping culture unconsciously. The immigrant, as a stranger, can be more objective. "Because he is not rooted in the peculiar attitudes and biased tendencies of the group," says Simmel, "he stands apart from all these with the peculiar attitude of the 'objective,' which does not indicate simply a separation and disinterestedness but is a peculiar composition of nearness and remoteness, concern and indifference." [34]

The immigrant, as a stranger, is also relatively free from conventions. He has left behind his old environment with its traditional controls. Since he has accommodated himself only to the externalities in American life he neither knows nor feels the pressure of the proprieties and local conventions. Since he has not been given full *entrée* into the primary-group life of the native Americans, he is not expected to live according to their standards. "He is the freer man," in the words of Simmel, "practically and theoretically; he examines the relations with less prejudice; he submits them to more general, more objective, standards, and is not confined in his action by custom, piety, or precedents." [35]

[32] Unpublished life history.

[33] Cf. E. V. Stonequist, *The Marginal Man: A Study in Personality and Culture Conflict*, pp. 155–56.

[34] Quoted in R. E. Park and E. W. Burgess, *Introduction to the Science of Sociology*, p. 324.

[35] Quoted in R. E. Park and E. W. Burgess, *op. cit.*, pp. 324–25.

Because of his enigmatic position, the marginal man may be stimulated to creative activity.[36] The uncertainty of the dual life makes it necessary to take thought.[37] As Stonequist puts it,

> To be poised between two groups demands mental agility. The individual is not permitted to come to rest and possibly vegetate. The necessity for continual adjustment prods the mental functions into swift activity. There may be pain and even tragedy at times—but there is also interest and excitement.[38]

The marginal man plays an important interpretative rôle between two groups because he understands them both. Rebekah Kohut, as an example, was marginal and had rather free access to both cultures. In that situation she did much to interpret Americans and Jews to each other.[39]

The marginal man plays an important rôle in the fusion of cultures.[40] According to Stonequist,

> It is in his mind that the cultures come together, conflict and eventually work out some kind of mutual adjustment and interpenetration. He is the crucible of cultural fusion. His life history recapitulates something of the processes described in the race relations cycle; [41] at first he is

[36] Reactionary organizations like the Ku Klux Klan usually do not develop out of a marginal situation. The marginal man's objectivity saves him from such a social myopia.

[37] This may account for the intellectual achievements of the Jew.

[38] E. V. Stonequist, *The Marginal Man: A Study in the Subjective Aspects of Cultural Conflicts,* unpublished dissertation, University of Chicago, p. 94.

[39] Cf. *op. cit., passim.* The value of the marginal man became evident in an immigrant community. "They must have churches and must have ministers who could speak Dutch. There were but two ways in which they could obtain enough men for these pulpits. One was to bring them from the Netherlands, and this was attempted but with indifferent success. The other was to train in the West men who were themselves immigrants and who knew and could meet the needs of the people. Time has abundantly proved that this was the wiser plan." A. J. Pieters, *op. cit.,* p. 136. Jerome Davis says of immigrant religious workers among the Russians and Ruthenians who have been trained in America, "They can reach the hearts of their fellow-countrymen as almost no one else can." From *Russians and Ruthenians in America* by Jerome Davis, copyright, 1922, by Doubleday, Doran and Company, Inc., New York, p. 94. Cf. A. Mangano, *op. cit.,* pp. 182–90, for church leadership among the Italians.

[40] This has become evident in the Hawaiian Islands. Cf. W. C. Smith, "The Hybrid in Hawaii as a Marginal Man," *American Journal of Sociology,* XXXIX (January, 1934), 459–68; E. V. Stonequist, "The Marginal Man in Hawaii," *Social Process in Hawaii,* May, 1935, pp. 18–20.

[41] According to Robert E. Park, "In the relations of races there is a cycle of events which tends everywhere to repeat itself. . . . The race relations cycle which takes

unaware of the cultural conflict going on; then through some experience or series of experiences he becomes aware of it and the external conflict finds an echo in his mind; and finally, he tries and sometimes succeeds in making some kind of adjustment to his situation.

As he learns that his personal destiny is linked with a cultural conflict which he did not create, he seeks to find some way out of his predicament. In these efforts at personal salvation he consciously or unconsciously includes or affects the interests of others involved in the situation. His efforts at adjustment make him an innovator or leader in the larger process of cultural fusion. Whether he takes the rôle of the nationalist or functions as a conciliator, interpreter, teacher, or reformer, he plays a part in promoting acculturation.[42]

The marginal man tends to become a leader. When the dominant group refuses to accept him he begins to deliberate. In the words of W. O. Brown,

This refusal impugns his personal status, violates his ego, makes him race conscious. As a sophisticated and educated person he resents being treated as an outcast.[43] In time, unable to penetrate the social order of the upper race, he turns to his own masses, who likewise are victimized by the situation creating the marginal man. He articulates their grievances and, as their experiences and aspirations become increasingly similar to his, they respond to his leadership.[44]

the form, to state it abstractly, of contacts, competition, accommodation and eventual assimilation, is apparently progressive and irretrievable." For fuller discussion, see *Survey Graphic,* LVI (May, 1926), 196.

[42] *The Marginal Man: A Study in the Subjective Aspects of Cultural Conflicts,* unpublished dissertation, University of Chicago, p. 315. Cf. E. V. Stonequist, *The Marginal Man: A Study in Personality and Culture Conflict,* pp. 221–22.

[43] An immigrant wrote: "A few days ago my wife and I offered a concert to our local club, the members of which I have known for the last three years. The following was the introduction of the chairman: 'We are extremely glad to have with us two foreign artists from Czechoslovakia.' The sentiment of such an introduction was fully appreciated by us, though the fact that we were brought to the plane of a foreigner was somewhat resented by me. That, of course, immediately reminds one that he is nothing more than an outsider." *Sociology and Social Research,* XVII (January–February, 1933), 244.

[44] In E. B. Reuter (editor), *Race and Culture Contacts* (New York, 1934), p. 44. By permission of McGraw-Hill Book Company.

CHAPTER XIX

THE SECOND GENERATION

Our concern in the following chapters is with the American-born children of immigrant parentage. In reality, however, we must include children who were born in the old country and came here in infancy or early childhood—those who have no memories of the Old World and culturally, though not physically, are of American birth. They are in the same situation as children born on American soil; they have the same problems to face, except in the case of groups not eligible to citizenship. Foreign-born Chinese and Japanese [1] who came here as infants may not become citizens, while Italian, Lithuanian, Bulgarian, and other children from Europe may be naturalized and enjoy the full rights and privileges of American citizenship.

Numerical significance. Comparatively little has been written on the second generation. On the basis of the available literature one might conclude that this group is relatively of slight importance. Numerically, at least, it is significant. In our population of 123 million about thirty million belong to this second generation.[2] Although nearly all of them are faced by certain common problems, they do not form a homogeneous aggregation and roughly may be broken into several age groups, each with some outstanding characteristics. The age group, 45 and over, totaled more than five and one quarter million in 1930. The vast majority of these are of "old" immigrant stock and because of length of residence and similarity of culture

[1] Cf. Kazuo Kawai, "Three Roads, and None Easy," *Survey,* LVI (May 1, 1926), 164–66, for a Japanese who came to America at the age of six.

[2] According to the Census of 1930 the total population of the United States was 122,775,046. There were 26,082,129 native born of foreign or mixed parentage. To this number should be added those who came in infancy, but numerical data are lacking. Furthermore, when we add the increase by births since the 1930 census we may safely set the total at thirty million.

they are now quite thoroughly assimilated. The second group, 25 to 44, in the most active period of life passes seven and one half million. While those in the top of this bracket are largely of the "old" immigration there is a tapering off toward the lower years. Although this group has much in common with the one above 45 years, it has been touched more closely by the disturbances of the World War. Changed conditions in the Old World and the exaggerated patriotism in America affected their parental homes and retarded their assimilation. The age group, 15 to 24, numbering more than five and one quarter million has its source very largely in the "new" immigration. Members of this group were either born after the beginning of the World War or were small children and thus have lived practically all their lives in a rapidly changing world. The age group below 15, with a total approaching seven and one half million, was born since the outbreak of the War and their parents belong almost exclusively to the "new" immigration.

These thirty millions are the offspring of immigrants representing a wide diversity of ethnic groups. That fact alone is of great significance. What will this heterogeneous group do to America?

Cultural significance. It is becoming evident that out of this welter of cultural backgrounds are coming influences that will touch us on every hand. When the parents were reared in the old-world culture and the children are conditioned by American ways of life, there is considerable likelihood that the two generations will find it impossible to see eye to eye. Ancestral habits and attitudes are prone to be misunderstood and unappreciated by the native generation. Likewise the parents usually fail to comprehend the outlook of their Americanized children. This chasm between parents and child has made comradeship and parental guidance impossible and has been no small factor in the comparatively high rate of delinquency and crime among the native-born. The problem of crime alone should be sufficient to direct attention to this group.

Furthermore, another development is bringing the second generation into the lime light. According to one writer, this group is taking over the rule of our large cities and is not doing it entirely on the basis of altruistic motives.

The employees were not in the socialist sense class-conscious. The great majority of them were trying to climb the ladder of conventional success. But they had become keenly conscious of an assumption on the part of the older stock that it owned the country. The new Americans were aware that the old stock did not wish them to dispute its leadership, or to ruffle the smooth perfection of its traditions or vulgarly to interfere with its plans for their social and political betterment. They resented this attitude and they showed their resentment unequivocally and effectively. They will . . . . keep on showing it in the future more frequently and more generally than they have in the past. These upstart half-breed Americans seem destined to rule the larger American cities, for many years in spite of the discomfiture, the dismay and the intellectual protests of the former ruling class.[3]

Peculiar problems of second generation. Decreasing immigration has made it possible to focus greater attention upon the second generation and its problems, and it is significant that articles, chapters, and even books on the second generation have begun to appear.[4] Old agencies and institutions are gradually shifting their activities from the immigrant group to the second generation.[5] New organizations are also developing to assist these young people in making wholesome adjustments to our life. According to E. C. Sartorio,

The second generation needs special attention . . . . for to it belong those who stand in the greatest need of guidance. They are neither fish nor flesh. They have not the traditions and the love of the old country and they imperfectly possess the traditions of the new one. . . . . American freedom is dangerous to youth of Italian blood. That is why, according to experts on immigration questions, the second generation is the one which should be most carefully trained. They represent the period of transition; they are at a critical stage of development similar to that of adolescence.[6]

[3] "Rise of the New American," *New Republic*, XXX (May 10, 1922), 301–02.

[4] A selected bibliography on the second generation may be consulted in the appendix.

[5] The Foreign Language Information Service is centering largely on the second generation. The Y.W.C.A. has also made considerable adaptations.

[6] E. C. Sartorio, *op. cit.*, pp. 69–71.

To ignore this second generation group which comprises about one fourth of our total population and to remain ignorant of its problems and of those created by its presence in our country is neither a wise nor a practical public policy. Much attention has been paid to the immigrant but practically none to his American-born children. In the words of John Valentine, "The hardships endured by the immigrant have often been pictured, but the mental agonies undergone by the children of immigrants, born in the United States but of old-world citizens, are ten times more poignant." [7] As Eugene Lyons puts it:

> Hard as may be the accommodation of the first generation of aliens to the American environment, it is not so tragic as that of the second generation. The Swede or Greek or Russian just arrived may retire into himself and into the group of which he is a part—tens of thousands of them do this despite the almost compulsory proselytism attempted from time to time. They remain essentially unchanged. But a deeper, more harrowing struggle awaits the child of alien parents born into an alien home in America. Unavoidably in school, in the streets, in the moving-picture theater, in the cheap reading matter it finds that which the people at home cannot understand no matter how hard they try.[8]

If the immigrant finds a certain situation intolerable he may move away from it, but his child is practically helpless. If the immigrant is mistreated by Americans he may retreat to the colony of his compatriots where he will find a warm welcome and needed counsel. But his child—that's different! Members of the ethnic community cannot understand him and revile him for behavior at variance with their code, and on the other hand the Americans ridicule him and call him a "Wop," a "Sheenie," or a "Dago." And there is no peace within his soul!

Marginality of the second generation. A member of the second-generation group is the marginal man *par excellence*. Theodore Abel wrote of a group in a New England community:

[7] John Valentine, "Of the Second Generation," *The Survey*, XLVII (March 18, 1922), 956.

[8] Eugene Lyons, "Second Generation Aliens," *The Nation*, CXVI (April 25, 1923), 490.

The young Poles . . . . are no longer Polish, since they lack the feeling of allegiance to the Polish community; nor are they Americans since they are excluded from social intercourse with the natives. They do not belong to either society but rather form a society of their own, unorganized, it is true, and without purpose, but enough to satisfy their desire for response.[9]

Pauline V. Young presents a case which illustrates vividly the marginality.

You see, we young people live in two worlds,[10] and learn the ways of both worlds—the ways of our parents and the ways of the big world. Sometimes we get mixed up and we fight, we fight our parents and we fight the big world. Sometimes I feel I am not much of an American. I was raised by Russians, I understand Russians, I like Russians. At other times, I think that I am not much of a Russian; except to my parents, I never speak Russian, and all my friends are Americans. Well, I am American, we live in America—why shouldn't we take their ways? When my parents object to my American friends, I say: "I work with them. I do everything with them; why shouldn't I go out with them?" Then they come back at me and say: "Why don't you sleep with them?" They think they would disgust me with Americans, but I get mad and say: "Well, I will!" and they have nothing more to say.

I almost always have a good comeback. I say: "This isn't Russia. When you go to Russia, you can be Russians; but you can't be Russians in America." I have learned American ways. I can't go against my friends and do the Russian way. . . . .

Many times I get mad, and then I leave the house. You see, I don't want to hurt my parents and still I want to live like I see is right—that is, right according to American ways. They can't see it my way, and I can't see it their way.[11]

[9] E. deS. Brunner, *op. cit.*, p. 242.

[10] This condition is not restricted to one or two groups but is quite general. An Eastfriesian said: "I grew up in two cultures: On the one side was the school life and the intimate contacts with the friends and playmates of the school and playground. Even during the summer vacations my only daily companions were from the English-speaking homes, few of whom attended church or Sunday School regularly. On the other side was the church group. Consequently I was on the margin between the two—more German than the playmates in one group, and more Americanized than my companions of the other group." J. A. Saathoff, *The Eastfriesians,* unpublished dissertation, University of Iowa.

[11] P. V. Young, *op. cit.*, pp. 114, 115. See also pp. 114–18, the entire case from which these excerpts were taken. Another document illustrating the marginality is found on pp. 160–74 which ends thus: "It sure is strange. I don't like to live like

Dr. Young comments on this document:

The old and the new are plainly at war in Alex. The conflict is irrepressible and bitter, but inevitable. Reflection makes the issues intelligible to him, and at the same time intensifies the struggle. Emotional attachments to his home are not to be destroyed at will,[12] even though there should be a desire for such a rupture. His mental conflict is the precise counterpart of the social conflict into which life has precipitated him.[13]

When the factor of race is added to that of culture difference, the situation becomes more complicated. An American-born Japanese girl in a college of California gives an insight into their marginality.

We belong to two groups, the Japanese and the American. In ancestry and in physical appearance we are Japanese, while in birth, in education, in ideals, and in ways of thinking we are Americans. Nevertheless, the older Japanese will not accept us into their group because, as they see us, we are too independent, too pert, and too self-confident, and the Americans bar us from their group because we retain the yellow skin and flat nose of the Oriental. Thus we stand on the border line that separates the Orient from the Occident. Though on each side of us flow the streams of two great civilizations—the old Japanese culture with its formal traditions and customs and the newer American civilization with its freedom and individualism—the chance to perceive and to imbibe the best things from each has been withheld from us.[14]

It is in this second-generation marginal person that the culture conflict rages most bitterly. The immigrant has a past in which he can live, but the youth cannot sail his barque into any such sheltering cove. Stern wrote:

my mother does, but I can't live like the Americans. Sometimes I think I am 'advanced,' as my parents say; but sometimes I just don't fit in anywhere." Chapter VIII, in its entirety, pp. 160–83, brings out the culture conflict and marginality.

[12] Anzia Yezierska, in *Arrogant Beggars* (New York, 1927), shows the dualism. This is a novel of a New York born Polish girl who worked and struggled to improve her status. She left the Polish people in the slums for a time and had an opportunity to break away, but she was not perfectly at ease among the outsiders. Her heart was with her own people; she had her roots there and could not leave. In the tenements were warm hearts that understood her and it was there she found her real life.

[13] *Op. cit.*, pp. 117–18.

[14] W. C. Smith, *Americans in Process: A Study of Our Citizens of Oriental Ancestry*, p. 250.

Father could not even see that what I hated nor why I loathed it. . . . . As he said, all his friends, his synagogue, were in the neighborhood. All his memories during the last eighteen years were centred in those crooked streets. Mother could not alter him. For him the ghetto, so real to me and to other young people like me, does not exist. For father lives in a world altogether cut off from the world about him; his is a world of the past, a world built by the ancient rabbis in whose footsteps he walks. He said to me one day slowly, "I belong to the fifteenth century—and you, my daughter, to the twentieth." Mother and I could not make him understand.[15]

Most immigrant parents realize that they cannot go far in America. If they can get on tolerably well and can live more comfortably than in the old country, they are satisfied. The children, however, make contacts with American life at more points and are desirous of gaining a status higher than that held by their parents. The school stirs them and sets high goals for them, but obstacles of different kinds hinder and mental conflicts arise. At times this struggle becomes all the more bitter because of parental urging and stimuli to move on and up. This pain of marginality, however, is one of the prices which the younger generation must pay that we may advance.

15 From E. G. Stern, *My Mother and I* (New York, 1917), pp. 139–40. By permission of The Macmillan Company, publishers.

CHAPTER XX

BEHAVIOR OF THE SECOND GENERATION

Members of the second generation often behave in "outlandish" ways, neither like Americans nor like their immigrant parents. A Russian newspaper in Pennsylvania carried this item:

It is a sad occurrence, but it illustrates that some of our youth, even when born here, are not really Americanized. They do imitate Americans, but do not strive to inhale the very spirit of true Americanism. They take what is worst in the American youth, instead of getting the best and noblest traits. . . . . As a result, our youth is neither Russian nor American. It is a mixture of stupidity and pomposity.[1]

An editorial in a Polish paper presents the more vulgar characteristics of the youthful group:

A young Pole reared in a Polish-American environment . . . is neither a Pole nor an American in any genuine sense of either word, but a species of transitional being. . . . . Having heard a great deal about liberty in America, he translates the notion into a license to do what he likes. He is impertinent and disagreeable to everybody (except to the policeman who carries a club and can put him in jail), and his behavior toward other people is such as to make a farmhand in the old country blush with shame. He thinks it perfectly proper to snub his parents, who are nothing but ignorant foreigners in his estimation, while he is a modern and progressive young person. He sneers with contempt at Poland, its language and civilization. All this makes him feel vastly superior to his elders and he accompanies this display of his emancipation with oaths that would astonish a pirate and with a talent for long-distance spitting that would make a professional marksman gasp. Doubtless he believes that all this is American and calculated to win him the approbation of Americans. How should he know, poor soul, that decent Americans have

[1] Quoted by Josephine Roche in *National Conference of Social Work*, 1921, p. 483.

a great deal more respect for a Pole who is genuinely and unaffectedly a Pole.[2]

Ravage tells of the behavior of the younger generation of Roumanian Jews in New York City. Since they had learned more of American life than their elders, they assumed an attitude of superiority and threw off parental restraint. They copied crudities of all kinds. They made love on park benches, according to the American pattern, and thronged the dance halls. Houses of prostitution drew recruits from the ignorant and "untamed daughters" of immigrants. Jewish young men were becoming delinquent and criminal.[3]

A second-generation Mennonite recounts how the younger group invented an institution unlike anything either in the immigrant or American culture in order to circumvent the taboo of the parental group which would keep the youth of both sexes from intermingling.

To give the whole problem of acquaintance a semi-legal status in the community, the young people devised the so-called "crowd" at which the "sins of youth" could be indulged in *en masse* without throwing the burden of responsibility on any particular individual. Not even the host was held accountable because the "crowd" was generally a self-invited affair. In an invisible way the word would be passed around that there would be a "crowd" at such and such a place—usually on a Sunday evening. When the appointed evening came, young people from far and wide arrived at the designated home. Everybody was there, invited or otherwise, and then the fun commenced. Since this was everyone's affair, and no one was responsible, convention was somewhat thrown to the wind. So-called swinging games were in special favor. Since dancing was tabooed, these games were not called dances—so much the better—for a dance generally follows a more or less conventionalized form, but a swinging game is catch-as-catch-can, and the fine balmy darkness of the summer night furnished an excellent setting. As the night advanced, the

[2] *Kuryer Polski,* Milwaukee. Quoted by E. B. Reuter and C. W. Hart, *Introduction to Sociology* (New York, 1933), p. 374. By permission of McGraw-Hill Book Company, Inc., publishers. Cf. also E. deS. Brunner, *op. cit.,* pp. 241–43.

[3] M. E. Ravage, *op. cit.,* pp. 79–80. Cf. L. Lewisohn, *Upstream,* pp. 287–88, for some interesting contrasts between immigrants and their sons. C. M. Panunzio, *The Soul of an Immigrant,* p. 255.

"crowd" became hilarious. Couples paired off from time to time, and there occurred much of what was called "schmugen" (necking).[4]

Park and Miller point out that "the term 'Americanization' is not used popularly among the immigrants as we use it. They call a badly demoralized boy 'completely Americanized.' "[5] This, however, need occasion no surprise when we observe the behavior of the second generation youth.

Delinquency. Not all children of immigrants become disorganized and demoralized, but the number is sufficiently large to arouse considerable apprehension. The behavior has a wide range, all the way from slight disagreements with parents to serious offenses which require court action.

Even though no adequate statistical data are available, it has been quite generally agreed that the criminality of the second generation of immigrant parentage exceeds that of the immigrant group and of the native born of native parentage. Certain samples and special studies have supported this contention. According to L. G. Brown, juvenile delinquency and vagrancy on the part of the second generation of Irish and German parentage had become a problem in 1850. "Of the fifteen hundred truant and vagrant children in Boston in 1850, slightly over ninety per cent were from foreign homes."[6] Breckenridge and Abbott found that 72.8 per cent of the 14,183 delinquent children brought before the Juvenile Court in Chicago between July 1, 1899, and June 30, 1909, had foreign-born parents.[7] A special study of 584 boys in this group showed that 66.9 per cent had foreign-born parents.[8]

A comparison of the nativity of these wards of the Court with the married persons in each population group in Chicago indicated that the number of parents of delinquent children in the foreign-born group was disproportionately high. The foreign-born constituted 57.0 per cent of the married population of Chicago, while at least 67.0 per cent of the parents of the delinquent boys were of

[4] Unpublished life history.

[5] *Op. cit.*, pp. 288–89.

[6] Lawrence Guy Brown, *Immigration* (New York, 1933), p. 109.

[7] Edith Abbott and Sophonisba Breckenridge, *The Delinquent Child and the Home* (New York, 1912), p. 57.

[8] *Ibid.*, p. 61.

foreign birth.[9] A Census Bureau study showed a higher ratio of commitments for those of foreign or mixed parentage than for those of native parentage in the age-group from 10 to 17 years. The number per 100,000 of the same parentage and age-group was 153.3 for those of foreign or mixed parentage and 99.8 for those of native parentage,[10] making a coefficient of difference of 1.5. The Immigration Commission also supported this when it stated that the statistics indicated "the American-born children of immigrants exceed the children of natives in the relative amount of crime." [11] Dr. Clairette P. Armstrong's data from the Children's Court of New York City for 1930 assign the highest ratio of delinquency to the native-born of foreign parents.[12] On the basis of the inmates of the Massachusetts Reformatory the Gluecks concluded:

Clearly our figures bear out the proposition that native-born sons of foreign-born parents contribute considerably more than their share to the criminal ranks. There are two and a half times (53%:22%) as many persons native-born of foreign or mixed parentage in our Reformatory group as are found in the general population.[13]

In their later study of 1,000 cases the Gluecks found the native sons of one or both foreign parents had the highest delinquency rate. Next in order came the native sons of native parents and the foreign-born children of immigrant parentage had the lowest rate.[14]

Alida C. Bowler wrote:

Practically every law-enforcement officer who was interviewed in the course of this study, whether he were a police officer, a prosecutor, a probation officer, or a judge, expressed the opinion that it was not the immigrants themselves but their sons that constituted the big problem at the present time.[15]

[9] *Ibid.*, p. 62.

[10] *Prisoners and Juvenile Delinquents in the United States, 1910,* Table 206, p. 191.

[11] *Reports of the Immigration Commission,* Vol. XXXVI, p. 1.

[12] "Juvenile Delinquency as Related to Immigration," *School and Society,* XXXVI (July 8, 1933), 61–64.

[13] Reprinted from *Five Hundred Criminal Careers* by Sheldon Glueck and Eleanor T. Glueck by permission of and special arrangement with Alfred A. Knopf, Inc., authorized publishers, New York, p. 119.

[14] *One Thousand Juvenile Delinquents* (Cambridge, 1934), p. 85.

[15] National Commission on Law Observance and Enforcement, *Report on Crime and the Foreign Born* (Washington, 1931), p. 157. *Ibid.*, Table VII, p. 158, however,

On the basis of data supplied by sixty-five juvenile courts for 1928, the Children's Bureau concluded that "the delinquency rate among native-born boys of foreign or mixed parentage was high." [16] For the year 1933 sixty-seven juvenile courts reported a disposition of 37,467 delinquency cases of white boys and girls. Of this number 45 per cent of the boys and 34 per cent of the girls had one or both parents of foreign birth.[17] This figure for delinquents is considerably higher than the percentage (20.7 per cent [18]) which the native-born whites of foreign or mixed parentage bear to the total white population. This is also much higher than the percentage (23.7 per cent [19]) which those of seven to twenty years (within which limits the majority of juvenile court cases fall) bear to a like age-group in the general white population. In 1934 out of a total of 37,274 delinquency cases disposed of by sixty-five courts, 15,823 or 42 per cent were those of children with foreign or mixed parentage.[20]

Thomas and Znaniecki state: "It is a well-known fact that even the number of crimes is proportionately much larger among the children of immigrants than among the immigrants themselves." [21] Bogardus noted a high delinquency rate among the second-generation Mexicans in the Southwest.[22] Dr. Pauline V. Young found in her study of the Molokans of Los Angeles that members of the immigrant generation presented relatively few problems to American urban agencies, but the younger group was making increasing contacts with the law.[23]

In any treatment of the children of immigrants, however, it is

does not necessarily support this contention. For most offenses in Detroit those of foreign parentage have a better record than sons of native parents. In Buffalo the ratios are somewhat more favorable to the latter.

[16] *Juvenile Court Statistics,* 1928, Children's Bureau Publication, No. 200, p. 10.

[17] *Juvenile-Court Statistics and Federal Juvenile Prisoners,* 1933, Children's Bureau Publication, No. 232, Table 4, p. 30.

[18] *Fifteenth Census of the United States, 1930 Population,* Vol. II, Table 2, p. 26.

[19] *Ibid.,* calculated from Table 8, p. 1097.

[20] Data from the Children's Bureau.

[21] W. I. Thomas and F. Znaniecki, *op. cit.*, Vol. II, p. 1659.

[22] E. S. Bogardus, "Second Generation Mexicans," *Sociology and Social Research,* XIII (January-February, 1929), 276.

[23] *Op. cit.*, pp. 184–216. Cf. also *American Journal of Sociology,* XXXV (November, 1929), 400. Cf. W. C. Smith, *Americans in Process,* pp. 211–26 for second generation Orientals.

well to bear in mind that they are more likely to be brought before the courts than those of native parentage, even for the same offense. It is a well-known fact that the foreign-born are the objects of discriminations by our legal machinery,[24] and it is not unlikely that unconscious nationality prejudices of judges, juries, and court officials are extended to the second generation to increase their commitment rates.

Maurice R. Davie has this to say: [25]

> In the case of organized crime which has received much public attention, it appears that comparatively few of the gangsters are foreign-born but that a high proportion are sons of foreign-born parents, reared in the slums of American cities. At least seventeen of Chicago's well-publicized twenty-eight "public enemies" are native-born sons of immigrant parents; eight are foreign-born, and in the case of three birthplace or parentage is unknown.[26] On the Cleveland police "black list" of 121 criminals of a dangerous character, seventy-four are natives of the United States whose parents had been born abroad, as against thirty who were themselves foreign-born.

Some of the more recent findings, however, are challenging these usually accepted conclusions. Certain data furnished by the Children's Bureau for 1934, as presented in Table I, raise some questions, at least.

The figures in Table I show in general the relation between the proportion of the male population, fifteen to nineteen years of age, that were foreign-born or of foreign or mixed parentage in a group of cities which had 20 per cent or more foreign-born white population and the number of cases of boys of foreign birth or of foreign or mixed parentage (less than 10.0 per cent were foreign-born) dealt with by courts in areas in which these were the principal cities. In these ten representative cities, 65 per cent of the male population, fifteen to nineteen years of age, were foreign-born or were of foreign or mixed parentage. In the area served by the courts in these cities, 59.0 per cent of the cases were of boys of

24 Cf. R. H. Smith, *op. cit.*

25 From *World Immigration*, by Maurice R. Davie (New York, 1936), pp. 274–75. By permission of The Macmillan Company, publishers.

26 Cf. John Landesco, *Organized Crime in Chicago* (Chicago, 1929), pp. 1061–87, for a "Who's Who" of organized crime in Chicago.

foreign birth or with foreign or mixed parentage. These are all the cities in the Juvenile Court Statistics reporting area of 100,000 or more population which fall in the class (20.0 per cent or more of total population foreign-born or foreign and mixed parentage).

TABLE I

BOYS OF FOREIGN BIRTH OR WITH FOREIGN OR MIXED PARENTAGE IN TEN CITIES IN 1934

Data from the United States Children's Bureau

	Male population 15–19 years of age			*Boys' cases disposed of*		
	Total	*Foreign-born or foreign or mixed parentage*	*Ratio*	*Total*	*Boys of foreign birth or with foreign or mixed parentage*	*Ratio*
Bridgeport, Conn.	21,117	15,172	1.4	489	318	1.5
Hartford, Conn. ..	20,801	14,032	1.5	575	317	1.8
San Francisco	58,430	27,054	2.2	463	188	2.5
Detroit, Mich. ...	200,581	111,037	1.8	(Wayne Co.) 2,269	1,256	1.8
Jersey City, N. J.	45,114	26,274	1.7	(Hudson Co.) 741	521	1.4
Trenton, N. J. ..	17,620	10,659	1.7	(Mercer Co.) 449	273	1.6
Buffalo, N. Y. ...	75,999	40,904	1.9	(Erie Co.) 1,089	674	1.6
New York City ..	875,785	613,848	1.4	5,328	3,213	1.7
Rochester, N. Y. .	41,688	23,425	1.8	(Monroe Co.) 167	117	1.4
Yonkers, N. Y. ...	18,990	11,738	1.6	(Westchester Co.) 341	182	1.9
	1,376,125	894,143	1.6+	11,911	7,059	1.7

The data presented in Table I have a limited value, to be sure, since three groups are lumped together. Nevertheless, ratios indicate that this combined group contributes only a small fraction above its quota to the delinquency column.

The Bureau of the Census in a recent publication [27] gives the old idea a telling blow. On the basis of returns from twenty-six states the native white males have a commitment ratio of 144 as compared with 120 for those of foreign parentage and 91 for those of mixed ancestry. In seventeen of the states those of mixed parent-

[27] *Prisoners in State and Federal Prisons and Reformatories, 1933* (Washington, 1935), p. 26.

age have a lower rate than those with both parents foreign-born. In the other nine states the reverse is true. This is contrary to the usual expectations, since disturbing conflicts might be expected with mixed marriages, particularly where there is considerable divergence between the cultures. "Yet, curiously enough," writes Donald R. Taft, "the nine states where people of mixed parentage have relatively high commitment rates, have an unusually large proportion of the 'old' as compared with the 'new' immigrants." [28] These census tabulations depart most widely from the usual expectation in the fact that the sons of immigrants, taken as a whole in the twenty-six states, show rates of commitment below those of native parentage. In only nine states of the twenty-six do the latter have the lower ratio.

When further refinements are made in the statistical comparisons, it is probable that very little difference will be found between the second generation and those of native parentage. It would be greatly to the advantage of the children of immigrants if they could be compared with natives on the same low economic level. Since immigration has been considerably reduced within the last decade, it is also probable that at the time of this enumeration in 1933 the children of foreign parentage have more favorable conditions for adjustment than those who appeared in the earlier studies.[29]

Whatever conclusion may be drawn relative to the amount of crime committed by the second generation, the Immigration Commission discovered another significant fact.

> It appears that a clear tendency exists on the part of the second generation to differ from the first or immigrant generation in the character of its criminality. It also appears that this difference is much more frequently in the direction of the criminality of the American-born of non-immigrant parentage than it is in the opposite direction.[30]

[28] D. R. Taft, "Nationality and Crime," *American Sociological Review,* I (October, 1936), 726–27.

[29] Cf. D. R. Taft, "Nationality and Crime," *American Sociological Review,* I (October, 1936), 724–36; T. Sellin, "Crime and the Second Generation of Immigrant Stock," *Interpreter Releases,* XIII (May 23, 1936), for further discussion.

[30] *Op. cit.,* Vol. XXXVI, p. 14; cf. also pp. 14–16 and 67–86; E. H. Stofflet, "A Study of National and Cultural Differences in Criminal Tendency," *Archives of Psychology,* No. 185 (May, 1935), 54.

This propensity may be illustrated by a comparison of the rates of conviction of the first and second generation Irish and the native whites of native white parentage in the New York Court of General Sessions from October 1, 1908, to June 30, 1909, with reference to five crimes,[31] as given in Table II.

TABLE II

DEVIATION OF THE IRISH SECOND GENERATION FROM THE PARENT GROUP

Offense	*Irish*		*Native White of Native parentage*
	Immigrants	*Second Generation*	
Forgery and Fraud ...	0.0	1.3	5.3
Gaming	1.2	2.7	3.6
Homicide	2.3	1.0	0.5
Rape	0.0	0.3	0.7
Simple Assault	25.6	11.0	7.9

The Irish second generation adheres more closely to this rule than any of the other groups studied, but nevertheless the bias is quite distinct. On the basis of data from the Massachusetts Department of Correction, 1914–1922, Sutherland found the same situation among the Italians with reference to crimes of violence. "This seems to show that the tendency to commit crimes of personal violence which is seen so clearly in the Italian immigrants is a matter of tradition—a tradition that is not passed on to the second generation." [32]

On a basis of a study of crime in Buffalo and Detroit, Alida C. Bowler, concluded:

The sons of the immigrants show a tendency to take on American ways in crime. In these two cities the sons of the foreign-born were arrested, charged with serious crimes against person and property, very much more frequently than their foreign-born parents in proportion to their numbers. Moreover, the types of offenses of which the sons of the foreign-

[31] *Reports of the Immigration Commission,* Vol. XXXVI, table 8, pp. 14–15.

[32] E. H. Sutherland, *Principles of Criminology* (Chicago, 1934), p. 116. By permission of J. B. Lippincott Company.

born stood accused with great frequency did not, as might have been expected, take on their parents' pattern.[33]

Governor C. C. Young's Mexican fact-finding committee in California reached a similar conclusion. "Forgery, rare among native-born Mexicans, was practically as common a cause for commitment among these Mexican boys at Preston who are mainly American-born as among the other boys and doubtless reflects the greater familiarity among the American-born with handwriting and banking." [34]

The writer found the same tendency among the second generation of Oriental ancestry in the Hawaiian Islands. Chinese immigrants had a high rate of convictions for violations of the narcotic laws while the American-born group committed practically no such offenses. Japanese immigrants infringed upon the prohibition laws while their sons did so only rarely.[35]

These are samples of the facts on the basis of which Alida C. Bowler generalized:

> Even these limited figures will prove disconcerting to the intellectually honest thinker. He will find himself speculating as to what it is in American attitudes, institutions, conditions, and practices that seems to take stock that has demonstrated its relative respect for laws for the protection of property and to mold it into new patterns of predatory lawlessness.[36]

[33] National Commission on Law Observance and Enforcement, *Report on Crime and the Foreign Born* (Washington, 1931), p. 160.

[34] *Mexicans in California* (San Francisco, 1930), p. 200.

[35] Cf. W. C. Smith, *op. cit.*, pp. 216–20.

[36] *Op. cit.*, p. 161. According to Evelyn Hursey, "Settlement house directors shake their heads over the noisy, painted girls and groan at the sneering, hats-over-the-eye 'smart alecs' that swarm over their thresholds. Can these be the children of the thrifty, quiet, dignified peasants living in the next block?" Manuscript paper, read at the meeting of the National Conference of Social Work, May 21, 1934.

CHAPTER XXI

FACTORS IN THE BEHAVIOR OF THE SECOND GENERATION

When facts concerning delinquency of the children of immigrants are observed, it is all too easy to blame heredity for any failures. "Some persons think that delinquency and crime are in some way due to foreign stock from which these boys sprang." [1] As proof of this contention, it is possible to point to American-born gangsters of immigrant parentage. But an explanation on the basis of heredity has an unpleasant backfire. How can we explain the fact that adult immigrants have a better record than native Americans of old stock, criminalistically speaking? Immigrant children, in the main, comport themselves better than American children. Immigrants and their children do not monopolize social failure. We have the well-known families—the Jukes, the Kallikaks, the Nams—with their long lines of criminals, prostitutes, and social parasites. And they are of old American stock! [2] The situation is entirely too complex to be explained on the basis of an inferior heredity. A number of factors condition the young person's behavior.

Urbanization. The majority of recent immigrants have settled in the cities of the northeastern portion of the country.[3] When we consider that, in general, crime tends to increase with the density

[1] *Institutional Treatment of Delinquent Boys,* Part 2, U. S. Children's Bureau, Publication No. 230, p. 21.

[2] Alarmists are often blind to the marked upward trend of the descendants of immigrants. They move out of the slums in which their parents were unwilling settlers and leave criminal ways behind them. They advance in the occupational field. They have forged ahead to occupy positions of trust, honor, and prominence in our American life.

[3] According to a Census Bureau study (*Prisoners in State and Federal Prisons and Reformatories,* 1933, p. 26), the highest delinquency ratios are found in the more highly industrialized areas and, except for Illinois, they are concentrated in the northeast. Cf. D. R. Taft, "Nationality and Crime," *American Sociological Review,* I (October, 1936), 724–36.

of a population,[4] we are brought face to face with the fact that the children of immigrants are located in a situation favorable to delinquency. City life is conducive to anti-social conduct on the part of the native-born of native parentage and it bears down more heavily on the child of the immigrant: his parents do not understand American life and are unable to help him.

> Frequently the parents are entirely ignorant of our laws and possess little appreciation of the social life about them. Their attitudes, ethical standards, language, manners, and outlook on life are those of the Old World. Thus the immigrant family, although rich in Old World traditions and culture, has little to offer the child which will prepare him for participation in the activities of the larger American community.[5] Not infrequently . . . . the child, through his contacts outside of the home, develops attitudes and forms of behavior which isolate him from his own family. In many such cases the child's relationship to his parents assumes the character of an emotional conflict, which definitely complicates the problem of parental control, and greatly interferes with the child's incorporation into the social *milieu* of his parents. In this situation the family is rendered relatively ineffective as an agent of control and fails to serve as a medium for the transmission of cultural heritages.[6]

It should by no means be assumed that the immigrant parents of delinquent children in these urban areas are necessarily indiffer-

[4] For a discussion of this, see E. H. Sutherland, *Principles of Criminology*, pp. 122–25.

[5] "The lack of understanding between the girl and her parents, the lack of confidence in each other, the inability of the older generation to grasp the meaning of the new world so strange to them in its differing customs and attitudes is pictured again and again in the scenes of the court room on immigrant day. Observation of juvenile court sessions is convincing proof of the breach that is ever widening." Dorothy Reed, *Leisure Time in a Little Italy* (Portland, Oregon, 1932), p. 31.

[6] National Commission on Law Observance and Enforcement, *Report on the Causes of Crime* (Washington, 1931), Vol. II, No. 13, pp. 111–12. Cf. E. H. Sutherland, *Principles of Criminology*, pp. 146–48, for case studies.

The new environment brings changes in rôles within the family, thereby having a disorganizing effect. "The children have learned to speak, read, and write in English. They begin to feel superior to their parents because they can speak a language which the parents cannot understand. The normal parent-child relationship becomes reversed. Whereas normally the parent interprets the world to the child, in these families the child has to interpret all the important happenings to the parents. Often he is even called upon by neighbors to interpret for them. This gives the children an idea

ent to the conduct and welfare of their children. The techniques, however, that were effective in the Old World are of slight avail because of powerful influences operating in complex urban environments.[7]

The slum. Furthermore, since the average immigrant is poor, he settles in the slum, not because of its attractiveness but from sheer economic necessity. Immediately on arrival the immigrant must find work and husband his slender resources. Usually the employment agency collects a large fee. He then is forced to rent insanitary and vermin-infested quarters that have been abandoned by other immigrants who have climbed to a higher rung in the economic ladder. Hence his children live in tenements, attics, or cellars, in unlighted and unheated rooms, with defective plumbing and overfilled garbage cans. Many of these conditions are due to a disregard for and a lack of enforcement of laws, all of which indicate to the child that flouting of law is acceptable and even proper.

The majority of immigrants come from small villages or farms in Italy, Ireland, Roumania, or Serbia and settle in blighted urban areas. Thus their offspring are slum children—their attitudes and reactions are fashioned by the slum environment.[8]

Delinquency areas. A considerable fund of literature has accu-

that they are very important and superior in their own social group. They have no one to respect, no authority to guide them. They realize that in many ways they know more than their parents. . . . . The child who feels he is the intellectual superior in his family and knows that he can outwit his parents by such simple devices as misinterpreting a communication, will naturally later sneer at other kinds of authority and try to outwit other laws and rules.

"These two factors, the feeling of superiority and power in his own group on the one hand and the feeling of inferiority which results in resentment toward the outside alien world on the other, form the basis for the mental attitude of the gangster. He can bully his own world and he also wants to impress and bully the people whom he considers superior and of whom he is really afraid." Joseph Miller, "Foreign-Born Parentage and Social Maladjustment," *Psychological Clinic,* XIX (March, 1930), 20.

[7] Cf. National Commission on Law Observance and Enforcement, *Report on the Causes of Crime* (Washington, 1931), Vol. II, No. 13, p. 139; Jane Addams, *Twenty Years at Hull House* (New York, 1911), pp. 252–53.

[8] Cf. Abraham Myerson, "Descendants of the Foreign-Born," *The Annals,* CLI (September, 1930), 150. According to Harold Ross, the native born of European parentage seem to have a higher rate of criminality only because the statistical tabulations disregard the various income levels. *Journal of Criminal Law and Criminology,* XXVIII (July–August, 1937), 202–09.

mulated recently to show the demoralizing effect of slum conditions on children. Clifford R. Shaw analyzed several series of statistical data on juveniles in Chicago and found that certain areas had maintained high delinquency ratios consistently for several decades, even though the ethnic composition of the population had changed almost completely during the period. When the Swedes and Germans were located in the Lower North Side their children had high delinquency records. When the Italians and Poles replaced them the ratios in the locality remained practically unchanged, while those of the Germans and Swedes decreased as they moved northward into the better districts. Furthermore, the ratio of any particular immigrant group, the Poles for instance, tends to follow the general tendency for the total population, that is, to decrease gradually from the center of the city outward to the periphery.[9] Clifford R. Shaw and Henry D. McKay studied six other cities in different sections of the country. These cities showed marked differences in geographic conditions, in size, in rapidity of growth, in commercial life, and in composition of population, yet all presented the same general pattern of distribution of juvenile delinquents as Chicago.[10] "In each of the six cities, the highest rates of delinquents are found in the areas adjacent to the central business district, while the lowest rates, with few exceptions, are in the residential communities farther removed from the major commercial and industrial centers." [11] Shaw and McKay delineate the delinquency-producing areas of Chicago as characterized by "physical deterioration, decreasing population, high rates of dependency, high percentage of foreign-born and Negro population, and high rates of adult offenders . . . . by marked disintegration of the traditional institutions [12] and neighborhood organization. In this type of area, the community fails to function effectively as an agency of social control." [13] According to the same authors,

[9] Cf. C. R. Shaw, *op. cit.*

[10] National Commission on Law Observance and Enforcement, *Report on the Causes of Crime* (Washington, 1931), Vol. II, No. 13.

[11] *Ibid.*, p. 188.

[12] Cf. J. Landesco, *Journal of Criminal Law and Criminology*, XXIII (July, 1932), 238.

[13] *Op. cit.*, p. 108.

Children who grow up in these deteriorated and disorganized neighborhoods of the city are not subject to the same constructive and restraining influences that surround those in the more homogeneous residential communities farther removed from the industrial and commercial centers. These disorganized neighborhoods fail to provide a consistent set of cultural standards and a wholesome social life for the development of a stable and socially acceptable form of behavior in the child. Very often the child's access to the traditions and standards of our conventional culture are restricted to his formal contacts with the police, the courts, the school, and the various social agencies. On the other hand his most vital and intimate social contacts are often limited to the spontaneous and undirected neighborhood play groups and gangs whose activities and standards of conduct may vary widely from those of his parents and the larger social order. These intimate and personal relationships, rather than the more formal and external contacts with the school, social agencies, and the authorities, become the chief sources from which he acquires his social values and conceptions of right and wrong.[14]

These areas of social disorganization are not only lacking in facilities for prevention and suppression of delinquency but . . . . they show a general indifference to the problem of delinquency and crime. Generally speaking, violations of the law are no longer shocking. Delinquency, particularly various forms of petty stealing, may be generally accepted or tacitly condoned. Sometimes these delinquent activities are engaged in openly without any organized attempt to suppress them. This is especially true of pilfering, jack-rolling, stealing junk.[15]

There are certain areas of the city in which stealing from freight cars and markets is a common form of delinquency. In many instances . . . . the practice is encouraged by the parents. It is sometimes practiced openly and apparently has the sanction of the neighborhood, at least no action on the part of the neighborhood is taken against it.[16]

One particular type of delinquency shows a close relationship to the physical environment in which it occurs. The deteriorated sections of the city are fruitful fields for junking and its various

[14] National Commission on Law Observance and Enforcement, *Report on the Causes of Crime* (Washington, 1931), Vol. II, No. 13, p. 111.

[15] *Ibid.*, p. 124.

[16] *Ibid.*, p. 132.

related activities. As Thrasher suggests,[17] such stealing, often instigated by junk dealers, is frequently an initial step in a delinquency career.[18]

According to Bolitho, stealing by the immigrant child came from the anachronistic ways of his parents.

> The initial theft, in Chicago, is quite usually one of coal, fallen on the track from passing wagons, or indeed anything of consumption value, taken—this is the significant thing—only it must be from a mass, and from an impersonal owner. To this his parents have sent him, often encouraged him. . . . . The coal looting of Chicago is simply the old-fashioned "gleaning" of backward rural Europe. Possibly it may even be a reminiscence of some complicated village communism, such as the Basuto still practice. But in any case, it is as Ruth did, with the tacit approval of the Almighty, and which the Christian Church has repeatedly hallowed in the Middle Ages. . . . . And so the first step in crime of a gangster may have been a strict compliance with laws that his first teachers, his parents, never dreamed had become out of date, a crime.[19]

Each group of immigrants has a moral code of its own, a standard of right and wrong, and a conception of what is social and what is anti-social. These ideas, however, may vary strikingly from the statutes in America and children who have been brought up to do what is right fall into the toils of the law simply because the American law is different.

Very often there is an attitude of indifference on the part of the people of the district toward such activities—they are accepted as matters of course.

> Delinquency persists in these areas not only because of the absence of constructive neighborhood influences and the inefficiency of present methods of prevention and treatment, but because various forms of lawlessness have become more or less traditional aspects of the social life and are handed down year after year through the medium of social contacts. Delinquent and criminal patterns of behavior are prevalent in these areas and are readily accessible to a large proportion of the children.

[17] F. M. Thrasher, *op. cit.*, pp. 148–58.

[18] *Ibid.*, p. 134.

[19] William Bolitho, "The Psychosis of the Gang," *The Survey*, LXIII (February 1, 1930), 505.

The extremely high rate of crime among the young men between 17 and 21 years of age living in the areas with high rates of juvenile delinquency is convincing proof of the presence of criminal influences surrounding the boys in these areas. . . . . The presence of a large number of older offenders in a neighborhood is a fact of great significance for the understanding of the problem of juvenile delinquency. It indicates, in the first place, that the possibility of contact between the children and hardened offenders is very great. These older offenders, who are well known and have prestige in the neighborhood, tend to set the standards and patterns of behavior for the younger boys, who idolize and emulate them.[20] In many cases the "big shot" [21] represents for the young delinquent an ideal around which his own hopes and ambitions are crystallized. His attainment of this coveted ideal means recognition in his group and the esteem of his fellows.

In many of the delinquency areas of the city, crime among the older offenders is often highly organized.[22] These organizations become a very powerful influence and perpetuate criminal traditions in the whole area. The members of these groups and their criminal practices are known to the younger boys. . . . . For the most part, this knowledge is secured through their contacts in the neighborhood and thus reflects the kind of world in which they live.[23]

These areas not only fail to provide a sufficiently consistent cultural background and neighborhood organization for the development of desirable forms of behavior, but they possess many elements that contribute directly to the formation of delinquent habits and attitudes among the children. It appears that in many cases the delinquent and criminal behavior of the boy represents an adjustment to the traditions, behavior standards, and expectations of the neighborhood groups with which he has contact.[24]

One of the significant factors with reference to delinquency in the disorganized areas is that of cultural heterogeneity. When mem-

[20] Cf. F. M. Thrasher, *op. cit.*, pp. 252–76.

[21] The grandiose funerals of gangsters are not without effect upon the under-privileged youth in the areas of disorganization. At the funeral of Dion O'Banion in Chicago, 20,000 people crowded in to see the "Irish Robin Hood" borne away in his $10,000 silver casket. *The Survey,* LXIII (March 1, 1930), 662. Cf. J. Landesco, *Organized Crime in Chicago* (Chicago, 1929), pp. 1025–39.

[22] Cf. J. Landesco, *Organized Crime in Chicago,* pp. 825–1087.

[23] National Commission on Law Observance and Enforcement, *Report on the Causes of Crime* (Washington, 1931), Vol. II, No. 13, pp. 126–28.

[24] *Ibid.*, pp. 138–39. Cf. M. Gold, *op. cit.*, and S. B. Ornitz, *op. cit.*, for realistic descriptions of life on the East Side in New York City.

bers of several cultural groups live interspersed in a district there is no single pattern or code to define the situation and control the behavior of the youth. Dr. Mabel A. Elliott's study of Chicago shows that localities having high rates of juvenile delinquency were those with a high degree of racial [25] heterogeneity.[26] Furthermore, "The greater the potential resemblance of the heterogeneous racial group to the American group, the lower the rate of delinquency." [27] Likewise Lind's researches indicate a high rate of delinquency among the Japanese in a section of Honolulu with a heterogeneous population. An adjoining area, occupied entirely by Japanese, had a low delinquency rate. Here the Japanese culture was dominant and exerted a stabilizing influence over the children.[28]

Shaw and McKay located one area in the near down-town section of Seattle which did not run true to theoretical expectations.[29] This district has, it would seem, a sufficiently compact oriental population, overwhelmingly Japanese, to maintain its cultural patterns with some degree of success.[30]

Evelyn Buchan Crook mapped the "delinquency triangles" [31] of 700 cases of sex delinquency from the records of the Juvenile Court in Chicago and concluded:

[25] The term "racial" is used of the various European groups, such as English, German, Irish, Russian, etc. The term "cultural" would be preferable.

[26] *A Correlation Between Rate of Juvenile Delinquency and Racial Heterogeneity* (Springfield, Ill., 1926), p. 25.

[27] *Ibid.*, p. 42.

[28] A. W. Lind, "The Ghetto and the Slum," *Social Forces*, IX (December, 1930), 209. For the situation in the Hungarian colony of Detroit, cf. *Journal of Criminal Law and Criminology*, XXV (January, 1935), 762. Cf. also Eleanor T. Glueck, "Culture Conflict and Delinquency," *Mental Hygiene*, XXI (January, 1937), 46–66.

[29] National Commission on Law Observance and Enforcement, *Report on the Causes of Crime* (Washington, 1931), Vol. II, No. 13, p. 184.

[30] A citizen of Seattle is quoted as making this comment on the delinquency spot map: "So Seattle was white where it ought to have been black, because it was yellow!" Albert W. Palmer, *The Oriental in American Life* (New York, 1934), p. 57.

These facts tend to support the hypothesis formulated by Park: "It is the immigrants who have maintained in this country their simple village religions and mutual aid organizations who have been most able to withstand the shock of the new environment . . . . In some sense these communities in which our immigrants live their smaller lives may be regarded as models for our own. . . . . Our problem is to encourage men to seek God in their own neighborhood. These immigrant communities deserve further study." R. E. Park and E. W. Burgess, *The City* (Chicago, 1925), pp. 121–22.

[31] The "delinquency triangle" is constructed by locating three points—the home of the girl, the home of her male companion, and the place of the delinquency.

Most significant . . . . is the frequent concentration of delinquency cases in areas where two or more language or racial groups occupy homes near each other.[32] . . . . Our findings clearly reveal the cultural marginality of the habitat of juvenile court sex delinquents and their partners, as well as the marginality of their rendezvous.[33]

These marginal or "socially interstitial areas," as Thrasher calls them,[34] are the gangland of the city. Borderlands between residential and manufacturing or business districts, between city and country, between immigrant or racial colonies constitute the cultural "no-man's-land" in which the gang thrives.[35] Furthermore, ganging is inevitable in such situations.

Since these deteriorating areas are populated for the most part, by immigrants,

The gang in Chicago is largely though not entirely, a phenomenon of the immigrant community of the poorest type. Of the 880 gangs for which data have been secured as to race and nationality, only 45 are given as wholly American; while 63 are negro; and 25, mixed, colored, and white. Of those remaining, 351 are of mixed white nationalities, while 396 are dominantly or solidly of a single nationality group.[36]

Here now is the significant fact for our study: "A few of the members of these gangs are foreign born, but most of them are children of parents, one or both of whom are foreign-born immigrants." [37]

We must, however, treat these data with care. Thrasher puts it thus:

A superficial conclusion might easily be drawn from the statistics . . . . that the immigrant peoples of the city are responsible for gangs and all the problems related to them. Such an inference would be entirely erroneous. Native white American boys of the same economic and social classes as the children of immigrants enter into gangs just as readily,

[32] "Over 86 per cent of all points (of the triangles) fall on frontiers, including 69.14 on boundaries, 3.7 in interstitial areas, and 13.58 in overlapping areas." P. 499.

[33] "Cultural Marginality in Sex Delinquency," *American Journal of Sociology*, XXXIX (January, 1934), 500.

[34] F. M. Thrasher, *op. cit.*, p. 22.

[35] *Ibid.*, p. 23.

[36] *Ibid.*, p. 191.

[37] *Ibid.*, pp. 191–92.

but their identity is lost because of the vastly greater number of the children of foreign-born parentage in the regions of life where ganging takes place. It is not because the boys of the middle and wealthier classes are native white that they do not form gangs but because their lives are organized and stabilized for them by American traditions, customs, and institutions to which the children of immigrants do not have adequate access. The gang, on the other hand, is simply one symptom of the immigrant's traditional social system without adequate assimilation to the new.[38]

These are the conditions in the delinquency areas. Since immigrants, and particularly the more recent arrivals, have taken up their residence in these sections, it has been but a normal expectation to have a disproportionate number of delinquents of foreign-born parentage making contact with the juvenile court in Chicago and in other cities. These high delinquency ratios cannot be explained in terms of nationality, race, or heredity because the populations in many of these districts in Chicago have changed while the rates of delinquency have remained relatively unchanged. The delinquency rate, we may conclude, is a function of the area rather than of the class of people resident there.[39] Dr. Pauline V. Young's study of the Molokans in Los Angeles supports this contention. In the early days of the colony (founded in 1905) only 5 per cent of their children made contact with the juvenile court; five years later the percentage rose to 46.2, and after another ten-year period 82.5 per cent of their children made appearances before the court. There was no change in the hereditary factor, but the opportunities for contacts and assimilation of delinquency patterns in a slum environment had increased.[40]

[38] *Ibid.*, pp. 217–18.

[39] Cf. National Commission on Law Observance and Enforcement, *Report on the Causes of Crime* (Washington, 1931), Vol. II, No. 13, p. 98.

[40] *Op. cit.*, pp. 201–11; "Urbanization as a Factor in Juvenile Delinquency," *Publication of the American Sociological Society*, XXIV (1930), 162–66.

CHAPTER XXII

CULTURE CONFLICT AND THE SECOND GENERATION

Physical and social conditions in the slums, as presented in the foregoing pages, have an important bearing on the behavior of the offspring of immigrants; they affect all slum dwellers, whether they be of recent immigrant or of old native stock. But we must go beyond these factors to a cultural analysis which will be more fundamental and more fruitful in its results. The cultural factor affects all, but particularly the children of immigrant parentage.

Culture conflicts and mental conflicts. Healy introduced the term "mental conflict" into general usage. He defined it as "a conflict between elements of mental life, and occurs when two elements or systems of elements, are out of harmony with each other." [1] Sociologists have introduced the term "cultural conflict" which is an extension of Healy's idea in that it takes into account the social and cultural influences in a larger measure.[2] Mental conflicts often arise in cultural conflicts.[3] When the child of foreign parentage meets with sneers and jibes because he belongs to a group which is considered inferior—mainly because it is different—he is disturbed, and he may turn to anti-social behavior. This inner conflict is not necessarily due to some unlearned behavior pattern or innate weakness, but rather to contradictions and incompatibilities inherent in the two or more differing cultures to which the person has been exposed. These contradictory and incompatible elements

[1] William Healy, *Mental Conflict and Misconduct* (Boston, 1917), p. 22.

[2] The cases of Stasia and Stanley Andrews, Case 17, Series I, *Judge Baker Foundation Studies,* could have been analyzed more adequately from the cultural point of view.

[3] Cf. R. E. Park, "Personality and Cultural Conflict," *Publication of the American Sociological Society,* XXV (1931), 95–110; Evelyn W. Hersey, "The Emotional Conflicts of the Second-Generation," *Interpreter Release,* XI, No. 14 (July 10, 1934).

come to grips within the person.[4] He finds it difficult to reach a decision because grave moral problems are often involved; he finds it difficult to conform to the accepted social code because the required behavior is not consistent with his conception of himself as a well-ordered member of the group.

Most of us hold membership in several social groups, each one of which has a culture of its own. Not infrequently these cultures, or elements in them, are widely divergent. The church says, "Love thy neighbor as thyself," but the trade association says, "Charge all the traffic will bear"; the pietistic Swedish immigrant home taboos dancing, but, when the boy joins the college fraternity, he must dance or be labeled queer; the public school orders all children to leave their hats outside the classroom, but the orthodox Jewish home requires the boy to keep his head covered at mealtime. The necessity of playing such antipodal rôles often necessitates such marked and abrupt readjustments that many break under the strain.[5]

[4] Ruth Shonle Cavan presents the case of a young Jewish man who is torn by an inner struggle. "As often in mental conflicts, the conflict is not merely between two individual desires, but between two sets of social codes or mores held by two different groups in both of which the person has membership. As a Jew the man has acquired the belief that parents should be honored, cared for, and obeyed. As an American, he feels that his married life should be given precedence over other considerations. He is both Jew and American; he shares both attitudes and he cannot reconcile them. The situation is complicated because he has emotional attachments to members of each group. The Jewish group is personified in his mother; the American, in his fiancée. He desires the affection and respect of both. He is experiencing not merely a contest between the attachment to his mother and to his sweetheart, but a genuine conflict between two sets of attitudes regarding his 'duty,' both of which he has accepted and in both of which he believes. It is possible for a person to subscribe to several moral codes so long as they are not brought into conflict with each other. This man probably found nothing incongruous in the ideas that a man owes a duty to his parents and also owes a duty to his wife until the two came into sharp conflict in his own experience. When such a conflict does occur there is often involved not only a moral decision as to which set of attitudes shall take precedence over the other, but consideration of the losses and gains involved in accepting wholeheartedly the creed of one social group and discarding the creed of, and with it membership in, another social group. In this case, if the man decides in favor of his fiancée he will undoubtedly lose the respect of his mother and her Jewish friends; if he clings to his mother, the American girl and her friends will scorn him." *Suicide* (Chicago, 1928), pp. 160–61. Cf. J. I. Kolehmainen, "A Study of Marriage in a Finnish Community," *American Journal of Sociology,* XLII (November, 1936), 377.

[5] A young Hungarian related his experience:

"When I started to school I knew not one word of English; all family conversation was in Hungarian. I was not allowed to speak English at home at all! And my

Situations producing conflicts. Not one but many situations may be fertile soil for cultural conflicts.[6] We may give a number of situations as follows: (1) living in an area of high mobility, like a slum in which there are no stable forms of social organization to set definite behavior patterns; (2) membership in a group where practices do not conform to the enacted laws or where there is a divergence between precept and practice; (3) membership in an organization like a gang which is in conflict with the larger community; (4) membership in a group which sanctions conduct violative of the mores of another group of which he is also a member; [7] (5) membership in a group in which a different meaning is placed upon certain forms of conduct which externally, at least, resemble those of the dominant group, and where there is a difference in emphasis upon values; [8] (6) membership in a family in which there is a cultural tension because the parents represent different cultures; [9] (7) membership in a group which one considers inferior to

first grade teacher used to shake me vigorously, evidently believing that she could transfer knowledge of English to me by that method. Later, as I picked up some English, she would still become furious if I would thoughtlessly use a Hungarian word. It was like the dual character in the book, Dr. Jekyl and Mr. Hyde, for me to be always alert to the fact that English was forbidden at home, and Hungarian was forbidden at school." S. C. Newman, *op. cit.*

[6] Cf. *Social Forces,* IX (June, 1931), 491–92; *Publication of the American Sociological Society,* XXV (1931), 216–17.

[7] This may be illustrated by the Jewish boy who enjoys eating a ham sandwich with his playfellows at school, but who has the wrath of Abraham, Isaac, and Jacob brought down upon his head at home if he is even suspected of tasting pork.

[8] This is shown by a second-generation Polish girl. "My parents are foreigners and many of their manners and means of doing things conflict with the ways I have learned in and out of school. For example, my girl friends think nothing of holding a boy's hand while walking along a public highway from school. I did this one day, and—my father saw me. If you had been present to hear the scolding I received you would have thought that the boy and I had committed some penitentiary offense. He said that if I were in Poland, he would send me to a convent where I would not be permitted to see young men." Unpublished life history.

[9] This situation usually is productive of a high rate of delinquency. The native-born children of mixed parentage (one parent native-born and the other foreign-born) usually have a higher delinquency ratio than the native-born children with both parents foreign-born or both native-born. This general statement relative to different cultures in the home needs some qualification. In Hawaii the Chinese-Hawaiian offspring have a good record. The important factor is that there is no superior-inferior relationship in this situation. Both groups have high status and, fortunately for the children, they are accepted and granted status in both. Hence there is no conflict. A census bulletin shows that in seventeen out of twenty-six states the children of mixed parentage have a lower delinquency ratio than those

the dominant group and from which one cannot easily escape into a group which is considered superior and satisfying.[10]

Conflicts in immigrant home. Everywhere there is conflict between the older and younger generations, and particularly in a country like ours where change is unusually rapid. If it is present where both generations have substantially the same tradition, it rages more fiercely where alien and American generations dwell under the same roof.[11] The children of immigrants respond readily to stimuli in the new environment while their parents, in large measure, remain static. "The change came for them when their world was fluent and plastic, when they had not yet grappled other souls to theirs with the steel hoops of long love and firm-set will." [12] Conflicts, therefore, between the age groups that have been bred in different cultures are intensified and are more disorganizing to the family and to the personalities of the individual members than among those of native stock.

The immigrant home offers an excellent laboratory for the study of culture conflicts between the two generations. Within the confines of the family circle are concentrated all the contradictions, incompatibilities, and dissonances that can be found to exist between any two cultural groups, no matter how unlike they may be. This battle may be glossed over by politeness as it usually is by the Japanese or may be repressed by a sense of filial duty as with the Chinese, but nevertheless it rages on. At this point we shall present a case which shows the conflict as it appears from both sides.

with both parents foreign-born. *Prisoners in State and Federal Prisons and Reformatories, 1933,* p. 26. According to W. R. Tylor, mixed marriages may indicate a cessation of culture conflict between the parents. Hence, the children encounter no serious adjustment problems. *American Sociological Review,* I (October, 1936), 726–27.

[10] In California a hybrid Japanese-Mexican boy was not accepted by the Japanese. He considered them superior to the Mexicans and was desirous of status among them. His facial features, however, resembled, in considerable measure, those of his Mexican mother and so it was difficult to escape the inferior relationship. To gain status he attached himself to a group of younger Japanese boys whom he domineered. His behavior was such that he made contact with the juvenile court. Probably the cultural confusion in his home was a factor, but his unhappiness at being compelled to associate with inferiors was more important.

[11] Cf. E. deS. Brunner, *op. cit.,* pp. 239–43; Anzia Yezierska, *Bread Givers* (New York, 1925), for this conflict.

[12] Horace Bridges, *On Becoming an American* (Boston, 1919), p. 3.

An elderly man, with black derby and gray beard, accompanied by his wife entered the office of the social service agency. They were dejected and frightened. The woman spoke while the man wept: "This morning he hit him with a bottle. He didn't want to come here because he felt it was a disgrace, but I said we could stand it no longer; that he might kill us both and that we had to do something about it. We ask nothing from him, only that he should leave our house and never come to see us again. He is a wild bull; he isn't a human being."

In Yiddish they told a long story of their peaceful life in Poland, of their religious devotion, their prosperity and their family loyalties. The pogroms brought them to America. The father set up a little repair shop in the "back-of-the-yards" district of Chicago. That was in 1908. They sent their eldest son, then six, about whom they were now complaining to *Cheder* for his religious training and to the public school for education in the secular field. There were only a handful of Jewish children in the public school which their son attended: most of the others were Poles and Irish, but to the parents they were just gentiles or Americans. The father regained his composure sufficiently to go on with the story. He motioned to his wife to let him talk and he continued: "We had no trouble with him in Europe. He was a fine child; he was bright and everybody in the family was fond of him. I thought that if he would grow up all right and be healthy he would be a good Jew and be of some help to me in my old days because I am not a rich man. He could say the prayers when he was just six years old and I had great ambitions for him to become an educated man, maybe a doctor or a lawyer or a rabbi. But all my hopes have gone to pieces. I haven't even got a family any more. My word counts for nothing with him and he is teaching the younger boy to be as bad as he is. I never could imagine what bad children mean to parents but now I can see that it is the greatest penalty God can inflict. He went to *Cheder* for a couple of years or so and then he quit. He knows nothing any more about praying or the Jewish religion. He is as bad as the gentiles he runs around with. He hasn't been in a synagogue even on the holidays for several years. We made him be *Bar Mitzvah* (confirmed), but that is all. I don't expect him to be my *Kaddish* (say the memorial prayers) when I am dead because by that time he will be married to some gentile girl that he runs around with. I can't even tell you what he does for a living. He always wears fancy clothes and jewelry and I am sure he doesn't get it in any honest way. He never gives a cent to the house, although we need it. I wouldn't expect him to pay any board if he lived with us and never have, because that isn't done in my family. He has broken up my home and I don't care now if the police will get him because he will be a robber or burglar anyway. He can't disgrace me any more than he has already. My wife and I are heartbroken because in our old age we got to go through such troubles as that. We never expected that could happen to us. That is America, where children are not children but wild animals. You can do what you please, only keep him away from us: we want to forget him."

That same day after the parents had returned home, the boy telephoned and said that he would come down to tell his side of the story. He came. He was dressed in a natty suit and had all the outward signs of fashion and refinement. He said: "I hope you won't believe all the bunk they told you. I don't need to ask you what they said. I know them better than you do. They are just a pair of old cranks that think they are living in Europe. If you were in my place you wouldn't act any different. It's true that I threw a bottle at him, but he got me so mad that I could have killed him on the spot. I'm really surprised at myself that I didn't."

He asked not to be judged until he could tell his story and he was urged to talk frankly. He began with Europe about which he remembered little. He only knew that they were fairly well off and that he wasn't expected to do very much work. His father and mother were both very religious, as was the whole community of Jews in the town. No one worked on Saturdays and the synagogue was the main center of life. He recalled how the young children played in the spare rooms and in the yard of the synagogue while their elders prayed or studied.

Yiddish was the only language he knew, although he could say the prayers in Hebrew. But he did not know what they meant. When his folks moved to America he entered school and in a few months knew English as well as the other children in the neighborhood. He graduated from grammar school and took a two-year commercial course in high school. He hoped to become an accountant, and took a correspondence course for which he paid out of his earnings as a junior book-keeper in a large firm. He recalled that people used to call his father names in the little repair shop and that he had scarcely any Jewish companions. His playmates often called him names, too, and he was very much affected by that. He often wished that he wasn't born a Jew, and promised himself that when he grew up he would try not to have any of the characteristics by which a Jew could be identified. He went to public school willingly, but to *Cheder* very unwillingly. He was bored by what went on at the religious school and realized that the non-Jewish children in the neighborhood were very much freer than he was. Furthermore the *Cheder* was quite a distance from his father's shop, in the rear of which they lived.

His folks would try to keep him in the house as much as possible, but he would create such mischief that they would be glad to let him go out, in order to be rid of him.

They had no close relatives in Chicago, but the family made friends with some of the other Jews living in the neighborhood and attending the same synagogue. They were all very poor people and all very orthodox. His father kept the store closed on Saturdays at first, but later found that he would have to keep open in order to do any business, because that was the best day of the week.

He told of his many experiences at home and on the street at play when he would be insulted because he was a Jew or because his father looked so funny. When he graduated from grammar school he entered a high school which was located outside his district, so that he could start anew and be taken at his worth rather than as a Jew or the son of his father. He said that he looked no different from the rest, although he had many of the outward characteristics of the Jew, but that his distinctly Jewish name gave him away. He made few friends, although he tried very hard. He tried never to be seen in company of his parents. When anyone came to his father's shop that he knew, he would try to get away to the rear rooms before being discovered, because he was ashamed to be seen in such a place. He complained that there wasn't even a bathtub in his house and that he never had a toothbrush until he was about fourteen years old. "But there were many prayerbooks and other Jewish things lying around." While he was ashamed of his parents he was envious of the non-Jewish children whom he knew and he realized what a handicap it was to be not only a foreigner, but also a Jew. "And I knew just as much about America as they did: they were mostly Poles and Irish anyway."

He stopped attending *Cheder,* at first without telling his parents, but later, when they found out that he wasn't going he was defiant and told them that there was no sense in it; that no one else he wanted to be like went, and that this was not Poland. His father punished him on several occasions and shortly after his confirmation made him take lessons from a private teacher. He decided to go through with that, but promised himself that it would be the last thing that he would do to please his parents. He did it only because his mother pleaded with him, and not because of his father. "He could never get me to go. I hated him and as I looked at him I sometimes would say to myself 'the damned Jew.' "

As soon as he earned enough money he took as few meals at home as he could, because he didn't like the greasy Jewish food, which was always the same. His folks suspected that he was eating non-Kosher food but could do nothing about it. His father quit speaking to him for a while and he didn't mind that a bit, because it saved arguments.

He sometimes felt sorry for his mother, but thought it was too late for him to try to change her. They were just old-country people and nothing could be done about it. The best thing he could do was to leave them alone and go his own way.

He related several incidents of collisions with his father after some irritations. He acknowledged that the slightest move his father would make to get him to do something he did not wish to do, irritated him. At first they were just matters of religious practice, but later it was everything. "He didn't like my clothes, he didn't like my looks, he didn't like my going out nor my coming in. One Saturday afternoon after I got through with the office and I had a date I got out the flat iron to press my pants. He was sitting there reading and wanted to take the iron away, because he said it wasn't necessary to do that on the Sabbath in his house. I had a fight with him then and I hit him. I was sorry afterwards, because I realized that that was the end, that he wouldn't stand to have me around any more. So I decided to get out. But my mother held me back."

"This morning's fight was just about like that. I haven't eaten at home for some time, except a glass of tea occasionally. I brought home a bottle of milk and a sandwich and started to eat. He saw me and got up to tell me that I couldn't eat meat and milk in his house at the same time, and especially meat that wasn't Kosher. I told him that it was none of his business. He grabbed the bottle away from me, and in a moment of excitement I threw it at him. I can see now that it will be impossible for me to stay there any longer. I am too far away from them and they are too far away from me. They are still living in Europe and I am in America and East and West don't meet." [13]

Cultural analysis of conduct. Culture conflicts have a wide range and not all situations are charged so heavily with emotion or end

[13] L. Wirth, *Culture Conflicts in the Immigrant Family,* unpublished dissertation, University of Chicago.

in actual violence. This case, however, shows how precarious is the situation in many immigrant homes where bitterness between parents and children may develop out of what appears to be mere trifles. Conflicts like this can neither be understood nor resolved unless it be clearly recognized that fundamentally they are due to the clash of cultures or of irreconcilable elements in those cultures. In the case presented above, the economic situation and the physical aspects of the home were fairly satisfactory and there were no mental deficiencies or significant defects in personality. Hence, analysis of the behavior cannot be made in these terms. If, however, it is realized that the tensions between father and son are basically conflicts between attitudes, sentiments, traditions, and practices which have their roots in antagonistic cultures, the attendant behavior becomes intelligible. If it is recognized that the children of immigrants are living in two, or even more, cultural worlds, much that has been peculiar and perplexing in their behavior can be understood.[14] When two or more discordant cultures make their impacts upon a person, the problem of adjusting the inconsistencies may be too great for the individual concerned and may lead to misconduct. This applies to all, both to those of native and of immigrant stock, but the problem is greatly accentuated in the case of the children of immigrants. As a result they have less stability than their elders and much of their behavior is nondescript—it follows no known patterns. Wirth has made this statement.

> The fact that second-generation crime should be even more prevalent than first-generation crime does not seem difficult to understand when we note that the immigrant himself, living as he generally does, in an isolated immigrant colony, even though he has not assimilated New-World standards, is at least supported and controlled by Old-World traditions, which are, to a large extent, reproduced in the immigrant colony, be it Chinatown, Little Sicily, or the Ghetto. Under these circumstances, whatever the differences between native and immigrant culture may be, personal morale and community control are maintained. But the second generation is differently situated. The immigrant child, especially if born in America, does not have the life-long and exclusive

[14] Cf. *Publication of the American Sociological Society,* XXV (1931), 216.

attachments to the folkways and mores of the Old-World group that the parents have, who have been reared in the customs and traditions of their people and in whom the memories of the Old World call forth a strong emotional response. The child, because of the relative weakness of his attachment to the Old-World culture, and because of his greater mobility, has greater opportunity of making intimate contacts with the American social world than the parent whose contacts are generally confined to the society of his own countrymen, often within the confines of the immigrant colony itself. What is of greatest significance, however, is the circumstance that the child soon becomes incorporated into a neighborhood-, a play-, and a school-group, frequently into a gang, where he establishes primary relations with other foreign and native children. It is under conditions such as these—in the course of intimate and spontaneous contacts that assimilation takes place.[15]

In this process the child is exposed to several cultures, all of which may be, and frequently are, at variance with the culture of his parents. This confuses him and clashes in the home are inevitable. When conflicting social codes bid for the allegiance of the youth, confusion results—they do not know which course of action is right. Where standards are thus in conflict many children who are haled before the court feel no sense of guilt. Miriam Van Waters says of this:

When young people violate sacred family traditions and smile complacently, with no loss of self-esteem, it is not because they have become anti-social; it indicates probably that they dwell in some other island of social-culture which smiles upon their activities, and which is endorsed by some powerful group of adults. Almost all delinquencies of youth are the expressed social standards of a part of the adult community which is under no indictment, and which flourishes without condemnation.[16]

Culture conflicts are the "stuff" out of which much misconduct develops. Sutherland has concluded that

The conflict of cultures is . . . . the fundamental principle in the explanation of crime. . . . . The more the cultural patterns conflict, the

[15] L. Wirth, "Culture Conflict and Delinquency," *Social Forces*, IX (June, 1931), 487.

[16] Miriam Van Waters, *Youth in Conflict* (New York, 1925), p. 128.

more unpredictable is the behavior of a particular individual. It was possible to predict with almost complete certainty how a person reared in a Chinese village fifty years ago would behave because there was only one way for him to behave.[17]

We must not conclude, however, that every culture conflict results in misconduct. There are several other possibilities open to the person who is unable to resolve the conflict: he may work out a scheme which is far superior to the accepted code; he may become a reformer and try to bring about changes in one or both cultures that the dissonant elements may no longer bring strife; he may withdraw into a world of phantasy; he may become mentally deranged and commit suicide.[18]

[17] E. H. Sutherland, *Principles of Criminology* (Chicago, 1934), J. B. Lippincott Company, p. 52. Cf. T. Sellin, *Culture Conflict and Crime,* pp. 78–106.

[18] Philip Davis reported the following case: "A hideous story comes from New York of a young Russian Jewess who was employed as a stenographer in a downtown office, where she became engaged to be married to a young man of Jewish-American parentage. She felt keenly the difference between him and her newly immigrated parents, and on the night when he was to be presented to them she went home early to make every possible preparation for his coming. Her efforts to make the menage presentable were so discouraging, the whole situation filled her with such chagrin, that an hour before his expected arrival she ended her own life. Although her father was a Talmud scholar of standing in his native Russian town, and the lover was a clerk of very superficial attainment, she possessed no standard by which to judge the two men." Philip Davis, *Immigration and Americanization* (Boston, 1920, Ginn and Company), pp. 12–13. Quoted from *The Commons,* Vol. X, No. 1 (January, 1905).

CHAPTER XXIII

LANGUAGE AND CULTURE CONFLICT

Bitter conflicts between immigrants and their children rage about language. Language, as a means of communication, plays a basic rôle in bringing the individual into contact with his social group. In a homogeneous society, with a language understood by all, the members are not even aware of their medium of communication; they become conscious of it only when confronted by persons who cannot use the current speech. A common language is a prime factor in the establishment of a "universe of discourse," since in it are embodied the cultural symbols peculiar to that sector of the population. It is indispensable to assimilation; it is a pre-requisite for group life and group solidarity. "The barrier of language," Shaler comments, "puts a curious limitation upon the sympathies," [1] as in this Molokan home.

My little brother comes home from school and starts telling her [mother] something of what had happened during the day. She listens to him, but cannot make out what he is saying, and he repeats to her, but she says: "Well, what are you talking about? I can't understand you." And he gets impatient: "Well, I am trying to tell you. Why can't you understand?" And both of them get mad. He runs out on the street and tells the boys all about it, and she never knows what happened. You see, they just don't speak the same language. The older children learned Russian, and they speak half English and half Russian to their parents, but they get along.[2]

The school and language. When the children of immigrants enter the American school a barrier at once begins to develop which impedes free communication with their parents.[3] They progress in the school language but retrogress, or at least stand still, in the

[1] N. S. Shaler, *The Neighbor* (Boston, 1904, Houghton Mifflin Company), p. 37.
[2] P. V. Young, *op. cit.*, p. 169.
[3] Cf. K. Bercovici, *On New Shores*, pp. 156–57.

language of the home. Several factors are responsible for this. Teachers are eager to have their pupils use good English. Miss Mahon in Rölvaag's novel [4] may be considered typical of many when she told the boy of Norwegian parentage that he had a bad accent and that he should discontinue the use of his foreign speech. Later she told Peder's mother that he must get rid of his foreignism immediately lest it blight him for the remainder of his life.[5] And the continual goading of the schoolmistress made its impression. Peder heard an address in English which caused his fists to clench involuntarily and he vowed that he would learn to speak as beautifully as that man. His teacher was right—he must use less Norwegian at home. Hereafter he would use it only when conversing with his mother.[6]

Disdain of foreign languages. There is also the characteristic American attitude that any foreign language is inferior. "When my mother visited me in my sophomore year," said a college girl, "and my sorority found that English was not one of the six languages she spoke, they snubbed me. I was different and, therefore, necessarily inferior." [7]

Not until college days did this daughter of refined German parents realize the dignity of their mother tongue.

> My father made me learn German and always was wanting me to read it. I hated to have anything to do with it. It seemed to me something inferior. People in the West call a thing "Dutch" as a thing of scorn. It was not till I was in college that I realized what German literature and philosophy have meant in the world, and that to be a German is not to be a thing to be ashamed of.[8]

Parents with little education, or those using a language that does not have the high standing of the German, face a far more difficult situation. A child will say with emphasis, "I ain't no Bohunk; I'm an American."

Children are eager to escape anything that stigmatizes them as

[4] O. E. Rölvaag, *Peder Victorious* (New York, 1929), p. 91.

[5] *Ibid.*, p. 138.

[6] *Ibid.*, p. 129.

[7] Evelyn W. Hersey, manuscript copy of paper read at the National Conference of Social Work, May, 1934.

[8] E. G. Balch, *op. cit.*, p. 414.

inferior. Many have had their pride wounded by the speech of members of the immigrant group. One girl said:

I have never wished my parents were of another race, but they have hurt me beyond words. I have brought friends of mine to visit or have a meal with me. My parents are always genial enough, but they often address each other in Italian, which of course is not understandable to guests. They feel at sea, and I feel even more embarrassed.[9]

The broken English of this Jewish mother mortified her son.

I don't like to bring my American friends around. My mother speaks "English" to them, and they make fun of her. When I ask her to leave them alone she says: "They are only *goyim* (Gentiles); ain't I good enough to entertain them?" Sure, she "entertains" them—at my expense. . . . . It's awfully embarrassing to bring any American friends to the house.[10]

The young people wish to use English so well that no foreign accent or peculiarity can be detected to label them. Because of this sensitiveness many have their composure disturbed when an immigrant tries to speak the language of America. The mispronunciation of words, the errors in grammar, and the garbled sentences make them hang their heads.[11]

Language and personality problems. Language idiosyncracies are serious matters to children. In the words of Levy,

Even when the language difficulty is slight, a foreign accent, lack of facility in speaking, imperfect understanding of the full idiom of the new tongue may place a child definitely outside the pale. He never truly becomes "one of the boys," and frequently adjusts to this situation of essential conflict in a manner that brings him to the attention of the psychiatrists. Especially is variation in accent a source of conflict when the accent derives from an "inferior" culture. The speech idiosyncracies of the child may then remind his associates at every turn that here is an enemy or a person to be scorned. He functions, not as an individual, but as the representative of a hated race.[12]

[9] H. G. Duncan, *op. cit.*, p. 743.

[10] P. V. Young, "Jim's Own Story," *The Survey,* LIX (March 15, 1928), 777.

[11] Cf. O. E. Rölvaag, *Peder Victorious,* pp. 129–30.

[12] John Levy, "Conflicts of Cultures and Children's Maladjustment," *Mental Hygiene,* XVII (January, 1933), 44.

The upshot of it all is that many reject the parental language; they do not want it known that they can use it. Addressed in the mother tongue, they pretend they do not understand. Theodore Abel observed that the young Pole in a New England community deliberately avoids the use of the Polish language; he tries to eliminate all traces of his foreign extraction, which he considers a stigmatizing shortcoming. Only reluctantly will he admit his relationship to his own group, preferring to call himself French or Irish. Such a person will speak few words in Polish! [13]

According to a second-generation Mennonite, the old language brought serious problems in their colony, and a dislike for the German developed.

> The daily intercourse with friends is non-German. School lessons are learned in English and perchance some religious philosophies have been thought out that are more dynamic than customary. On returning home and to the church, the very medium of linguistic intercourse is the one that has all along brought difficulties. The religious philosophy expounded by the church in the German is conservative, in the main, and does not grapple with the daily life problems of the young people. Without any thorough-going analysis, impractical religious aphorisms, social difficulties experienced in the home, and feelings of inferiority are lumped together and charged to the account of the German language, with the result that the mother tongue becomes a hated symbol of the old order.[14]

The child of immigrant parentage encounters many impediments in his efforts to master the English language: he hears one speech at home and another outside and thus he has no steady pattern to follow. In such a situation language perplexities at times give rise to personality problems. Some children of immigrants find it difficult to acquire status in certain groups because of language peculiarities. Then they may turn to misconduct to gain recognition.

Language and family tensions. The language situation is the source of many problems in the home that develop into conflicts. Ability to read American newspapers exposes the child of the immigrant to a wide range of want-creating suggestions to which

[13] E. deS. Brunner, *op. cit.*, p. 240.

[14] Unpublished manuscript.

his elders are not attuned and, when they cannot understand and appreciate these new desires, tensions develop. His parents, he concludes, are, after all, just ignorant foreigners. Furthermore, the additional demands come to be a serious drain upon the slender financial resources of the home. Since the majority of the immigrants belong to the low-income class that can ill afford such increased expenditures, the children are prone to consider their parents inferior to the Americans they see on every hand. All this makes inroads upon family harmony and solidarity.

With the acquisition of the English language, the children can develop a private life of their own—think and act in ways their elders do not comprehend. Often this leads to the building up of life organizations beyond the ken of the parents. This result comes not only from participation in English-speaking play groups and gangs, but also through behavior patterns learned less directly through reading—particularly trashy novels. These patterns deviate widely from those of the old country. Oftentimes the parents are so far removed from the children that they are not even aware of the existence of the world in which the younger generation lives.[15] When parents and children live in such antipodal worlds, estrangements frequently come. When the children learn to speak English, they adopt American ways and have American friends with the inevitable result that there is little sympathy between the two generations. One boy said:

> I don't want to be green all my life. . . . . I've got my friends and go to their homes, but what would be the use of bringing them to see my folks? It would only make for trouble: they would think I am a gangster, because they don't know that we talk about all sorts of things that are harmless.[16]

The learning of English, which gives the children ideas foreign to the parents, brings misunderstandings, especially since the children are unable to translate these new notions into the terminology of their elders. When, however, the children turn away from the mother tongue and refuse to speak it at home, that is a

[15] Cf. O. E. Rölvaag, *Peder Victorious*, p. 151.

[16] L. Wirth, *Culture Conflicts in the Immigrant Family*, unpublished dissertation, University of Chicago.

still heavier cross to bear. Rölvaag shows the anguish this brought to one mother. She saw that more and more her children were using English while she never heard them mention anything that pertained to them as Norwegians. She came to realize that slowly, nevertheless surely, her children were being taken away from her. She dreaded the outcome, but saw no escape.[17]

Language conflicts often bring factional strife into the home. Some of the older children, who are foreign-born and speak the mother tongue fluently, take sides with the parents against the younger children who are American-born and English-speaking.

Language is so deeply embedded in the emotional life and in the case of the immigrant so closely entwined with memories of the Old World (where children were obedient) that it is a sacrilege to give it up. Language is a most precious heritage linking them with a hallowed past. When the old language is connected with religion, then it is doubly sacred. A second-generation Mennonite writes of his group: "Some of the older and more determined folks have insisted that the very foundations of the Mennonite religion were being undermined by the dropping of the German language.[18] In some mystical way, to them the word 'Gott' means far more than the word 'God' and 'Glaube' carries with it a subtle strength that the word 'faith' cannot possibly have." [19] A Norwegian immigrant mother spent a sleepless night when the minister gave her boy an English Bible. How could God's word conceivably be revealed in any language but the Norwegian! [20] A Jewish boy spoke English at the table on Friday evening, the important meal before the Sabbath, and that was an unforgivable offense; Yiddish was the only language to use on such an occasion.

Reversal of family rôles. Through his ability to use the English language the child becomes the interpreter, the instrumentality through which the parents communicate with Americans.

[17] Cf. O. E. Rölvaag, *Peder Victorious*, pp. 194–95.

[18] The Mennonite elders are not alone in their point of view. According to Arthur Ruppin, "One may say that the Jewish religion is on firm ground only where Yiddish is the mother tongue." *The Jews of Today* (New York, 1913), p. 117.

[19] Unpublished manuscript.

[20] Cf. O. E. Rölvaag, *Peder Victorious*, pp. 211–16.

"Me no know," accompanied by a shrug of her shoulders is the characteristic answer an American receives from a foreign woman. Then she adds, "Me call Mary." Little ten-year-old Mary comes and smilingly explains, "My mudder she don't know anything. What you want?" Mary has been to school and has learned the English language and some American customs; she is her mother's mouthpiece and very often must offer her mother advice in making the transition from the old world to the new.[21]

A parental rôle was virtually assumed by this youth of Ukrainian parentage.

My father had to depend upon me for many things. After my mother's death he had to use me more and more as a contact with the world of English-speaking people; he had learned very little of the language since he worked in a Jewish bakery in New York and thus had little occasion to use English. We consulted together about what should be done with this or that family matter. I accompanied him when he paid his gas bills, when he visited the offices of the insurance company, when he went to the union headquarters, or to other places. Often I acted as interpreter. On other occasions I merely accompanied him as a sort of advisor. Thus, in certain ways, I matured more rapidly than did other children of my age.[22]

The immigrant parent, in a greater degree than the native parent, is dependent upon his child. The child as the interpreter makes the necessary explanations for his mother to the landlord, the grocer, the visiting teacher, and the probation officer. The child also interviews the "boss," finds a job for his father, and explains all the "red-tape" connected with the necessary union membership. If the truant officer inquires concerning an absence or the policeman warns about a window-breaking escapade, usually the scamp himself serves as interpreter between officer and parent.

This situation complicates the problems in the immigrant home since it leads to a reversal of the usual relationship between parent and child. The parents in the old country were the sources of

[21] B. O. Pehotsky, *The Slavic Immigrant Woman* (Cincinnati, 1925), p. 39.

[22] Unpublished life history. Cf. also P. V. Young, *op. cit.*, p. 170, for an interesting case.

wisdom, but here the child becomes the fountain-head of knowledge and the parents learn to trust the child's version. Oftentimes in an interview the child interpreter gives the questioner his own ideas rather than what the parent tries to say when he answers questions directly without referring them to the parent.[23] But the parent usually is helpless. An Italian mother was displeased with her daughter for going to the settlement house when she was needed at home as interpreter. When Carmella returned, the mother grabbed her by the arm and scolded her. This outburst brought forth the retort: "You lick me again and I forget English." [24] A new threat had been evolved and it frightened the mother. The whipping did not materialize. The girl was afraid of her father who had not yet discarded the old-world attitude of patriarchal dominance in the household. But that was not all.

> It would not have been good for her, at thirteen, to know that he also was afraid of her; that he was afraid of all his English-chattering children. But chiefly afraid of Carmella, she being the oldest and the one on whom both parents relied to interpret their wishes to a world that did not speak their language.[25]

Thus the child in the immigrant home comes to play a more important rôle than the one in the native home. The latter is usually more or less dependent and makes little contribution in the family councils, while the former becomes at least a partner, if not a leader, in family enterprises. Oftentimes he arrives at a position of dominance. The parents, even though they may use English fairly well, are often baffled by the apparent irrationalities in our customs and need guidance in making adjustments to our complicated life. The child consequently comes to hold the whip hand.

In such situations of dependency one frequently sees expressions of humiliation on the faces of parents, particularly of the father. In the old-world he was the source of wisdom and authority, and

[23] An interesting picture of this situation is given by Walter S. Ball in *Carmella Commands* (New York, 1930). Carmella interpreted for her Italian parents and often took matters entirely into her own hands.

[24] W. S. Ball, *op. cit.*, p. 31.

[25] *Ibid.*, p. 32.

obedience was expected from the children. Such a reversal is a blow to his pride and dignity. Contrariwise, as the child observes the helplessness of the parent, he frequently assumes an air of patient condescension. He is not slow to realize his importance and comes to regard his own opinions on any and every subject as superior to those of his parents. He soon learns that he can circumvent his elders in ways that are seemingly of advantage to himself. Parents thus lose prestige in the eyes of their offspring and parental control is inevitably weakened. Delinquency and crime are often the direct results, or, at least, this anomaly is a predisposing and complicating factor. Certain control devices which are useful in the native homes are impotent in immigrant homes where the parents do not read English. School report cards, letters from teachers, attendance officers, or probation officers will not necessarily be translated accurately to the parents when the culprits themselves serve as interpreters. If a boy is having difficulty at school and his teacher writes a letter to his mother, he may tell her it is a circular letter advertising a new brand of breakfast flakes or the latest can-opener.

The language barrier in the immigrant home stands in the way of a wholesome parent-child relationship. According to Ruppin, when Jews adopt another language this "cuts away at a single stroke the chain by which the Jewish tradition was handed down for centuries in unbroken continuity from father to child. Children and parents no longer understand one another. Yiddish—the sole language of the parents—is despised by the children." [26] Because of this situation, many children lack proper parental counsel and guidance. Since there is no adequate means of communication, only matters of routine are discussed.

[26] A. Ruppin, *op. cit.*, p. 117.

CHAPTER XXIV

THE SCHOOL AND CULTURE CONFLICT

The American school is the nursery, *par excellence,* of culture conflicts. Through the teachers and other persons in authority the school dictates, in large measure, the conduct of the child during his waking hours. In all probability the immigrant parents had no idea of the far-reaching influence of this institution under whose jurisdiction their children come immediately on reaching school age. But they do not have to wait long before the results become evident.

The school and language. The school is the instrumentality above all others that functions in connection with the acquisition of language by the child of foreign-born parentage, and in that capacity it drives a big wedge between the two generations living under the same roof.

When the child, through the magic of the public school, learns the language, he then readily imbibes the traditions and ideals of the American epic. America becomes a living experience, while tales of the old country that he hears at home are but curious fragments of something remote and strange. They may even seem old-fashioned, tiresome—irritating. This is particularly true when the young person feels that his wishes are thwarted by misunderstanding parents who insist that old-world traits be followed closely.

Ability to read, write, and speak English introduces the child to a world that is alien to his parents. He reads the sport column in the newspaper when Babe Ruth, Jack Dempsey, "Dizzy" Dean, and the all-American quarter-backs become his heroes, while Huss, Sobieski, and Mazzini, who are all but worshipped by his parents, are nothing but ignorant "dagoes," "wops," and "hunkies" to him. As the children learn English they tend to prefer everything American to that of Bohemia, Poland, or Italy.

This larger world intrigues the children and entices them away from the parental group. Peter A. Speek observed that in a Polish farming colony the parents were greatly distressed over the prospect of losing their children as Poles after the public schools inoculated them with the idea that everything American was preferable to everything Polish.[1] Drachsler expressed this misgiving: [2]

> The fear of losing the children haunts the older generation. It is not merely the natural desire of parent to retain influence over child. Nor is it simply the dread that the wayward offspring will mar the good name of the immigrant group by abuse of his newly found freedom. It is a vague uneasiness that a delicate network of precious traditions is being ruthlessly torn asunder, that a whole world of ideals is crashing into ruins; and amidst this desolation the fathers and mothers picture themselves wandering about lonely in vain search of their lost children.

American superiority complex. The school reflects with remarkable accuracy the typical American feeling of superiority. The Italian child is assured that no greater good fortune could befall him than that of becoming an American.

> His geography lesson shows him how big this country is; his history lesson thanks Columbus for discovering us . . . . and explains how Washington and Lincoln and a few lesser lights made this world what it now is; his civics lesson assures him that America, if not still the refuge of the oppressed, is indeed the home of the free.[3]

[1] P. A. Speek, *op. cit.*, p. 153.

[2] From Julius Drachsler, *Democracy and Assimilation* (New York, 1920), p. 80. By permission of The Macmillan Company, publishers. This idea is borne out by Rölvaag. "The school seemed to exert an influence that Beret [the mother] could not understand. . . . . Evenings as soon as they had swallowed the last bite, they would clear the kitchen table and sit down to their books. In a moment they were off in a world where she could not follow. And they would act as if possessed; they neither heard nor saw. . . . .

"At first, she had not realized what was taking place, feeling contented because she had the children at home, right there by the kitchen table. . . . . At times she would think of questions to ask just to make them come out of their world. What were they doing now? What was the lesson about? Yes, but couldn't they say it in Norwegian? . . . . Either she would be ignored altogether, or she would get an answer so nonsensical that it vexed her. . . . If the two younger were called upon to explain, they would stammer or stumble over the words, and immediately switch into English; then they weren't stuck for words!" O. E. Rölvaag, *Peder Victorious*, pp. 193–94. See also pp. 137–41, 151–52.

[3] Ida L. Hull in *National Conference of Social Work*, 1924, pp. 288–89.

That point of view is further accentuated by the characteristic attitude of belittling everything foreign. This idea literally exudes from the pages of some school books. Oftentimes they present certain phases of life in other countries as being queer—even ridiculous. Children in American homes acquire this bias with their mother's milk, as it were, and then saturate the schools with it. An American-born girl of Russian-Jewish parentage encountered this narrow-mindedness.

> Often in class when we were discussing one thing or another, I would bring up, as examples, quaint customs that my mother used to perform in her country. Immediately, their faces would light up with ridicule, and instead of appreciation for the variety of ways of doing things, they would only laugh at customs different from their own.[4]

Teachers in the schools, both consciously and unconsciously, reflect the same attitude, as evidenced strikingly by the experience of a Jewess. In the opening exercises one morning, the teacher read a selection from the "literature book" and followed this by a brief talk in which the Jews were designated a "peculiar" people. A number of the pupils discussed the matter in earnest and concluded that even though the teacher knew everything else, she was quite mistaken about them. It hurt to be held up as strange.[5]

The schools, unwittingly or otherwise, put pressure on the children to turn away from everything belonging to the culture of their ancestors. They endeavor to shape the children of immigrants into a standardized American mold as rapidly as possible. Brunner studied seventy rural communities and in not one had the school adapted its program to the particular needs of the immigrants and their offspring. No attempt had been made to use the music, folk dances, folklore, or any of the customs of the various nationality groups to enrich the cultural life of the community and incidentally to dignify the parental cultures in the eyes of the children. Such activities on the part of the school would probably be useful in

[4] H. G. Duncan, *op. cit.*, p. 775.

[5] Elizabeth G. Stern, "What It Means To Be a Jewess," *Ladies' Home Journal*, XXXVI (April, 1919), p. 129.

releasing the usual tension between foreign-born parents and their American children.[6]

The school and behavior. Sufficient data have accumulated to show that our schools are not producing the most commendable results in dealing with the children of immigrants. Many parents keep their children away from school, not because of innate depravity or ignorance, as some would have us believe, but from an earnest desire to have them grow up as well-behaved, orderly citizens. According to Dr. Miriam Van Waters, some immigrants say that their children learn wickedness at school.[7] "My mother," remarked a Molokan girl, "was dead set against my plans [of going to school], and she would say: 'Well, look what happens when we send our children to school. All they learn is to despise us. Look how they talk back to us'!" [8] Further evidence is given by the distressed man who conferred with Panunzio about his thirteen-year-old nephew. Two years ago, according to the uncle, when the boy came from Italy, he was exemplary in his attitude toward his elders—he was affectionately attentive to his mother. Now, however, he is unmanageable; he is disrespectful, keeps late hours, and uses the most vile and profane language. After this recital the man asked if the schools in America taught boys to be bad.[9]

The schools have often been responsible for developing in the children impoliteness, rudeness, and vulgarities that brought heartaches to the parents. Such crudities stand out all the more glaringly in young persons from immigrant homes because they do not have a sufficiently wide acquaintance with our life to temper individual acts to the occasion. Leiserson reports a case.

> A native American woman drove over to the house of a Polish neighbor to inquire if the daughter of the Polish family would accept work as a servant. . . . . The American woman was displeased with the attitude of the Polish girl, but she thought the old Polish woman was "nice." The

[6] E. deS. Brunner, *op. cit.*, pp. 106–07. Cf. G. H. von Koch, *op. cit.*, pp. 37–48, for the effect of the school as observed by a visitor from Sweden.

[7] *Op. cit.*, p. 16. Cf. also K. Bercovici, *On New Shores*, p. 194, relative to the Amish of Ohio.

[8] P. V. Young, *op. cit.*, p. 168. Cf. also pp. 145–46.

[9] C. M. Panunzio, *The Soul of an Immigrant*, p. 255.

girl did not seem at all pleased about the opportunity to work as a servant. The mother, however, was quite evidently anxious that the daughter should get the work. The girl asked in good English about the wages offered and the privileges as to days off and evenings out, and she stipulated the kind of work she would do in the household and what she would not do. The mother, in broken English, apologized for her daughter's attitude, apparently fearing that her questions might lose her the job. But the daughter explained that her teacher in the public school told her to be independent like an American and to ask questions like that.[10]

In an atmosphere where everything of foreign origin is rejected on the pretext that it is inferior, a severe handicap is imposed on the child. When small boys in the play group find ego security in boasting about what "my father" says and does, the young son of the immigrant soon detects that his father's animated gestures, his long beard, his broken language, and his queer shoes are causes of derision.[11] He learns that his father is a "wop," a "sheeney," a "bohunk," or a "dago" and although he does not know what these epithets signify, he realizes that they bear with them opprobrium and stigma. When he discovers that the larger community accords his father a low status, he begins to lose respect for him.[12] Other boys can feel proud of their parents and boast about them, but he must feel ashamed of his and apologize for them. This brings a terrific struggle, for he knows that he should respect and honor his elders. On every hand—in the church, in school, and in the books he has read—the sacredness of father and mother has been instilled into him as a holy idea. He may succeed in hiding this shame, but in many instances it breaks out in the ugliest of conduct that brings heartaches to the distraught parents.[13] In

[10] W. M. Leiserson, *op. cit.*, pp. 19–20.

[11] A young Molokan in Los Angeles said of the street-car conductors: "They holler 'Whiskers Boulevard' when they stop at Utah Street. Many times the people in the street cars would look at the Russian men and say, 'Baa-baa.'" P. V. Young, *op. cit.*, p. 170.

[12] The case of Nick is a good illustration of an attitude of contempt and superiority toward the parents. National Commission on Law Observance and Enforcement, *Report on the Causes of Crime* (Washington, 1931), Vol. II, No. 13, pp. 3–20.

[13] Drucker and Hexter present a case of a Russian mother who was dejected because of the behavior of her children. "I am so unhappy," she said. . . . . "My eldest son is lost to us forever. . . . . I am afraid—afraid of this America." *Children Astray* (Cambridge, 1923), p. 74. See entire case, pp. 67–85.

the old country obedience and respect were normal expectations. How different here when twelve-year-old Tony stamps his foot and shouts at his Sicilian father, "I'll take nothing off a damn Dago like you." [14]

An Americanization worker indicates the general course of the culture conflict which is accentuated by the school.

As time goes on, the children of the "foreigner" realize that their parents' whole mode of living—the food they eat, their strict views on amusement, social intercourse, marriage and other subjects—differs markedly from American ideas and practices. Under the stimulus of this new environment, the children make their own plans and gradually leave their fathers and mothers out of the picture. They resent questions relative to their conduct and, if parents try to exercise their traditional authority, clashes result. The first quarrel leads to harsh words and to contempt for the non-American parents. Then comes the juvenile court, and the parents' pitiful, "I can't do anything with him." Too often the cleavage is complete and the children are never reunited in spirit and sympathies with their parents, at least not until they have grown to maturity and see with the eyes of bitterly acquired wisdom. Keeping in step with their children is the most difficult problem facing foreign parents today.[15]

Furthermore, it often becomes painfully evident to the boy that because his father is rejected he, too, is rated as an inferior and many uncomplimentary epithets are attached to him. He is subjected to stinging jibes and taunts. A second-generation boy was interested in examining the new barn of a neighbor when the owner's son of the same age said, "Look all you please, only don't scare the cows—they ain't used to Norwegians!" [16]

The child of immigrant parentage has many earmarks that set him apart from other children. School lunches often cause distress. "My neighbor's little boy," observed a Mexican in California, "is

[14] That the school indoctrinates the child thoroughly with American patriotism is made evident from the report on an Italian boy who resisted when his father tried to punish him. When brought into the juvenile court and questioned about the matter, he asked: "Well, Judge, honest now, do you think an American ought to let himself be licked by a foreigner?" Edward R. Lewis, *America: Nation or Confusion* (New York, 1928), p. 133.

[15] Adapted from *The Interpreter,* IV, No. 3 (March, 1925), 9–11.

[16] O. E. Rölvaag, *Peder Victorious,* p. 96.

ashamed to take *tortillas* to school for his lunch and often does not eat his lunch. Everyone laughs about *frijoles.*" [17] A Molokan girl in Los Angeles said of her brother: "He dislikes my mother's lunches. She can't make any dainty sandwiches for him. She fries something for him, gives him two thick pieces of Russian bread, and the boy is ashamed to take that to school. They make fun of him." [18]

Insult is added to injury when these lunches are wrapped in tell-tale foreign-language newspapers. Because of this, paper, lunch, and all have been thrown away rather than face the taunts and ridicule of the children. Elizabeth G. Stern related her experience when she opened her first lunch parcel at school. The girls gasped in sympathy when she unwrapped the newspaper and spread out the mass of fried potatoes, thick, unshapely slices of bread, a crushed tomato, and a big piece of filled fish. They concluded that the lunch had been crushed and must be thrown away, whereupon they gave her fruit, pie, and sandwiches. After that first day she threw all her mother's lunches in the trash can at school, even though she was hungry for the bread and fish prepared by her mother.[19]

Since the child finds, to his sorrow and chagrin, that anything which labels him as different also stamps him as an inferior, he makes every effort to remove distinguishing marks. The Finnish newspaper was a source of embarrassment to a second-generation Finn. "On the occasion of its arrival at the post office," he wrote, "I would wrap it in an English paper, or else hide it under my coat while taking it home." [20] The child feels the loss of status which is his by virtue of his attachment to an immigrant home. To gain the desired acceptance he must make every effort to conform to this new, strange, and unknown American pattern. This may lead to a wholesale rejection of everything foreign, even of his own parents in many instances. "This rejection of their natural

[17] *Survey of Race Relations.*
[18] P. V. Young, *op. cit.*, p. 168.
[19] E. G. Stern, *My Mother and I*, pp. 89–90.
[20] H. G. Duncan, *op. cit.*, p. 791.

backgrounds and the breakdown of parental authority produces many types of personal and social maladjustment." [21]

The child may even ridicule his parents and the parental culture in order to put himself on the side of the Americans against the immigrants. But this bravado does not at once give him status in the American group and he finds himself trying to live in two social worlds at the same time. In the words of Zorbaugh:

> The same situations are defined in contradictory terms by the school, for example, on the one hand, and by the family, on the other. If the child conforms to the American definition he is a delinquent in the eyes of the family; if he conforms to the family definition he is a delinquent in the eyes of the American law.
>
> The child cannot live and conform in both social worlds at the same time. The family and colony are defined for him in his American contacts by such epithets as "dago," "wop," "foreign," and the like. He feels the loss of status attached to his connection with the colony. In his effort to achieve status in the American city he loses his *rapport* with family and community. Conflicts arise between the child and his family. Yet by virtue of his race, his manner of speech, the necessity of living in the colony, and these same definitive epithets, he is excluded from status and intimate participation in American life. Out of this situation . . . . arises the gang, affording the boy a social world in which he finds his only status and recognition. But it is by conforming to delinquent patterns that he achieves status in the gang. And every boy in Little Hell is a member of a gang. This is substantially the process of disorganization of the Sicilian boy of the second generation. Out of it grows all manner of social disorganization.[22]

The imputation of inferiority to the immigrants and everything pertaining to them by the schools influences their conduct through the effect it has on occupational choices of the children.

> The practical result of their teaching seems to be so to turn the desires of children as far as possible from manual labor, and inspire them all with the ambition to be teachers, clerks, stenographers, attendants in stores, or at least factory workers. The young Italian boy will rather

[21] *The Social Work Yearbook* (New York, 1935), p. 197.
[22] H. M. Zorbaugh, *op. cit.*, pp. 176–77.

loaf on a street corner than go into unskilled, manual work; and where opportunities are as crowded as they are in the lines he wants to follow, the chances are that he, and many like him, will loaf a long time, and learn many vices that are likely to lead to pauperism.[23]

Many children of immigrants feel that they are an out-cast group. "This growing feeling of inferiority," as Wirth puts it, "deprives the individual of the group sanction which is necessary to preserve personal morale." [24] This leads to a divided life. To quote Eugene Lyons:

A system of hypocritical makeshifts is forced upon the boys and girls whereby they seek to hide from their friends the nature of their lives at home and from their families the nature of their lives outside the home. The tragedy lies in this: the child, taught to spurn foreign ways, renounces not only what is intrinsically objectionable in the home, but everything. The finest expressions of its parents' life experiences or racial traditions, sometimes the profoundest manifestations of religion or social idealism, it throws indiscriminately into the limbo of "foreign."

Anyone who has looked without blinking at life in our foreign sections can quote examples a-plenty of young people unable to reconcile the two phases of their existence and encouraged arbitrarily by the educational mechanism to despise their alien families.[25]

Inevitably the schools of America, be they the public grade schools or colleges, build barriers between the immigrant parents and their children, and it is more noticeable in those groups whose cultures differ most widely from the American norms. The Jews are deeply affected.

The children may attend religious schools until the age of six or eight, but after this age they must attend public school, and if they continue both their religious and secular education at the same time a conflict usually arises. The "cheder" is a religious institution representing a definite set of social values; the public school represents a cosmopolitan group and tends to wean the child away from his old culture. The

[23] K. H. Claghorn, "Immigration and Pauperism," *The Annals,* XXIV (July, 1904), 204.

[24] Louis Wirth, "Culture Conflict and Misconduct," *Social Forces,* IX (June, 1931), 491.

[25] Eugene Lyons, "Second-Generation Aliens," *Nation,* CXVI (April 25, 1923), 491.

school cannot set itself to make better Jews; its prime function is to make better American citizens. The children learn a new and different moral code through their associations at public school. They begin to live simultaneously in two different worlds: their home, their religious and communal life represent one culture, and the public school and the larger community represent another.[26]

The problems of Jewish children, particularly those from orthodox homes, tend to be accentuated because of certain ceremonial observances. The uncompromising Jew wears under his vest a small praying shawl, the *arba kanfoth* (four corners), with a woolen fringe on each corner. This garment is worn by a boy from his earliest years and because of this he is singled out and made the butt of ridicule in the school. The following experience related by an immigrant boy reveals the genesis of a religious conflict.

I didn't know any better when I came here. I was a regular *Zaddik* (extremely pious person). I had been brought up that way and didn't know any better. I even wore an *arba kanfoth.* I didn't think there was anything queer about it. I really didn't think about it at all, just as I don't think about eating or sleeping or breathing. But one day I got into a fight in the schoolyard and in the tussle my *arba kanfoth* was pulled out. The boys who watched us fight began to make fun of me. I found out that most of the American Jewish boys didn't wear them at all. The next day when I got to school a bunch of the boys pulled my *arba kanfoth* out. I didn't feel so bad the first day, but the second day I felt ashamed of myself. The first day I was sore at them for making fun of it. I made up my mind then that I wouldn't wear it any more and the next day I left it off. My mother found it and when I came home that night I got an awful bawling out. I told her that I wouldn't wear it any more, that other Jewish boys at school weren't wearing it and that I wasn't going to have them make a fool out of me again. It made her awful mad and she was afraid to tell my father at first. When he found out he gave me a beating, but I wouldn't wear it anyway. But that was just the beginning. I found out that there were lots of things that I was doing that other Jewish boys weren't. It started me thinking about the Jewish religion and the more I thought about it, the less I believed in it. I thought that my father and mother were very

[26] Pauline V. Young, "The Reorganization of Jewish Family Life in America," *Social Forces,* VII (December, 1928), 239.

old-fashioned, and I had many arguments with them. They don't think much of me any more and I don't think much of them.[27]

Wirth makes this comment:

In the above case the reaction to a particular situation involving one religious element led to a changed attitude toward the body of traditions as a whole. The tension arising from an incident involving one cultural element led to a redefinition of the individual's set of values and to a cultural conflict with his parents and the code which they represent. This seems to be a tendency which is manifest in most of the cases of cultural conflict. The cultural element around which the tension first centers becomes generalized into a set of reactions toward the culture as a whole. If that reaction be of an antagonistic nature, the chances that a culture conflict will emerge out of the situation are very great.[28]

Higher education and culture conflict. Many children of immigrants are eager to go on through high school and even college in order to gain a status higher than that accorded their parents, but the farther they go the wider becomes the chasm between themselves and their parents, as evidenced by a Japanese college student in Hawaii:

Sometimes I wish I had not come to college. With those persons who are going to college, education just widens the gap between the parents and their children. When my mother urged me to go to college, she was thinking only of me, but little did she foresee the consequences. My brother was the first one to leave home. He is at present in San Francisco, and probably will not return to Hawaii. Now, I am just about in the same situation; I am away from the control of home. My parents thought that when my brother and I graduated from high school, they would enjoy old age. I fear their wish is still unanswered; for, instead of happiness, they may have to face the hard struggle of life for many more years. Between these two forces, the school and the family, there has not been much coöperation. I guess this is the lot of children of immigrant parentage; it is an inevitable consequence. Perhaps, if our parents foresaw this outcome before they came here, they would not

[27] L. Wirth, *Culture Conflicts in the Immigrant Family,* unpublished dissertation, University of Chicago, 1925, p. 93.
[28] *Ibid.,* pp. 94–95.

have taken such a chance. But it is too late; we are here and we have to make the best of it.

To meet the situation we children of oriental parentage try to live a dual life. At home we try to act and speak like typical Japanese. Outside the home we try to act and speak like "Old Americans." We are criticized by our parents for speaking an imperfect Japanese; we are, also, criticized by the Americans.[29]

When a second-generation Jewess returned to her parental home in the ghetto after four years in college she found the situation unbearable. Her parents, too, were deeply distressed by the change that had come over her. After some heated discussion her father blurted out:

Pfui on all your American colleges! Pfui on the morals of America! No respect for old age. No fear for God. Stepping with your feet on all the laws of the holy Torah. A fire should burn out the whole new generation. They should sink into the earth, like Korah.[30]

After more harsh words he addressed his wife who had tried to pour oil on the troubled waters.

Fool woman, ... stop laying yourself on the ground for your daughter to step on you! What more can you expect from a child raised up in America? What more can you expect but that she should spit in your face and make dirt from you? . . . . The old Jewish eating is poison to her; she must have *trefa* ham—only forbidden food. . . . .

Woman, how you patted yourself with pride before all the neighbors, boasting of our great American daughter coming home from college! This is our daughter, our pride, our hope, our pillow for our old age that we were dreaming about! This is our American teacherin! A Jew-hater, an Anti-Semite we brought into the world, a betrayer of our race who hates her own father and mother like the Russian Czar once hated a Jew. She makes herself so refined, she can't stand it when we use the knife or fork the wrong way; but her heart is that of a brutal Cossack, and she spills her own father's and mother's blood like water.[31]

Language schools and behavior. Much has been said and written about the language and parochial schools of immigrant groups in

29 Unpublished life history. Cf. H. G. Duncan, *op. cit.*, pp. 770–73 for a similar experience of a Polish student.

30 A. Yezierska, *Children of Loneliness*, p. 103.

31 *Ibid.*, p. 108. Cf. also pp. 101–16.

America. "Until the Asiatics met with so much prejudice on the Pacific Coast," writes Duncan, "many of the parents opposed the language schools. They wanted their children to grow up as good American citizens in every respect." [32] This assertion does not present the situation adequately. The first Japanese language school in Los Angeles was organized for the express purpose of helping the children of the immigrant Japanese become good citizens. Japanese had observed the disorganization of children in other immigrant groups and advocated the language school as an instrumentality to aid the two generations in understanding each other, thereby reducing culture conflicts and resultant misconduct.[33] Kum Pui Lai brings further evidence from Hawaii: "The function of the language schools, according to the early Chinese, was to prevent the rapid acculturation of their youths and their eventual estrangement from the first generation and their ancestral land, China." [34] Delinquency ratios of the Japanese and Chinese children both on the Pacific Coast and in Hawaii make it evident that their idea was sound. The Japanese have been remarkably successful in controlling the conduct of their children, and the language school, without doubt, has been a factor of no small importance.[35] Many immigrants have seen, to their sorrow, the results of a rapid denationalization of their offspring. The public school by itself tends to accelerate the process unduly. An immigrant woman pleaded with Panunzio not to send her children to an American school. She had observed that as soon as children learned English they became estranged from their parents, and she did not want to lose hers. She asked that they be sent to a school where they might be taught the Italian language so she would be able to converse with them.[36]

On the basis of such experiences, demoralization comes to be synonymous with Americanization so far as many immigrants

[32] H. G. Duncan, *op. cit.*, p. 700.

[33] Cf. Y. Ichihashi, *op. cit.*, pp. 325–33, and *Sociology and Social Research*, XVII (January-February, 1933), 259–64, for discussions of the Japanese language schools. Cf. W. I. Thomas and F. Znaniecki, *op. cit.*, II, pp. 49–56.

[34] Kum Pui Lai, "Attitudes of Chinese in Hawaii toward Their Language Schools," *Sociology and Social Research*, XX (November–December, 1935), 141.

[35] Cf. W. C. Smith, *op. cit.*, pp. 211–26.

[36] C. M. Panunzio, *The Soul of an Immigrant*, p. 254.

are concerned,[37] and this situation is at least one reason for the existence in America of the many schools where foreign languages are used almost exclusively.[38]

Hitti is aware of the enigma:

One of the main problems of Syrian family life in America is that of how to span the gap between the old-fashioned Arabic-speaking parents, on the one hand, and the American-born English-speaking children on the other. How hard it is for a public school child, who has all of a sudden discovered that he is superior to his father in point of education and linguistic attainments, to reconcile himself to an attitude of obedient respect is easy to imagine.[39]

Duncan also states that the prime purpose of parochial schools "appears to be to teach the religion and language of the parents." [40] That, too, is an inadequate statement. Religion and language are not necessarily taught as ends in themselves, but as means to an end—to the end that the chasm between the generations may be bridged and the culture conflicts be materially reduced. If the children can understand and appreciate the language and religion of their parents, they will not necessarily hold to them, but will develop more wholesome attitudes toward them.

Conclusion. On the basis of the available data we are forced to the conclusion that the American school, although well-intentioned, has not dealt wisely with the children of immigrants. Unknowingly it has been actually ruthless in ignoring and belittling the cultural heritages of the diverse elements in our population while glorifying the dominant civilization, thereby bringing about permanent and often tragic estrangements. The school should have paid some attention to counteracting the various influences in the community which tend to produce conflicts between the two generations. It might well have turned to the delicate task of reëstablishing and reenforcing between the two generations a sympathy which, under conditions in the new environment, was in danger of waning.

[37] Cf. R. E. Park and H. A. Miller, *op. cit.*, pp. 288–89.

[38] Cf. C. M. Panunzio, *The Soul of an Immigrant*, p. 254.

[39] From *Racial Studies of the New American Series,* by P. K. Hitti, copyright, 1924, by Doubleday, Doran and Company, Inc., New York, p. 80. Cf. also E. E. Ledbetter, *op. cit.*, pp. 27–28.

[40] *Op. cit.*, p. 700.

CHAPTER XXV

RECREATIONAL CONFLICTS

Immigrant groups come to our shores with a host of recreational customs and traditions all of which differ from the forms common to America. According to Roberts,[1]

> There is one characteristic which differentiates Americans at play from the people of southeastern Europe on pleasure bent: it is the intensity with which the native-born throw themselves into their games. There does not seem to be any relaxation in the amusement of our people; the tension before mentioned, which characterizes labor in the United States, is also carried into the pleasures which are enjoyed. The Italians play a ball game and they enjoy themselves in a leisurely manner. They smoke, chat, laugh, and stroll along quietly and without haste after the balls; but a ball game among the native-born is "no good" unless the field rings with shouts and the players exert themselves to the utmost. A game of cards played on the lawn of a summer's evening by a group of Slavs is enjoyed by each of the players; they chat, smoke cigarettes, and possibly have a bottle of beer to pass around. But a game of cards on a railroad car among Americans is a serious thing; the players seldom smoke, they are quiet or swearing, they study their hands very seriously, and the whole performance appears as if much depended on the game then going on. The same is true of the dance; the foreigners move leisurely, they smoke and chat, they have a good time in a pleasant way; but the American dance hall is not up to standard, unless the pace on the floor is exhilarating, the whirl exciting, men and women in perspiration, and the dancers so exhausted that they are glad to find a seat to rest themselves.

American patterns of play are acquired rapidly when children of the immigrants enter school, and very early this becomes a source of conflict in the home. One sees this among the German Amish in Ohio.

[1] From Peter Roberts, *The New Immigration* (New York, 1912), p. 265. By permission of The Macmillan Company, publishers.

The youngsters go to school not because they love school but because they refuse to be different from the other boys. I have seen them look on enviously at baseball games around the school. Games are *verboten* by the Amish religion. All amusement is *verboten.* Work. Food. Bed. Meditation. It is the law. They go to bed at sunset. Hardly a house that has a kerosene lamp. It is true the boys kept apart, but there was a flame in many a boy's quiet eye as he watched the game. A Polish boy leaned over and told me confidentially: "Gee, it's hard on them kids! But Jacob there has already organized a baseball team of his own, and they practise secretly on the other side of the woods where their fathers do not see them." [2]

Old-world heritages. The immigrants have continued some of the play activities to which they were accustomed in the Old World. A number of Italians have earned a livelihood by playing hurdy-gurdies on the street. But that is work and not the most pleasant kind. After a day of this they feel the need of relaxation, and then they turn to a traditional outlet. Robert A. Woods tells how in the north end of Boston a group will gather in a court where they have Italian music and dancing. "There, indeed, the *tarantella,* the favorite and famous dance of southern Italy, is performed exactly as it is among the crags of Capri." [3] These scenes from the home country life are not enacted before the public gaze, but in places that are sheltered from curious American eyes.

Many of the recreational activities of the immigrants revolve around religious festivals. Weddings and christenings also receive considerable attention. The Italian's love of the dramatic and his loyalty to his fatherland home blossom out into a variety of folk festivals. Anniversaries and holy days provide opportunities. Italy is also the home of music, particularly the opera, and not even work on the railway track or in the grimy factory has crushed out their interest in Caruso and Tetrazzini. Immigrants from northwestern Europe have demonstrated their love for music through the organization of bands, orchestras, choirs, and male choruses. Gymnastic and dramatic societies have come largely from central Europe.

[2] K. Bercovici, *On New Shores,* p. 198.
[3] Robert A. Woods, *Americans in Process* (New York, 1902), p. 227.

When immigrants came to America and began to work, for the most part, at hard, monotonous labor, they needed relaxation. But they could not participate in the leisure-time programs of the old Americans. The natives accepted them as utilities in the mine and steel mill, but not in social and recreational life where mingling is more on the basis of equality. The immigrant would also feel more ill-at-ease there than at his work. He, therefore, had to devise means to provide for his play needs, so he transplanted certain forms in which he had participated in the homeland. Not all types, however, could be used. Many were suitable only in colonies of considerable size. The extent to which imported diversions could survive depended in some measure on the degree of their divergence from those of America. The north European immigrants encountered less difference, nevertheless they had to discard some traditional divertisements. "Even the British worker . . . . found on his arrival that tea drinking was ridiculed, ale illegal, football of a different variety, and cricket a gentlemen's pastime reserved for exclusive country clubs." [4] However, in many of these leisure-time activities there was no conflict with Americans particularly in those that were carried on within the groups and were not displayed to outsiders. To be sure, Chinese gambling, a traditional activity of the Cantonese, ran afoul the law in California, and the use of alcoholic liquors came into conflict with prohibition laws. In the main the immigrants did not have to make changes in this sector of their lives in order to hold jobs, except in some measure. When the Slavs and Lithuanians would not work on the festival days of the church and when the Magyars, Poles and Roumanians would have weddings that lasted for several days, certain employers might object.[5]

The immigrants were not particularly interested in American forms of play. In Iowa, "Hollanders take very little interest in the forms of recreation and amusement so popular in American towns and cities: they are such poor patrons of 'shows' of every kind that traveling companies habitually pass them by as un-

[4] Donald Young, *American Minority Peoples* (New York, 1932), p. 276.
[5] Cf. C. A. Galitzi, *op. cit.*, p. 137.

profitable."[6] Certain immigrant groups have taken a strong stand against specific American play activities. The Swedish immigrants to Texas had come under the influence of the great religious awakening in Sweden. The reformers had inveighed against the worldliness of the state church and had put the patterns of the old forms of recreation out of their lives because they were sinful, as measured by the standards of the new faith. All kinds of amusement were considered wrong.[7] Pihlblad wrote of the Swedes in Lindsborg, Kansas:

The pietistic attitude, an inheritance from the old country, interpreted nearly all forms of recreation as sinful. The heavy labor and toil of the early period made it relatively easy to prevent the devil finding work for idle hands. Dancing, card playing, gambling, the theatre, etc., were strictly tabooed during the early days, and are even today considered to be somewhat immoral. No theatre existed until the coming of the movies, which at first were regarded as questionable, no pool hall existed until last year [1931] and then only after the revocation of a city ordinance forbidding such places. This was accomplished after a conflict which split the community into two warring factions. Dance halls have always been forbidden by ordinance.[8]

The Molokans of Los Angeles have been an austere, hard-working group and the older people have considered play a means of wasting valuable time that should be devoted to honest labor —the only visible result is mischief and disrespect for both God and the elders. One put it thus:

Our children always play, play, play. They tell us that we don't give them enough time to play. Why, they play at school, they play after school, they even make them play at Juvenile Hall. Ball-playing does not help you in life. It's baby stuff.

I don't let my children go any place. And my girl came home and told me they invited her to a dance. She told them she could not come because her parents think that "dancing is a sin." So they told her: "Your mother is old-fashioned, you are in America now and you must

[6] Jacob Van der Zee, *The Hollanders of Iowa* (Iowa City, 1912), p. 328.

[7] Cf. C. M. Rosenquist, *op. cit.*

[8] C. T. Pihlblad, "The Kansas Swedes," *The Southwestern Social Science Quarterly,* XIII (June, 1932), 12–13.

change according to our customs. We don't have any wicked dancing here." That was the last time she has been to that club. She never learned to dance, and has never gone to public dance halls.[9]

Immigrant children and recreation. For the most part the children of immigrants neither appreciate the old-world forms of play nor do they comprehend the antagonistic attitudes of their parents toward the common American practices. The parents do not understand the children's play and call it foolish, wasteful, ridiculous even immoral. "Often in my younger days," commented a second-generation Polish girl, "I have wanted to play but father would not permit me to do so. He would say: 'Idleness is the devil's workshop. If you want to do something, go and shell peas for mother, or fetch a pail of water from the well.' "[10]

Despite opposition, the younger generation is turning to the American forms. Van der Zee observed that

> The young people tend more and more in their everyday life to adopt the ways of the American public and to break with the orthodox views of their elders, and thus exert a softening influence on the hard tone of community life; but parents continue to hope and pray that their children will retain the traditional hardihood, industry, frugality, thrift, morality, and religion for which the Hollanders are famous as a people.[11]

But even then the break with the old order is not a violent one; the indoctrination by the older generation has been too thorough for that. "Skating rinks, moving picture shows, and dances attract the younger folks, but dancing is rarely indulged in because it shocks and antagonizes the older people."[12]

According to Rosenquist,[13] the younger generation Swedes in Texas have appropriated in large measure the American forms for their leisure-time activities, many of them being unchanged acquisitions from the American folkways.[14] Bridge parties, al-

[9] P. V. Young, *op. cit.*, p. 140.

[10] Unpublished life history.

[11] J. Van der Zee, *The Hollanders of Iowa*, p. 329.

[12] *Ibid.*, p. 328.

[13] *Op. cit.*

[14] O. A. Benson found a similar situation among the Swedes in Chicago. *Op. cit.* The second generation Hungarians in Lorain, Ohio, have likewise adopted the current American uses of their leisure time. S. C. Newman, *Immigrant Adjustments of the Hungarians in Lorain, Ohio,* unpublished dissertation, Oberlin College.

though comparatively rare in the Swedish community have been adopted. This indicates a break in the Swedish mores which have indiscriminately condemned card playing.[15] Dancing, however, has encountered such strenuous opposition that it has not gained admission.[16] There was considerable controversy over this matter in the community at one time. The church, supported by a majority of its members, denounced dancing. A considerable number of the young people with the knowledge of their parents, if not actual consent, attend dances, but they have to go outside their own community to participate. The attitude against dancing has been taken over in considerable measure even by the young people. Rosenquist found that some of the Swedish students in the University of Texas were opposed to dancing; the old attitudes had not yielded to American influences even under the pressure of their extended school life. On the whole the evidence indicates that there has been a gradual shift in the recreational activities of the Swedes of Texas from the old-world patterns to American ones, except where the new forms have been contrary to the mores.[17]

[15] Swedish immigrants of the pietistic group were definitely opposed to card playing. In one rural colony in Nebraska, the young folks played but not openly—they would play in the haylofts. One immigrant mother, with tears in her eyes, implored her son to give her the deck that she might burn it. Another woman in the same colony saw a group of the younger set playing "Rook." Plaintively she pleaded with them to stop. When her son pointed out that the "Rook" cards had numbers and not the usual symbols of the devil's own game, the fun was permitted to continue undisturbed. Another means of circumventing the "card" taboo was to play "Forty-Two" with dominoes.

[16] Among the Swedish immigrants of the Separatistic group, disapproval of the dance extended even to the violin, which was the musical instrument used. An immigrant in Nebraska returned to Sweden on a business trip. After one of his sons had taken him to the railway station he bought a violin and brought it home. His mother pleaded with him to burn the instrument. The violin, however, was kept and was gradually assimilated into the home until nothing was said about it. About twenty years later the minister's daughter introduced violin music into the Swedish church where this immigrant mother had been a member for some twenty-five years. When asked how she liked the violin music, she replied, not with unbounded enthusiasm, "Oh, it's beautiful music, is it not?."

[17] In a Swedish community in Nebraska a number of boys constructed croquet grounds. Boys from neighboring farms would meet and play, usually on Sunday, because a half-holiday for recreation was unknown. The immigrant parents would speak disparagingly of this useless play, but there was no open conflict. This particular game was not in their old-world experience and had not come under the interdiction of a homeland taboo at the time of the great awakening in the church. One of the immigrant fathers, however, seemed to have won a great moral victory one autumn when his corn crop overtaxed the available crib space and several

Thus the surprise party and picnic have been accepted, while dancing and Sunday sports are still under taboo. There they will remain so long as the church, the guardian of the mores, is able to exercise control. In this group the conflict between the generations has not been so violent and disorganizing as in those with cultures differing more widely from that of the old American stock.

Nels Anderson found difficulties in a colony in rural Virginia.

> The scruples against dancing which the Bohemians have taken over from the Protestants, as Protestantism is interpreted to them by the missionary societies, have tended to divide families. The young people cross the line to dance with Catholics and Free Thinkers. Some attend the public dances. The other groups not only condone dancing but whole families attend the dances, which vary little from country dances elsewhere, except for the fact that all ages are present and all ages take part. The music is superior and does not include jazz.[18]

Pieters shows the conflict among the Dutch in Michigan.

> Card playing, dancing, and theater going were forbidden as a matter of course. Not that these had been unknown and unpractised in the Netherlands, but they were not in the least compatible with the religious beliefs in the community and had, therefore, been condemned. Many a father and mother suffered heartache over the spiritual degeneracy of the sons, who all too soon forsake the straight and narrow way of the church for these worldly amusements.[19]

hundred bushels of ear corn were unloaded on the croquet ground, thus obliterating it for several months and removing the temptation from his sons.

In this same community the theater was under condemnation. This, however, was no serious problem for there were practically no theatricals. An occasional medicine show would come to town but the taboo evidently did not cover this. The young men, in particular, attended these shows and no protest was raised.

Membership in lodges or secret organizations was not proper for a Christian. Some of the younger men, however, joined in face of the opposition, but they did not proclaim the fact of their membership from the housetops. Some of the immigrant elders favored the dismissal of these men from the church. The proposal did not carry and gradually the opposition died away and the matter was forgotten.

Sunday baseball was not approved, but since there was no provision for playing, except on holidays, such as Memorial Day or Fourth of July, the boys played. The old men talked about the foolishness of that activity but there was no serious conflict. Some of the boys considered they had gained a decided advantage when one of the old immigrant men, a pillar in one of the churches, was seen at a Sunday afternoon ball game.

[18] E. deS. Brunner, *op. cit.*, p. 201.

[19] A. J. Pieters, *op. cit.*, pp. 103–04.

The older generation of Molokans is bewildered and perplexed by the "shameful, pagan conduct" of their children as they participate in the fascinating street life about them. The elders discuss the problems but they can summon no past experience to their aid, and the conditions out of which conflicts arise are aggravated.[20]

Nevertheless, in spite of conflicts and parental opposition, there is noticeable on every hand a decided trend toward American patterns of play on the part of the second generation of immigrant heritage. Among the Italians,

> The street piano, which is an ever-present, ever-welcome entertainer, starts the children dancing. Their feet have already forsaken the steps of Italy. It is not any peasant dance through which they flit, with the native lightness and aptness of their rhythmic land; it is the prancing, burlesqued grace of the Afro-American cake walk.[21]

The same writer stated that as the boys and girls deliberately choose to obliterate their foreign origin through a change of names they also shift their tastes in amusements. In the north end of Boston one

> would find the polyglot Russian boys preferring to discuss "craps" in English, rather than to conduct some European game in their inherited Yiddish or Slavic tongues. If a dramatic club is formed, the children choose American plays; and in all entertainments their national airs give way to the street songs of the city and the patriotic hymns of the school.[22]

Recreational conflicts and delinquency. The relationship between culture conflicts in the recreational field and delinquency is shown by the experience of a Jewish boy.

> My father won't allow us to play ball on the lot. He says it's a waste of time and a disgrace to make such a lot of noise over nothing. He was raised in Poland. . . . . I hate to stick around here with no friends and nothing to do. My mother reported me to the judge of the Juvenile Court. He told me to stay off Augusta Street, and I did for a couple of

[20] Cf. P. V. Young, "The Russian Molokan Community in Los Angeles," *American Journal of Sociology,* XXXV (November, 1929), 401.

[21] R. A. Woods, *op. cit.,* pp. 225–26.

[22] *Ibid.,* pp. 318–19.

days, but I wasn't going to be lonesome all by myself, and when I started to long for the guys, I ditched school and went out there to join them.

They sure are a slick bunch, and we have a lot of fun together. We can play ball all we want to, besides there are many playgrounds in that neighborhood, and the directors are congenial fellows, but we don't stick around there all the time. . . . .

Once a bunch of boys got arrested for trying to get money from milk bottles to go to Venice and have a good time. It cost at least a dollar to have fun. It costs fifty cents to rent a bathing suit. Sure I have one but it got many rips and is the New Yorker kind. My mother figures that if I don't like that suit I won't go to the beach, but she has another guess coming. Then when you are at the beach you want to have fun at the beach Fun House, or at a show and some food. My parents don't believe in beaches and never go swimming. I don't like to stay home, and my parents don't understand what boys need, and they expect me to be old-fashioned and go to *shuhl.*[23]

The story of Nick as presented by Shaw and McKay [24] is an excellent illustration of culture conflict in the play aspect of life. Nick was brought to the juvenile court charged with various forms of misconduct. His mother made the following statement to the judge:

Nick no wanta work. He big man, 14, and wanta play ball all day. Father say, "you go to-day and work in restaurant with your uncle. . . . ." He makes faces, cusses, laughs, and runs out to play ball. . . . . He very bad boy. . . . . He no wanta work. He tell me "go to hell," "shut your mouth," "why don't you holler all the time?" He get up at noon and go out to play. That not right. I go out to the ball game and say, "Nick come home with me from these bad boys and work." He laugh at me, make a face, tell me to go home and to mind own business. He like nothing but ball. . . . . The father work hard. Have heart trouble. Nick ought to help. His father work hard when he was only 11 years old. That would be right way for Nick.[25]

[23] P. V. Young, "Jim's Own Story," *The Survey,* LIX (March 15, 1928), 777.
[24] National Commission on Law Observance and Enforcement, *Report on the Causes of Crime* (Washington, 1931), Vol. II, No. 13, pp. 4–20.
[25] *Ibid.,* pp. 4–5.

Nick's story shows that the parents and other older persons have no appreciation of the world in which he lives; they behave toward him as if he were an Italian in Italy. The boy told his story:

I've had a lot of trouble at home. They all fight me and hate me. They don't want me to play or have any fun with the fellows. They say I ought to work all day and then only play a little at night. The other fellows my age don't work and I don't see why I have to if they don't. My married sister . . . . can't keep her nose out of my business. . . . .

My uncle tries to boss me and make me work. . . . . My mother makes me mad when she won't let me play baseball. She always goes out to where we play ball, and she whips me, and then the boys laugh at me, and when she goes away they say, "You've got a heck of a mother. Our mothers don't make us stop playing ball." She always whips me out there and then scolds me and the other fellows. That's what makes me sore, and then the fellows have the laugh on me.

They don't want me to play baseball. They want me to work. . . . . All was going well until I stole $2.00 from my mother and bought a baseball glove. . . . . I couldn't even get a glove, or ball. About a year ago my mother started to hide my gloves and baseballs. About a week ago I found my glove which was hidden. I gave it to a friend of mine to take care of. . . . .

The other night when I was playin' ball with the guys out in the street my ma came out, began scolding me, broke up the game, and made me come in. Then she whipped me with a big stick. The next time I met the guys they made fun of me and asked me if I asked my ma if I could come out. I whaled into Irish and beat him up, but I got a black eye. Then my dad beat me for fighting and for not askin' ma if I could go out and play.

That's the way they are all against me. I feel like I don't belong there. They tease me and nag me and I get mad and feel like I could kill them. . . . . I can't have any fun. If I work hard they still fuss at me and don't give me any of my money. I get filled up with mad feeling and tear into them; I can't help it.[26]

Nick's family, which was on a lower economic level than the neighbors, lived in an area largely populated by Irish and German-Americans. Furthermore, they were the only ones of that particular

[26] *Ibid.*, pp. 5–8.

nationality in the neighborhood and there was an attitude of hostility against them which excluded them from participation in local activities. As Nick was striving to acquire status in the neighborhood, his mother, in particular, humiliated him and made his problem of adjustment all the more difficult.

At the time of Nick's appearance in court he was a member of a large play group in his immediate vicinity in which he was an enthusiastic participant. The play interests and activities of the boys, consisting largely of various forms of athletic games, particularly baseball, were of a wholesome nature. Practically all of them attended school regularly. Nick identified himself with this group and was keenly sensitive to the attitudes of approval and disapproval of its members. His interests and his attitudes are indicated by his own story:

I started to play with the guys around my home. These guys are my best friends. We like to play ball the most. We always play ball. Gee, I like to pitch and I like to catch. We play over in Clyde Park and beat another team there nearly all the time last summer. I'd rather play ball than anything else. It's the most fun I ever had. Every boy likes to play ball, I guess. . . . . We used to smoke a lot. . . . . I don't like to smoke much because it hurts my lungs and kills my wind and then I can't be a good ball player. I'd like to be a big league player like Babe Ruth and I can't, if I smoke.

I like to play baseball. I want to be a great ball player. Babe Ruth is the kind of player I'd like to be. He's a great player. Everybody knows him and the fellows all talk about him. He's a great swatter. I wish I could bat like him. That would be great. But nobody likes me to play ball; that's what makes me mad.

The fellows used to call me "Dago," but since I'm a good player on the team they don't call me this name. Everybody thinks we are wops and dagos. They don't know we are not wops. It doesn't make any difference to them. That's what I used to fight about a lot. I wouldn't let them call me such names. I can lick every kid on this street. I don't like to box or wrestle, but I'd rather fight with my bare fists.

I don't read much but the sports section in the newspaper. That's the best part of the paper. I could read it all the time. I don't tell the guys I have to work all the time. I don't want them to make fun of me all the time because of my pa and ma. I tell the guys that I go to the

Cubs and White Sox Parks and that I run off and go swimming. I read all about the games in the papers and tell the guys about them so they'll think I've seen them.[27]

Shaw and McKay summarize the case as follows:

It is clear that the parents had very little appreciation of the nature of Nick's problems and the sort of social world in which he was living. Although his behavior was, for the most part, strictly in conformity with the socially approved standards of the play group and neighborhood, it was a violation of the family tradition and expectations. He was torn between the demands and expectations of two conflicting social groups. On the one hand, we have in the family background a persistence of an Old World family pattern, the outstanding features of which consist in the exercise of paternal authority, rigorous discipline, and the subordination of the individual member to the ideals of economic security. In accordance with this tradition the boy must go to work at an early age and contribute his wages to the family budget. On the other hand, the boy has grown up in an American community; his attitudes and interests have been defined in terms of the activities and values of a more or less typical American group. His interests are centered chiefly in sports and high-school attendance, both of which are in direct conflict with family expectations. This conflict is made more acute because the boy was conscious of the economic and social inferiority of his family and had accepted the contemptuous and superior attitudes of the neighbors toward his family. It is in this conflict of values, attitudes, and interests that the boy's temper tantrums, stubbornness, and open defiance of authority occurred. From this point of view it may be assumed that his behavior problems were incidental to the larger cultural conflict between the family and the prevailing social values of the neighborhood.

In addition to the behavior problems associated with Nick's rebellion against parental authority, it was known that he had stolen money from home on two occasions. In each of these instances he used the money to purchase athletic equipment for his team. His parents were unwilling to contribute money for this purpose. As far as could be ascertained, Nick had no definite interest in stealing as such, nor any emotional drive toward such behavior. It appeared, in the light of the total case study, that stealing represented the only, or perhaps the easiest,

[27] *Ibid.*, pp. 12–13.

means for securing those objects which were essential to a satisfactory adjustment in the group in which his major interests were defined and in which he desired favorable status.

While it is quite possible that there were important contributing factors which were not disclosed in our study of Nick's behavior problems, the materials secured suggest very strongly that his behavior was inextricably involved in his personal relationships in his family, his play group, and his neighborhood.[28]

In this bitter conflict which raged between persons living in antipodal cultural worlds, the adult members of the family considered baseball a foolish waste of time which should be devoted to hard work. To Nick it was not merely something enjoyable—a pleasurable activity; it was the one thing above all else that could make him an American and give him status. Because of his ability to play baseball the boys quit calling him a "dago." To him this was serious business—it was all-important. Had he followed the family orders and worked in the restaurant, he would have been a nobody, merely a despised "dago." By his exploits on the baseball diamond he had gained the right of admittance to that American brotherhood of which Babe Ruth, the boy's great hero at that time, was the exalted master. This was worth fighting for, even against great odds. In such a situation, a bitter conflict was inevitable.

[28] *Ibid.*, pp. 19–20.

CHAPTER XXVI

RELIGION AND THE SECOND GENERATION

Religion is a fruitful source of conflict between the generations, particularly in groups with religions diverging definitely from American Protestantism. Bitter culture conflicts are likely to rage around those values in the two systems which are most incongruous and out of harmony with other aspects of the experience of youth in the American environment. Certain practices and rituals, which have no rational basis, come to be burdensome and appear ridiculous in the new setting. Since religious practices have their roots buried deeply in the lives of the immigrants, they cannot and will not make changes in this sector of their lives as readily as in matters which are more nearly on the surface.[1] Distinctive religious characteristics cannot be abandoned at once, even though a conscious effort were made to do so—and they remain to plague the children.

Embarrassing practices. The Molokan immigrants of Los Angeles are fervent in their religion. Holy jumping is an experience in which the believer feels the mystic presence of God. The young people, however, are not carrying on the religious traditions of the elders except in a limited way.

They are affected by the emotional tone of the ritual but are greatly embarrassed by the ceremony of the "brotherly kiss." They are imbued with the presence of the Holy Ghost but they quit going to church as soon as the "Holy Ghost makes them jump." They consider it humiliating to jump and cannot reconcile this behavior with American practices and attitudes.[2]

[1] E. Corsi, *In the Shadow of Liberty: The Chronicle of Ellis Island* (New York, 1935), p. 267, for an interesting description of the immigrants as they discard old-country clothes, valises, and bags on landing in New York.

[2] P. V. Young, "The Russian Molokan Community in Los Angeles," *American Journal of Sociology*, XXXV (November, 1929), 399.

A Molokan girl gave her reaction to this traditional practice:

> Then my folks have that crazy old religion; they are Holy Jumpers. I don't go to church; I just hate to go. When I do go I just sit there on the bench and don't take part. The folks don't like it because I don't go to church. They feel awfully bad about it.[3]

Of all immigrant groups from Europe, the Jews, undoubtedly, have the most widely divergent religion, and it literally teems with possibilities for culture conflicts. It has a large number of rituals which are observable and thus there are more points which may actually prick and arouse antagonisms. To the American-born Jews, the orthodox synagogue with its oriental and medieval atmospheres may be so remote from their everyday experiences as to become actually repulsive.

Growth of contradictions. Whether born in this country or elsewhere, the child of orthodox Jewish parents spends his earliest years in a family atmosphere which is deeply devout, where religious observances are a most important part of the daily life. He learns to say his prayers every morning and evening, either at home or in the synagogue. But in America, even before he begins to go to the public school, the Jewish child finds himself in contact with a new world which is in violent contrast to the environment of his first few years. In the home he is taught that there is nothing more wonderful than to be a Jew. But early in life he is made to feel that he is different and that being a Jew is something that the non-Jew does not envy him. Almost unnoticed in the beginning, from his playmates in the streets, he picks up a little English and becomes aware of the difference between himself and those about him. With his entrance into the public school he comes in contact with a system of education and a set of influences which are widely divergent from those of his home life. The religious element is entirely lacking. English becomes his most familiar language; he begins to forget his Yiddish. The home influences over him gradually weaken. He begins to look upon the ceremonial life of his home as rather ridiculous. As he becomes more saturated with American ideas and practices in the school,

[3] Unpublished life history.

he comes into open conflict with his parents—the teachings of the home and school are contradictory. For instance, we may note the orthodox Jewish custom of wearing a hat or cap in the home. Quite evidently this is at variance with the American practice as taught in the school. While this may appear to be an inconsequential trifle, it still provides a basis for conflict.

In our home everybody keeps his hat on. When my father takes off his hat he puts on a little skull-cap, so that his head will be covered. That is the Jewish law. We boys used to do that, too. But how can you keep on doing something at home that you don't do anywhere else and not think about it? You learn to take off your hat at school, and if you don't take it off everybody will laugh at you, and think you haven't any manners. You get in the habit of doing it and you can't help it. My father objects to sitting down at the table with us when we have our caps off. It's caused many quarrels and will cause a lot more until he gets over it.[4]

A person may hold opinions, attitudes, and sentiments which would be considered heretical by his group, should he openly admit them. That, however, is impossible in the case of overt practices which others can observe. Attendance at synagogue or church, observance of the Sabbath and other holy days, the practice of public prayer, the giving of alms, and the following of ritual cannot be hidden. Ritual is essentially an outward demonstration and cannot be discreetly concealed like contradictory opinions. What the Jewish boy may think about the wearing of a hat at meals need not necessarily be known and cause conflict, but failure to wear the hat is evident to all and releases the wrath of the orthodox father.

To the Jews, particularly those from the Pale in Russia where life had been severe and uncertain, there was a tendency to cling tenaciously to their religion. The cruel Russians might deprive them of everything, but their religion would yield not even to the blows of the Cossack. There was no assurance that they could bequeath worldly goods to their children, but they could give them the priceless treasures of their religion. In a situation where the Jewish children were not accepted by the dominant group, there

[4] L. Wirth, *Culture Conflicts in the Immigrant Family,* unpublished dissertation.

was no choice and they followed the traditions of the fathers. The social and political ostracism of both old and young drew them all more closely together and this created a situation that tended to foster an adherence to the established forms of the orthodox faith. America loosens the old group solidarity and pulls the children away—they begin to revolt against the stereotyped religious observances. Certain parents have said that they would never have migrated to America had they known that their children would become Gentiles in the new land. With feeling the child responds that his parents are unreasonable and old-fashioned, living in a world they brought with them. This is America, and old-country customs are out of place. Upon the heels of this follow resentment, rebellion, misunderstanding.

Conflicts arise when the parents attempt to set up their age-worn institutions for giving the children instruction in religion. Conditions here differ so radically from those across the sea that they do not attract the youth. In Russia there were such serious limitations on educational opportunities for the Jews that all Jewish boys went to *Cheder* (Jewish school); there was practically nothing else available. In America, however, all, no matter what their race or creed, have to attend the public schools, or private institutions which measure up to certain definite standards. Many Jewish pupils become inoculated with Americanism right early and conclude that the public school gives them everything worth knowing. They resent having to go to *Cheder* after a full day when the other children are playing or doing their home work. Furthermore, the children who make contacts with well-trained teachers in the public institutions do not appreciate the crude methods in the Hebrew school.

> Whom have you got to teach you in *Cheder?* An old fellow that doesn't know how to teach. He doesn't even know how to talk English. All he knows is how to beat you, and nobody pays any attention to him. It's all right for the kids who just come over from Europe, but not for me.[5]

Orthodox Jews make much of the confirmation of their children. The religious ceremony in the synagogue at which the boy

[5] *Ibid.*

must read a Scripture portion from the original Hebrew is followed by a family reunion and celebration in the home. Traditionally this has been a ceremony of great importance to the family, but in America it has often been a source of conflict between the parents and children and has brought sorrow and dismay. If the boy would not respond and do his part in a creditable manner, his immediate family would be disgraced in the presence of the relatives or larger family circle. A father said of his boy:

> We made him go to *Cheder* for several years, but he made lots of trouble for us. He went on and off. When it got close to his *Bar Mitzvah* (confirmation) we knew he didn't know enough so we hired a teacher to give him private lessons. We have so many relatives in the city that it would be a great shame for us not to have him know anything. We got everything for him. We bought him new shoes, new clothes, and promised him a bicycle. All our relatives, of course, expected to be invited, but he wouldn't learn. So we had to call it off. It was a big disgrace for me and my wife to have such a son who wouldn't learn even for his *Bar Mitzvah*. I wouldn't do another thing for him.[6]

The orthodox Jewish home has so much ceremonial that oftentimes it surrounds the children with irksome restrictions. After they have become accustomed to the comparative freedom of the school and playground, this ritualism makes the parental abode much like a place of confinement. A delinquent boy who had been paroled to his parents from a reformatory, ran away from them immediately. When apprehended he said that he would rather be returned to the institution than to live with them, because his home with its thousand and one regulations was more prison-like than the regular place of incarceration.[7]

Factors affecting conflict. A number of factors affect the severity of the religious conflicts. The age of the parents at the time of their arrival is important. If they are young, they assimilate more readily and do not cling so doggedly to the hoary customs and are less perturbed when the children deviate from them. Furthermore, since they adjust themselves to American life and give up some of the time-worn practices that embarrass the younger gen-

[6] *Ibid.*
[7] Cf. *ibid.*

eration, their children react less violently against the old religion. Settlement in a colony is another factor. In a homogeneous immigrant settlement the younger set can carry on more of the traditional life without discomfort. Where a few immigrants settle among those of native stock there is more pressure on the children to conform to American behavior patterns as a Jewish boy living outside the ghetto learned.

I have never taken very much stock in religion. I don't see any sense in it. Our Sabbath begins Friday at sunset, but my father works in the shop all day Saturday. Oh, he sighs and hopes to be in the land of the "faithful" before he dies, but that don't help him any. I don't see why a faithful people should suffer and be laughed at like we are. My parents nag at me to go to *shuhl* on holidays. They make many sacrifices to keep this tradition, but they don't mean anything much in life. It's different with my brother. He got a start in New York in a Jewish community, but I can't be friends with Gentiles at school and at work and stick up for European ways too. That's just why I don't like to stay at home. I don't want to hurt my parents and I can't follow their advice.[8]

Weak hold of the church. The church does not seem to have the same hold on the children of immigrants that it does over the youth of the same group in the homeland. In the old countries there is a greater homogeneity in religion than in America. Usually there is the state church, together with some smaller dissenting groups. In Sweden, for instance, all were born into the Lutheran state church and it was more difficult to get out of the church than to stay in. Because of this there is a quite stable behavior pattern with reference to religion which may be followed without difficulty. When the immigrant settles in America he cannot carry on his religious activities exactly as he did in the old country; hence the pattern set before the children is less steady than the one left behind. Commonly the immigrant must seek employment in the open market where he has to compete with others who have been in America longer. The Jew, for example, who persists in keeping the Sabbath is at once at a disadvantage. If he compromises on Sabbath observance but clings to the holy days and

[8] P. V. Young, "Jim's Own Story," *The Survey,* LIX (March 15, 1928), 777.

the dietary laws, he still faces a serious handicap. If he is to live and support his family, he must make changes. This brings confusion and interferes with the religious training of the children. To be sure, not all even in the homeland were equally orthodox and some, as soon as they left the old home and its surroundings, began to break away from certain old customs. They adjusted themselves to the new environment in America quite readily and made no special effort to keep their children loyal to Judaism.[9] Furthermore, there are many religions and sects in America with which the immigrant family makes contacts. The children of immigrants, then, live in a sort of interstitial religious area in which they mingle with several religious groups and ally themselves whole-heartedly with none. A young Jew who participates freely in activities with Gentiles is in danger of losing his interest in and enthusiasm for Judaism.

Religion and earning of a livelihood. When the young people secure work and begin to learn the English language, usually they are swept irresistibly away from the old religious moorings. The Jewish boy yields to environmental influences and practically dissociates himself from all of Judaism.[10] Likewise the Catholic youth yields to pressure and leaves his church, turns his back upon the beauty in his parental religion,[11] learns to sneer at all obedience to constituted authority, be it Pope or policeman, "only to take on the most superficial veneer of some new-found cult." [12] A considerable number of young Jews have forsaken Judaism in order to earn a livelihood more easily. They change their names and remove identification marks so far as possible. Many persons join churches to enhance their social standing. Pihlblad writes of a Swedish community in Kansas: "In general, there still prevails the attitude that church membership is synonymous with good citizenship and non-church members are likely to be regarded

[9] Cf. Mary Antin, *op. cit.*, pp. 241–47.

[10] Cf. Chapter XI, pp. 151–52.

[11] "These American-born seem to have given up the good traits which their parents imported from Italy, and to have retained the bad ones, and on the top of this they have absorbed the worst customs of the American life. A. Di Domenica, *Missionary Review of the World*, LVIII (February, 1935), 73.

[12] From Maurice R. Davie, *World Immigration* (New York, 1936), p. 553. By permission of The Macmillan Company, publishers.

by neighbors with some misgiving." [13] Some even consider church membership to ease the struggle for bread, as did a young man of Polish-Jewish ancestry:

In my present state of mind I am considering my brother's attempt, and think that I shall follow him. That is, I believe I shall try to make myself an "American." It will be necessary for me to attach myself to some church, since everyone these days wants to know your religion. Every employment office and company asks the question. Then will come my real conflict. It will be cowardly—i. e., against my convictions—to become anything, Protestant or Catholic. Why should I join either church when I neglected my own, since I believe no more in either of them? I am afraid that I am going to consult my personal interests, be a coward, and live a lie.[14]

Some of the young people have discontinued their attendance at the foreign-language churches because they felt they would acquire a higher status by going to churches where the services were conducted in English.

Critical attitude toward the church. Frequently young people become critical of the church and religion in general. Among the young Chinese and Japanese on the Pacific Coast and in Hawaii one finds many who are cynical and even bitter. They have heard official Christianity talk about equality, brotherhood, and the absence of a color line in heaven. The practices, however, of the church folk do not square with their professions. For instance, an American-born Japanese girl on the Coast, a member of a Presbyterian Church, made application at two hospitals to enter nurses' training. The application was bluntly rejected because of her Japanese ancestry. This incident aroused considerable feeling in the Japanese Christian group and the local Buddhist Church secured a number of additions as a result. A young Japanese man, who was familiar with this case and had seen other discriminations expressed his reaction to Christianity in the word "tripe." [15]

While some young people are dissatisfied with the foreign-

[13] C. T. Pihlblad, "The Kansas Swedes," *Southwestern Social Science Quarterly,* XII (June, 1932), 9.

[14] H. G. Duncan, *op. cit.,* p. 788.

[15] Cf. *Japanese-American Courier,* Sept. 8, 1934. Also W. C. Smith, *op. cit.,* pp. 141–58.

language churches and disagree with their elders, yet they have a sentimental attachment and loyalty to the parental group and resent slights and discriminations. This tends to bring reactions against the American churches toward which they would otherwise be drawn. A young woman of Spanish ancestry recommends an improvement:

The change I would suggest in the church is to treat foreigners in *this* country (not in Spain or Turkey) as if they had souls—it is taken for granted that they have souls when they are thousands of miles away. Americans seem to think that the ocean voyage has caused the immigrants to lose their souls—they may have lost their stomachs but not their souls. The American churches should be the same as other churches. I should think Christ's teachings would be the same the world over.[16]

While many young people with Jewish and Catholic backgrounds in their homes are dislodged from the parental faiths, large numbers of them are in no way attracted by the American Protestant Churches because of the narrow-mindedness and bigotry of so many of the sectarians. This young woman was repelled:

Up to the time of my entrance into high school, I received my religious instruction in a Protestant Sunday School because we lived too far from a Catholic church to attend services. In my first two years of high school I lived with an Irish Catholic family. The third year I boarded with a narrow-minded Protestant family which switched between Baptist and Methodist doctrines. I suffered real persecution that year, but only became more steadfast in my Catholic beliefs and practices for in them I received true consolation. Irish ancestry and Catholic faith became almost synonymous to me, and I mistrusted anyone who bore an Irish name and professed a non-Catholic belief—possibly because of my experiences of that year. A roomer in the house where I lived boasted of being Irish, but he was the most ignorant, hardest-shelled Baptist I have ever known—so unenlightened that he never greeted me except by a disparaging epithet.[17]

The following paragraph from a youth of Russian-Jewish parentage is tinged with skepticism:

[16] Unpublished life history.
[17] Unpublished life history.

My relations with the synagogue are very limited, but I do not feel any loss. The trend of modern thought is too far advanced for all the churches, barring none. They refuse to recognize new knowledge that has arisen, and thus fail to adjust to the present modern conditions. Instead they accept the old worn-out dogmas, or else find very silly excuses to make the new knowledge coincide with the old. The whole religious situation is like an individual trying to push back a locomotive, and saying all the while, "No, you shall not go forward; our fathers never rode in or saw a locomotive, and therefore you shall not exist." The child of the immigrant has enough of an antiquated system of theology. If the church limited itself to the teachings of morality as given by Jesus and the prophets, including Moses, there would not be any need for more than one church. . . . . Why should the child of an immigrant go to church, as this institution teaches hatred or abhorrence of another religion different from its own? [18]

Another member of the same group added:

Religion is getting to be "old-fashioned." The Jewish religion is passing out fast. I see it, but my parents don't. And I think my children will be left to do as they please, but—who knows—I might have just enough religion to remember my parents and do as they did and thus keep our world from progressing.[19]

Young Jews are not the only ones who are cynical with reference to the church. A second generation Swede was critical: "The church certainly does not meet my needs: I want intellectual questioning in search for truth, and not ritualistic ballyhoo." [20] A second-generation Irish woman was denunciatory: "I believe the churches have not in the least kept march with educational advance or other progress of civilization. I also think in the case of foreign groups they hinder both education and Americanization." [21] A young woman of English-Irish ancestry was censorious: "I feel that there is nothing so destructive to intelligence as religion the way we present it to the mind of the child. I should like

[18] H. G. Duncan, *op. cit.*, pp. 780–81.
[19] Unpublished life history. Cf. Louis Wirth, *The Ghetto* (Chicago, 1928).
[20] Unpublished life history.
[21] Unpublished life history.

to see one generation reared with adequate ethical and moral training, free from hampering, outworn dogma." [22]

Even though some are rather caustic concerning the church, they cannot break away completely. They are still marginal and have some sentimental ties to the ancestral church while they are not completely accepted in the outside world. A second-generation Finn could not cut the old bonds:

My own situation is especially difficult. Mother, being uneducated and very religious, found my ideas heart-rending. I assumed the attitude that she knew nothing, and preferred a dance with English-speaking people in preference to going to church. Although completely broken from the church, I now go sometimes in order to see the Finnish people. I feel an outsider. I know it would break her heart if she knew the real situation. Nevertheless, I do derive much pleasure from my ancestry. Once when working I learned from the boss where to find a bunch of Finns. Many pleasant evenings I spent listening to old Finnish folk songs, mythology, and superstitions. I became so interested that I have since spent many happy hours reading Finnish literature. There is something that makes my flesh reach out into their very existence. I now have the background for the Finnish culture.[23]

While some break completely with the parental religion to the point that one young woman stated, "I try to conceal the fact that I was ever connected with that church," [24] others are happy there. "My parents are Catholics and I was brought up as a Catholic," writes an Italian boy, "and I am perfectly satisfied with this church." [25] His parents were fairly well assimilated; his father was a skilled worker; they did not live in a slum section; and there were no serious conflicts between him and his parents. Evidently this boy had not been embarrassed by his parents and had not become cynical about their religion. A girl of German-Jewish ancestry agreed that "the church of my parents entirely meets my needs at present and I can suggest no change in it." [26] She, too, lived in a home where there were no destructive conflicts be-

[22] H. G. Duncan, *op. cit.*, p. 712.
[23] *Ibid.*, p. 793.
[24] Unpublished life history.
[25] Unpublished life history.
[26] Unpublished life history.

tween parents and children. A young woman, reared in a Swedish community of Minnesota, who had moved to California where she was teaching, said: "Several have expressed their surprise at finding that I still attend a Swedish church. In this respect I have not become Anglicized because I love the language, the church, and the people of my own group, not, however, to the exclusion of all others." [27] She had not been in a position where she had been embarrassed by her group and when she moved out to enter the teaching profession she encountered no difficult problems. America had been good to her and had not forced her into situations where the conflicts had been serious burdens.

Immigrant churches tend to be conservative. Most immigrants have to adjust themselves to the American industrial machine in order to earn a livelihood. This means a break from the old and familiar. They are compelled to send their children to school—they must conform to the American practices. In the realm of religion, however, they are under no such compulsion; they are left free to their own devices. Here is the one anchor which keeps them in touch with fond and tender memories of the past. In their work-day activities they are compelled to use some English, but in their religious worship they are usually free to use the mother-tongue. They pay little heed to the American churches about them. In their isolation they are not even touched by the currents that tend to make for progress in the homeland. This backward look does not help the churches to gear into the American life in which the children are living.[28]

Language and religious conflict. Much of the religious conflict centers about language. "When I was a little girl," wrote a second-generation Swede, "an English word spoken in church was a desecration." [29] Many parents have made great efforts to hold to the mother tongue in connection with religion, for it has seemed

[27] Unpublished life history.

[28] "Among the second generation of Russians, I found many who seemed to be drifting, without really substituting anything in the place of the church. These people are waiting for a strong, virile religion, whose first approach shall be through ministering to the needs of every day." From *Russians and Ruthenians in America* by Jerome Davis, copyright, 1922, by Doubleday, Doran and Company, Inc., New York, p. 80.

[29] Unpublished life history.

to be the only language in which God could speak to them. The struggle of many of the older generation to maintain the traditional religion and keep the younger generation within the fold is oftentimes pitiable. A Jewish mother, who sought the aid of a social worker to induce her boy to go to the school for religious instruction, which was conducted in Yiddish, said:

I never went to school myself, but my father hired a private teacher for us in Russia. He wasn't so rich either, but he wanted all his children to be good Jews. Now I am poor and I have no husband and I can't afford to get a private teacher, so I want him to go to *Cheder* until he is *Bar Mitzvah* (confirmed). Maybe if I had come here when I was young I wouldn't care so much about it, but I lived in a nice religious home all my life until I came here at the age of thirty-eight and it is too late for me to change now. He would be a disgrace to my family if he did not go. I would be willing to save every penny to get a private teacher if you can't get him to go to *Cheder*.[30]

Many parents have been quite insistent that their children attend the immigrant churches. "In only one respect," said a Jewish boy, "had father ever been strict: we must attend church day, and if we do not, he considers any variation as a lack of personal respect." [31] "Every night after work," writes Dr. Van Waters about some Russians, "father and mother and the eldest son go to church. As long as the children are in arms they, too, go to church." [32] When some of them, however, grow older and begin to think for themselves, they quit as did this girl:

At first I attended a church of my own parental language, but when I became old enough to have a few ideas of my own, I changed to an American church. This was much more liberal and more of my friends attended it. The Swedish church was run by people of the older generation who had been brought up under the strict discipline of the Lutheran Church and attempted to run their own in the same way. I think that children born of foreigners should attend American churches as they are a help in Americanization. The foreign-language churches endeavor to keep the customs and languages of the old country.[33]

[30] L. Wirth, *Culture Conflicts in the Immigrant Family,* unpublished dissertation.
[31] H. G. Duncan, *op. cit.,* p. 784.
[32] M. Van Waters, *op. cit.,* p. 13.
[33] Unpublished life history.

Oftentimes this defection on the part of the children brings anguish to their parents. "When finally I left the parental religion, so to speak," wrote one girl, "I was quite completely ostracized from the home circle and still am. Mother vows she loves me but that I have left the family and am no longer one of them." [34] At times it is not merely a peaceful departure from the foreign-language church, but the parents see their children assume a haughtily contemptuous attitude toward that which to them is most sacred. There is a tendency on the part of the American-born Jew, who believes himself emancipated from parental traditions, to despise the stern morality which the immigrant has brought with him from the land of his birth. Orthodoxy does not appeal to the younger generation.

Sometimes, however, members of this group, out of sympathy, continue the formality of attendance at the parental churches. "The church is small," comments a girl, "mostly old German people and it does not satisfy me. I attend seldom and then only to please my people." [35] "My parents are still avowed Catholics," states one boy, "and I am not telling them my ideas. I still go to church when I am home. I shall not make them unhappy by leaving them until they are gone." [36] A Jewish boy does not like the parental religion but conforms in some measure.

> I can quite easily recall the time that I went to a synagogue and all the men wore hats. "What an odd custom and how un-gentlemanlike," I said audibly to my parents. With angry looks they asked me not to voice my opinions. We are accustomed to going to the reformed church and this visit to the orthodox one was a new experience for me. Then, we have some holidays which I consider altogether useless but I conform in order to please my parents. I can remember the time when I just would not eat the required kind of food for Passover but when I saw that it hurt my parents so deeply, I ate it.[37]

The dogged clinging to the foreign language, often to the point of fanaticism, tends to alienate many young people. It is a rather costly procedure, as one girl shows:

[34] Unpublished life history.
[35] Unpublished life history.
[36] Unpublished life history.
[37] Unpublished life history.

The matter of attendance at the Swedish church services had always been a bone of contention in our home, but we children always went to please our parents—we never argued or demanded our rights as American children do, and Swedish parents are not American parents. They love their children just as much but teach them submission always. The church we attended was made up of families like ours, of typical hard-working Swedish people. All those children felt the same way as I did but went to please their parents. Needless to say they are unhappy—they have practically no religious inclinations and have a longing to belong to an American church. I think all churches should have only one language—and that is American.[38]

In spite of all their efforts, however, to retain the mother tongue in the churches, the older generation has recognized the handwriting on the wall. Among the Eastfriesians,

Parents found it difficult to interest their children in religion when it was presented to them in a foreign language. The wish for a single class in the Sunday School in English soon found expression. The older people looked with alarm upon the innovation, but it meant losing the young people from the church unless their wishes were granted. Some churches persevered in using German exclusively and saw their young people drifting away. Others experienced bitter feuds as a result of the language question. A few churches split over it. The war hastened the coming of the inevitable.[39]

Where the older group refuses to yield, it loses the younger element. Among the orthodox Jews the congregations at the synagogues are made up almost entirely of the immigrant generation. The pathetic plight of some of the loyal ones is described by Ray Stannard Baker:

I have visited many of them [synagogues] on Friday evenings and Saturday mornings—the two principal services of the week. Often I

[38] Unpublished life history.

[39] J. A. Saathoff, *op. cit.*, pp. 73–74. Cf. also pp. 74–75.

"What was once the Dutch Reformed Church dropped the word 'Dutch' some fifty years ago to make it appear a purely American organization. It is now known as the Reformed Church in America. It is an intensely American body, though hailing from the land of dikes and dunes." *The Wisconsin Magazine of History,* II (1918–1919), 465.

Cf. A. Bergin, *Lindsborg efter Femtio År,* pp. 146–47, for the shift in language in a Swedish church in Kansas.

have found a dozen bearded men waiting there—for what reason at first I could not understand. . . . . Sometimes one of the number will go out on the street and beseech passing Jews to come in and help them with their quorum. (They must have ten for a prayer quorum.) I never shall forget one of these old Jews—his wistful eyes, his gentle, ineffectual movements—whom I saw one day stepping out like some patriarch from his fifteenth century synagogue and seeking to stop with a call to prayer the tide of the twentieth century as it rushed through the streets.[40]

Attendance at the foreign-language church means more than the mere loss of the sermons they hear but cannot understand. In such a group they are in a measure isolated from the life about them and their problems of adjustment are thus accentuated. A girl who attended the Swedish church said:

I felt so strange among Americans that I was embarrassed in speech and manner with them. Now I attend an American church entirely and enjoy its activities. I attended the Swedish church and was left without direct American contacts. Finally I came to the conclusion that I wanted to be a real American. Since I had my own life to live it was really my right to choose an American church.[41]

[40] R. S. Baker, "Spiritual Unrest," *American Magazine*, LXVIII (October, 1909), 595.

[41] Unpublished life history.

CHAPTER XXVII

TREATMENT OF CULTURE CONFLICTS

Culture conflicts between the generations have a disorganizing effect upon the traditional life of the immigrants. Aware of this situation the parents face the problems in several different ways.

Resistance to change. Many parents cling to the old-world traditions with a tenacity that compels admiration—though it be tinged with pity. This has been true, in particular, of those who, because of bitter disillusionments, have lived almost completely in memories of the homeland. Nothing in the United States is worthy of consideration: things American can be endured only because of their potentialities in the acquisition of more of the good things of life that flow out of their old-world heritages. They are saddened when their children accept anything from the new environment. This is exemplified by a Norwegian woman who was grieved when her son gave his baby boy the American name, Randolph Osborne. She was so much annoyed by this that she had occasional spells of crying. She declared that there should have been greater respect for tradition, for that which is sacred to a people, than to give the child such a name.[1] Furthermore, many immigrant parents, because of their own meager educational attainments, lack the resources to stimulate in their children an appreciation of the old-world culture. Moreover, they make no effort to share the new interests of their offspring. But with their traditional background, they see neither virtue nor need in paying attention to such folly. Nor could they give their children the proper training even if they would, because they do not have the necessary time—the long day at the furnace in the steel mill or in the bowels of the coal mine leaves no margin for other than bread-getting activities.[2] While the children are small, no special difficulties are encountered,

[1] O. E. Rölvaag, *Peder Victorious,* p. 327.

[2] Cf. E. deS. Brunner, *op. cit.,* p. 240.

since parental authority directs them. However, as they grow up, they revolt against the austerity of their elders.

Pieters states that one point of view among the Dutch immigrants in Michigan was

that the settlers should come to America but not be of it. They should maintain a little Holland, retaining their own language, customs, and religion. The writer well remembers, when a child, being told by the widow of one of the early settlers that this was their intention, and that, therefore, they did not wish to speak English. The sadness in her tone will never be forgotten as she added, "But we made a mistake." The sadness was all the more touching since this old woman had not wished to learn English and could not converse with her own grandchildren as they could not speak Dutch.[3]

Sometimes the parents in their bewilderment strike out blindly in all directions in frantic efforts to control situations which have gotten out of hand. In one instance,

The mother nags persistently and complains in an ineffectual way, and Catherine responds with growls and such remarks as "You don't understand anything anyway." The father seems to let things run their own course in his family over long periods of time, looking on rather helplessly, and then suddenly gets into a frenzy of "trying to do something about it," punishes the children excessively and does many rash things which he later regrets.[4]

Healy reports the pitiable case of a Polish man who could not adjust to the new conditions. He was gradually backed off the stage and the mother, by holding the purse strings, played the dominant rôle. After this dethronement in the family, the father bought an expensive phonograph which he kept covered with a sheet in the front room. He carried the key in his pocket and permitted no one but himself to touch or play it. That was a "face-saver," a symbol of his vanished patriarchal authority.[5]

Resigned toleration. Some parents try to maintain ancestral domination over their children but are unable to do so and finally

[3] A. J. Pieters, *Dutch Settlement in Michigan* (Grand Rapids, 1923), p. 130.

[4] Joseph Miller, "Foreign Born Parentage and Social Maladjustment," *Psychological Clinic,* XIX (March, 1930), 21.

[5] *Judge Baker Foundation Case Studies,* No. 17 (Boston, 1923).

resign themselves to the inevitable. It is an abandonment of the old system, so far as the children are concerned, but they develop nothing new and vital to take its place. Moreover, these parents, for the most part, are like hens that raise ducks—invariably astonished and alarmed at the manner in which their children behave.

> The Molokan elders, however, due to an ardent desire to maintain their traditional life and scheme of social control, have developed no mechanisms for dealing effectively with cultural hybridism. In an urban environment systemization of life and traditional behavior are cumbersome and highly ineffective. Still that is all the older generation understand and hence they are forced to a policy of passive resistance and aloofness in the face of the invasion of the strange culture.[6]

The parents do not change their point of view but, in the interest of a tolerable peace, surrender and even allow the children to dominate the home.[7] The internal arrangements are made over to suit the younger generation; its routines are Americanized in considerable measure. English becomes the official language of the family. The situation of the parents in such homes is often pathetic. Among the Swedes of Texas the father may continue the Swedish newspaper, but he is obliged to keep it in the bedroom; the mother may have her afternoon coffee, but she must sip it on the sly in the pantry.[8] In a Polish community in New England,

> The usual solution found is a parting of the ways, resignation on the part of the parents as to the doings of their children, avoidance of parents on the part of the children. Americans frequently wonder at the freedom given to the children of the Polish immigrants and the lack of supervision, little realizing that leniency in this case is the only way out of what would otherwise be an intolerable situation. The prevalent opinion of the community is opposed to the doings of the younger generation, but shows its lack of power in resigned toleration.[9]

[6] P. V. Young, "The Russian Molokan Community in Los Angeles," *American Journal of Sociology*, XXXV (November, 1929), 398–99.

[7] Cf. W. C. Smith, *American Journal of Sociology*, XXXIII (May, 1928), 928, on the second generation of oriental ancestry.

[8] Cf. C. M. Rosenquist, *op. cit.*

[9] E. deS. Brunner, *op. cit.*, p. 241.

Mutual toleration. In some instances parents resist a complete revolution of their ways of life and compromise on a bi-cultural basis. In the matter of communication a bi-lingual accommodation is worked out: [10] the parents address the children in their vernacular while replies are made in English. The immigrants, who do practically all their thinking in their own concepts, speak English haltingly and under great strain. Furthermore, they have a strong sentimental attachment to the old folk speech and are unwilling to give it up for the new. The children, however, persist in using English and in paying less and less attention to the foreign idiom.

Quite commonly the first-born in the family use the mother tongue. This is absolutely necessary since the parents have had insufficient opportunity to learn English. Furthermore, these children are exposed to the parental language and nothing else within the confines of the household. By the time younger children arrive, both the older ones and their parents have acquired greater facility in English.[11] The younger siblings, then, have a double exposure to English—in the school and in the home. In such a situation, when conversing among themselves, they use nothing but English, but communication between parents and children is bi-lingual.

Many families continue for years on a bi-lingual basis. In some instances the parents finally capitulate and converse with the children in a broken English. Among the Swedes in Kansas, the young people frequently manifest an attitude of hostility toward the old speech and customs. In one home, the mother used a Swedish expression in asking that a certain dish be passed to her at the table. The grown daughter immediately offered reproof, telling her mother not to "talk Swede," because it was unpatri-

[10] Cf. *ibid.*, pp. 172–73.

[11] A gradual change takes place in other aspects of the home life as well. A Chinese high-school girl in Honolulu wrote: "In my early years my mother didn't believe in letting my sisters marry as they pleased. She wanted a match-maker to find husbands for the girls. But now, mother and father let the girls choose their own husbands with their consent. Everything is almost completely changed to the American style now and I know there will be no conflict between my parents and myself." Unpublished life history.

otic.[12] This transitional stage of bi-lingualism may be somewhat awkward but it can usually be passed without serious conflict. To be sure, the parents are disappointed by the disregard—and at times contempt—evidenced by the children toward the mother tongue, while the children themselves are humiliated by the halting speech and foreign customs of their parents. Yet this accommodation makes it possible to live together without serious disorganization.

Conscious adjustment. In some instances the parents have analyzed the problems with which they have been confronted and have set about to redefine the situation in such a way as to prevent conflict and consequent family disorganization. Among the Poles in New England,

> Harmonious relations between parents and children are exceptional. In these exceptional cases the parents have got away from traditional modes of behavior and show open-mindedness in accepting new values.[13] They have adopted a higher standard of living, speak the English language well, have widened their horizon of knowledge, and are willing to disregard traditional standards of a religious and moral nature. They do not persist in holding up national solidarity as a duty, and are desirous of having business and social contacts with Americans.[14]

A Jewish mother is reported as saying:

> Believe me, times have changed. My boys make twice as much as my husband did when we were married. We are too old to change. Our children are wiser and more independent. I can't say: "Look here, Jack, you can't run around and think as you please." All the young people are ahead of their parents these days. There is no use fighting with them all the time. You might as well give in and make them realize they are

[12] Cf. C. T. Pihlblad, *op. cit.*

[13] The writer is reminded of a Swedish immigrant man. A church in a Swedish community had become bi-lingual: the young people used the English language in all their activities. A new minister advocated the adoption of Swedish in the young people's society. This immigrant man understood the situation and was opposed to the suggested change. "If the proposal is made to adopt Swedish," he said, "I shall oppose it. I shall argue for the continuation of English. But in arguing for English I shall have to speak in Swedish: I can use that language more readily."

[14] E. deS. Brunner, *op. cit.*, p. 239.

welcome in the home, and they can keep in contact with a little bit of Jewishness.[15]

Some parents realize that they cannot expect to hold the respect of their children if they are ignorant of the English language. Rebecca Kohut's father did not wait for tensions to develop but endeavored to anticipate any likely causes of conflict. Immediately on his arrival in America he began to read the newspapers with the aid of a German-English dictionary. He insisted that English must become the speech of the household, even though the older children found it easier to use the mother tongue. In Hungary he would have resented any pressure to force him to use English, but in the United States he considered it the proper language and determined to master it.[16]

Sophus Keith Winther [17] shows how a Norwegian immigrant woman set about to learn English in an endeavor to keep close to her children. A Jewish immigrant woman said:

> My oldest child is now seven years old and I know I will have trouble with him, if I don't know English. A neighbor of mine told me that I was foolish to try to learn English at my age, but I told her that she would not have such bad children if she knew what they were doing. I can see that my oldest boy is already getting away from me and he will do what he wants to and go with bad boys if I can't check up on him.[18]

Abraham Cahan tells of a Jewish woman who tried to Americanize herself in order to prevent estrangement from her daughter. When the girl began to read in school the mother felt a sense of inferiority. She said to herself that her daughter would grow up an educated American and then would be ashamed of her. She had seen tragedies where the parents had slaved to educate their children only to be treated as ignorant greenhorns by them. She firmly resolved to keep the respect of her child, and with determination entered upon the task of learning to read and speak English.

[15] P. V. Young, "The Reorganization of Jewish Family Life in America," *Social Forces*, VII (November, 1929), 242.

[16] R. Kohut, *op. cit.*, p. 13.

[17] *Take All to Nebraska* (New York, 1936), pp. 249–52, ff.

[18] L. Wirth, *Culture Conflicts in the Immigrant Family*, unpublished dissertation, University of Chicago.

As the girl began to use more English and less Yiddish, the mother struggled on so that at the end of the first year she spoke the new language with considerable fluency. As the two worked together in this way, there developed between them a close companionship.[19]

Some parents make great efforts to Americanize with their children, but in spite of all they may do, they cannot keep pace with the youthful generation. "Mother," wrote Elizabeth G. Stern,[20] "was doing her utmost to 'move on' with my sisters and me. She tried breathlessly, as it were, to catch up with us, with the new, and yet not to lose the old, to be American for us, and still not to leave her husband behind." But with all her trying they slowly drifted apart. "Mother and I," she wrote, "did not speak so freely as we used to speak. And she began to look at me often in a manner that brought a tightening to my throat." [21] At times these efforts of the parents are pitiable. The experience of a Russian mother bears this out. "They said," according to her, "they are ashamed of us because we were greenhorns and couldn't speak like American people. . . . . I did all I could to learn how to speak English —I even went to night school—but the language wouldn't come to me." [22] In the words of Pauline V. Young,

> Many parents make a desperate effort to adopt some American customs, but they are rarely emancipated from the old group in the first generation. Their attitudes, their philosophy of life remain hyphenated, and they seek to gain status in American groups. Their accent, their mannerisms, their inability to understand American jokes . . . . their failure to appreciate the niceties of polite conversation, their indifference to American forms of sport, and the whole character of American life give them a feeling of strangeness and discomfort.[23]

It is all but impossible for the parents to keep pace with the children. They have strong attachments to the traditional culture, are less plastic on account of age, are less mobile, form compara-

[19] A. Cahan, *op. cit.*, pp. 182, 242–46, 253–54.

[20] From E. G. Stern, *My Mother and I* (New York, 1917), pp. 129–30. By permission of The Macmillan Company, publishers.

[21] *Ibid.*, p. 130. By permission of The Macmillan Company, publishers.

[22] S. Drucker and M. B. Hexter, *op. cit.*, p. 74.

[23] *Social Forces*, VII (December, 1928), 240.

tively few, if any, primary contacts outside the home or immediate ethnic group, and rarely attain fluency in the language which the children acquire with relative ease. When all the factors in the situation are considered, it is surprising that immigrants and their children fare as well as they do.

CHAPTER XXVIII

ASSIMILATION AND THE SECOND GENERATION

The process of assimilation usually goes on with considerable rapidity in the children of immigrants. Several factors are responsible for this. In the first place, they are a marginal group—on the margin between two cultures where the "melting-pot" boils most briskly. In this interstitial culture region they are subjected to situations which bring conflicts and these force them to face situations and deliberate. These deliberations result in certain accommodations to the American group which make it possible for assimilation to take place. If Abie Goldstein, with his lunch wrapped in a Yiddish newspaper, goes to school with a large number of Irish children, ridicule and lack of acceptance will be his lot. If, however, he changes his name to James O'Brien and brings ham sandwiches wrapped in plain paper, the chances of being accepted are greatly increased, and once within the play group at school he will unconsciously move in the American direction. As an outsider, the butt of ridicule, his mental state would not be particularly receptive to contributions from his schoolmates. When once admitted within the circle, tensions tend to be released and avenues of communication are opened.

Slowly but surely absorbed. In the main, the second generation of immigrant parentage is well along in the assimilative process. "I never considered myself as the daughter of an immigrant," wrote a girl, "until I was asked to write this life history." Another spoke thus: "For the first time in my life I have the disagreeable sensation of being considered other than wholly American." These statements may be considered typical of a large number, particularly of those from culture groups close to the American, as shown by the two following excerpts:

Because of my English descent I have never looked upon myself as anything but an American. My life and problems, as far as I am able to judge, have been typically American, too. Our home was the home of the average middle-class American. My playmates were from the same type of home.[1]

All through school and college, and through all my contacts, I cannot see that I have been handicapped because of my French parentage: I do not see that anything has been closed against me because of it. Nothing has ever been said about my ancestry. Born an American and brought up to respect America I have no inclination to be anything else. I can say the same for the other members of the family. My parents still cherish memories of the past, but they too have become loyal Americans, as proven by the fact that father became a citizen shortly after his arrival here. I cannot see that I differ from any person of native parentage. I was brought up in an American community and taught to respect its laws and its schools. I have never felt different from anyone whose whole family tree had originated here.[2]

Many are so thoroughly assimilated that they are imbued with the characteristic attitude of superiority. An English immigrant woman commented on her son: "He has the American complex against England. One day he told me very proudly, 'Mother, you used to be English, didn't you? Well, we beat the English up in the Revolutionary War.' He is an American and even resents any allusion to a nationality we might have had before becoming naturalized." "I was born and raised in America," said an Italian boy, "so I consider myself one. I have been brought up among Americans and my relations with them have been very intimate." This apparent assimilation was aided, no doubt, by the fact that his parents, as he stated, "had lost all the old-country customs and ideas."

Because of their separatistic religion Jewish immigrants encountered many difficulties but, nevertheless, many of the second generation are able to make quite satisfactory adjustments. "My friends, associates, in fact my environment," remarked a second-generation German Jew, "are and always have been American in spirit. It is little wonder, then, to know that I am at ease and at

[1] Unpublished life history.
[2] Unpublished life history.

home amongst Americans. America is my home." Russian Jews usually find it harder to make accommodations, but many children in that group are accepted, as was this one:

> I went to public schools until I came to the University. I was vastly interested in my work ever since I can remember—as well as in play. I was always happy in whatever I did—and was always accepted as being "as good as the next one." I never encountered any difficulties because of my race or the fact that my parents were immigrants. We've always lived in a fine neighborhood with people who took you for what you really were.[3]

Slowly but surely the leaven works and they become a part of the life about them,[4] as did this girl of Russian-Jewish parentage: "My cousin from Europe has lived with us for a year. We are friendly, but still I feel uncomfortable in his presence as we have nothing in common. My friends are Americans; they are my own people."[5] "No one," according to Bercovici, "could tell a Finn from an American after the second generation. Slow as they are to assimilate, they merge perfectly."[6] The same author testified of the Italians: "Though they everywhere form little groups, the second generation spreads out and merges with all other populations, bringing into the lives of the others whatever of color and of song and of smiles and of laughter there is in them."[7] Among the Armenians, "the second generation is thoroughly Americanized. Descendants of the small band of early arrivals have all been assimilated beyond recognition."[8] "Most of the second-

[3] Unpublished life history.

[4] "America takes this firm old cloth, saying, 'this pattern is old, we want to stamp a new one on it.' The younger generation of our Italians are pleased, and say, 'Yes! We like the new pattern, throw the old one away, and show us how to use the new.' But the old people are sad, for they remember how their parents used the same cloth and were proud of it. They think now to themselves, 'It may not be fashionable, but we like it, we feel queer in the new pattern, it does not suit us.' And as time goes on the pattern slowly, almost imperceptibly changes; so slowly that for a time no one realizes that it is fading." P. H. Williams, *The Religious Mores of the South Italians of New Haven*, unpublished dissertation, Yale University.

[5] Unpublished life history.

[6] K. Bercovici, *On New Shores*, p. 118.

[7] *Ibid.*, p. 94. N. L. Sims makes much the same statement relative to the young Italians in Arkansas. *Op. cit.*, p. 180.

[8] From *The Armenians in America*, Malcolm, M. V., (Boston, 1919), p. xiii. *The Pilgrim Press.* Used by permission.

generation Slavonians," avers a college girl, "are quickly absorbed into the American group. In fact I cannot myself tell a second-generation Slavonian from an American, except in a few cases. There doesn't seem to be any race distinction, at least I've never come across any." [9] Emily G. Balch writes of some American-born Dalmatians in Galveston: "One is an American pure and simple; there is no evidence of a foreigner about him. Another is a great ball player and a thorough American in spirit." [10]

Not interested in parental culture. "True Americanization," asserts Antonio Stella, "takes place effectively in the second generation, as the absorbing influence of the American public schools upon the children of foreign parents is so great, that they show little, if any ties toward the country from which their elders come." [11] "Though the national spirit is still strong in the hearts of the older generation," observes Mary L. Zahrobsky, "it is still of small influence in the lives of the younger people. They have not had to undergo the hardships which their parents experienced in the defense of their national rights and traditions." [12] As a general rule the American-born group evinces slight interest in the parental homeland or its affairs. Among the second-generation Eastfriesians,

> there is very little interest in the native land of their parents. To them Eastfriesland is a foreign country known only through stories and traditions. The memories and meanings that would make them one with the people of that land are lacking. They are happy in the new home; they know no other, nor do they desire another. "America is good enough for me," voices the unanimous opinion of this group. They maintain a few customs of their fathers but they think in terms of America, not in terms of Eastfriesland. However, they do believe that their people have made a contribution to the economic and social well-being of their communities in the Middle West.[13]

[9] Unpublished life history.

[10] E. G. Balch, *op. cit.*, p. 197.

[11] Antonio Stella, *Some Aspects of Italian Immigration to the United States* (New York, 1924), p. 21.

[12] *The Slovaks in Chicago*, unpublished dissertation, University of Chicago.

[13] J. A. Saathoff, *op. cit.*

A boy of Norwegian descent affirmed: "I am an American and America is my native country. My desire to see the native land of my parents is as a tourist." On the other hand, a girl of Irish parentage has not even had a desire to visit Ireland and second generation Bohemians pay scant regard to old-world heritages.

Are Čech children not interested in the birthland of their parents? Or, to state the case more pointedly, are they indifferent about their ancestry? The answer is simple: the American Čech youth—American not only by cold statistics, but by sympathy as well, for all that is born in America belongs to America—are neither better nor worse than the children of Swedish, French, or Irish parentage. Their schooling is American, their mother tongue is English. . . . .

When Frances Gregor's English version of Božena Němcová's masterpiece *Babička* (Grandmother) came off the press, the Čech papers in the United States were deeply chagrined that the book, notwithstanding flattering newspaper notices, did not appeal more strongly to the younger generation. "We are keenly disappointed that our American-born children feel so little interested in the work of our authoress," commented one newspaper. "If *Babička* had been published here in Čech we should have condoned the apathy of our young folk, but Miss Gregor's *Babička* they should all understand." Yet is it reasonable to expect from our American children and grand-children, reasoned the same journal, whose heads are full of fractions and algebra, to love our adorable *Babička,* to listen patiently to her artless tales of rustic life, to evince curiosity about the contents of that wondrous, decorated dowry chest of hers? [14]

It is not uncommon for immigrants to lament the indifference of the Americanized second generation. A Korean editor expresses himself in these words:

Regarding the second problem—that of racial pride—it must be admitted that most of these hyphenized Koreans have very little knowledge of and appreciation for their ancestral connections. They are not to be wholly blamed for this. Born and raised in a foreign land, where civilization is entirely different, we could hardly expect them to manifest the same spirit of nationalism possessed by seniors; but again the sad part of the narrative comes where many of them don't give a rap

[14] Thomas Čapek, *The Čechs in America* (Boston, 1920, Houghton Mifflin Company), pp. 101–02.

for it. To them only the glimmer and comforts of American life appeal; nothing else matters. They are incapable of stretching their imaginations beyond that.[15]

Sometimes acquire thin veneer. Florian Znaniecki cautions us, however, not to draw conclusions too hastily:

Do not let the Americans illusion themselves that, because the second or third generation of Polish or German immigrants talk American slang and know how to vote they are assimilated psychologically and have acquired the American ways of feeling and thinking. More is needed to attain such a result than most people are inclined to imagine.[16]

Oftentimes some of the external evidences of assimilation are merely a thin veneer. To quote Willa Cather: "It's curious, too; on the outside Emil is just like an American boy,—he graduated from the State University . . . . , you know,—but underneath he is more Swedish than any of us. Sometimes he is so like father that he frightens me; he is so violent in his feelings." [17]

Certain groups encounter obstacles. In some places certain immigrant groups in particular have been kept at a distance, but their children are breaking through the barriers. Kazia Natupski, a Polish girl, met Susy Perkins.

Susy was now in high school, and she wanted Kazia to come and help her in a theme. Once it would have meant something revolutionary for a Natupski to enter the Perkins house by any but the back door, but Kazia was now considered to have lived down her family.[18]

The Chinese have been in America for many years, but still the native-born group retains elements of the old culture, even though there may be no scruples against following American fads and fashions to the extreme. American-born Chinese attend American schools, read Hearst newspapers, devour Hollywood films, dance to jazz music, smoke Chesterfield cigarettes, and vote the Republican ticket like any of the other native sons of

[15] *Korean Student Bulletin,* May, 1930, p. 1.
[16] *Immigrants in America Review,* II (July, 1916), 32.
[17] Willa Cather, *O Pioneers* (Boston, 1913, Houghton Mifflin Company), p. 117.
[18] E. M. Miniter, *op. cit.*, p. 291.

the "Golden State." Many of them speak English without trace of foreign accent and their ideas and ideals differ very little from that of the native whites. If there were no special disturbing factor, the children of Chinese could be assimilated as well as those of English, German, or Swedish ancestry. But there is a disquieting difference. The yellow skin, a distinction more apparent than real, is an obstacle which keeps the Chinese, and other Orientals, from feeling perfectly at ease in America. Because of his color, the young Chinese is treated much the same as his immigrant father. This makes him conscious of the fact that he must be different. That raises barriers between him and Americans and he actually becomes dissimilar. He becomes conscious of his race and his assimilation is retarded. This race consciousness has in some instances transformed native-born Chinese who once considered themselves American into Chinese.

Some small children, even though of different race, play with American white children and no distinctions are made. They are happy in that relationship and no questions are asked—they belong. A small Japanese girl in California came home from school one day and informed her big sister that there were entirely too many "Japs" in their school. When asked to name them she did not include herself or other members of their family. It had not occurred to her yet that they were Japanese. A nine-year-old son of Portuguese parents came to his father about a class in weekday religious instruction and said, "Dad, I don't want to go to that class—they're all Portuguese." These pleasant associations usually continue through the grade school and often through the high school. Even there, however, some lines begin to be drawn, for the young people then are becoming sensitive as to status and they begin to avoid persons that may endanger them. Persons from divergent racial or cultural groups usually are not received with the warmest cordiality by parents and older members of the family. Theodore Abel speaks of the Poles in a New England community:

The younger Poles do not mix with the American youth nor are they received in American homes, with the exception of two college boys whom Americans invite on their camping trips and to home entertainments. . . .

The natives resent the Polish youth because their conduct and manners are not to their liking. They urge their children not to associate with their schoolmates of foreign parentage; so that contacts established in schools, where mixing is indiscriminate and ethnic differences are disregarded, are not kept up after the children leave school.[19]

A Jewish girl tells of the change that came to her, particularly in college.

During my eighteen years I have had only American acquaintances, and we have been the very closest of friends. We have slept at each other's homes and have practically lived together for months at a time. When I was in high school I always went around with an American group, joined their societies and social groups. At college it is different. I am affiliated with a Jewish sorority, and I am ever so happy with my choice. My belonging to this order should not and will not conclude my relationship with my American friends as they are very dear to me.[20]

[19] E. deS. Brunner, *op. cit.*, p. 241.

[20] Unpublished life history. Cf. W. C. Smith, *op. cit.*, pp. 186–210.

CHAPTER XXIX

INDICES OF ASSIMILATION

As we observe the second generation of immigrant parentage, certain elements are noted in their behavior which indicate that they are becoming assimilated into the native group. We may point out a number of these indices.

Changes in externals. Children of immigrants are eager to remove labels of any kind that set them off as being different. They make changes in personal appearance to accord with current American usage. Practically all the Syrians in Pittsburgh who came over as adults are tattooed but no one in the native-born group follows the practice.[1] A school teacher said of the young Mexicans: "Very seldom do we see a young fellow with a moustache or wearing a big sombrero, not if he has lived in California very long. He insists upon dressing in the same style as the American youth."

Changes in dress at times bring conflicts in the home, but that does not deter the young persons from adopting the current American styles. In an urban environment, where contacts are casual and on the basis of secondary relationships, externalities are highly important. A person's status depends on personal appearance rather than on intrinsic qualities. Because of this, the young people try to conform to prevailing fashions. A Molokan girl describes her struggle.

We quarreled over my buying a hat. I wore a shawl to work as long as I could. I did not want people to think I had just come back from a parade. Once I mustered up enough courage to buy a hat for one dollar and ninety-eight cents. When my mother heard about the hat, she cried and carried on something terrible. "A hat? And what next?" To avoid trouble at home I left my hat at a girl friend's house and called for it

[1] M. Zelditch, *op. cit.*

every morning, ditching my shawl. I was determined not to go to work any more in a shawl. I continued that for six months. But my girl friend moved away. And I said to my hat: "Well, here you go home with me, and we will suffer together." When my mother saw that hat, she started to carry on again. She said she would burn it. And I told her frankly that I did not mean to wear a shawl to work any more, and if she burned that hat I would buy another.[2]

Changes are made in food habits. According to Ravage, "nationality is principally a matter of diet." [3] Hence changes tend to come slowly in this sector of life.[4] A teacher reports relative to her school:

Many mothers come to school with food for their young children, but the older children patronize our school cafeteria, and give evidence that they have made adjustment in the matter of food. Lunches brought from home have to be kept out in the hall, for the odor of garlic, fish, etc. is repulsive to the gentile teacher.[5]

[2] P. V. Young, *The Pilgrims of Russian-Town,* p. 163.

[3] M. E. Ravage, *An American in the Making,* p. 226. A man of Danish parentage supports this contention. "The 'clabber' and 'gravy' eating habits that grew around early life in Kimball county, especially in Deerfield, must have left deep impressions on my neurones, because my wife says I am 'Danish as the deuce' in spite of having been away from the Scandinavian associations for nearly forty years." Unpublished manuscript.

[4] One of the first changes comes through the adoption of pie. Cf. P. A. Speek, *op. cit.,* pp. 15–51.

"There are only 32 per cent of second-generation Jews who observe the Jewish dietary laws outside their homes. This means that only one third of our informants will not eat in a non-Jewish restaurant." Nathan Goldberg, *Changes and Persistence of Cultural Traits among Second-Generation American Jews,* unpublished dissertation, University of Pittsburgh.

The second-generation Hungarians do not break completely: "We girls started introducing English dishes we learned at school. When mother died I did the cooking and did it part English. Today, in my own home, I cook about 50–50, which is typical among the second generation Hungarians I know. The 'kids' (third generation) really prefer the Hungarian dishes; they are always after me to bake Hungarian cakes." S. C. Newman, *op. cit.*

This shows a difference between the behavior of the second and third generations. The former, in order to gain status, tend to break away from parental practices, be they good, bad, or indifferent. The latter are in no danger of being classed as queer immigrants and can select elements from the old-world culture with impunity. Even if members of the third generation may be found using more of the parental practices than some of the second generation they may be much farther along in the assimilative process, since these traits have been selected on the basis of deliberation.

[5] Unpublished manuscript.

Oftentimes the young people take over the most crude and undesirable traits of the Americans. Theodore Abel comments on a group of young Poles that, in their eagerness to be considered Americans, have accepted certain superficialities from our culture which set them off in sharp contrast to the youth of old stock. There is a lack of refinement in their conduct; they do not have a sufficiently rich background for evaluating and selecting from the multitudinous stimuli that crowd in upon them.[6]

Change of names. Foreign names cause difficulty and bring mental conflicts because they are labels that invite ridicule. The adoption of a common American name, by removing traces of ancestry, tends to make life more tolerable and provides a more ready approach to the American group. Oftentimes a native child selects a new name or begins to use a nickname which is finally adopted.[7] A second-generation girl did not like her Italian name of Carmella. Some of her friends called her Kate. Her reaction was: "I get so damn' sick of this wop stuff. You can't imagine! My name, when I get to be an American, is going to be Catherine." [8] Miniter shows some of these changes.

Wajeich went to Mifflin Grove peddling one Saturday, and came home accompanied by a youth whom he introduced as Tommy Donahue. Despite his name, *Tommy Donahue* discoursed very ably in Polish until he became convinced that most of the family knew English.
"Tommy Donahue," laughed 'Statia. . . . .
He laughed back. "Oh, I had another name. Only no one could say it and I couldn't spell it.[9] What is it your father called you—Stacy?"

[6] Cf. E. deS. Brunner, *op. cit.*, pp. 241–42.

[7] Changing of names is a common practice among children of Orientals in Hawaii and on the Pacific Coast. Cf. W. C. Smith, *op. cit.*, pp. 247–48. Cf. also M. Van Waters, *op. cit.*, p. 13.

[8] W. S. Ball, *op. cit.*, p. 17.

[9] Some second-generation Eastfriesians changed the spelling of their names because outsiders misspelled them. E. T. Hiller, F. E. Corner, and W. L. East, *op. cit.*, p. 77. Many have adopted other names because of the difficulty of pronunciation. This, however, has exceptions, as pointed out by Dorothy Krall. "It is more than likely, for example, that when names such as Cohen, Kaplan, Levy, and Levine, which are both easy to spell and to pronounce, and certainly as euphonious as most American names, are changed to American-sounding substitutes often far removed in spelling and pronunciation from their originals, the object is in most cases the desire to discard a cognomen that is too Jewish." *The Second Generation Immigrant in America,* unpublished dissertation, Yale University.

"My name," she returned, with great decision, "is Annie S. Natupski. Miss Annie S. Natupski."
He understood and nodded. "Good enough," he said. "I think Miss Annie S. is an awful handsome name." [10]

Many of the young people have found by sad experience that an American name is worth dollars and cents to them.[11] One of them protests:

I did not consider that immigrant or Polish parentage would make any difference in a profession. I now realize that it makes a world of difference. I have tried desperately hard for three months to secure a teaching-coaching position, but so far I have secured no offer. The other day I went and interviewed the president of a teachers' agency. He suggested that I change my name. Many of the superintendents of schools think that because my name ends in "ski" that I am Jewish, and they don't want a Jew. One of my Polish friends was unable to secure a position for two years after his graduation from college. Then he changed his name, taking a familiar English name, and immediately secured a position. I hate to change my name. It will hurt my folks and make them mad. They would never be able to understand my plight. I am going to try it a little longer, but I may have to change it. I hate to do so not only because of my folks and friends, but also because it is part of me and would affect my personality. Can a man be true to himself and change his name that way? [12]

Rölvaag shows how a changed name had been of value.

The name of the teacher was Ted Gilbert. . . . . That he was a Norwegian the Irish did not know at the time they hired him. The name had fooled them, though he had come by it rightfully enough. His father's name, at the time of landing in America, had been Knut Gilbertson; but prompted by a desire to be a real American from the start he resolutely cut away the last syllable of the surname—easier and much more handy that way, Knut thought. The son had been baptized Theodor, which name the boy bore until he entered school; but the first

[10] E. M. Miniter, *op. cit.*, p. 215.

[11] This seems to hold true in different walks of life. Lou Ambers, lightweight champion of the world, was born in New York, and christened Luigi d'Ambrosio. *American Magazine,* CXXIV (June, 1937), 107.

[12] H. G. Duncan, *op. cit.*, p. 771. A second generation Hungarian lawyer in Detroit changed his name to an Irish one to help him in politics. *American Journal of Sociology,* XLI (January, 1936), 433.

schoolma'am under whose care he came, meaning to do the boy a real kindness, shortened Theodor to Ted.[13]

Even in the business world a foreign-sounding name is a handicap. A successful caterer of Czech origin, when asked why he had changed his name to Allen, replied:

"Economic necessity. The élite of this city would not trade with a man with a Slavic name—I tried it." "Don't the old folks mind your dropping of the family name?" A shadow passed over his face as he answered: "It nearly killed my father, but he sees now it was necessary." It is to these experiences that we owe numbers of Bakers, Smiths, Davis's and Cabots in the Polish, Czech, Hungarian and Italian communities.[14]

Occupational adjustments. In the matter of adjustment to occupations, the second generation gives evidence of shifting away from the parental group and moving closer to the native population. The Immigration Commission [15] found that the children of foreigners are not much more disposed to earn their living by unskilled manual labor than are the offspring of native Americans. Those nationalities with an exceptionally high percentage of laborers in the first generation show a marked reduction in the second. This is notably true of the Italians, Poles, Irish, and Hungarians. The building trades, for the most part, employ skilled labor and command, in general, better wages and more favorable employment conditions than do many other fields. In this occupation, however, the immigrants do not attain the same prominence as they do in the less desirable ones, and their percentage varies but slightly from that of their sons.

The Immigration Commission concluded that even though there was a movement away from unskilled manual labor and from work in factories and mines there was no drift into the skilled trades but rather into the "white-collar" occupations. The percentage for clerks, stenographers, book-keepers, and salesmen

[13] O. E. Rölvaag, *Peder Victorious,* p. 315. Cf. E. T. Hiller, F. E. Corner, and W. L. East, *op. cit.*, pp. 76–77, for the Eastfriesians.

[14] E. W. Hursey, *Interpreter Release Clip Sheet,* Vol. XI, No. 14 (July 10, 1934), 85.

[15] Cf. *Reports of the Immigration Commission,* Vol. XXVIII, pp. 18–56; Elin L. Anderson, *We Americans* (Cambridge, 1937), pp. 57–58.

runs high. The percentage of the second generation in professional pursuits is much higher than that of the immigrants and practically the same as the percentage for the total number of male breadwinners in the United States.

Niles Carpenter furnishes certain data relative to the second generation in occupations:

> The daughter of the immigrant plays a distinctly different rôle in the economic life of the country than does her mother. Instead of entering into gainful occupations with relative infrequency, she is unusually heavily employed. . . . . A larger percentage of native white women of foreign or mixed parentage than any other group of females, excepting the negroes, are found in gainful occupations. . . . . It is possible that the immigrant woman, through unfamiliarity with American customs and the English language, is unwilling to venture as far from her home in search of work as her native-born daughter. It is more likely, however, that the larger percentage married among the foreign-born is mainly accountable for this situation. The immigrant woman is typically a wife and mother and is amply occupied at home. Her American-born daughter, however, remains unmarried for a considerable period and so is able to leave her home and earn her own living.[16]

In general, Carpenter says of the second generation:

> Whereas 26.2 per cent of the native-born of native parents and 34.6 per cent of the native-born of foreign or mixed parentage are engaged in manufacturing and mechanical industries, 46.9 per cent of the foreign-born are so occupied. The extraction of minerals employs 2.4 and 1.8 per cent of the foreign-born, while domestic and personal service engages 5 per cent and 6.1 per cent, respectively, of the former and 9.9 per cent of the latter.[17]

On the basis of the data presented by Carpenter, it would appear that the foreign-born are engaged in more arduous, disagreeable, and, probably, less skilled and less remunerative work than are their sons and daughters.[18]

In statistical data on the second-generation Italians, Mariano

[16] N. Carpenter, *op. cit.*, pp. 269–70. Cf. R. I. Kutak, *op. cit.*, pp. 21–22, for occupations of the second-generation women.

[17] N. Carpenter, *op. cit.*, p. 271.

[18] Cf. *ibid.*, pp. 271–75.

indicates that Americanizing influences are working rapidly. "The day is passing when most of the physical work, such as digging, building and heavy construction work is to be done chiefly by our Italian element." [19]

According to E. D. Beynon, the American-born Hungarians in 1930 were represented in the public service, clerical, and professional occupations by a higher percentage than the total of the gainfully employed in Detroit. The latter had only 18.8 per cent in these three occupational classes, while the second-generation Hungarians had 21.1 per cent.[20] In another connection he states that "those Hungarians of the second immigrant generation who become lawyers, doctors, or dentists, or enter other professions, usually are the children of working-class families." [21]

Information from non-statistical sources support the conclusions of the studies to which reference has been made. The children of immigrants give evidence of adopting the occupational pattern of the native group, and have been moving upward into the more preferred occupations. Among the Molokans of Los Angeles, the majority of the men are unskilled or semi-skilled laborers—many work in the lumber yards of the city. Their sons, however, are not following in their footsteps.

The younger-generation Molokans engage in a greater variety of occupations than do their parents. The young men drive delivery trucks, work as master mechanics in automobile shops or in movie studios, print shops, laundries, and the like. At least one has entered the jewelry trade in the down-town section of the city. One or two of the younger men have become professional prize-fighters and some have become "dancers for society folks," to the great scandal of the older generation. Few of

[19] John H. Mariano, *The Italian Contribution to American Democracy* (Boston, 1921), p. 36. Cf. also pp. 31–36.

[20] E. D. Beynon, "Occupational Succession of Hungarians in Detroit," *American Journal of Sociology*, XXXIX (March, 1934), 608.

[21] *Ibid.*, LXI (January, 1936), 433. "In the case of the second generation, the principal factor in the occupational 'rise' of the child has been the desire to regain the status lost by the father after migration. Maladjusted parents who were unable to capitalize their previous occupational experience gave to their growing children imaginative descriptions of the status they had enjoyed in the old homeland. The consequences are to be found in the rise of the sons and daughters into the professions. . . . . The dissatisfied immigrant worker has been probably the principal factor in the unusually rapid ascent of American-born Hungarians into the professions." E. D. Beynon, *American Journal of Sociology*, XXXIX (March, 1934), 609.

the younger men go into the lumber yards, even when work in their own lines is scarce.

The girls work chiefly in laundries and in biscuit, prepared-food, and chocolate factories. A few have drifted into offices; a limited number are salesladies; some work in textile establishments; two girls hold stenographic jobs; two are assistants in a bookkeeping department; and a few occasionally substitute in the movies, keeping this work a secret from their parents.[22]

Pick and shovel no longer harden the hands of young Italians along the railway tracks of our country. Hands are used, if they must be, in industries with higher wage scales.[23] Among American-born Slavs there is a marked trend away from manual labor to the "white-collar" jobs. "Thus while the older Czechs of New York are cigar-workers, pearl-button operatives, and mechanics, the younger generation is found downtown in the stores and offices . . . . or in professional life." [24] Among the Jews in Chicago, "the modern business man on Halsted Street represents the ideal of the sons of the push-cart owners on Maxwell Street." [25] And furthermore, "the sons and daughters of these former push-cart owners are now conducting fashionable shops in other parts of the city, or are lawyers, or doctors, but their parents in many cases still stick to the gold mine on Maxwell Street." [26]

Available data relative to Chinese and Japanese on the Pacific Coast indicate that the second-generation is not following the vocational pattern of their parents.[27] Lind concludes that "among the Orientals in Hawaii the rate of transmission of occupational status from father to son is exceedingly low. . . . . The sons of oriental immigrants abandon the occupations of their parents to enter the fields of endeavor which, in the eyes of their parents, afford status." [28]

[22] P. V. Young, *Pilgrims of Russian-Town*, p. 27.

[23] G. E. Schiavo, *The Italians in Chicago*, p. 52.

[24] K. D. Miller, *Peasant Pioneers* (New York, 1922), p. 78.

[25] L. Wirth, *The Ghetto* (Chicago, 1929), p. 232.

[26] *Ibid.*, p. 235.

[27] Cf. Edward K. Strong, *The Second-Generation Japanese Problem* (Stanford University, 1934), pp. 208–23; W. C. Smith, *op. cit.*, pp. 88–101.

[28] A. W. Lind, "Occupational Attitudes of Orientals in Hawaii," *Sociology and Social Research*, XIII (January–February, 1929), 255. Cf. W. C. Smith, *American*

Rose C. Feld summarizes the occupational situation:

If the Czech or the German or the Pole or the Italian or Swede or Scotchman does not get the stride and the rhythm of the country when he comes here, then certainly his son gets it. If the first digs a ditch, the chances are that his son will become a builder or architect; if the father works in a factory the first son may own one; if the new immigrant regrets his illiteracy, the son, it is fair to assume will be a professor in a college. Invariably, almost, the son of an immigrant rises several degrees above his father in the social and the industrial scale of American life. The lowest class of yesterday becomes the better class of today, its place being in turn taken by new groups of struggling immigrants.[29]

Journal of Sociology, XXXIII (May, 1928), 926–27, for the parental influence in this rise in the occupational scale.

[29] Rose C. Feld, "Sons of Immigrants Remind Us," *Century,* CXV (January, 1928), 363.

CHAPTER XXX

INDICES OF ASSIMILATION
(*Concluded*)

Marriage. Carpenter's study reveals some significant facts relative to marriage in the second generation. The sons and daughters of immigrants display a lower percentage of married persons than either the foreign-born or the native-born of native parentage.[1]

The maximum difference in both males and females between this and the other population classes is at the age-group 20–29 years and that it grows smaller with succeeding age periods. In other words, the immigrant's native-born children not only marry less frequently than either the foreign-born, or the sons and daughters of the natives, but those who do marry tend to postpone their marriages for a relatively long time.

The explanation for this condition can only be conjectured. It may, however, be observed that the postponement or foregoing of marriage involves the deferment or avoidance of the financial obligations involved in marriage, more particularly in the support of children. It may be further pointed out that the second generation immigrants are particularly likely to seek relief from financial pressure in this way, for they are passing over from the social position and economic level of the foreign to the native group and could materially accelerate their progress by keeping themselves free, temporarily or permanently, from family burdens. In other words, to many of the children of the foreign-born it seems to be of more importance to bridge the gap between the social and economic level in which they were born and that attained by the sons and daughters of the native Americans than it is to marry and have children. . . . .

It is worth noting that the women as well as the men among the native-born of mixed and foreign parentage display a disposition to delay or to

[1] Andrew Granstedt found a high percentage of bachelors among the oldest of the second-generation Scandinavians in a Kansas community. *Scandinavian People and Americanization,* unpublished dissertation, University of Kansas.

avoid marriage. It may be, indeed, that the daughters of the immigrants have a special motive for postponing marriage in that by waiting until they might have improved their economic status and broadened their social contacts they would widen the field from which they might choose their prospective husbands.[2]

The postponement and avoidance of marriage by the daughters of immigrants, when contrasted with the practice of their mothers, betoken a veritable revolution in attitudes toward marriage and the home and indicates a rapid Americanization in this respect, at least.[3]

The native-born Swedes of Texas, according to Rosenquist, did not follow the general rule formulated by Carpenter.

They marry two or three years earlier in life than did their parents. Doubtless the reasons for this difference are to be sought in the customs of the country, which among the farmers of the South generally sanction early marriages. The acceptance of this custom by the second generation would indicate that the desire for higher status had not yet become the dominant force sometimes observed in the children of immigrants. The early marriages of the second-generation Swedes may therefore be adequately accounted for by assuming their acceptance of the customs of the community they live in, which customs provide for early marriages and a low standard of living. A slight tendency to increase the age at marriage is, however, noticeable both in the case of men and of the women.[4]

Intermarriage. Intermarriage may be considered the most rigid test of assimilation.[5] When the descendants of immigrants may marry into the dominant group without opposition, it may be assumed that they are accepted and are permitted to participate freely in the life of the older population. So long as relations are restricted solely to economic activities, there is little or no intermarriage. It is only as social contacts of a more intimate nature are permitted that lines are crossed in seeking mates.

Before this rapprochement develops, usually there is disappro-

[2] N. Carpenter, *op. cit.*, p. 217.

[3] *Ibid.*, pp. 217–18.

[4] C. M. Rosenquist, *op. cit.*

[5] In America the crucial question usually asked is: "Would you have your daughter or your sister marry into that group?"

bation of intermarriage, both on the part of the natives and of the immigrants themselves.[6] The following letter to the editor of the *Jewish Daily Forward* is illustrative of the emotional turmoil and struggle which frequently takes place when an out-marriage may be in the offing.

Dear Editor of the *Forward:*

I am not able to express my feelings, yet try I shall so that you may understand me.

I have a daughter, a very good child. But something which I had never in all my life imagined happened. She went with a girl friend of hers to a party in a very pious Jewish home and she enjoyed it very much. Then the young men took them home. A week passed. The second Sunday one of the young men called her up, he wanted to come to our house with another couple. So she asked me, if I was satisfied. What mother is not satisfied, when her daughter has company? So I asked her what sort of a young man is he? Says she, "You'll see him." And I saw him. I wish I had not seen him. A handsome, tall and nice boy. I was the happiest person in the world. And so he used to call her up and always make dates when to come, and they would always be in each other's company . . . . and I was very happy. Everything then seems all right, but the end is, that it is not all right, and what an end! I must have been made of iron, of something stronger than iron to have lived through the past week. He confessed that he is a Gentile. But before she decided to tell me that, she lost six pounds in a few days. She became ill of aggravation. She understood what it meant when we would find that out, how much health it would cost us. It is not half bad with me. I relieve myself by crying when my husband is away, but my husband became wild when we told him. He is a nervous person. And I am in a position where I do not know how to begin to deal with these three people. I try to talk kindly to the girl; she should not ruin my life. So she says, that she likes him, but to please me she will not ever go with him again. But he does not leave her alone. He calls her every day on the telephone. But she does not even answer the telephone. . . . . He talks to me in a manner which frightens me. He speaks no evil, but he says that he cannot live without her and he will never forget her. So I will try my best to explain to him with kind words, but only

[6] Elin L. Anderson discovered considerable antagonism on the part of the French Canadians in Burlington, Vermont, to out-marriage. *Op. cit.*, pp. 187–201. According to Caroline F. Ware, the Irish Catholics were opposed to marriages with Protestants. *Op. cit.*, p. 219. Cf. also pp. 134–42.

God knows what the end will be. He says he is willing to do anything in the world for her, even to become a convert to Judaism. But we are not satisfied with that. We are not pious but we are far from anything (who would consent to) a Gentile as a son-in-law.

Dear Editor, no one can heal my wound, but your kind wise answer will perhaps relieve me. I am very much afraid for my husband. So I beg once more not to make me wait too long for your answer. I remain your reader,

The Despondent Mother from . . . .[7]

An Irish Catholic girl, in whom a second-generation boy had become interested, brought vexation of spirit to the lad's immigrant mother—that was more than the staid Norwegian Lutheran widow could bear. "If the day should come," said she, "that you get . . . . yourself mixed up with the Irish, then you will have lost your mother—that I could not live through!" [8]

The Molokans of Los Angeles have been vehement in their condemnation of out-marriage.[9] Parents considered themselves disgraced if their children found wives or husbands outside the sect. One father among them was deeply distressed:

My daughter recently married a Mexican. I can't understand what possessed her to take this step. If she were crippled or old, or could not find a nice Russian boy, there would be some reason for it. Our family was never disgraced before. People come up to me and ask: "Anna married?" I say: "Yes," "Whom she marry?" I choke; I can talk no more. She wrote us a letter after it was all over. I went around crazy. I thought I would lose my mind. My wife was sick in bed for days. I forbade the whole family to talk about Anna. She is dead to us. We have not gone to see her and don't care to know where she lives. It would be better if she were dead.[10]

A number of intermarriages have been failures. The difficulty in such a new and culturally different group like the Molokans is that the young women have no adequate opportunity to meet the better class of men of other nationalities; they meet those on the

[7] Quoted by Dorothy Krall in *The Second Generation Immigrant in America,* unpublished dissertation, Yale University.

[8] O. E. Rölvaag, *Peder Victorious,* p. 258. Cf. also p. 192.

[9] Cf. P. V. Young, *The Pilgrims of Russian Town,* pp. 172–73, 187–92.

[10] *Ibid.,* p. 188.

fringes, as it were. A girl, weary of the conflicts and suppression at home, elopes with a man of brief acquaintance and soon the marriage goes on the rocks. Under such conditions prejudices against intermarriage develop quite naturally.

Nevertheless, in spite of parental opposition out-marriages take place, and where the person of immigrant ancestry has become fairly well Americanized, so the culture differences are not great, the unions work out satisfactorily. We must not, however, jump to the conclusion that the young people are completely ignoring the wishes and the attitudes of the older generation. Despite bold assertions and a certain amount of blustering the young people cannot completely shake off the influences of the parental culture system. If they were freely accepted by the outside world it would be far easier, but the grudging welcome of the native stock makes them hesitant—some more than others. A second-generation Jewish college boy was perturbed:

> If I didn't love my parents too dearly to hurt them, I would marry a certain American girl with whom I kept company one summer. The danger is not over, however. The more girls I know, the more I love the "certain one." But I know well it would kill my parents and I would much rather suffer myself.[11]

Intermarriage is a serious matter in the eyes of many parents, particularly when religious lines are crossed. A Jewish girl disregarding the threats and pleas of her parents married a young gentile with whom she had fallen in love. On the day of her marriage her father forbade his family to mention her name again and, according to the custom at the death of a loved one, he sat *shivah* for seven days (the mourner with his shoes removed sits either upon the floor or a box and prays) and mourned his daughter as dead. Those who have been reared in the traditional home find it difficult to disregard the old culture completely.[12]

Pihlblad, in his study of the Swedes of Lindsborg, Kansas,

[11] Unpublished life history.

[12] Leah Morton (Mrs. E. G. Stern) in her book, *I Am a Woman and a Jew* (New York, 1931), introduces us to the situation. Her father, an orthodox Hebrew scholar, was broken-hearted when she married a gentile and forsook many practices of Judaism. She was as if dead to her father—he never wrote to her after her marriage. Cf. also E. G. Stern, *My Mother and I,* pp. 153–69.

found that in the upper grades of the school the percentage of children of mixed parentage was low, while in the lower grades it had increased considerably. This seems to indicate that the younger parents had become more thoroughly assimilated.[13] In the early days of the colony, marriage with non-Swedes was not favored, but the younger generation apparently offers no opposition now.[14]

Rosenquist reports a considerable number of out-marriages among the second-generation Swedes in Texas. A scarcity of immigrant women led to a number of unions with outsiders, and thus was forestalled any rigid taboo against the practice. For the most part those marrying outside have been lost to the Swedish group and have become assimilated into the American community.

> In the vast majority of cases, English is the language of the family resulting from an intermarriage; the children are not taught Swedish; and the family customs approximate the American. The relations of such families with the Swedish community are apt to be broken off almost entirely. Newly established families often move away from the vicinity of the former homes of the husband and wife. This gives the Swedish partner an opportunity to break ties with the Swedish group and join an English-speaking church and American groups, both formal and informal. Contacts with the old group tend to be limited to perfunctory visits to and from blood relatives.[15]

E. T. Hiller's study of a French-Canadian rural group in Illinois indicates an increasing tendency on the part of the young people to marry outside the local cultural group, particularly when there were no wide differences in wealth to act as barriers.[16] Mariano presented data to show that intermarriage of the second-generation Italians with the Irish was progressing rapidly, particularly on the

[13] C. T. Pihlblad, *op. cit.*

[14] C. T. Pihlblad, "The Kansas Swedes," *The Southwestern Social Science Quarterly,* XIII (June, 1932), 6. A group of second-generation Swedes in Chicago have been entering into out-group marital alliances increasingly. The outside matings were with those of north-European ancestry. O. A. Benson, *op. cit.*

[15] C. M. Rosenquist, *op. cit.*

[16] E. T. Hiller, F. E. Corner, and W. L. East, *op. cit.,* p. 129. Cf. B. B. Wessell, *op. cit.,* pp. 144–69; Hattie Plum Williams, *A Social Study of the Russian German* (Lincoln, 1916), pp. 77–87.

middle west side of New York City.[17] The process is also going on in Boston. In these cities the Irish may be considered natives of old stock, but the Catholic religion is undoubtedly a factor in drawing these two groups together.[18]

Romanzo Adams in his study of intermarriage in Hawaii [19] found that, in the main, cultural and racial similarity favor intermarriage. There are, however, several conditioning factors. In the early days of Chinese immigration into Hawaii a considerable number of Chinese men married Hawaiian women for the simple reason that Chinese brides were not available. In recent years, however, as the sex ratio has been approaching a balance, a decline in out-marriages has become evident. Furthermore, the Chinese group, now largely resident in Honolulu, is developing a community life in which a definitely adverse attitude toward out-marriage is in process. The Chinese are obviously opposed to marriages that will not enhance their status. When they are freely welcomed into the prestige-giving interracial organizations they will, in all probability, let down the bars against outside matrimonial alliances.[20]

There is comparatively little statistical data available on intermarriage among the second generation of immigrant parentage. Brunner made a significant study of intermarriage in the rural areas of Nebraska, Wisconsin, and New York, the three states having the records with the necessary information. For the purposes of this study five divisions were used: Anglo-Saxon, Scandinavian, Teutonic, Slavic, and Latin. If a person married within his own group this was called "in-choice." If he married a native-stock American this was called "out-choice." If, finally, he married an immigrant of another race or the American-born child of

[17] J. H. Mariano, *The Italian Contribution to American Democracy*, p. 27.

[18] In out-marriage a common language is very important. Dress is a factor. If the wife dresses in some outlandish fashion, the husband will be embarrassed. Similarity in food and household arrangements tend to make both more comfortable. Racial identity so the partner will not be particularly noticed is a predisposing condition.

[19] Romanzo Adams, *Interracial Marriage in Hawaii* (New York, 1937). This is a thorough-going study of the situation in Hawaii. However, conditions there differ markedly from those in continental United States.

[20] Cf. *ibid.*, pp. 142–59.

such an immigrant this was called "inter-choice." The following conclusions were reached:

1. Sons of immigrants born in this country show tendencies quite similar to those of the foreign-born; but they are more than twice as likely to marry the daughter of American-born parents as are the immigrants. . . . .
2. The tendency for both the foreign-born and the native-born sons of foreign parents to marry native-stock Americans seems to be increasing. . . . .
3. The tendency of men from northern Europe and their sons to marry native-stock women is much greater than that of Southern Europeans. . . . .
4. In the main these tendencies are duplicated among the women . . . . except that there is less out-choice.
5. Because immigrants practice in-choice and marry many American-born daughters of immigrants in their group, the native-born men, to that extent, are forced outside for mates. . . . . These native-born sons have no language barrier to overcome; they mingle freely with the children of natives in school and in the workaday world. Frequently they desire to have done with all things foreign.
6. While there was considerable out-choice among the sons of immigrants, nevertheless in-choice and inter-choice combined were in the majority. This means that even among the sons of immigrants the attraction of that which was foreign bulked large.
7. The tendency toward out-choice is gaining among both the foreign-born and the children of immigrants. . . . .
8. The proportion of out-choice marriages varied considerably between the five "racial" groups. In general, Anglo-Saxons are more likely than any other group to marry native brides, the Scandinavians and Teutons come next in order, and the Slavs [21] and Latins show least out-choice. Recency of arrival is undoubtedly a prime factor affecting the Slavic and Latin groups.
9. In the main the women tend to duplicate the tendencies followed by the men, except for a lower rate of out-choice. . . . .
10. A comparison of the pre-war with the post-war period shows a de-

[21] The Poles have stayed more to themselves and married out less than the Germans, Irish, Norwegians, or English in Portage County, Wisconsin. *Proceedings of the State Historical Society of Wisconsin,* 1907, pp. 281–82.

cided tendency among both brides and grooms for the proportion of in-choice to decrease and for inter-choice and especially out-choice to increase. . . . .

11. Certain of these data must be used with caution. . . . . These so-called brides of native stock may be granddaughters of aliens of the same "racial" group.[22] The unmistakably foreign names of many native-stock brides support this contention. This is amply shown by the Pennsylvania Germans who for two centuries have maintained their peculiar dialect and certain customs. In such a situation, marriages with women of native stock would be largely endogamous and would have no particular value from the point of view of assimilation.[23]

Bessie Bloom Wessel has presented data on intermarriage in Woonsocket, Rhode Island.[24] She found that 12.1 per cent of all first-generation, 20.9 per cent of all second-generation, and 40.4 per cent of all third-generation individuals had intermarried.[25] She found among the French-Canadians, a group which tends to cling tenaciously to its cultural values, a rapidly increasing rate of intermarriage, particularly in the third generation. Willingness on the part of this ethnic group to enter into marriage relations with persons from outside the group connotes a fairly complete acceptance of the out-group folkways and mores. On the other hand it indicates that the French Canadians have been accorded status in the larger community.

Julius Drachsler, in his study of intermarriage, found a readiness on the part of persons of the second generation to marry those of different national descent. He concluded that "the irresistible leveling influences of American life have stamped persons of the second generation as unmistakably alike." [26]

The birth rate. Robinson, in a Chicago study of selected census tracts which are mostly Polish or Italian, found the rate of reproduction to be approximately twice as high in the families of

[22] Elin L. Anderson found this to be true in Burlington, Vermont. *Op. cit.* p. 190.

[23] E. deS. Brunner, *op. cit.*, pp. 75–91.

[24] *Op. cit.*, pp. 103–74.

[25] *Ibid.*, p. 107.

[26] From *Democracy and Assimilation* by Julius Drachsler (New York, 1920), p. 106. By permission of The Macmillan Company, publishers. Cf. pp. 87–145. Cf. also J. Drachsler, *Intermarriage in New York City* (New York, 1921).

immigrants as in those of the second generation.[27] Stouffer's study seems to point in the same direction. According to this, the Catholic confinement rates are highest among the unskilled, next among the skilled, and lowest in the white-collar group. This latter class contains a much higher percentage of the second generation than of foreign-born.[28] Census data support this conclusion. The median size of all white families in 1930 was: foreign-born 3.74; foreign or mixed parentage 3.28; native-born of native parentage 3.37. In the urban areas the figures are 3.76, 3.19, and 3.13, respectively.[29] These averages indicate that the birth rate in the second generation has fallen considerably below that of the immigrant generation and the size of the family is nearing the American pattern.

Racial gestures. Dr. Franz Boas, in his study of motor habits as expressed in posture and gestures,[30] found that the Italian and Jew change in the second generation. Mayor Fiorello H. La Guardia of New York City, of Italian-Spanish ancestry, gesticulates freely but his movements and postures are American. In private conversations or under excitement, however, Italianisms become evident. Governor Herbert H. Lehman of New York is of German Jewish parentage, but he uses even fewer gesticulations than the average American Protestant.[31]

Crime. Even the criminality of the children of immigrants is an index to their assimilation. They become assimilated to the native group in this respect. The Immigration Commission found that "the movement of second generation crime is away from the crimes peculiar to immigrants and toward those of the American of native parentage." [32] Furthermore, children of immigrants be-

[27] Gilbert Kelly Robinson, "The Catholic Birth-Rate," *American Journal of Sociology,* XLI (May, 1936), 757–66.

[28] Cf. Samuel A. Stouffer, "Trends in Fertility of Catholics and non-Catholics," *American Journal of Sociology,* XLI (September, 1935), 143–66.

[29] *Fifteenth Census of the United States, 1930: Population,* Vol. VI, p. 16, Table 21. Cf. also pp. 13–16 for other data which point in the same direction.

[30] Cf. "The Effects of American Environment on Immigrants and Their Descendants," *Science,* LXXXIV (December 11, 1936), 522–25.

[31] *The Literary Digest,* CXXI (May 9, 1936), 19.

[32] *Op. cit.,* Vol. XXXVI, p. 14. See chapters XX, XXI *supra.*

come partners with others in crime; they cross ethnic lines in their delinquent activities. According to Wirth,

> One of the most significant signs of the relationship between the Jews and their neighbors in the ghetto is found in the contacts between the members of the younger generation. They mingle not only in school but they are members of the same gangs. The recent outbreaks of gang warfare in Chicago show that in many instances the Jews, the Irish, and the Italians are engaged in joint illicit liquor enterprises, or combine their forces in "hi-jacking." [33]

[33] L. Wirth, *The Ghetto,* pp. 229–30.

CHAPTER XXXI

FACTORS IN ASSIMILATION

A. Retarding Factors

In brief we may note some of the factors that exert a retarding influence upon the assimilation of the second generation. The common tendency of a group to consider itself superior and to express contempt for all others and their cultures is a serious hindrance to the incorporation of newcomers. This touches the immigrants but the American-born children tend to feel the thrusts of the various opprobrious epithets more keenly than do their parents. Parents can take refuge in memories and console themselves that these prejudiced, crude persons do not represent America. They realize that they are different and are not expecting to become like Americans. The children, however, have no past; they are Americans and are eager to be accepted by Americans. These expressions of contempt produce mental conflicts and restrict free and open communication with the native group, thereby retarding assimilation.

Race differences. Race differences are closely related to prejudice since physical dissimilarities constitute permanent labels that serve as reminders of a one-time imputed inferior status. Many years will pass before American-born Chinese and Japanese in California will be accepted by the white group, no matter how thoroughly Americanized they may become. Skin color and the slant of eyes categorically classify them with their alien parents. Children of immigrants from southeastern Europe encounter more opposition than those from the northwestern countries. Members of the second generation who are set apart by distinctive physical characteristics usually find that prejudices against the parental group are directed also against them. Such opposition has made it impossible for many to identify themselves with the American group, even though they have wished to do so. Many second-generation Orientals, growing up as Americans in the schools with American ideals, attitudes, and sympathies, considered themselves American and never wanted to be anything else. Race prejudice, however, has thwarted them and forced them to shift their aspirations.[1]

Sometimes the disillusionment is a cruel one. W. E. Priestly tells of a Seattle-born Japanese who "in every respect but features was as American as buckwheat cakes. In his conversation he used all the conventional slang phrases, and, if occasion demanded it, he could swear with a fluency that would have shocked his ancestors." He was graduated from the University in electrical engineering and tried to get a job only to be turned down repeatedly because he was Japanese. A fellow classmate, with a much lower record, was given one position for which he applied. From Bellingham to San Diego he tried in places where he knew there were openings, but without success. As he bluntly expressed it, "They slam the door in my face and call me a damned Jap." Because of his features he was forced into the anomalous position of being an Oriental. He decided to go to Japan. But his inability to use the Japanese language readily and his ignorance of things Japanese made his adjustment most difficult.[2]

An Hawaiian-born Chinese girl, who had been accepted as an American in Honolulu, came to California for her university work —and soon her disillusionment began. She had a Chinese face and was not accounted an American.

> I gradually learned that I was a foreigner—a Chinese—that I would be wiser to admit it and to disclaim my American citizenship, particularly when I was in a Chinese group. I accepted my title as a *foreign* student more graciously. I became more accustomed to the stares of the American people, to their remarks, and to their sneers. I did not feel inferior to them; I did not feel antagonistic toward them; but I was disappointed and deeply hurt.[3]

[1] Cf. W. C. Smith, *Americans in Process,* pp. 186–210.

[2] *The Japanese-American Courier,* September 8 and 15, 1934.

[3] *Survey of Race Relations,* Document A–310. For her later experiences see W. C. Smith, *Americans in Process,* pp. 243–44.

Segregation in colonies. Segregation in colonies affects the immigrants and it also leaves its marks on the children. Peter A. Speek reported that "a considerable number of the American-born drafted men who could not speak, write, or even understand English" [4] came from certain colonies where the immigrants had kept alive their old-world traditions through their schools, churches, and libraries which had cut them off from direct contact with American life.[5] Dr. Young [6] points out some of the difficulties encountered by the young Molokans. Because of the comparative isolation in the colony they cannot lose themselves in the larger community. They may resent the heavy hand of tradition, but they have no way of escape. Sorties into the outside world have found it cold, impersonal, unsatisfying. A second-generation Mennonite wrote of the colonies established by his group.

In such closed settlements the cultural traits, including the language, remain intact for a long time. This isolation carries with it many ossifications which stand in bad stead when the group finally essays forth into the larger world, as it invariably must. Due to the isolation there was a slow turn-over, not only of otherwise fleeting fads, but of nearly every phase of life, so that whenever young people from this closed community went beyond its confines, they were for a time marked.[7]

The language barrier. Ability to read, understand, and speak the language of the country is most important. Without language the process of assimilation cannot go far. Embarrassment frequently comes to the person who takes on certain externals by observation without knowing the full meaning behind the overt behavior. Etiquette, as an example, can be learned only with the greatest difficulty, if at all, without language. Etiquette is important in connection with assimilation, for the person who breaks

[4] P. A. Speek, *A Stake in the Land,* Carnegie Corporation of New York, p. 131.

[5] According to Morris Zelditch, "The degree to which the children of Syrian parents cling to old-country customs and attitudes seems to vary with each family and in proportion to the degree of participation with which that family partakes in the activity of the rest of the Syrian community in Pittsburgh." *Op. cit.*

[6] P. V. Young, *The Pilgrims of Russian-Town,* pp. 177–78.

[7] Unpublished manuscript.

rules of etiquette with flagrance will not be accepted readily, and it is in the small, primary groups where the assimilative process goes on most effectively.

B. Factors Aiding Assimilation

All elements which are favorable to the assimilation of the immigrants are aids to the younger group also. There are, however, certain additional factors which affect the children, some of which we may consider at this point.

The school. Undoubtedly the school is the most potent Americanization agency that touches the native-born children of immigrants. In the school the children of all nationalities meet both in the classroom and on the playground, and because of this contact traditional differences are reduced to a minimum and finally obliterated. Stephenson quotes an item from the *Minnesota Chronicle and Register* of September 23, 1850, to the effect that the school

> takes the child of the exile of Hungary, of the half-starved emigrant from the Emerald Isle, and of the hardy Norwegian, and places them on the same bench with the offspring of those whose ancestors' bones bleached upon the fields of Lexington. . . . . As the child of the foreigner plays with his school fellow, he learns to whistle "Yankee Doodle" and sing "Hail Columbia" and before he leaves the school-desk for the plough, the anvil and the trowel, he is as sturdy a little republican as can be found in the land.[8]

Rosenquist has pointed out how the school aids the assimilation of the children of Swedish immigrants in Texas.

> They go to a school where English is spoken and taught. The subject-matter of the books used is taken from American life. The children know all about the Mayflower before they hear of Ellis Island; they learn to worship our heroes and to idealize all that is American. Now it is a fact that it is impossible to love one culture more without loving others less. It follows as a matter of course that as the children of these immigrants become more American they become less Swedish. They may even and usually do regret that they are of Swedish origin instead

[8] G. M. Stephenson, *History of American Immigration* (Boston, 1926), Ginn and Company, p. 101.

of colonial American. They learn to despise things Swedish and to be ashamed of the foreign ways of their parents.

At school also the children of Swedish parents meet children of American parents. Often, though, by no means always, these American children come from homes a little more cultured, or at least on a slightly higher economic level than those of their Scandinavian neighbors. Children are democratic in their associations, to be sure, but they sense class differences. And since the native children, in the main, belong to a higher class, Americanism itself becomes associated with the upper levels of society. Desirous of attaining these upper levels, the children emulate and imitate American ways.[9]

Not infrequently the child of the immigrant is Americanized too rapidly and too superficially by the school. Pressure is brought to bear to have him set aside all that is foreign and take on everything American. In this hasty process he tends to lose the finer elements of the parental culture and take on a thin veneer of Americanism in which the crude and gaudy characteristics all too often predominate.

A trend is noticeable in the schools now which may decrease, or at least change in some measure, their Americanizing influence. In the early days, the schools were staffed by those of north-European stock, but there has been a decided shift. The Immigration Commission in their study of the schools in thirty of the largest cities found that the second-generation Irish teachers constituted the largest group with the Germans next in order. The Irish ranked first in twenty and second in eight of the thirty cities. In Shenandoah, Pennsylvania, 56.8 per cent of the teachers were Irish, in Worcester, Massachusetts, the percentage was 46.2, and in Scranton, Pennsylvania, it was 35.1. In eight of the thirty cities more than one fourth of the teachers were of Irish parentage.[10] Scandinavians, Jews, Italians, and others have been increasing in numbers. Eleanor Ledbetter found in her study of Cleveland that many Czech girls went to the Normal School to prepare for teaching. While some of them may speak English with an accent, they should be able to sympathize with the children of immigrants and

[9] *Op. cit.*

[10] *Reports of the Immigration Commission*, Vol. XXIX, p. 139.

may be able to provide more wholesome conditions that will make for a more healthy assimilation.

Whatever may be the assets and liabilities of the American school as an assimilative agency, it does provide the most favorable opportunity for mastering the English language.

Language. Ability to use the common language is basic in assimilation. The children usually can learn a new language more easily and have favorable conditions in school and in their other contacts for acquiring it. Hence they quite early come into possession of this most valuable instrument of assimilation. This opens avenues of communication both through speech and the printed word.

Age of parents on arrival. The age of the parents at the time of arrival is an important factor. If they are comparatively young they tend to assimilate more readily and thus can make the setting more favorable for the children's assimilation. They will be in a better position to understand and appreciate the American culture and can assist the children in making their adjustments with a modicum of disorganization. The situation will be favorable for a minimum of culture conflicts and the unhappy results that often follow in their train.

Birth order of the children. The birth order of the children plays an important part in assimilation. Of two native sons of foreign parentage, one born after the parents have been resident in the country for many years has a more favorable situation for thorough assimilation than one whose birth is dated only a few months after the parents' arrival. The younger child will be assisted not only by his parents but by his already assimilated brothers and sisters.

Parental attitudes. Many parents do all they can to make conditions favorable for a wholesome assimilation of their children. So far as possible they remove distinguishing marks that might be sources of embarrassment. They strive to give them suitable and stimulating contacts. They encourage them in school. In California some Japanese parents, even though they knew practically no English, tried to help their children with school work. They are watchful to see that the necessary supplies are provided. They coöperate with the school in order to make conditions the best possible for the pupils.[11] A number of parents do not insist that their children maintain the mother tongue lest it interfere with school work.

Economic status of parents. If the economic situation of the family is such that it can avoid slum dwelling and can live in a respectable neighborhood, the chances for assimilation are increased. The slum with its heterogeneity is not the place to find well-defined American behavior patterns. Furthermore, a favorable economic status makes it possible to use more readily the various agencies and instrumentalities that provide contacts with American life. It also enables them to discard externalities, such as foreign clothes, which tend to restrict contacts with Americans.

[11] Cf. W. C. Smith, *Americans in Process* (Ann Arbor, 1937), pp. 164–70.

CHAPTER XXXII

ASSIMILATION OF PARENTS THROUGH THEIR CHILDREN

The children of immigrants are important agents in the assimilation of their parents. Wirth even ventures to say that, "The Americanization of the immigrant parents takes place, if at all, through the medium of the children. In the immigrant family the child thus comes to play a rôle not unlike that of the missionary between cultures." [1] In another connection Wirth shows the influence of children upon their parents.

In most instances it is the children who discover the ghetto for their parents. They go to school; they work in the stores and offices in the Loop; they make friends; they go to dances, and the girls are seen home by escorts; they are mobile, and the world of the ghetto begins to shrink, then to bore and finally to disgust. In contrast with the sweep of Michigan Boulevard, the gawdy splendor of the Trianon Ballroom, and the grandeur of the Oriental Theater, the ghetto streets look narrow, dark, and filthy.

Sometimes parents, who feel at home because they have never been outside, resist for a time, but then family conflicts arise that make life intolerable. They eventually yield, and the exodus begins. What ten years ago was a slow westward movement has now developed into a veritable stampede to get out of the ghetto.[2]

Angelo Patri placed importance on the influence of children: [3]

I have been a part of many movements to Americanize the foreigner, but I see that the child is the only one who can carry the message of democracy, if the message is to be carried at all. If the child fails to make the connection between the ideals of the school and the funda-

[1] *Social Forces,* IX (June, 1931), 487.

[2] L. Wirth, *The Ghetto,* p. 234.

[3] From Angelo Patri, *A Schoolmaster of the Great City* (New York, 1917), p. 218. By permission of The Macmillan Company, publishers.

mental beliefs of the people, there is none other to do it. The children are the chain that must bind people together.

This contention seems to be borne out by the fact that family men tend to assimilate more readily than single adult men who live by themselves or with other unmarried men. In groups with a large preponderance of males there are few children to make the essential contacts that indirectly bring changes in adult attitudes.[4] Where the sex distribution approaches the normal, more family life with children exists and opportunities to touch the enveloping American life at vital points are thereby increased. The Japanese in California had a more normal family life than the Chinese and they have gone further in the assimilative process. The presence of children usually stimulates parents to work harder in the achievement of a more secure economic status and thus provide better opportunities for the children. Furthermore, as many parents have seen their children becoming Americanized they bury their hopes and intentions of returning to the native land—they realize that their Americanized children could not make adjustments there. Bercovici wrote of some Polish immigrants that "their children, having grown up in this country, refused to leave for an unknown land." [5] Hence these immigrants

[4] Cf. E. Abbott, *Immigration: Select Documents and Case Records* (Chicago, 1924), p. 548; *Reports of the Immigration Commission,* Vol. I, p. 42. In a group of Swedes studied in Chicago, the English language crowded out the Swedish most rapidly in the homes with children and thus assimilation was accelerated. "Devoted as the normal parent is to his offspring, the immigrant parent cannot fail to be profoundly influenced by the thoroughly American interests and activities of his American-bred child. Perhaps reluctantly but none the less inevitably, he will accustom himself eventually to speaking the language preferred by the son or daughter. One by one his native prejudices will yield to the opinions of the children, and rather than create the suspicion that he does not share the American outlook of the younger generation, he will gradually abandon some of his most cherished traditions. The conversation between foreign-born parents and American-born children, if indeed they are to converse at all, must concern American subjects, about which alone they have common knowledge. This tends still further to concentrate the parents' minds on matters that pertain to their adopted country and to familiarize them with its life, thus doing much to stimulate assimilation. Children are very effective agencies in the Americanization of their alien parents." O. A. Benson, *Accommodation of the Swede to American Culture,* unpublished dissertation, University of Pittsburgh.

[5] K. Bercovici, *On New Shores,* p. 120.

are less insistent on retaining their old-world traditions and are more receptive to the culture of their children.

Predisposing factors. The child, especially if born in America, has excellent qualifications to serve as this culture missionary. He is more nearly free than his parents. He does not have the habits formed by many years of life in an old-world environment to hamper him in his adjustments. He does not have his emotions aroused by some new experience as do his parents when called upon to break with the traditional mores. Old-world memories restrict the activities of adults who are less receptive to new stimuli. The child is in the formative stage and is more plastic and impressionable. Ability to use the common language makes the child more mobile; he can make contacts which are beyond the range of his parents, who, in large measure, are restricted to relations with members of their own ethnic group, usually confined within a colony. In their work-day activities the adults make contacts of a formal, impersonal and secondary nature in the process of working out accommodations that may render their bread-winning activities tolerable. The child, however, is accepted forthwith into a play group at school or in the neighborhood or even admitted into a gang where he participates on the basis of primary relationships. In these intimate, face-to-face interactions assimilation takes place rapidly. It is frequently through these activities of the children that the immigrants make their first contacts with their neighbors, since the development of friendship between two children may result in their parents becoming acquainted.

The rôle of the school. American culture penetrates the foreign-language community most deeply and effectively through its impact upon the child of the immigrant, which is the most sensitive and plastic area of family life. Since the child learns the common language in the school he carries this into the home. He is desirous of having his parents use the English language and become like the people they meet on the street. He comes to be the medium through which his parents make their contacts with the new world and through which American conceptions and practices are infiltrated into the home. The child interprets to his parents the various customs, ideas, and ideals which he has learned in school; he instructs them with reference to American standards of health, civic rights and duties, and moral codes as he learns them in school; he gives them lessons in geography and shows how big this country is; and he explains how Washington and Lincoln and other notables made this America what it now is. He has new experiences in the school which he shares with his parents and in this way they come to participate in the life about them. The child reads the newspaper and thus keeps the family informed relative to the happenings in this country. The parents are eager for news from abroad, but the child is insistent on keeping them informed about events in his America. Thus, willy-nilly, they are exposed to a battery of Americanizing influences. An excellent illustration may be gleaned from the experience of an old immigrant group.

Conservative as the Pennsylvania Germans are by nature, and as strongly inclined as they are to maintain fundamentally unchanged their religious beliefs and practices, still they are slowly, if not always perceptibly, being more or less influenced by the spirit of the times which seems to be affecting religious thought and church relations generally, everywhere. This is especially true with regard to the young people, and true to an extent, too, of such young people as have been raised in the strict faith of the Mennonites. All of which tends to explain the tendency of many to abandon the wearing of a distinctive religious garb and to do some things heretofore deemed sinful, but which most people now do, or look upon as innocent.

No small part of the subtle influence affecting beliefs and customs is attributable to the contacts of the children with other children and with new ideas at the public schools. Indeed, owing to the part that the state has taken in establishing and maintaining schools and in promoting education, there has been a greater change among the Pennsylvania Germans in regard to education than in almost any other fundamentally important respect. Moreover, it is significant that it has been said that a large proportion, if not most, of the children "despise" the so-called "Pennsylvania Dutch" (Pennsylvania-German) language or dialect.[6]

Changes in externals. Children are eager to bring the first changes in externals that cause them embarrassment, because

[6] Jessie L. Rosenberger, *In Pennsylvania German Land, 1928–1929*, pp. 39–40.

they, too, are hit by jibes directed at peculiarities of their parents. In a community in Iowa where the Dutch were in the majority the language and many of the old customs were continued. A college, located in the area, drew students from distant points and these outsiders made some of the younger generation sensitive about the old Dutch customs. "One of my cousins," said a young woman of the group, "tried to get grandfather to quit wearing his wooden shoes—he told grandfather that he would take the shoes away from him, if he would not quit wearing them." Most utensils are left in the home and are not noticed, but a person's dress goes with him and is observable whithersoever he wanders. Children notice when others stare at their parents and make caustic remarks. Hence, they often insist that their parents adopt American dress—a change not always easy to make.

One Sunday as we were starting for church, Aurora, our eldest daughter, then ten years old, asked why I did not wear a hat like the other women in place of my black *rebozo*. What a thought! How could I go on the street without that? It was out of the question! For several weeks after I watched the women. One day while passing a second-hand store I saw a pretty hat. I went in to see how much it was. It was very cheap, so I bought it and went home. I had planned to put aside my *rebozo* the next Sunday. Each day, after the children had gone to school, I put on my hat to see how it felt. On Sunday, how happy the girls were to see me in a hat! But how sad at heart I felt. I, too, was giving up part of my life in Mexico.[7]

Peculiar actions and gestures are also noticeable and come within the children's province of reform. "My mother," wrote a Lithuanian boy, "used her hands freely when she spoke. Often I went shopping with her and was always sorely chagrined when she pointed to an article she admired with awkward gestures, and expressed her opinion of it in a rising voice." [8]

Many children are embarrassed when their parents use the mother-tongue in the presence of Americans or when they make

[7] Unpublished document.
[8] H. G. Duncan, *op. cit.*, p. 733.

efforts to use English.[9] Some of them try to teach the parents to speak English. In many homes the parents gradually learn the new language from the children as the old speech falls into disuse.

Many, perhaps, are unduly sensitive about their homes and will not invite friends or acquaintances to go there. The statement of one person that she would die of shame if one of her college friends should open the door [10] would apply to many. Some leave

[9] The following poem published in a newspaper (source unknown) shows the desire of the child to break away from anything which might label him as a foreigner. At the same time, it is evident that the father is proud of his "American" boy.

THE DAGO

I, mysel', I feela strange
  Een dees contra;
I no' can make mysel' agin
  An' change eento 'Merican
An' so I am wot you calla me,
  Shust a dumb ole Dago man.
Alla same my boy ees be
  Smarta younga 'Merican.

Twalve year ole, but alla same,
  He has learna soocha lot,
He can read an' write hees name.
  Smarta Keed? I tal you wot!

He no' talk Italian,
  He say, "Dat's for Dago speak,
I am younga 'Merican;
  Dago langwige make me seek."
Eef you gonna tal heem too,
  He ees leetle Dago, my!
He is git so mad at you,
  He gon' punch you een da eye.

Mebbe so you try to make fool weetha heem,
  An' mebbe not,
Queek as flash he sass you back.
  Smarta keed? I tal you wot!

Evra time when I go out weetha heem
  I no' can talk to somebody;
"Shut your mout',"
  He weel tal me pretta queek,
"You weel give yoursal' away
  Talking Dago lika dat.
Try be 'Merican," he say.
  Smarta keed? I tal you wot!

[10] A. Yezierska, *Children of Loneliness,* p. 103.

the parental roof, but others stay and gradually remake the home [11] according to the American pattern.[12]

Immigrants cling tenaciously to their old-country diet, but even in this area of life the children bring changes. According to Peter A. Speek,

The first breach is usually occasioned by pie—the American national dessert. The immigrant children learn about it and taste it in school

[11] A good case is reported by H. G. Duncan, *op. cit.*, p. 763.

[12] Edith M. Miniter, in her novel of a Polish family, paints a vivid picture of the transformation of the home into an American one. The father objected, but he could not stand out against the children. " 'Statia installed white iron beds with National springs complete, and papa and mamma actually slept thereon, though they first muttered 'Tin!' when they creaked, and mamma thought she could never be really comfortable on anything but a tick fresh stuffed with straw. Fly screens, too, appeared in every window, and papa was made properly apologetic whenever he forgot and propped the door open. Nor did 'Statia feel peeved when, of an evening, she trimmed the Rochester lamp and set it cozily on the round table in the front room, with the Morris chair and willow-rocker hard by, only to see their natural occupants making excuses to seek a congenial atmosphere. She followed to the vicinity of the hog-pen and said reproachfully, 'Papa, I don't like it for you to let me spend money on tables and chairs 'less you use 'em.'

"If papa made an exclamation that sounded very profane it was in a language 'Statia was rapidly forgetting, and he looked ashamed directly afterward.

"Another day, 'Papa, I made for you a *punkin pie*. It's like the American's eat.'

"And she sat smiling at his right hand until a wedge disappeared.

"Again, 'Oh papa, see how splendid I scrubbed the floor. With sand, like Mrs. Slocumb, showed me.'

"He truthfully admired the shining boards, glad this day he was not made to eat another pie; he felt akin to a criminal when he managed to slop a few quarts of swill on them. 'Statia said he ought to—and the pantry was no place for a swill barrel, anyway.

"With mamma she felt she should have no difficulty, for mamma had once, on a never-to-be-forgotten occasion, the birth of Yadna, emancipated herself from certain Old-World customs, and they had never been resumed when Yan came along two years later. So in her presence 'Statia cheerfully went about sniffing at the cooking pots, and remarking that a single shirt wasn't clothes enough for a five-year-old Yadna even in summer. 'Statia gave orders further, that mamma was to do no more field work, but sit on the piazza for hours making embroidery like Mrs. Bowes and Mrs. Perkins. Mrs. Natupski's fingers were somewhat stiff for the needle, but she seldom lifted her eyes from its shining point—not even when she suspected the hired boy was pulling up the vegetables and hoeing the weeds.

" 'Statia, being possessed with the energy of youth and hopefulness of a nation that ventures to emigrate, enjoyed herself in this self-appointed mission. How much better it was for her papa to spend money now, than to hoard it as he had done. Presently she would prove to him that he did want a coat of paint on the house and a rambler rose over the door. She had already told him to feel shame for uprooting the woodbine when he bought the place from Mrs. Judson Buckland the year she—'Statia—was born. As for eating from the kettle, and wearing a night-shirt, 'Don't papa!' and 'It ain't correct not to do so,' had become words she repeated,

cooking classes and also in the neighboring American families, insisting that their mothers make it also. As a result the pie appears on the immigrant table, though in the poorer families only on holidays.[13]

Together with changes in food came modifications in table manners. A Lithuanian boy related some of his mother's table manners and ways of setting the table.[14] He said that his sisters had tried to "mannerize" their mother and had succeeded in some measure. A Filipino boy in Hawaii indicated the changes in his home.

Several years ago my parents used to eat with their fingers—they paid no attention to the spoons, forks, and knives that were placed before them. I was then in school and knew something of American etiquette. I explained to my parents that since we were in America, we should try to adopt American modes of living, customs, and table manners. Gradually my advice was put into effect. They began to realize that I was learning something good at school, and little by little they dropped the practice of eating with their fingers, and are using the forks, spoons, and knives more and more.[15]

Less visible changes. The children, however, do not stop after bringing about changes in the more apparent externals; they are desirous of making their parents American in all ways. In their study of history and civics in school they learn about citizenship and want their parents to be citizens. Mary L. Zahrobsky in her survey of the Slovaks in Chicago found that an attempt had been made to prepare a number of the immigrants for citizenship through an English class, but with very little success. Most of the men, however, were naturalized after a few years, and it usually came about through the influence of the children.[16]

Angelo Patri recalls the changes that came over his father when he served as his parent's teacher.[17]

parrot-like, all day long." *Op. cit.*, pp. 209–11. Also pp. 131, 141, 339–45. Cf. also Jane Addams, *op. cit.*, pp. 253–54.

[13] P. A. Speek, *op. cit.*, pp. 150–51.

[14] Cf. H. G. Duncan, *op. cit.*, p. 734; also A. Yezierska, *Children of Loneliness*, pp. 101–09.

[15] Unpublished life history.

[16] *Op. cit.*

[17] From Angelo Patri, *A Schoolmaster of the Great City* (New York, 1917), p. 218. By permission of The Macmillan Company, publishers.

When my father came to America, he thought of America only as a temporary home. He learned little or no English. As the years went by he would say, "It is enough; my children know English." Then more years rolled by. One day he came to me and asked me to help him get his citizenship papers. He and I began reading history together. Month after month we worked, laboring, translating, questioning, until the very day of his examination.

That day I hurried home from college to find a smiling, happy father. "Did you get them?" I asked.

"Yes, and the judge wanted to know how I knew the answers so well, and I told him my son who goes to college taught me, and the judge complimented me."

Parental attitudes. Some parents bitterly oppose the changes urged by their children; they refuse to become Americanized. They are hesitant about giving up the time-worn customs in which they have grown up. Furthermore, yielding to the children is against their traditions; this distorts the old order in which the children were to be seen but not heard. Some men object violently because it means the surrender of a patriarchal prerogative. Anzia Yezierska presents one of the extremes:

"All my teachers died already in the old country," retorted the old man. "I ain't going to learn nothing new no more from my American daughter. . . . ."

"You, witch, you!" he cried in a hoarse voice tense with rage. "Move by yourself! We lived without you while you was away in college, and we can get on without you further. God ain't going to turn his nose on us because we ain't got table manners from America. A hell she made from this house since she got home." [18]

On the other hand, many parents welcome the innovations brought into the home by the children; they realize, at least in some measure, the significance of these new ideas in the lives of the younger generation. Schiavo writes of the Italians in Chicago that with the growing up of their American children many of them become dissatisfied with "Little Italy." They do not wish to humiliate their boys and girls. Hence they furnish their homes according to approved American patterns so that the young folks

[18] A. Yezierska, *Children of Loneliness*, p. 101.

of the neighborhood may be invited in without hesitation. These parents want their sons and daughters to be proud of them.[19]

If the children do well in school and win any distinctions or honors, the parents are pleased; this reflects favorably upon them and enhances their status. While Mary Antin was in the public school one of her poems was published in a Boston newspaper.

> When the excitement in the house had subsided, my father took all the change out of the cash drawer and went out to buy up the "Herald." He did not count the pennies. He just bought "Heralds," all he could lay his hands on, and distributed them gratis to all our friends, relatives, and acquaintances; to all who could read, and to some who could not. For weeks he carried a clipping from the "Herald" in his breast pocket, and few were the occasions when he did not manage to introduce it into the conversation. He treasured that clipping as for years he had treasured the letters I wrote him from Polotzk.[20]

If, after several years of happy experience in school, the children make satisfactory economic adjustments, the parents speak with pride about their success in America. This admiration, reluctant though it may be at times, leaves them more open to suggestions and they yield more readily to the notions of the children. In this receptive mood they unconsciously begin to participate more freely in American life.

Mary Antin's father had difficulties in making accommodations to America. The language barrier limited him in his acquisition of many values he knew were available in his new surroundings. But that did not stop him. If some of these higher things of life were denied him directly, he could acquire them vicariously by sending his children to school, perhaps even to college. Then his house would be filled with books and with intellectual company. With a swelling heart he took the children to school and delivered them over to the teacher. In this way he took possession of America.[21] He did everything he could to help the children in their Americanization and, incidentally, that aided his own. He

[19] G. E. Schiavo, *The Italians in Chicago*, p. 45.

[20] Mary Antin, *The Promised Land* (Boston, Houghton Mifflin Company, 1912), p. 237.

[21] *Ibid.*, pp. 204–05.

did not permit their more orthodox mother to put hindrances in their way. He permitted her to keep a Jewish kitchen, but encouraged the children to accept invitations to dine with their gentile neighbors. He was desirous that they mingle freely in the life about them. On the holy days and the Sabbath, the mother could carry on the usual religious activities but her orthodoxy must in no way interfere with the Americanization of the family.[22]

Even though the mother was more conservative than the father, she too longed to possess some of the good things which the other members of the family were enjoying. In the evenings she became a pupil in a school which the children conducted around the kitchen table. They borrowed books from school, the father gladly supplied the necessary pencils, and Mary served as teacher.[23]

The experience in the Antin home seems to support the conclusion of Angelo Patri when he said: [24] "I have told about parents growing because they sought growth for their children. I saw them grow through the initiative of the school."

[22] *Ibid.*, pp. 247–48.

[23] Cf. *ibid.*, pp. 252–53. Cf. A. Cahan, *op. cit.*, pp. 242–46, for an interesting case.

[24] From Angelo Patri, *A Schoolmaster of the Great City* (New York, 1917), p. 218. By permission of The Macmillan Company, publishers.

CHAPTER XXXIII

THE IMMIGRANT'S CONTRIBUTION TO AMERICA

When we pause to consider the large number of immigrants within our gates, several questions arise: What have they brought? What contributions have they made? What effect have they had upon our life?

A variety of answers has been given. According to some, all our numerous ills were brought by these hordes from across the seas.

Biological problems. The Nordic myth has been worked overtime in an effort to show that the biological level of our population was lowered through a process of mongrelization. Furthermore, it was argued that the birth-rate of the old native stock was forced to decline and it would be only a matter of time until those of north European ancestry would be engulfed.[1] These alleged facts, however, have not been fully accepted.

Economic problems. Immigrants unquestionably have accentuated our economic problems. The influx of large numbers with low standards of living has depressed wages. They have been used as strike-breakers. Several employers not only drew upon the supply of workers already here, but also imported others directly from Europe to displace Americans and older immigrants who had begun to ask for better conditions.[2] The presence of many ignorant foreigners weakened the labor organizations so they could not maintain standards and wage scales. Many aliens who

[1] Long discussions on this question have produced a considerable fund of literature. André Siegfried, on the other hand, indicates how immigration restriction may decrease the birth rate. Domestic servants are becoming increasingly difficult to get—the wealthy can secure them through the payment of high wages, but those of the middle class will be forced to do their own housework. When family life is thus made difficult, there will be fewer children. *America Comes of Age* (New York, 1927), p. 125.

[2] E. A. Ross, *The Old World in the New* (New York, 1914), pp. 195–227; W. Halich, *Ukrainians in the United States,* pp. 17, 29.

contemplated a return to the homeland were eager to work even at low pay. Since they came from non-industrial areas and lacked acquaintance with the trade-union idea, they could see no advantage in paying the required dues. Organized labor, consequently, has quite consistently opposed immigration while the employers have displayed no great enthusiasm for restrictive measures. In general, immigrants have been detrimental to the wage-earners with whom they have been in direct competition while they have added to the prosperity of those who were in a position to profit through the cheapening of labor. With a large number of needy and tractable workers it has been easy for American employers and foremen to become autocratic. Moreover, when it is possible to hire and "fire" "wops," "hunkies," and "dagoes" without compunction, the situation is favorable to the development of attitudes that are not conducive to harmonious relationships in industry. Furthermore, this situation has provided no incentive to regularize employment. So long as an employer has access to an elastic body of alien workers, why should he attempt to spread production evenly over the year in order to provide employment for family men with local attachments? The form of industrial organization has also been changed: more sub-foremen have become necessary in industrial establishments to act as interpreters. A certain amount of specialization has also resulted and unskilled immigrants have been used for routine work.

Despite these objectionable features, certain benefits have accrued to American workers. A considerable number, at least, had opportunities to leave poorly-paid, unskilled drudgery and rise to the preferred occupations. Immigrants have also acted as a steadying influence on the labor market and thus have eased the shock of depressions. With a decrease in the demand for workers, the inflow from other countries automatically, as it were, was reduced. Furthermore, many returned to their native villages in slack seasons, in periods of depression, or when too old and helpless to continue at work. This elastic element in the labor supply diminished the pressure on the native workers in some measure and hastened the return to normal conditions. These departures, however, were at best tardy and incomplete; the more prosperous ones left, leaving upon us the burden of a large residuum of unemployed and needy aliens.[3]

Social problems. We have been told time and again that our crime problem is almost entirely due to the influx of foreigners. A number of studies, however, indicate that the foreign-born have a better record than the native-born.[4] The presence of immigrants, nevertheless, has tended to increase crime in the native-born population. As different groups settled in America, inevitable culture conflicts led to a breakdown of standards and behavior patterns. But this cultural confusion has not been all loss, for it brought new stimuli and led to new evaluations—it has been a price paid for relief from stagnation. Donald R. Taft is not disturbed about a modicum of criminal behavior on the part of our immigrants because the very characteristics which cause some to fall into crime leads others to make significant cultural contributions. New ideas are valuable and we can afford to pay dearly for some of them.[5]

Brawn. Others, more generous, admit that immigrants brought strong, rugged, and healthy bodies which enabled them to toil at the blast furnace and in the mine, and thus play a part in our industrial development. Their brawn, sweat, toil, and skill—crude perhaps, but fresh, vital and strong—were indispensable in the exploitation of our natural resources.[6] The immigrants do a large part of America's work; they erect our office buildings, construct our tunnels and highways, mine our coal, iron, and copper, and make our steel, our machines, our automobiles, and our clothes. Many of these "hewers of wood and drawers of water" have sacrificed life and limb as they toiled that we might reap the advan-

[3] This problem has been discussed quite thoroughly in a large number of books on labor problems.

[4] See *supra*, chapter VI.

[5] D. R. Taft, *Human Migration*, p. 216.

[6] According to C. M. Panunzio, "The United States has, without doubt, developed too rapidly industrially, and this expansion has given the country a temper of motion and has raised standards which seem at times to be destroying all perspective, all poise, and all sense of values. Economic possessions, economic power, and prestige are our gods. . . . . If all this is true, it would seem as if the presence of the new immigrant which has so largely contributed to rapid economic development has been an ill rather than a good, except for one thing: the new immigrants are the most strenuous opponents of this economic god worship." *The World Tomorrow*, XIII (July, 1930), 301–02.

tages of a higher standard of living. Yet thousands upon thousands of these "unknown soldiers" in the industrial army will have no monuments erected to honor them—they will be known as dirty "bohunks," damned "dagoes," and lousy "wops."

Eminent men. Others concede, rather grudgingly, to be sure, that a number of America's great personages have come from the horde of immigrants. But, they say, these men and women are merely biological accidents, and since accidents happen anywhere they are of no particular significance. We may consider a few of them.[7]

John Ericsson, a Swede, came to America in 1839 and the next year won a prize for the best design of a fire engine. For a number of years he experimented with the screw propeller and was the first to make it successful in connection with water navigation. He built the iron-clad *Monitor* which won the important battle with the Confederate *Merrimac* in 1862. This vessel brought a complete break with the past in design and construction of warships. It had a revolving turret for the guns, was propelled by steam, and the power was applied through the screw propeller. Without doubt, the appearance of the *Monitor* at this particular time had a decided effect upon the outcome of the Civil War and the future direction of our history. Andrew Carnegie came from Scotland in 1848 at the age of thirteen and began work as a bobbin-boy in a Pennsylvania cotton mill from which he gradually moved up to develop the steel industry into the giant that it is today. Olaf Huff came to the United States in 1879 from Norway and for many years was one of our outstanding engineers. He devised the method for tunneling the Detroit River in Michigan, and planned the subway tunnel under the Harlem River at New York City. Michael O'Shaughnessy, a native of Ireland, was city engineer of San Francisco from 1912 to 1932 and built the system which brings water from the Sierra mountains two hundred miles distant. Leo Hendrik Baekland, born in Ghent, Belgium, came to America in 1889. He received a number of distinctions for his researches in

[7] Cf. Annie E. S. Beard, *Our Foreign-Born Citizens* (New York, 1922); Joseph Husband, *Americans by Adoption* (Boston, 1920), for brief biographies of citizens born in other lands. Cf. F. J. Brown and J. S. Roucek, *op. cit.*, for names of eminent persons in the various immigrant groups.

chemistry and was granted many patents, both here and abroad, in the fields of organic chemistry, electric insulation, synthetic resins, and plastics. John Stevens, born December 4, 1840, in Wales, came to Wisconsin in 1853 where he worked in a flour mill. Stone-grinding, which produced only 20 per cent good white flour, was the usual method at the time. Stevens began experiments with rollers and in 1880 patented a device which revolutionized the milling industry. The introduction of the roller system into the mills of Minneapolis made that city the flour center of America and brought an addition of 100,000 people to the community within five years. It also attracted large numbers of hardy pioneers to the northwestern prairies to grow wheat to supply grist for the new machine.[8] Alexander Graham Bell, inventor of the telephone and the outstanding figure of his generation in the education of the deaf, came from Scotland in 1870. His first activity was with the deaf in Boston. Meanwhile his experiments with telegraphy resulted in the invention of the telephone over which the first message was transmitted in 1876. Louis Agassiz, a Swiss, was outstanding in the fields of geology, palæontology, and ichthyology. He did much to open the eyes of America to the book of nature and we are indebted to him for that great institution, the American Museum of Natural History. Cesar Ritz, another Swiss, raised standards of hotel management in America as well as elsewhere so that the adjective "ritzy" is accepted in the dictionaries and stands for a high grade of excellence in hotel service. Dr. Alexis Carrel came from France in 1905 and in 1912 was awarded the Nobel prize for success in suturing blood vessels and in the transplantation of organs. Many soldiers of the World War are grateful to him for his work in aseptic surgery which alleviated their suffering and saved their lives. In 1931 he was winner of the Nordhoff-Jung cancer prize.[9] D. W. Griffith, the moving-picture magnate, is a Welshman. Wales also gave us the labor leaders John Mitchell and John L. Lewis. Andrew Furuseth, a Norwegian, for many years president of the International Seaman's Union of America, was in large measure responsible for

[8] *Proceedings of the State Historical Society of Wisconsin,* 1907, pp. 244–45.
[9] Cf. *American Magazine,* CXXI (March, 1936), 20–21, 142–44.

the passage of the La Follette Seaman's Act of 1915 which blotted out the last vestige of slavery under the American flag. March 4, 1915, is considered by the sailors as their "emancipation day." [10] Jacob Riis, a Dane, through his newspaper reporting and books, aroused New York City so that slums were cleared, parks established, and better housing laws enacted. Little Holland gave us Edward Bok, and what would America be without the *Ladies' Home Journal!* Birger Sandzen, who ranks among our foremost painters, was born in Sweden in 1871. He has specialized on the rugged mountain landscapes of the Southwest and has exhibited his paintings in Sweden, Paris and in several American cities. He has been director of the art department of Bethany College, Lindsborg, Kansas, since 1894.[11]

But some one will say that these men came from northwest Europe and were of close kin to our old stock. We may turn, however, to the so-called "new" immigration and find a considerable array of talent, even though these groups have been in America a shorter time. We may enumerate a few of them.

From a garlic-growing town in Hungary came a boy, so poor that at first he slept on a park bench in New York City. One cold winter night he entered a hotel lobby to get warm but was thrown out. Twenty years later he bought that hotel for $635,000 and somewhat later acquired the newspaper, *The World,* for $340,000. This was Joseph Pulitzer who became journalistic king of the metropolis.[12] Dr. Ales Hrdlicka, a prominent anthropologist connected with the National Museum in Washington, was born in Bohemia. Michael Pupin, whose researches made possible the long-distance telephone, was a Serb. Nikola Tesla, a Yugoslav, emigrated to the United States in 1884 and shortly thereafter developed the arc light and made important inventions in connection with the alternating current in electrical transmission systems.

[10] Knut Gjerset, *Norwegian Sailors in American Waters* (Northfield, Minnesota, 1933), pp. v, vi, 179–80.

[11] Adolph B. Benson and Naboth Hedin, *Swedes in America, 1638–1938* (New Haven, 1938), pp. 494–95.

[12] C. E. Schaeffer, "Perspective in Evangelical Hungarian Work," *Annual Report, Home Missions Council,* 1934–1935, p. 39. Cf. Don C. Seitz, *Joseph Pulitzer: His Life and Letters* (New York, 1924).

Franz Boas, the dean of American anthropologists, Simon Flexner of the Rockefeller Institute for Medical Research, and Felix Frankfurter, associate justice of the Supreme Court, are Jews. Henry Morgenthau, who was entrusted with several important governmental missions, was a Jew from Germany. The late Albert A. Michelson, one of the world's eminent physicists who gave the most fruitful years of his life to America, was also a Jew from Germany.[13] Hideyo Noguchi, a native of Japan, came to the United States in 1899 for advanced study in medicine. His published report on snake venoms established his reputation and in 1904 he began work with the Rockefeller Institute. He devised a new and important method for diagnosis of syphilis and gave the last ten years of his life to a study of yellow fever. He came to be recognized as the leading microbiologist since Pasteur and Koch.

Probably no one will deny the fact that these immigrants have made valuable contributions to our life and that we would have been heavy losers if they had not come. The benefactions of these men, however, have not been foreign elements added to our culture; they worked in science and in the various fields in the same manner as other men. In some instances, to be sure, it is probable that their training in the homelands gave them particular fitnesses for making these contributions.

Changes due to immigrants. According to some, the immigrant must undergo all the transformation while the true American does not change at all—there is no give-and-take in assimilation. The immigrant went into the melting pot and was remade, but this did not affect our institutions or our culture in any way. Some will say that this should be so but admit, almost tearfully, that it is not. Sufficient evidence has accumulated to show that assimilation is a two-way process—there is an interchange of cultural elements. Anthropological data from a wide field substantiate this. When the colonists settled in America they took not only the land from the Indians but much of their culture as well. Note but one instance, that of the maize culture complex. The colonists adopted the

[13] Cf. George Cohen, *The Jews in the Making of America* (Boston, 1924), for other Jews.

methods of growing corn from the aborigines and we still plant it, cultivate it, store it, and eat roasting ears and hominy as they did.[14] We have been influenced by the Indians and by immigrants as well. Benjamin Franklin noted the reciprocal influencing and feared the dangerous effect of large numbers of foreigners. After 4,317 Germans had arrived in Pennsylvania in 1750 he wrote to a friend in England asking

> why the Pennsylvanians should allow the Palatine Germans to swarm into our settlements, and by herding together to establish their Language and Manners to the exclusion of ours? Why should Pennsylvania, founded by the English, become a colony of Aliens, who will shortly be so numerous as to Germanize us instead of our Anglifying them? [15]

The United States has always been a nation of immigrants and their contributions have, in large measure, been responsible for the development of our American civilization. The interplay and interstimulation of the diverse ethnic and national groups in the new-world setting have made our history and shaped our destiny. No one single nationality has directed our course to the exclusion of all others. Immigrant groups have profoundly influenced the material, institutional, and cultural aspects of our life, and we may give them credit in considerable measure for whatever of American idealism there may be. The great mass of migrants came not only because of economic opportunities, but because of dislike for religious intolerance, militarism, official injustice and tyranny. Inspired by these ideals, they did not rest until the tone of American thinking and political practice had been raised. When liberalism was crushed in Germany, thousands of revolutionary idealists took refuge in America, and brought with them almost the last vestige of democratic leadership. When this was strangled in the homeland they were all the more solicitous to nourish it here.[16]

[14] Cf. Clark Wissler, "Aboriginal Maize Culture as a Typical Culture-Complex," *American Journal of Sociology,* XXI (March, 1916), 656–61.

[15] E. R. Lewis, *op. cit.,* p. 199. Quoted from A. H. Smith, *The Writings of Benjamin Franklin.* Cf. Marcus W. Jernegan, *The American Colonies, 1492–1750* (New York, 1929), p. 316.

[16] Russell Blankenship, *American Literature as an Expression of the National Mind* (New York, 1931), pp. 21–26; Samuel P. Orth, *Our Foreigners* (New Haven,

Immigrants have done much to make and keep America democratic. The Federalist party with its aristocratic bias set about to stop any further spread of dangerous democratic doctrines by enacting the Alien and Sedition Acts and the Naturalization Law in 1798. It was also proposed to amend the constitution to bar naturalized aliens from holding federal office. The trend toward democracy, however, was too strong and the Federalist party was doomed.[17]

While the American language is English, it differs considerably from that of England and the impact of immigrants has been one factor in producing changes. A German dialect used since the early days of settlement in Pennsylvania is still in use and has modified both the vocabulary and pronunciation of English in the regions of these colonies. Likewise the everyday speech of lower Louisiana reflects a French contact. Texans have appropriated words from the Mexicans. In Minnesota and the adjoining states Swedish terms and idioms have been borrowed. The suffix *fest* of the sport writer's *swatfest* comes from the German. The word *spaghetti* has been admitted into the dictionaries and we use this Italian word as if it had been bequeathed to us by Tennyson or Browning. As we have adopted ideas, practices, or materials we have made additions to our language.[18]

Even cookery in America has not followed English traditions but shows the influences of several groups. One does not see English restaurants in a city but there are many French, Italian, German, Greek, Chinese, and Jewish eating places.

While we owe a greater debt to the aboriginal Indians than is usually acknowledged, yet the main roots of our life are buried in the soil of Europe and our culture is more than anything else an interweaving of elements from the old-world tradition and the American environment.

Need we feel that we are any less American because we have made certain cultural contributions so much our own that they

1928); Arthur M. Schlesinger, *New Viewpoints in American History* (New York, 1928), pp. 1–22.

[17] A. M. Schlesinger, *op. cit.*, pp. 7–8.

[18] H. L. Mencken, *The American Language* (New York, 1936), pp. 150–63; 212–22.

seem to be indigenous with us? The Scotch have impressed much of their culture on America. In face of that fact, need one be a Scot to join in singing "Annie Laurie" or "Comin' Through the Rye?" Need one feel unpatriotic if he joins a club to study the poetry of Tegner or of Tagore, the dramas of Ibsen or Goethe, the novels of Dostoievsky or Sienkiewicz?

The late Franklin K. Lane, when Secretary of·the Interior, wrote of the immigrant's part in the making of America:

America is a land of but one people, gathered from many countries. . . . . Whatever the lure that brought us, each has his gift. Irish lad and Scot, Englishman and Dutch, Italian, Greek, and French, Spaniard, Slav, Teuton, Norse, Negro—all have come bearing gifts and have laid them on the altar of America.

All brought their music—dirge and wassail song, proud march and religious chant. All brought music and their instruments for the making of music, these many children of the harp and lute. All brought their poetry, winged tales of man's many passions, folksongs and psalm, ballads of heroes and tunes of the sea, lilting scraps caught from the sky and field, or mighty dramas that tell of primal struggles of the profoundest meaning. . . . .

All brought art, fancies of the mind, woven in wood or wool, silk, stone, or metal—rugs and baskets, gates of fine design and modeled gardens, houses and walls, pillars, roofs, windows, statues and painting—all brought their art and hand craft.

Then, too, each brought some homely thing, some touch of the familiar home or field or forest, kitchen or dress—a favorite tree or fruit, an accustomed flower, a style of cookery, or in costume.[19]

Each group brings its national beverage. The Swedes brought their coffee,[20] the French and Italians their wines and the Germans their beer. The Scandinavians introduced snuff or "snus" into the lumbering regions of the Northwest. The use of tobacco, particularly through smoking, is common among laborers. In the

[19] Quoted by Allen H. Eaton, *Immigrant Gifts to American Life* (New York, 1932), p. 28.

[20] The Basques in Oregon are fond of coffee and prepare it in homeland fashion. "They usually drink it from huge cups. They place approximately a half cup of hot boiled milk in the cup and then fill the remainder with coffee. This is the familiar European *café au lait*." *The Commonwealth Review,* XX (March, 1938), 374.

logging camps and around sawmills, especially in the summer, smoking is dangerous and is forbidden by the insurance companies and operators. The Scandinavian habit of using tobacco in the form of snuff causes no forest fires. Some of the older non-Scandinavian workers chew tobacco, but the younger men have taken to snuff or "Copenhagen snus."

Many immigrant contributions are so intangible as to be incapable of measurement or even visible demonstration. We cannot arrange in tabular columns or in museum cases the religious faiths, the moral codes, the domestic virtues, or the prejudices which they brought. Some felled trees in our forests and the stumps testify to their activities while the ledger column totaled the number of tons of coal mined by others. Such results are amenable to a certain kind of quantitative analysis. Will anyone deny, however, that the Pilgrims, Huguenots, Quakers, German Pietists, and Swedish Dissenters, gave us "pearls of great price?" They came for more than bread and butter, but who will measure their influence with accuracy! Frederick J. Turner wrote:

> The democracy of the newer West is deeply affected by the ideals brought by these immigrants from the Old World. To them America was not simply a new home; it was a land of opportunity, of freedom, of democracy. It meant to them . . . . the opportunity to destroy the bonds of social caste that bound them in their older home, to hew out for themselves in a new country a destiny proportioned to the powers that God had given them, a chance to place their families under better conditions and to win a larger life than the life they had left behind. He who believes that even hordes of recent immigrants from southern Italy are drawn to these shores by nothing more than a dull and blind materialism has not penetrated into the heart of the problem. The idealism and expectation of these children of the Old World, the hopes which they have formed for a newer and freer life across the seas, are almost pathetic when one considers how far they are from the possibility of fruition. He who would take stock of American democracy must not forget the accumulation of human purposes and ideals which immigration has added to the American populace.[21]

[21] Frederick J. Turner, *The Frontier in American History* (New York, 1920), pp. 263–64.

Material contributions. On the material side, the foreigner has been an important factor in the development of America. On the farm and in the mine, on the railway and in the skyscraper, he has strained his muscles and carried the heavy burdens.

Undoubtedly the German has proved himself the most successful farmer in the United States and this success has been an object lesson to others.[22] The Germans, "fearing God and debt," reared large families which enabled them to cultivate their lands with diligence and care. W. Hense-Jensen pointed out the difference between the farmer of the old native stock and the German:

> To the former, his farm was only a means of support and an object of speculation; without regret he left it after the soil became worthless through his irrational farming—his continually raising one kind of crop. On the other hand, the German, with his tender home feeling, whose farm had been won by hard toil from an unbroken wilderness, petted it as a mother would her child. His only object was to improve his homestead and leave it unencumbered to his posterity. Look over the flourishing farms of Wisconsin today, and deny if you can that this German spirit has become characteristic of all nationalities in our state.[23]

A typical example of their systematic, steady work may be found in the story of Grimm alfalfa. In 1858 Wendelin Grimm, an immigrant to Carver County, Minnesota, sowed about twenty pounds of alfalfa seed he had brought from Germany. Most of this was winter-killed, but he saved the seed from the surviving plants and after several years of this selective process had a frost-resisting variety. This greatly increased the acreage and importance of the crop.[24]

The Germans are also given credit for adapting corn to both colder and warmer regions than those in which it had been grown before. They have done much to develop pure-bred horses, cattle, and hogs. They are considerate of their live-stock, feeding and housing them well. The barn on the German's farm is frequently more imposing than the house, and the big red barn can

[22] Cf. A. B. Faust, *op. cit.*, II, pp. 28–65; S. P. Orth, *op. cit.*, pp. 127–28.

[23] *Proceedings of the State Historical Society of Wisconsin,* 1901, p. 146.

[24] U. S. Department of Agriculture, *Yearbook of Agriculture* (Washington, 1937), pp. 1125–27; K. Bercovici, *On New Shores,* pp. 186–88.

be seen wherever the German resides. Others have gradually patterned after this.

The Mennonites from Russia, who settled in Kansas in the seventies, introduced hard wheat which made the supply more dependable and Kansas City began to prosper in the milling business as did also the other towns in the wheat belt.[25] Russian and Ukrainian farmers brought Kherson oats which are now grown advantageously in the Middle West.

The Scandinavians [26] and Bohemians have done much to promote agriculture on the rolling prairies of the Mississippi Valley. In Virginia a colony of Bohemians settled on rather undesirable land but through their persistent efforts made the soil yield and in a comparatively short time won the respect of the skeptical native Virginians.[27] The Pole also has been a successful agriculturist. "The Polish farmer has opened to cultivation areas that would not have been touched by other nationalities and he thrives and advances from poverty to prosperity upon lands where American farmers would starve." [28] Immigrants from countries where land is scarce have developed methods unknown to the American who has been accustomed to great stretches of land. In the words of E. A. Ross:

> Certain of the South Europeans who are upon the soil have something to show American farmers facing the problems of intensive agriculture. Italians are teaching their neighbors how to extract three crops a year from a soil already nourishing orchard or vineyard. The Portuguese raise vegetables in their walnut groves, grow currants between the rows of trees in the orchard, and beans between the currant rows. They know how to prevent the splitting of their laden fruit-trees by inducing a living brace to grow between opposite branches. The black-beetle problem they solve by planting tomato slips inclosed in paper. From the slopes looking out on the Adriatic the Dalmatian brings a horticultural cunning which the American fruit-grower should be eager to acquire.[29]

[25] *Kansas Historical Collections,* XI (1909–1910), 123.

[26] A. B. Benson and N. Hedin, *op. cit.,* pp. 75–91; E. deS. Brunner, *op. cit.,* 155–82.

[27] E. deS. Brunner, *op. cit.,* pp. 186–95. A North Carolina agricultural colony, constituted of six different nationalities, was so successful that some of the native-born cautiously adopted the practices of the immigrants. *Ibid.,* pp. 95, 139–54.

[28] *Proceedings of the State Historical Society of Wisconsin,* 1907, p. 280.

[29] E. A. Ross, *The Old World in the New,* pp. 202–03.

The Japanese on the Pacific Coast, through their indefatigable industry and high degree of efficiency in tilling the soil, have made it possible for Americans in all parts of the country to have fresh fruits and vegetables throughout the year. They have done much to reclaim rich lowlands, particularly in the San Francisco delta region. Their techniques of drainage, fertilization, cultivation, and coöperative shipping and marketing have made for greater efficiency in western agriculture. In certain areas non-Japanese have entered into coöperation with the Japanese to the mutual advantage of both groups.[30]

Our country has a highly developed dairy industry because our Danish settlers have shown the way. In the early seventies, when there was a heavy emigration from Denmark, dairying was changed into a large industry because of the results of researches and inventions by Danish scientists. The Danes applied the new ideas when they settled here and established dairies on an unprecedented scale. In addition to the coöperative creameries, the Danish communities have coöperative buying and selling organizations, and coöperative insurance companies. Some of these enterprises prove to be sufficiently attractive to draw non-Danish participants.[31] Because of the primacy of the Danes in dairying, it is not surprising to find that several from this group are experts in dairy science in our colleges of agriculture. The heritages of the Finns and Swiss also add to our stock of dairy products. According to Eugene Van Cleef, the Finnish immigrant soon buys a cow, gradually builds up a herd, and turns to dairying.[32] The mountain farmers of Switzerland who settled in Wisconsin in 1845, helped us win a high place in the production of cheese. Since they were expert in cheese-making they turned to that industry with the result that their product has captured the American market.[33]

[30] Cf. E. G. Mears, "The Land, the Crops and the Oriental," *The Survey,* LVI (May 1, 1926), 146–49; Y. Ichihashi, *op. cit.,* pp. 160–206; F. J. Brown and J. S. Roucek, *op. cit.,* pp. 472–93.

[31] Cf. K. Bercovici, *On New Shores,* pp. 22–24.

[32] E. Van Cleef, *op. cit.,* pp. 198–200. Cf. W. Seabrook, *These Foreigners,* pp. 75–79, for the Finns and coöperation.

[33] *The Wisconsin Magazine of History,* X (1926–1927), 42–49.

The Basques, who settled in southeastern Oregon, Idaho, and Nevada "have made their chief contribution to the life of the country through their efficiency in the sheep business." [34]

Pennsylvania is greatly indebted to the Germans for developments in horticulture. Turnips and cabbages were the main vegetables in the dietary of Philadelphia for a long time.[35] The Germans have also done much to develop fruit-growing. They were instrumental in establishing orange culture in Southern California on a large scale.[36] An Hungarian planted the first Tokay grapes in California.[37] In fruit culture we have had the help of the Spanish, Italian, and Portuguese settlers with their century-old experiences around the Mediterranean.[38]

Germans have paid considerable attention to food products, particularly to pickling and preserving, and the "57 varieties" of H. J. Heinz have been accepted in the American dietary.[39] In some places with large German populations, sausage-making has become important, and large quantities are sold to non-Germans. Not only have *sauerkraut* and *frankfurters* been accepted on American menus but many of the spicy articles of the delicatessen as well.[40]

Food habits, together with other heritages, of national, racial, and religious groups are sometimes commercially exploited and

[34] L. S. Cressman and Anthony Yturri, "The Basques in Oregon," *The Commonwealth Review,* XX (March, 1938), 368.

[35] F. R. Diffendorffer, *op. cit.*, p. 125.

[36] A. B. Faust, *op. cit.*, II, p. 52; Frederick F. Schrader, *The Germans in the Making of America* (Boston, 1924), p. 91.

[37] C. E. Schaeffer in *Annual Report, Home Missions Council,* 1934–1935, p. 38.

[38] A. H. Eaton, *op. cit.*, p. 90.

[39] A. B. Faust, *op. cit.*, II, pp. 65–73. This German influence is reflected in the large number of words related to eating and drinking that have been adopted in our American language. Such words as *pumpernickel, wienerwurst* (reduced to *wiener* or *wiene*), *frankfurter, hamburger, zwieback, delicatessen, lager-beer, beer-garden, stein,* and *rathskeller* show the effect of German immigration upon American habits. H. L. Mencken, *The American Language* (New York, 1936), p. 155.

[40] A. B. Faust, *op. cit.*, II, pp. 72–73. Among the Basques of Oregon, "A familiar sight each fall or early winter, after the cold definitely sets in, is a family group industriously working over a dressed hog to prepare their favorite *chorizos*. These are sausages made from pork cut up into small pieces and seasoned with salt, red peppers, and a touch of garlic, and preserved in shortening. *Chorizos* have become popular with other people also, but only the Basques are successful in achieving the individual flavor." *The Commonwealth Review,* XX (March, 1938), 373–74.

thus carried beyond the group of origin. Jewish dietary laws have influenced the meat-eating habits of New Yorkers. Advertising and salesmanship have developed a belief that *kosher* butcher shops sell the best meat. As a result a lucrative slaughtering business, catering both to Jews and Gentiles who prefer fresh to cold-storage meats, has grown up close to the metropolis.[41]

The production of beer is in German hands, but it is not necessary to produce statistical data to show that the consumption of this liquor is not restricted to the German group—it has been accepted quite generally in our American life.

According to Michael Choukas, the Greeks could poison a large portion of our urban population in any one day through the large number of restaurants they operate. Then the large number of Greek florists would provide flowers for the funerals. However, we need not fear such a calamity, for, if it should take place, the Greek shoe-shining establishments would have to close their doors. Greek boot-black parlors, with or without hat-cleaning adjuncts, are found all over the country.[42]

German immigrants stand out prominently in fields that require technical training. Engineering schools developed earlier in Germany than in America and sent out well-trained men. John A. Röbling built a number of big suspension bridges, among them the famous Brooklyn Bridge. They have been outstanding in piano-making as evidenced by the names Steinway, Weber, Sohmer, Wurlitzer, and Knabe.[43] George Gemünder, born in Würtemberg in 1816, made violins at his establishment in New York that rivaled the old Italian instruments.[44]

Swedes have made contributions in the mechanical field, in engineering, and particularly in the building trades. Many of the

[41] N. Anderson and E. C. Lindeman, *op. cit.*, pp. 104–05. It would be interesting to know to what extent non-Irish florists push the sale of shamrocks on St. Patrick's day. No Irish lassie has ever asked the writer to present a birth certificate from the Emerald Isle before she would sell him a shamrock. The custom of wearing the green on that particular day has become quite well established, at least in certain cities.

[42] F. J. Brown and J. S. Roucek, *op. cit.*, pp. 345–48.

[43] A. B. Faust, *op. cit.*, II, pp. 77–121; F. F. Schrader, *op. cit.*, pp. 242–43.

[44] George Gemünder, *George Gemünder's Progress in Violin-Making with Interesting Facts Concerning the Art and Its Critics in General* (Astoria, N. Y., 1881); A. B. Faust, *op. cit.*, II, pp. 111–13.

largest structures in Minneapolis, St. Paul, Seattle, Chicago, Cleveland, Dallas, and other cities have been erected by Swedish architects or contractors.[45]

Many Cornishmen became miners in America. In southwest Wisconsin they introduced the safety fuse for blasting, an invention used in Cornwall before the emigrants left for America.[46]

Norwegians for ages have been seafarers and when they migrated to America many of them stayed on the water or in closely related activities. In the days of sailing vessels they were on the Great Lakes and in ocean-going ships under the American flag. A considerable number are now on steamers, both as sailors and officers. Norwegians have served as harbor pilots, an occupation which can be undertaken only by expert seamen. They have engaged in ship-building and in deep-sea fishing on vessels plying from Gloucester, Massachusetts.[47] Norwegian sailors have been in great demand. When Sir Thomas Lipton's *Shamrock III* was defeated by the American yacht *Reliance* in 1903, of fifty-one men on the latter, forty-four were Norwegians, as were the first, second, and third officers. Sir Thomas said they were the smartest sailors he had ever seen.[48]

Much of Swedish tradition is also bound up with the sea and Swedes will concede equality to Norwegian seamen only. Many of the immigrants continued the sailor's life in America. The Matson Navigation Company which has a fleet operating from the Pacific Coast to Hawaii, New Zealand, and Australia was organized by Captain Wilhelm Matson who went to sea at the age of ten from his birthplace in Sweden.[49]

Effects on politics. Immigrants have had a decided effect upon

[45] A. B. Benson and N. Hedin, *op. cit.*, pp. 100–01; 382–434. Cf. G. Cohen, *op. cit.*, pp. 128–30, for the Jews in construction work; W. Seabrook, *These Foreigners* (New York, 1938), p. 131, for Italian builders.

[46] Louis A. Copeland, "The Cornish in Southwest Wisconsin," *Collections of the State Historical Society of Wisconsin,* XIV (1898), 320.

[47] Knut Gjerset, *Norwegian Sailors on the Great Lakes* (Northfield, Minn., 1928); *Norwegian Sailors in American Waters* (Northfield, Minn., 1933).

[48] Knut Gjerset, *Norwegian Sailors in American Waters,* p. 105. Cf. A. H. Eaton, *op. cit.*, pp. 89–90, for other contributions by immigrants. F. J. Brown and J. S. Roucek, *op. cit.,* have a section on "Contributions to American Life" of each group considered.

[49] A. B. Benson and N. Hedin, *op. cit.*, pp. 525–31.

our political life.[50] The Irish, one of the earliest and largest groups, made its influence felt in politics right early. For this there are several reasons. Our governmental system in large measure followed English models and with these the Irish were more or less familiar. Furthermore, they knew the English language and culturally were close to the so-called founders of the Republic. Hence, it was easy for them to enter into our political life. The fact that they had suffered from many oppressive measures in the homeland undoubtedly quickened their interest in politics in order to make conditions more favorable for themselves.

From early days the Irish indicated a preference for the Democratic party, for it was the Democrats who opened both their hearts and their jobs to the newcomers.[51] The Federalists found no favor in their eyes for the Alien and Sedition Acts, although aimed directly at French revolutionaries, touched the Irish also. The Jeffersonian ana Jacksonian Democrats were friends of the poor man and championed his cause against the ruling, propertied aristocracy. The impecunious Irish had for generations been engaged in a struggle with the upper classes in the homeland and this opposition was readily directed against the mercantile oligarchy in America. Two later developments tended to strengthen their allegiance to the Democratic party. Due to the large influx of Germans and Irish an antipathy to them of formidable proportions had developed by 1840 and particularly against the latter, both as aliens and as Catholics. This nativism gave rise to the Know-Nothing party which drew many recruits from the old Whig party.[52] In the midst of this turmoil came the Democratic

[50] Cf. E. A. Ross, *The Old World in the New*, pp. 259–81; John R. Commons, *Races and Immigrants in America* (New York, 1920), pp. 179–97; John P. Gavit, *Americans by Choice* (New York, 1922), pp. 296–376; Charles S. Bernheimer, *The Russian Jew in the United States* (New York, 1905), pp. 256–79; Gino Speranza, *Race or Nation* (Indianapolis, 1925), pp. 34–85; M. R. Davie, *World Immigration*, pp. 253–59.

[51] Cf. Edward F. Roberts, *Ireland in America*, pp. 110–30, 179; James Bryce, *The American Commonwealth* (New York, 1920), II, pp. 35–36.

[52] According to George M. Stephenson, "Many who joined the party were scheming politicians and young men over-ambitious for political office who played on the string of racial hatred to attract the hosts of political orphans after the demise of the Whig party and the defection from democracy." *The Mississippi Valley Historical Review*, IX (December, 1922), 188.

assurances of an unrestricted immigration policy and a more easy naturalization process. The slavery question was the second factor. Resentful at being classed by aristocratic Americans with the inferior black race, when they spoke of the "low Irish and the niggers," and fearing competition with free Negroes in the labor market, they stood firmly with the Democratic party in favoring the continuation of slavery.

The majority of Irish immigrants were poverty-stricken and had no resources for buying land. Furthermore, their agrarian life in Ireland left no pleasant memories. Hence they swarmed into the cities where they took a prominent part in the politics of these rapidly growing urban communities. In 1820 they captured Tammany Hall in New York City and in a few years compelled the state organization to take orders. The immigrants and the poor were now assured of a place in American politics, and aliens could vote almost as soon as they landed.[53] The Irish have exhibited a high degree of clannishness [54] in their politics and this has been favorable to the development of bossism. Through their geniality, wit, and flexibility they became the leaders of our urban democracy [55] and forged ahead until they controlled a large number of northern cities.[56] E. A. Ross concluded that the broadest mark left on American politics by immigrants has been the Irish domination of these urban communities.[57]

This reminds one of the campaigns in California in which office seekers capitalized on the hostile feelings against the Japanese.

[53] Cf. E. F. Roberts, *op. cit.*, pp. 85, 111–13, 115, 179–80.

[54] A striking example became evident on the day this was written. Douglas Corrigan, the American of Irish name and ancestry, who by "mistake" flew his airplane to Ireland instead of to Los Angeles, returned to New York where he was given a "noisy" reception in which the Irish were important participants. At the City Hall, Mayor La Guardia gave an address of welcome. While the Mayor undoubtedly enjoyed the occasion, it is not at all improbable that he had an eye on some additional votes which may be useful, if he is to keep Tammany out of the mayor's office. In the other cities visited by Corrigan, the Irish have also been prominent in the festivities.

[55] Cf. Harold F. Gosnell, *Machine Politics: Chicago Model* (Chicago, 1937); J. F. Salter, *Boss Rule: Portraits in City Politics* (New York, 1935); M. R. Werner, *Tammany Hall* (New York, 1931); Charles E. Merriam, *Chicago: A More Intimate View of Urban Politics* (New York, 1929); C. F. Ware, *op. cit.*, pp. 270–80.

[56] John P. Bocock, "The Irish Conquest of Our Cities," *Forum*, XVII (April, 1894), 176–95.

[57] E. A. Ross, *The Old World in the New*, p. 260. According to Edward F. Roberts, Irish influence had much to do with keeping organized labor out of politics. The Irish

The Irish, unquestionably, have been responsible for no small part of the corruption in municipal government, but they have, nevertheless, made some contributions to the other side of the ledger. While in most states they have furnished more than their share of bosses, they have also contributed a number of reformers. They gave us Richard Croker, the Tammany chieftain, and also Charles O'Connor who figured prominently in the overthrow of the Tweed Ring.[58] They rendered a valuable service in winning from the various states recognition of the American principle of religious equality and the abolition of religious qualifications for office holding. It is also significant that three partly Irish states —Kentucky, Maryland, and New Hampshire—adopted manhood suffrage between 1790 and 1815.[59]

Between 1830 and 1850 the German immigrants were second to the Irish in number of arrivals. After that date they moved into first place and remained there until the 1890 decade when the so-called "new" immigration became dominant. The Germans, too, entered into the political life of the country, but their activities differed greatly from those of the Irish. The language barrier restricted their early participation. Furthermore, they were not in-

controlled the political machines in the cities and they were unwilling to barter this control for the uncertainties of a labor party. *Ireland in America* (New York, 1931), pp. 175–77.

[58] Cf. E. F. Roberts, *op. cit.*, pp. 89–90.

[59] W. F. Adams, *op. cit.*, pp. 126, 180, 371–88; F. J. Brown and J. S. Roucek, *op. cit.*, pp. 91–92; 646–50; E. A. Ross, *The Old World in the New*, pp. 259–64. The almost undivided support which the Irish gave to the Democratic party has, without doubt, been of great significance both nationally and internationally. According to Edward F. Roberts, "It is demonstrably true that without Irish support the Democratic party could not have maintained its prestige and power as a national organization, and it is quite possible that if the Irish had not become traditional Democrats the two-party system of government would not have been maintained. Lacking the peculiar conditions under which nine Irishmen out of every ten joined the party of Jefferson and Jackson, the political development of the United States might have proceeded along the French lines of numerous minority parties or fallen under the undisputed sway of a Republican faction with the inevitable consequence of a dictatorship or monarchy." *Op. cit.*, pp. 110–11.

As a matter of fact, the framers of the Constitution made no place for political parties. More than a century of experience, however, has made it clear that a democratic government cannot function without a party system. That being true, the Irish are entitled to much credit for their share in making our country democratic. Cf. Samuel P. Orth and Robert E. Cushman, *American National Government* (New York, 1935), p. 165.

tensely interested in politics; they considered public office a burden rather than a distinction. Since they settled largely in the Middle West, they learned their practical political lessons in a rural environment. When they entered politics, however, they had a number of capable leaders from the group of revolutionary exiles of 1848, some of whom, like Carl Schurz, became national figures.

Prior to 1850 the Germans were Jacksonian Democrats because that party declared all men (white) free and equal while the Whigs had a strong nativistic element that placed restrictions on foreigners.[60] The passage of the Kansas-Nebraska Bill in 1854, however, brought the slavery issue to the front and caused the German idealists to rebel against the increasing domination of the Democratic party by the southern interests. When the new Republican party representing the anti-slavery factions came upon the scene in 1856, it gradually attracted the majority of these dissenting voters. They were slow, to be sure, in joining the new party because it had a nativistic tinge and a Puritanical element which was radical on questions of personal liberty, temperance, and Sunday observance. The Germans, together with the Scandinavians and other foreign-born voters in the Northwest, stated with unmistakable clearness their demands for homestead legislation and freedom from proscription which were accepted by the party. There are no exact figures on the number of Republican voters who were foreign-born, but the most conservative estimates show that unless the foreign-born had voted for Lincoln he could not have carried the Northwest, and he could not have been elected without the Northwest or if its vote had been divided in some other way.[61]

60 The Democrats interfered less with "their customs regarding the keeping of Sunday, the use of beer and wine, and similar things which may appear of small account to the highly educated, but are of great importance to the masses who have few sources of enjoyment." *Proceedings of the State Historical Society of Wisconsin*, 1901, p. 192.

61 Donnal V. Smith, "The Influence of the Foreign-Born of the Northwest in the Election of 1860," *The Mississippi Valley Historical Review*, XIX (June, 1932), 204. Cf. F. F. Schrader, *op. cit.*, pp. 95–96, 186–95; J. Bryce, *op. cit.*, II, pp. 36–37.

When we consider the heavy immigration in the decade before the Civil War and the fact that they massed in the North and were opposed to slavery, we cannot estimate the full consequences of this. Furthermore, they acted in accordance with their

While the Irish have been sticklers for party loyalty, mass voting, and granting favors to friends, the Germans have been the bane of machine politicians because of their independent voting. They have been in the forefront of the movement to improve the personnel in government offices. Carl Schurz, a severe critic of the spoils system as it operated during Grant's administration, applied the methods of civil service reform to his department when he became Secretary of the Interior under President Hayes. The Germans, accustomed to a class of civil servants who were faithful and honest, even though frequently overbearing, were dissatisfied with the practice of making appointments to federal positions on the ground of party loyalty and not on the basis of merit. Because of their stand for personal liberty and the non-Puritanical Sabbath, many have condemned them as being a corrupting influence. On vital issues, however, they have stood for improvement.[62] They have participated in municipal reform movements. Thomas Nast, the German-born cartoonist, was an important factor in the overthrow of the Tweed Ring in New York City.

The Germans have rather consistently remained under the Republican banner and have tended to be conservative. When Bryan led the free-silver movement, German leadership was prominent on the side of "sound money." In recent years, to be sure, large numbers of Germans as well as others have turned their backs on the "Grand Old Party." In spite of their general conservatism, however, their men have stood high in the councils of the Socialist and other radical parties. Socialism had its beginnings before the Civil War and was confined almost wholly to German immigrants of the working class.[63]

A considerable number of Jews arriving from Germany after

utterances. Both the Irish and Germans furnished, in proportion to their numbers, more soldiers to the federal army than did the native-born in the northern states. A. M. Schlesinger, *New Viewpoints in American History* (New York, 1922), pp. 12–13. One might speculate on the outcome if there had been some shifting in the immigrant vote and if John Ericsson's *Monitor* had not appeared.

[62] When Charles Evans Hughes as governor of New York was engaged in a fight against boss rule and race-track gambling, a German senator was carried to his seat in the capitol shortly after a surgical operation to cast the deciding vote for the passage of the reform bill.

[63] A. B. Faust, *op. cit.*, II, pp. 122–200, 360–63; F. J. Brown and J. S. Roucek, *op. cit.*, pp. 178–82, 650–54.

the collapse of the revolution in 1848 were opposed to slavery and participated in the organization of the Republican party.[64] Socialism has won a quota of adherents from the later Jewish immigration. Because of their intellectual alertness, the Jews have tended to be independent and liberal in politics.[65]

The Norwegians led the procession from the Scandinavian countries until they were outnumbered by the Swedes after 1870. Several factors combined to draw the Scandinavians into an almost immediate alignment with the Republican party. That party's liberal homestead policy appealed to the land-hungry people. Furthermore, they had a deep dislike for slavery. The Swedes that settled near Austin, Texas, shortly before the Civil War were not in sympathy with the southern cause. The leader of the colony did not hesitate to express his opinion on the matter and as a result threats were made to kill him. To save his life he fled to Mexico. Because of this attitude the Swedes were more or less shunned by the southern whites and remained outcasts until a considerable number of their young men enlisted for the World War.[66] The anti-slavery position of the Republican party was agreeable to the Scandinavians, and, in large measure, this has been their party ever since. The Swedish settlers in the Smoky Hill River Valley of Kansas were for a long time almost entirely Republicans. At the turn of the century, however, the solid front was broken but it was not a shift to the Democratic party, except for a small number. Populism, the Farmer's Alliance, the Socialists, the Progressives, and the Non-Partisan League were the attractions.[67] Much the same course was followed in the more northerly states, not only by the Swedes but by the Norwegians and Danes, where the defections from the Republican party did not ally themselves with the Democrats but with the more radical groups. The La Follette liberal movement in Wisconsin has leaned heavily upon the Scandinavian element and leaders from this

[64] G. Cohen, *op. cit.*, pp. 84–89.

[65] *Ibid.*, pp. 210–19.

[66] C. M. Rosenquist, *op. cit.*

[67] A. Bergin, *Lindsborg efter Femtio År*, pp. 142–43. Nils F. Brown says the Swedes are "Republican, Old Guard Republican." *The American Mercury*, VII (May, 1926), 11.

group have participated increasingly in the insurgent politics of the state. The rank and file of the elder La Follette's army was three-fourths agrarian.

> The farmers had rallied to his standards in thousands as he led his crusade against the railroad and lumber barons and their political errand boys, "the bosses." His most zealous followers were the Norwegian homesteaders who, having reached political maturity, were restless in the political obscurity to which the stalwart machine had confined them. German Lutherans, fretful under the Yankee oligarchy of the Republican party, swelled his ranks. The trend of economic forces also smiled upon him. The dairy farmers, whose special friend he was, were rapidly wresting primacy in the state from the lumbermen.[68]

In Minnesota the insurgent Farmer-Labor party sent Magnus Johnson, a Swedish immigrant, to the United States Senate in 1923. He had served on this ticket for several years in the state legislature. More recently the Farmer-Labor party with Governor Floyd Olson at the head was supported by the Scandinavians. In North Dakota the radical Non-Partisan League was a revolt against conservative Republicanism. In some areas the Scandinavian groups have exercised an influence greater than their numbers would warrant because they have held the balance of power and could make demands. In Lindsborg, Kansas, Swedish candidates could not be elected at first. This opposition developed a solidarity which actually placed control in the hands of the Swedes. After that both parties included Swedes on their tickets.[69]

The Norwegians, trained in the homeland since Norway gained her national independence in 1814, were prepared to exercise the duties of self-government in America. Furthermore, they did not gain their liberty through a single revolutionary blow but, like the English people, they won it by a long, persistent struggle. As they settled on the frontier, it frequently became necessary for them to set up and staff local governments immediately. From this they gradually moved up into state and national offices, many of which have been held by them. The Norwegians, taking their politics seriously, set high standards for participation. They have

[68] *The New Republic,* LXXX (October 25, 1934), 300.
[69] A. Bergin, *Lindsborg,* p. 316. Cf. A. B. Benson and N. Hedin, *op. cit.,* pp. 323–32.

made little headway in urban politics where bosses rule and where principles are all too often regarded as mere political stupidity.[70]

Many Swedish immigrants and their sons have rendered distinguished service in governmental offices and, for the most part, they have been allied with forces of constructive protest.[71] In Chicago they have, in the main, supported movements for the betterment of the city[72] and have been strongly independent in their politics.[73]

Slavs from the various countries, when taken together, form the largest group in the "new" immigration. Since they are of more recent arrival and settled more largely in the Irish-controlled cities of the North and East, there has been less opportunity for them to participate in politics than for the Germans and Scandinavians who settled on the frontier. Furthermore, language barriers, unfamiliarity with popular government, plans to return home, and an interest in the liberation of their fellow countrymen in the homelands delayed their entrance into our political life. Moreover, since they were largely employed in Republican-controlled mines and factories they usually voted as the employers dictated. Gradually, however, they came to realize that Republicanism did not meet their needs and shifted in large numbers to the Democratic party. When they became politically conscious, being urban dwellers, they came in conflict with the Irish and made them yield some of their control. Probably the most outstanding success was the election of Anton Cermak, an immigrant from Czecho-Slovakia, to the mayor's office in Chicago.[74]

The Italians are next to the Slavs in point of numbers in the later immigration and they, too, settled largely in the eastern cities where they first allied themselves with the Republican party,

[70] K. Gjerset, *History of the Norwegian People* (New York, 1915), II, pp. 607–08; *Norwegian-American Studies and Records,* VII (1934), 114–15.

[71] Cf. A. B. Benson and N. Hedin, *op. cit.,* pp. 321–37; G. M. Stephenson, *John Lind of Minnesota* (Minneapolis, 1935); N. F. Brown in *American Mercury* VIII (May, 1926), 9–13, disagrees.

[72] Fred Lundin, who was an important personality in the Thompson machine, may be considered a notable exception.

[73] C. E. Merriam, *op. cit.,* p. 142.

[74] Cf. E. G. Balch, *Our Slavic Fellow Citizens* (New York, 1910); E. deS. Brunner, *op. cit.,* pp. 394 ff.; C. E. Merriam, *op. cit.,* pp. 143–44.

largely through the dictation of their employers. Gradually, however, they began to lift this yoke and gravitate toward the Democratic party within which they have been an insurgent element, particularly in New York City where they helped defeat the Irish-controlled Tammany machine and place Fiorello H. La Guardia, one of their own, in the mayor's office.[75]

The presence of various immigrant groups in America has influenced our political life in many ways. Much political corruption in our cities has been due to their presence. J. T. Salter in his study of Philadelphia concluded that the "machine" works most effectively among the socially handicapped groups—the poor and ignorant—and these are found most numerously in the foreign-born and colored districts. Wherever there is want, an efficiently manned party organization is present to minister to the needy. In one river ward of Philadelphia with a majority of Italians, the boss conceded two of the three hundred and four votes to the opposition; he, "the people's friend" controlled the others.[76] Albert Hart Sanford wrote that the Polish voter in Wisconsin was easily corrupted and oftentimes even invited corruption.[77] Yet, one must not generalize too hastily on the relationship between corrupt government and the foreign-born. In the words of James Bryce,[78]

> The immigrants are not so largely answerable for the faults of American politics as a stranger might be led by the language of many Americans to believe. There has been a disposition in the United States to use them, and especially the Irish, much as the cat is used in the kitchen to account for broken plates and food which disappears. The cities have no doubt suffered from the immigrant vote. But New York was not an Eden before the Irish came; and would not become an Eden were all to return to green Erin, or move on to arid Arizona.

Ross has pointed out that many of our naturalized citizens have exhibited an intelligence that compares favorably with that of

[75] Cf. R. F. Foerster, *op. cit.*, p. 400; C. E. Merriam, *op. cit.*, p. 144; C. F. Ware, *op. cit.*, pp. 280–91.

[76] J. T. Salter, *op. cit.*, pp. 6, 55, 75 ff.

[77] *Proceedings of the State Historical Society of Wisconsin,* 1907, pp. 285–86.

[78] From James Bryce, *The American Commonwealth* (New York, 1920), Vol. II, p. 304. By permission of The Macmillan Company, publishers.

the native-born of old stock. The South has comparatively few foreign-born voters but that is precisely the section of the country in which prejudice has reigned and "delayed the advent of efficient and progressive government." [79] Furthermore, some of the cities with comparatively low percentages of foreign-born do not have records to be envied greatly.[80] In civic excellence, Kansas City, Missouri, with its low ratio of foreign-born certainly does not overshadow Minneapolis with a large percentage of naturalized citizens. In fact, it would be difficult to visualize a more boss-ridden urban community than Kansas City.[81]

Many foreigners expected much of America; to them America was "the symbol of justice, brotherly kindness, equal opportunity, personal liberty, free education, and square dealing." [82] But the new immigrant, according to Panunzio,

> has come to the United States at a time when these principles are being forgotten and actually repudiated. Having achieved economic success, this nation is now bending every effort to entrench itself in that success, to gain security in economic possession, forgetting, the while, the ideals that gave it being.[83]

Many immigrants are more idealistic than the old-stock Americans and, having suffered bitter disillusionments, they are making demands for something better.

Because of the immigrants, politicians have changed their actions and policies. Candidates for office have bowed to the Irish vote and have paid attention to conditions in Ireland.[84] According to Edward F. Roberts, an avowal of pro-British sympathies would be political suicide for an office-seeker in Boston or New York.[85]

79 E. A. Ross, *The Old World in the New*, p. 263.

80 Cf. C. E. Merriam, *op. cit.*, pp. 134–36.

81 Cf. Ralph Coghlan, "Boss Pendergast: King of Kansas City, Emperor of Missouri," *Forum*, XCVII (February, 1937), 67–72; E. A. Ross, *Old World in the New* (New York, 1914), pp. 263–64.

82 A. Mangano, *op. cit.*, p. 220.

83 C. M. Panunzio, "The Contribution of New Immigrants," *World Tomorrow*, XIII (July, 1930), 303.

84 Cf. E. F. Roberts, *op. cit.*, pp. 117, 185–97.

85 *Ibid.*, p. 209. Grover Cleveland was defeated in his second campaign because the Irish considered him too friendly to England. *Ibid.*, pp. 182–83. He regained Irish support when he took a strong stand against England in the Venezuelan boundary dispute. *Ibid.*, p. 184.

While the Germans have shown considerable independence in voting, the politicians have learned that there will be no scattering of votes on any measure which may endanger the "much-cherished beer mug." [86] Party leaders have made concessions. Carl Schurz was nominated for lieutenant governor of Wisconsin in order to attract the German vote and Hans Christian Heg was placed on the ticket to draw the Norwegians.[87]

Nativism, as exemplified by Know-Nothingism and the Ku Klux Klan, has arisen because of the presence of large numbers of poor, ignorant and *different* foreigners. It is based on fear. Nativism is no mere whim; it is a state of mind. This nationalistic chauvinism has a long history throughout which it has followed the same pattern. At the opening of the nineteenth century it defended us against un-American ideas. About twenty-five years later the Irish were the objects of attention. The climax was reached shortly after 1850 in the organization of the American or Know-Nothing party which arrayed itself against infidelity, skepticism, socialism, and Catholicism at the time when the German and Irish invasion was at its peak. The papacy was considered most dangerous, and this organization was determined that foreigners and Catholics should not rule America. The demand for Americanization of foreigners during the World War again aroused the dormant nativism and the agitation for a native, white, Protestant America was not conducive to the development of rationality on the part of large numbers of our citizens.[88]

Racial, national, and cultural heterogeneities of the various groups with different traditions have brought problems in connection with law-making and law-enforcement. When laws run counter to the mores of large blocs in the population, they cannot be enforced. The experiment with national prohibition is a case in point.[89]

[86] *Proceedings of the State Historical Society of Wisconsin,* 1901, pp. 144–45.

[87] *The Wisconsin Magazine of History,* IV (1920–1921), 297.

[88] James Ford Rhodes, *History of the United States* (New York, 1892), II, pp. 50–56; A. Siegfried, *op. cit.*, pp. 130–40; Charles A. and Mary R. Beard, *The Rise of American Civilization* (New York, 1930), II, p. 21.

[89] Cf. Frank Tannenbaum, *Crime and the Community* (Boston, 1938), pp. 25–31.

CHAPTER XXXIV

THE IMMIGRANT'S CONTRIBUTION TO AMERICA

(*Concluded*)

Effects on education. Our educational system has been influenced in great measure by several immigrant groups. The few schools and colleges established in the early days of settlement in Massachusetts gradually moved into ruts only to be revitalized by new ideas from abroad. Since compulsory education had been in vogue for a long time in Germany, the accessions from that country had a high rate of literacy and their respect for intellectual attainments touched our educational system from the kindergarten to the newly organized state universities. A number of German immigrant teachers introduced new methods from their homeland. The freedom-loving intellectuals who came after the revolution of 1848 exerted a powerful influence. Mechanical methods of teaching gave way to more rational procedures. Object lessons and singing were among the innovations.[1] They established a number of private schools which set stimulating examples before our public schools.[2] The German gymnastic societies with their trained teachers did much to popularize gymnastics in the curricula. The university system in the United States, particularly in graduate work, has followed German models. While immigrants lent their influence in making America receptive to new educational ideas, Americans themselves were the most important instrumentalities in the university field. Educators visited Germany and a considerable number of students went there for graduate work.

The kindergarten is an importation from Germany. Mrs. Carl

[1] *Proceedings of the State Historical Society of Wisconsin,* 1901, p. 146. Cf. F. F. Schrader, *op. cit.,* p. 183.

[2] A. B. Faust, *op. cit.,* II, pp. 239–49. Cf. pp. 201–49.

Schurz, a pupil of Froebel, established the first institution of this kind in the German community at Watertown, Wisconsin, in 1856. The first English-speaking kindergarten was opened in Boston in 1860 by Miss Elizabeth Peabody, who had come under the influence of Mrs. Schurz. In 1868 a training college for kindergartners was opened in Boston through the activities of Miss Peabody and two German women. Another German woman established a seminary for kindergartners in New York City in 1873. After 1883 the kindergarten idea spread rapidly.[3]

The Czech immigrants under the Komensky ("Comenius") tradition have been interested in education and have exerted an influence on our schools.[4]

The Swedish group has made a contribution to the public schools in the field of music. Bethany, Gustavus Adolphus, Augustana and other Swedish-American colleges through their musical departments have prepared a large number of public-school music teachers and at present these institutions cannot meet the demand for their trained products.[5]

Danish immigrants through their folk schools are exerting an influence on our growing interest in adult education as well as on so-called progressive education. Bishop Nikolai Grundtvig believed that both church and state would profit by a more popular education that would lessen the cleavage between the masses and the classes. To that end he organized a folk-school in 1844 out of which developed a movement that has done much to lift little Denmark out of the despair in which she lay paralyzed for a long time after losing bit by bit most of her one-time large empire. The new idea had taken root by the time of the heaviest migration to America and quite naturally a number of folk schools were established in the Danish communities of the Middle West. In the new environment, however, they have not lived up to the fondest hopes of the founders and several of them were discontinued. Atterday Folk School at Solvang, California, and Grand

[3] A. B. Faust, *op. cit.*, II, pp. 237–38; Ellwood P. Cubberly, *The History of Education* (Boston, 1920), p. 766; *Wisconsin Magazine of History*, XIV (1930–1931), 48–52.

[4] E. Hudson and H. R. Maresh, *op. cit.*, pp. 171–79; R. I. Kutak, *op. cit.*, pp. 65–66.

[5] A. B. Benson and N. Hedin, *op. cit.*, pp. 303–04. Cf. also pp. 300–14.

View College in Des Moines, Iowa, operate largely on the Danish pattern. The Ashland School at Grant, Michigan, established in 1882, continued as a Danish institution until 1920. In 1928 it became an American folk school and only a small percentage served have been of Danish origin.[6] The John C. Campbell Folk School of Brasstown, North Carolina, is based on Danish principles and adapted to local conditions. This was not organized by Danes but under the stimulus of Dr. P. P. Claxton, Commissioner of Education, who recognized that America might well look to Scandinavia for help in the solution of her rural problem. A Dane has been on the staff of the school and has been helpful in passing on Danish experiences. The Berea Opportunity School in connection with Berea College of Kentucky also is based on the Grundtvigian philosophy.[7]

Religious influences. It is customary to speak of the English tradition, particularly as exemplified by colonists settling around Massachusetts Bay, as being the essence of Americanism. Some of the early settlers came seeking religious freedom, but all too often such sectarians when removed from the old scenes forgot the original idea which prompted them to come and then became the most intolerant bigots. The settlers at Plymouth, including Roger Williams, were Separatists. The majority wanted merely to break from the Church of England and establish a bare, rock-ribbed church of their own, while Williams advocated absolute religious liberty. The Puritans set up several agencies to regulate the religious and moral lives of their people; they passed and vigorously enforced laws in an attempt to make folks saintly. When Roger Williams opposed this interference of the civil government in religious matters he was banished from the colony. The Puritans would tolerate no dissent and shortly thereafter a sentence of excommunication was pronounced upon Anne Hutchinson by the Reverend John Wilson:

> I do not only pronounce you worthy to be cast out, but I do cast you out and in the name of Christ I do deliver you up to Satan, that you may

[6] Personal letter from the director of Ashland College, July 31, 1938. Cf. John E. Kirkpatrick, "In Danish Shoes," *The Survey*, LX (June, 1928), 277–79, 310.

[7] *Mountain Life and Work*, VIII (April, 1932), 4–10, 25–26.

learn no more to blaspheme, to seduce, to lie, and I do account you from this time forth to be a Heathen and a Publican.[8]

Quakers who appeared in the colony were persecuted with an astounding venom. In 1660 several were hanged on Boston Common for the crime of being Quakers and preaching against certain Puritan practices. Others were flogged and driven away into the woods.[9] This spirit of intolerance persisted for a long time. "The year 1692 witnessed a woeful spectacle of priestly tyranny. Cotton Mather sat on horseback at the foot of a scaffold denouncing a brother minister, George Burroughs, who died before his eyes for no other crime than a denial of belief in witchcraft." [10]

One of the extremes of Puritanism is exemplified by the rigidity of Sabbath observance:

Thus in New London we find in the latter part of the seventeenth century a wicked fisherman presented before the Court and fined for catching eels on Sunday; another "fined twenty shillings for sailing a boat on the Lord's Day"; while in 1670 two lovers, John Lewis and Sarah Chapman, were accused of and tried for "sitting together on the Lord's Day under an apple tree in Goodman Chapman's Orchard." . . . .

Captain Kemble of Boston was in 1656 set for two hours in the public stocks for his "lewd and unseemly behavior," which consisted in his kissing his wife "publicquely" on the Sabbath Day, upon the doorstep of his house, when he had just returned from a voyage and absence of three years. . . . .

A Maine man who was rebuked and fined for "unseemly walking" on the Lord's Day protested that he ran to save a man from drowning. The Court made him pay his fine, but ordered that the money should be returned to him when he could prove by witnesses that he had been on that errand of mercy and duty.[11]

[8] M. W. Jernegan, *op. cit.*, p. 133.

[9] Cf. W. E. Woodward, *A New American History* (New York, 1936), pp. 41–58; M. W. Jernegan, *op. cit.*, *passim;* George L. Burr, *Narratives of the Witchcraft Cases* (New York, 1914).

[10] The Scotch-Irish Society of America, *The Scotch-Irish in America* (Nashville, 1892), p. 122.

[11] Alice Morse Earle, *The Sabbath in Puritan New England* (New York, 1891), pp. 246, 247, 248–49. Cf. also Alice Morse Earle, *Colonial Days in Old New York* (New York, 1926), pp. 261–65; Sydney G. Fisher, *Men, Women, and Manners in Colonial Times* (Philadelphia, 1897).

The Anglican Church, dominant in Virginia, held rigidly to the union of church and state, and permitted no variance in religious beliefs. As in Massachusetts a privileged class feared that toleration and freedom would undermine their power. Church attendance was compulsory for all and non-conformists were ordered to leave the colony.[12]

Maryland was Catholic and the first colony to stress freedom in belief. Persecuted Puritans of Virginia were invited to settle there. As the number of Protestants increased a spirit of hostility toward the Catholics developed and in 1692 the Church of England was established there imposing a tax on all Catholics, Quakers, and other Protestants to support the Anglican clergy.[13]

Such was the situation and one shudders to think of the outcome if the English tradition had continued unbroken. Changes would have come, to be sure, with the Industrial Revolution and other economic and social influences, but the arrival of other immigrants with different religious ideas tended to soften the harsh Puritanism.

The Middle Colonies were more heterogeneous in their ethnic and religious composition. The Dutch in New Netherland and the English Quakers in Pennsylvania attracted many who were interested in religious liberty and as they reacted on each other a spirit of tolerance and liberality developed quite at variance with the narrow provincialism of the Puritan colonies. Religious persecution and the witchcraft obsession did not disturb Pennsylvania. The Pietists—Mennonites, Moravians, Dunkards, Quakers—were opposed to a union of church and state, believed in freedom of conscience, opened their churches to all classes, and thus became an important democratizing leaven.[14]

The Scotch-Irish with their inherited antagonism against England were a liberalizing influence. Under persecution in the homeland they developed a militant love of liberty which they brought to bear in America, and, according to John S. MacIntosh, "The bitter sorrows of Ulster have given birth to much of our national

[12] M. W. Jernegan, *op. cit.*, pp. 99–103.
[13] *Ibid.*, pp. 103–04.
[14] *Ibid.*, pp. 227–34, 317–18.

joy." [15] One of their preachers, Francis Makemie, was imprisoned by the English governor of New York for preaching where nonconformity was not allowed. After a court battle waging for several days, Makemie gained a victory for religious freedom.[16]

The Scotch-Irish have exerted a powerful religious influence in America. This

> is not the stock from which spring poets, artists, philosophical idealists, or religious mystics. But it was precisely the stock most in demand in the backwoods of America. From them in time sprang great captains of industry, lawyers, soldiers, politicians, and pugnaciously orthodox theologians. Their theology fitted the view of life of the much-touted self-made man, the characteristic product of American frontier society, with his individualistic ethics, and his pathetic lack of social imagination. The conservative Scotch-Irish Presbyterians have served as make-weights and mediators rather than as innovators and radicals in the melting-pot of American culture. Nevertheless, they have played a rôle in our pioneer life out of all proportion to their numbers. Scotch-Irish culture traits passed over into other communions and today shape the pattern of the religious life and social ethics of Baptists and Methodists of the South and West.[17]

While the Scotch-Irish struck some telling blows in the cause of religious liberty, their memories, too, were beclouded and their idealism gradually waned as they became enamored of the flesh-pots in the land of plenty. Their theologians became more interested in fighting for orthodoxy than for freedom. An influence to counteract this growing severity of Scotch-Irish Presbyterianism and austere Puritanism came from over the seas. More than seven million immigrants came to the United States between 1865 and 1884, nearly one half of whom came from Germany and Ireland. These newcomers were mostly Catholic, Lutheran or rationalist and their impact on American Protestantism was marked by great changes.

[15] Scotch-Irish Society of America, *The Scotch-Irish in America* (Nashville, 1893), p. 130.

[16] *Ibid.*, pp. 122–30.

[17] Adapted from John M. Mecklin, *The Story of American Dissent* (New York, 1934), pp. 58–59. Cf. Clinton Stoddard Burr, *America's Race Heritage* (New York, 1922), pp. 47–48; William Warren Sweet, *Religion on the American Frontier* (New York, 1936), pp. 64, 75.

The Germans, both Lutheran and Catholic, brought with them the "Continental Sabbath," and in many places used the day as one of general merry-making, which soon became a cause for alarm among the evangelical churches. Ministers throughout the seventies denounced the growing tendency to forsake the Puritan Sabbath and warned their people that the very foundations of the Republic were being undermined. In 1872 when the Germans of Chicago opened their Turner Hall they boldly announced that they were giving to Chicago "the honor and felicity of an European Sabbath." [18]

The orthodox derived no pleasure from what they termed the "spectacle-wearing, beer-drinking, Sunday-despising German." With the opening of the next decade, however, even the most strict Sabbatarians admitted that it was no longer possible to maintain the Puritan Sabbath and gradually adjusted themselves to the change.[19] The liberal tendencies of German thought mellowed the austerity of the Protestant theology. E. A. Steiner has stated of the German that he has not done much to deepen the religious life of America, but he has played a part in making the life of the church more honest. He has such a strong hatred for hypocrisy that he seldom speaks of his own religious experiences.[20]

The Germans infused soul and beauty into the celebration of Christmas. They changed the Yuletide "from one of solemnity to joy, and impressed upon it the mood of peace and good will to men." They also introduced the Christmas-tree into America and developed the practice of giving gifts to children.[21] The American Christmas has also been enriched by the ingress of the hundreds of thousands from Sweden. A week of festivity, decoration of streets and homes, the wafting of music upon the air, and the *smörgåsbord* are the gifts from these northern folk.[22]

[18] W. W. Sweet, *The Story of Religions in America* (New York, 1930), p. 479.

[19] *Ibid.*, p. 480. According to E. A. Steiner: "The German has been the prime factor in dispelling the Puritan ideas of the Sabbath. . . . . Still he ought not to bear the blame alone, for the average American was ready to have his Sabbath broken for him and easily followed into the breach; just as it often takes four or five grown persons to escort one child to the circus, so one may find four or five natives at every Sunday base-ball game, helping the German to amuse himself." *On the Trail of the Immigrant* (New York, 1906), pp. 107–08.

[20] *Ibid.*, p. 108.

[21] A. B. Faust, *op. cit.*, II, p. 383.

[22] A. B. Benson and N. Hedin, *op. cit.*, p. 139.

In the westward movement from the Atlantic seaboard, New England Puritanism occupied the northern states while the Calvinism of the Scotch-Irish occupied the southern section. With these two streams flowing in,

> The West was Protestant; it is still Protestant in large part but its Protestantism is of a different type. The strongest single Protestant communion in Wisconsin, Minnesota, and the two Dakotas is the Lutheran Church. In Illinois, Michigan, Iowa, and Nebraska Lutheranism is second only to Methodism among the Protestant faiths. The strength of the Lutheran churches being relatively recent in the West, the influence of the Lutheran spirit, which is vitally different from that of Calvinism has not yet begun to be felt so widely or so profoundly as numbers would seem to promise. But it is an influence with which the future will be forced to reckon. In all these states and in many others the strongest church is not one of the Protestant denominations but the great Roman Catholic Church, which is today the most potent single moral force in that part of our country that we generally call the North.[23]

English Methodism which began to develop within the Church of England about 1730 and formally organized in 1744 also put its stamp upon the growing West. This sect did not partake of the religious traditions which held sway in Massachusetts and Virginia and did much to break their hold. John Wesley, the founder of Methodism and the great evangelist George Whitefield spent some time in the Georgia colony and from there the influence spread westward. The Methodist itinerants preached a doctrine that appealed to the frontiersman. It was a gospel of free grace, free will, and individual responsibility under which each one was the master of his own destiny. This theology which emphasized the equality among men fitted the democratic life of the West.[24]

The bulk of recent immigration has come from Catholic countries and has exerted an influence on the native population. The Catholic Church has brought more beauty, form, and dignity

[23] Lawrence M. Larson, *The Changing West* (Northfield, 1937), pp. 13–14. Cf. A. Bergin, *Lindsborg efter Femtio År,* pp. 137–38, for the influence of Lutheranism in a Kansas community.

[24] Cf. W. W. Sweet, *The Story of Religions in America,* p. 317; G. Speranza, *op. cit.,* pp. 118–19.

which has made an appeal to those not satisfied with the Puritan drabness of the Protestant Church.[25] A number of churches, as a result, have been paying increased attention to the æsthetic factor.[26]

Refinements of life. (1) *Music.* It took music a long time to develop in America. The New England colonists considered it a sinful diversion. In 1675 a law was enacted prohibiting the playing of musical instruments, except the drum, trumpet, and the jew's-harp.[27] The strait-laced Puritans and Separatist Pilgrims were not favorably disposed toward such a delicate art. Music was not tolerated for its own sake but only as an aid to worship, and even that was lamentably bad.[28] In such an environment no composers appeared for almost a century and a half after the landing of the Pilgrims; it was considered both worldly and vain to fashion a new tune. This period in the history of New England may be considered a musical desert, without any oases.[29]

Gradually a change came as newcomers from England raised the standards. After 1783 many foreign musicians arrived and took charge of our music. Italians came in considerable numbers and for some time had a monopoly in the secular field. President Jefferson recruited musicians in Italy who lifted the Marine Band from its fife-and-drum status to one of distinction. The first orchestras were introduced by Italians. When the Handel and Haydn Society was organized in Boston in 1815 the conductor was an Italian who remained in charge for several years. A number of Italians became teachers of music both in public and pri-

[25] The Protestant Church of America has for some time been largely controlled by prosaic men of means who have little feeling and no prophetic vision—they are more interested in a sizeable bank account than in any spiritual ideal. The rich emotional nature of the Italian which finds its outlet in the arts is a wholesome antidote to the common stolidity and materialism. Cf. A. Mangano, *op. cit.*, pp. 212–19.

[26] Cf. Carl R. Fish, *The Rise of the Common Man* (New York, 1927), p. 191; G. Speranza, *op. cit.*, pp. 86–122.

[27] G. E. Schiavo, *The Italians in America before the Civil War*, p. 228. Cf. pp. 228–44.

[28] Francis Trollope, *Domestic Manners of the Americans* (New York, 1927), p. 256.

[29] Louis C. Elson, *The History of American Music* (New York, 1915), pp. 1–25; John T. Howard, *Our American Music: Three Hundred Years of It* (New York, 1931), pp. 3–4.

vate institutions. Italian grand opera began in America in 1825 and in the operatic field the Italians have been outstanding; they have also furnished a number of directors among whom we find the incomparable Arturo Toscanini.[30]

Music and music-making, however, have in large measure come through German influence.[31] In 1694 a band of German pietists settled near Philadelphia and stressed music, both instrumental and vocal. Bethlehem, Pennsylvania, settled in 1741 by the Moravians, moved far ahead of Boston and Philadelphia and from its very beginnings to the present day has been a noted musical center. The other Germans also and the Swedes who settled in eastern Pennsylvania, even though many of them held to narrow, almost fanatical, sectarian beliefs, enjoyed music and encouraged good singing in their churches. One Swedish minister fined certain members of his congregation six shillings for "untimely singing." [32] The Pennsylvania Quakers were as much opposed to music as the New England Puritans and the history of music in Philadelphia is that of a continual struggle with this sect. Because of the large German population in the city and environs, however, music developed more rapidly than in other centers.

About 1848 there was a veritable invasion of musicians from Germany and they did much to raise our standards. In this migration was Carl Zerrahn who, in 1854, became director of the Handel and Haydn Society in Boston and continued with that organization for forty years. He also conducted many other events of importance.[33] The Germania Society, a group of twenty-five, held together for six years giving high-grade concerts far and wide. When this orchestra disbanded the members settled in different places and continued to have an influence. The Germans did much to popularize the art through their singing societies and orchestras. The three leading orchestras in Boston, New York, and Chicago were composed largely of German musicians under German leadership. Gradually the musical ambitions of other cities

[30] G. E. Schiavo, *The Italians in America before the Civil War*, pp. 231–44.

[31] C. R. Fish, *op. cit.*, p. 237; *The Wisconsin Magazine of History*, IV (1920–1921), 314; James Taft Hatfield, *German Culture in the United States* (Evanston, 1936), p. 63.

[32] J. T. Howard, *op. cit.*, p. 20.

[33] L. C. Elson, *op. cit.*, pp. 35–36.

were aroused and they organized orchestras in all of which the German element was prominent.[34]

Probably, when all is said and done, we shall have to give more credit to Theodore Thomas, the boy violinist who came to America from Germany in 1845, than to anyone else; he is an epic figure in American history.

> Compare the state of musical culture at the time of the Civil War with conditions today and thank Theodore Thomas for the difference. It is through his efforts that this country is the home of the best in orchestral music, that almost all of our major cities have symphony orchestras of the first rank, and, what is more important, that in each of these cities there is a public that will listen to the finest symphonic works.[35]

Thomas was a masterful conductor, but more important was his plan to educate our taste for good music. He was the first prophet of good music for the masses.[36]

The Czechs are also prominent in music and one cannot turn the radio dial far without hearing music played or composed by members of that group in America. Thomas Capek states that "a brass band or a symphony orchestra without a Cech is unthinkable."[37] Belgian settlers have also been great lovers of music and nearly every settlement in Wisconsin had a brass band and string orchestra.[38] Swedes and Norwegians have done much to give America more music. They have emphasized choral singing in particular.[39] Jews have participated as interpreters of music and as instrumentalists rather than as composers. "Violin virtuosity has become almost synonymous with Jewish musical genius."[40] Among them are Fritz Kreisler, Mischa Elman, Max Rosen, Efraim Zimbalist, and others. Ossip Gabrilowitsch, late conductor of the Detroit Symphony Orchestra, was born in Russia of Jewish

[34] A. B. Faust, *op. cit.*, II, pp. 250–93; J. T. Howard, *op. cit.*, pp. 216–17.

[35] J. T. Howard, *op. cit.*, p. 294. Cf. also pp. 294–305; J. Husband, *op. cit.*, pp. 74–91.

[36] *Ibid.*, pp. 295–96.

[37] *The Čechs in America* (Boston, 1920), p. 222. Cf. pp. 222–31.

[38] *Collections of the State Historical Society of Wisconsin*, XIII (1895), 387.

[39] A. B. Benson and N. Hedin, *op. cit.*, pp. 168–69; 435–52; 469–72; *Souvenir, Norse-American Women*, 1825–1925 (St. Paul, 1926), pp. 136–43, 258–59.

[40] Rachel Davis-DuBois and Emma Schweppe, *The Jews in American Life* (New York, 1935), p. 65.

parents.[41] The Ukrainians have stressed choral work and the Chicago chorus won considerable distinction in recent years.[42]

(2) *Painting*. Before the Revolution America had no fine art. The Indians on the Atlantic seaboard were far behind those of other areas in their artistic creations and the white settlers were in no frame of mind to learn from them even the little they had to offer. Furthermore, in most English colonies, they had little interest in music, sculpture, or painting. "People ate and drank, and built and reclaimed land and multiplied. But a bar of iron was of more value than the finest statue, and an ell of good cloth was prized more highly than the 'Transfiguration' of Raphael." [43] In general, the baggage of the early colonists contained no actual paintings while their minds brought exceedingly dim ideas about them.

Religious prejudice in the New England and Pennsylvania colonies was opposed to art in most forms. The Puritans considered it a product of the devil and placed a taboo on it. In the other settlements there was practically no opportunity to indulge in such activities. New York continued in her tradition of a trading post and disclosed no intention of becoming an intellectual and artistic center.[44] Some of the early Dutch settlers, who came from the land where Rembrandt and others were producing their masterpieces, brought paintings and portraits with them—but they brought no Rembrandt.[45] They were, however, more favorably disposed and cultivated the arts to some extent.

The French colonists were more advanced than the others in all that pertained to the refinements of life. There was a certain striving for a life adorned with the elegance and graces to which they had been accustomed. They, in striking contrast to the prosaic, incurious Puritan mind, drew pictures to illustrate descriptions of America and French New Orleans developed as an art center earlier than English Boston. Grand opera began in New Orleans in 1805. Yet strangely enough, when art did really begin

[41] Cf. G. Cohen, *op. cit.*, pp. 182–91.
[42] W. Halich, *op. cit.*, pp. 133–41.
[43] Quoted from Richard M. Muther by A. B. Faust, *op. cit.*, II, p. 293.
[44] Samuel Isham, *The History of American Painting* (New York, 1927), pp. 3–18.
[45] Lorado Taft, *The History of American Sculpture* (New York, 1930), p. 4.

to develop it was not through the French or the more cultured Cavaliers of the South but through its early persecutors, the Puritans of Boston and the Quakers of Philadelphia.[46]

American painting is in no way autochthonous; it has no archaic characteristics which it may claim as peculiarly its own. It is not national but cosmopolitan, for it has been more exposed to international currents than that of any other country.[47] It is almost wholly a European transplantation with one nation or school having at one time a preponderating influence to be followed by another. France and Italy have been the outstanding sources of artistic inspiration.

Painting has not been as firmly planted on American soil as music and this is doubtless due in large measure to the fact that the immigrant ships brought many musicians but comparatively few painters. Painting in America has largely developed through the native Americans who studied in Europe. Nevertheless, a number of foreign-born artists have made and still are making valuable contributions to our life.[48]

(3) *Sculpture.* Many strands in our tradition are English. When the colonies were founded, painting was in its crude beginnings in England and sculpture did not even exist. Hence the founders of America were without even a vestige of sculptural tradition. "The Pilgrim Fathers were elder brothers of those men who decapitated cathedral statuary, who burned paintings and tabooed the drama. Even their music was an unhappy sort. This world was to them a vale of tears, and art was a temptation to be strenuously resisted." [49] According to A. B. Faust,

> If the beginnings of music and painting in the United States were difficult, the case for sculpture seemed well-nigh hopeless. The Puritan and Quaker horror of the flesh and a peculiar unfathomable prudishness that held

[46] S. Isham, *op. cit.*, pp. 8–9.

[47] A. B. Faust, *op. cit.*, II, p. 293.

[48] G. E. Schiavo, *The Italians in America before the Civil War*, pp. 245–46; A. B. Faust, *op. cit.*, II, pp. 293–306; Allen H. Eaton, *op. cit.*, pp. 129–37; W. Halich, *op. cit.*, pp. 72–75; S. Isham, *op. cit.;* F. F. Schrader, *op. cit.*, pp. 250–51; G. Cohen, *op. cit.*, pp. 194–95; A. B. Benson and N. Hedin, *op. cit.*, pp. 488–501.

[49] From Lorado Taft, *The History of American Sculpture* (New York, 1930), p. 3. By permission of The Macmillan Company, publishers.

sway all over the country, compelled whatever talent there was in the land to seek refuge in fair Italy.[50]

When John Pine, an English artist, brought a cast of Venus de Medici to Philadelphia, there was such antagonism against it that it had to be kept in a case and exhibited only with care to a chosen few.

In such a setting, sculpture finally made a shy beginning after the passage of two centuries. The early sculptors were Americans who studied in Europe. While August St. Gaudens was born in Ireland in 1848 he came to America a mere babe in arms and must be considered an American rather than an immigrant. His preparatory training, however, came through work for French stone and shell cameo cutters in New York City, after which he spent several years in France and Italy.[51]

The World's Columbian Exposition in Chicago did much to develop an interest in pleasing forms. This, together with the reënforcement of the succeeding expositions, was largely responsible for increased opportunities in the field of architectural or decorative sculpture.

In this more "musical" expression of the sculptor's art, men from Austria, France, Germany, and Italy have been the leaders. Our bare and austere efforts in decoration lacked rhythm and grace of movement, while these men from across the sea with the tradition of centuries to guide their clever hands brought to new heights the delicate art of beautifying our architecture by means of sculptural adjuncts.

Karl Bitter, born in Vienna, came to the United States in 1889 and shortly won an award for the design of the bronze doors in the Trinity Church of New York City in competition with many Americans. This gave him an opportunity to design the embellishments for two buildings at the World's Fair in Chicago. Because of the recognition he gained from this, he was selected to direct the sculptural work for the Pan-American Exposition in Buffalo

[50] *Op. cit.*, Vol. II, p. 306.

[51] A. H. Eaton, *op. cit.*, pp. 117–19; J. Husband, *op. cit.*, pp. 121–39; L. Taft, *op. cit.*, pp. 279–309, 452–69.

in 1901, the Louisiana Purchase Exposition in St. Louis in 1904, and the Panama-Pacific Exposition in San Francisco in 1913.[52]

John Massey Rhind came to America from Scotland in the same year as Karl Bitter and he, too, made a beginning by designing a bronze door for the Trinity Church of New York City. He has done much to beautify our cities through statues and decorations on many buildings. He is one of our few adepts in ecclesiastical art.[53]

Philip Martini came from France at the age of twenty. His astonishing skill as a decorative sculptor on the agricultural building at the Columbian Exposition gave him a high place in America. He also modeled many monumental statues.[54]

Space limitations permit us to call attention to only a few sculptors from a considerable number that might be considered. They have come to us from Canada, England, Ireland, Poland, France, Germany, Norway, Sweden, Roumania, Czecho-Slovakia, Italy, and Ukrainia.[55]

(4) *Literature.* In the field of literature immigrants have made themselves felt. While there is a considerable list of writers that might be cited, we shall merely call attention to a few.

Ole Edvart Rölvaag enriched American letters with a new and discerning depiction of the immigrant pioneer in his *Giants of the Earth.* This, his most impressive work, "seems to be safely in the inner circle of great American novels." [56] He has portrayed more vividly than anyone else the struggle of the immigrant in rural America. This he could do because he was an immigrant and lived among his countrymen. *Peder Victorious* is a remarkable study of the second generation of immigrants. At the age of twenty Rölvaag

[52] L. Taft, *op. cit.*, pp. 456–62; A. H. Eaton, *op. cit.*, pp. 122–24.

[53] J. Walker McSpadden, *Famous Sculptors* (New York, 1927), pp. 249–53; Lorado Taft, *op. cit.*, pp. 462–63.

[54] L. Taft, *op. cit.*, pp. 453–56.

[55] A. H. Eaton, *op. cit.*, pp. 117–29; L. Taft, *op. cit.*, pp. 463–600; A. B. Faust, *op. cit.*, II, pp. 306–15; W. Halich, *op. cit.*, pp. 72–75; G. Cohen, *op. cit.*, pp. 192–94; A. B. Benson and N. Hedin, *op. cit.*, pp. 501–05; David Edstrom, *The Testament of Caliban* (New York, 1937); National Sculpture Society, *Contemporary American Sculpture* (New York, 1929).

[56] R. Blankenship, *op. cit.*, p. 718.

came to America from a fishing village in Norway. He worked at odd jobs and on farms in Dakota making it possible for him to attend school. At the age of twenty-eight he graduated from St. Olaf College in Minnesota where he became professor of Norwegian literature and continued there until his death in 1931.[57] Several other Norwegian writers have made contributions, but no one can be classed with Rölvaag.[58]

The Jews have given us a number of literary personages—poets, novelists, journalists, and writers of short stories. Mary Antin and Rose Cohen penetrated the lives of immigrants as they were making adjustments to American life. Anzia Yezierska came from Russia at the age of sixteen, and "worked her way from the sweat-shop to a well-established place in the American literary world." [59] Ludwig Lewisohn, critic, translator, and novelist, is "one of the finest masters of English prose among all the writers of America." [60] John Cournos, born in a Russian village, came to Philadelphia at the age of ten where he learned an expressive, if not elegant, language on the streets. After a number of years of struggle he went to London where he began to write. He has written novels, poems, and plays. While Joseph Pulitzer is not considered a literary man, he has exerted considerable influence through his provision for the Pulitzer prizes, the highest awards for different types of writing—the best play, biography, and novel.

Dhan Gopal Mukerji, a native of India, was awarded the John Newbery Medal for the most distinguished children's book in 1927. Through his books he has given us a far better understanding of the life of India than the shallow, disparaging accounts of the tourists.

Lola Ridge was born in Ireland, spent her early years in Australia, but has done her writing in America. In 1918 she published *The Ghetto,* a poem that pictures the brutalities and

[57] *Norwegian-American Studies and Records,* VII (1923), 53–73, 121–30; Stanley J. Kunitz, *Living Authors* (New York, 1931), pp. 348–49.

[58] *Norwegian-American Studies and Records,* V (1930), 61–83; VII (1934), 1–17; *Souvenir, Norse-American Women,* 1825–1925 (St. Paul, 1926), pp. 144–45.

[59] G. Cohen, *op. cit.,* p. 165. Cf. pp. 163–81 for other Jewish writers.

[60] Lee J. Levinger, *A History of the Jews in the United States* (Cincinnati, 1931), p. 482.

beauties of the city. One critic said of her, "Blood-drained, ravaged by illness, she is like a bright, untarnished double-edged sword in her courage and her integrity." Louis Adamic, the Yugoslav, saw his *Native's Return* develop into a best seller. Konrad Bercovici, the Roumanian, who spent his boyhood days among the gypsies in his homeland, came to the United States in 1916 and has gained recognition as a writer of short stories. Some of his literary productions have been translated into several languages.

The American-born generation of immigrant parentage has also produced writers who have frequently written on themes growing out of life in immigrant communities. Michael Gold, a Jew born in New York City, has become an apostle of the proletariat through his writings. Edna Ferber who was born in the Middle West of Jewish parentage has written of immigrants. Her *So Big* was awarded the Pulitzer Prize in 1924 and became a best seller.

Several Americans of old stock have also drawn upon foreign folk for their writings. Willa Cather as a girl played with Scandinavian, Bohemian, German, French, and Russian children and learned the ways of their parents during her early years as a resident of Nebraska. J. Frank Dobie of the University of Texas has used legends, ballads, and traditions of Latin Americans in his books.

Conclusion. America has given much to the immigrants, but she has also received abundantly. Our life has been changed by them in some ways undoubtedly for the worse, but it has also been enriched because of their coming. They are now with us by the millions and it will avail us little to weep over mistakes that have been made in the past. We need to understand them that we may learn what other contributions they can make to the enrichment of our national life in all its aspects.

BIBLIOGRAPHY [1]

General Works

Abbott, Edith, *Historical Aspects of the Immigration Problem.* University of Chicago Press, Chicago, 1926.

Abbott, Edith, *Immigration: Select Documents and Case Records.* University of Chicago Press, 1924.

Bogardus, Emory S., *Immigration and Race Attitudes.* D. C. Heath and Company, New York, 1928.

Brown, Lawrence Guy, *Immigration.* Longmans, Green and Company, New York, 1933.

Brown, Francis J. and Roucek, Joseph S., *Our Racial and National Minorities.* Prentice-Hall, Inc., New York, 1937.

Commons, John R., *Races and Immigrants in America.* The Macmillan Company, New York, 1920.

Davie, Maurice R., *World Immigration.* The Macmillan Company, New York, 1936.

Duncan, Hannibal G., *Immigration and Assimilation.* D. C. Heath and Company, Boston, 1933.

Fairchild, Henry P., *Immigration.* The Macmillan Company, New York, 1925.

Jenks, Jeremiah S. and Lauck, W. Jett, *The Immigration Problem.* Funk and Wagnalls Company, New York, 6th Edition, 1926.

Miller, Herbert A., *Races, Nations and Classes.* J. B. Lippincott Company, Philadelphia, 1924.

Park, Robert E., and Miller, Herbert A., *Old World Traits Transplanted.* Harper and Brothers, New York, 1921.

Ross, Edward A., *The Old World in the New.* The Century Company, New York, 1914.

[1] For excellent bibliographies, see the following: F. J. Brown and J. S. Roucek, *Our Racial and National Minorities* (New York, 1937), pp. 781–847; Donald Young, *American Minority Peoples* (New York, 1932), pp. 594–607; W. Ralph Janeway, *Bibliography of Immigration in the United States,* 1900–1930 (Columbus, Ohio, 1934). For bibliography of social fiction describing immigrant life in America see Maurice R. Davie, *World Immigration* (New York, 1936), pp. 568–71.

Stephenson, George M., *A History of American Immigration, 1821–1924.* Ginn and Company, Boston and New York, 1926.

Taft, Donald R., *Human Migration.* The Ronald Press, New York, 1936.

Warne, Frank Julian, *The Tide of Immigration.* The Century Company, New York, 1916.

Young, Donald, *American Minority Peoples.* Harper and Brothers, New York, 1932.

Autobiographies [2]

Adamic, Louis, *Laughing in the Jungle.* Harper and Brothers, New York, 1932 (Slovenian).

Adamic, Louis, *The Native's Return.* Harper and Brothers, New York, 1934 (Slovenian).

Antin, Mary, *The Promised Land.* Houghton Mifflin Company, Boston and New York, 1912 (Russian Jew).

Antin, Benjamin, *The Gentleman from the 22nd.* Boni and Liveright, New York, 1927 (Russian Jew).

Arrighi, Antonio A., *The Story of Antonio, the Galley Slave: A Romance of Real Life, in Three Parts.* Fleming H. Revell and Company, New York, 1911 (Italian).

Bartholdt, Richard, *From Steerage to Congress.* Dorrance and Company, Philadelphia, 1930 (German).

Birmingham, George A., *From Dublin to Chicago.* Doubleday, Doran and Company, New York, 1914 (Irish).

Bogen, Boris D., *Born a Jew.* The Macmillan Company, New York, 1930 (Russian Jew).

Bok, Edward, *The Americanization of Edward Bok.* Charles Scribner's Sons, New York, 1920 (Dutch).

Bridges, Horace James, *On Becoming an American: Some Meditations of a Newly Naturalized Immigrant.* Marshall Jones Company, Boston, 1919 (English).

Brudno, Ezra S., *The Fugitive.* Doubleday, Page and Company, New York, 1907 (Lithuanian Jew).

Carnegie, Andrew, *The Autobiography of Andrew Carnegie.* Houghton Mifflin Company, Boston and New York, 1920 (Scotch).

Clarke, Joseph I. C., *My Life and Memories.* Dodd, Mead and Company, New York, 1925 (Irish).

[2] For biographies of immigrants, see Maurice R. Davie, *World Immigration* (New York, 1936), pp. 567–68; Wilson *Bulletin,* IX (December, 1934), pp. 181–85.

Cohen, Rose, *Out of the Shadow*. George H. Doran Company, New York, 1918 (Russian Jew).

Cournos, John, *Autobiography*. G. P. Putnam's Sons, New York, 1935 (Russian Jew).

Damrosch, Walter, *My Musical Life*. Charles Scribner's Sons, New York, 1923 (German).

D'Angelo, Pascal, *Pascal D'Angelo, Son of Italy*. The Macmillan Company, New York, 1924 (Italian).

Davis, James J., *The Iron Puddler: My Life in the Rolling Mills and What Came of It*. The Bobbs-Merrill Company, Indianapolis, 1922 (Welsh).

Duncan, Hannibal G., *Immigration and Assimilation*. D. C. Heath and Company, Boston, 1933 (Various nationalities).

Edstrom, David, *The Testament of Caliban*. Funk and Wagnalls, New York, 1937 (Swede).

Ericson, J. A., "Memories of a Swedish Immigrant of 1852," *Annals of Iowa*, VIII (April, 1907), 3d Series (Swede).

Gemünder, George, *George Gemünder's Progress in Violin Making*. Astoria, New York, 1881 (German).

Gompers, Samuel, *Seventy Years of Life and Labor: An Autobiography*. E. P. Dutton and Company, New York, 1925 (English Jew).

Gordon, George A., *My Education and Religion: An Autobiography*. Houghton Mifflin Company, New York, and Boston, 1925 (Scotch).

Grove, Frederick Philip, *A Search for America: The Odyssey of an Immigrant*. Louis Carrier and Company, New York, 1928 (Scotch-Swedish).

Hasanovitz, Elizabeth, *One of Them*. Houghton Mifflin Company, Boston and New York, 1918 (Russian Jew).

Hindus, Maurice, *Green Worlds: An Informal Chronicle*. Doubleday, Doran and Company, New York, 1938 (Russian).

Holt, Hamilton (Editor), *The Life Stories of Undistinguished Americans as Told by Themselves*. James Pott and Company, New York, 1906 (Various nationalities).

Irvine, Alexander F., *From the Bottom Up: The Life Story of Alexander Irvine*. Doubleday, Page and Company, New York, 1910 (Irish).

Jensen, Carl Christian, *An American Saga*. Little, Brown and Company, Boston, 1927 (Dane).

Jorgensen, F. E., *Twenty-five Years a Game Warden*. Stephen Daye Press, Brattleboro, Vermont, 1937 (Swede).

Kang, Younghill, *East Goes West*. Charles Scribner's Sons, New York, 1937 (Korean).

Kenlon, John, *Fourteen Years a Sailor*. Doubleday, Doran Company, New York, 1923 (Irish).

Kin, Huie, *Reminiscences*. San Yu Press, Peiping, China, 1932 (Chinese).

Koerner, Gustave (Edited by Thomas J. McCormack), *Memoirs of Gustave Koerner*. The Torch Press, Cedar Rapids, Iowa, 1909 (German).

Kohut, Rebecca, *My Portion*. Thomas Seltzer, New York, 1925 (Hungarian Jew).

Kraus, Adolf, *Reminiscences and Comments*. Privately printed, Chicago, 1925 (Bohemian Jew).

Lane, Franklin K. (Edited by Anne W. Lane and Louise H. Wall), *The Letters of Franklin K. Lane, Personal and Political*. Houghton Mifflin Company, Boston and New York, 1922 (Canadian).

Leinweber, Martin, *One Man's Life*. Christopher Publishing House, Boston, 1938 (German).

Lewisohn, Ludwig, *Up Stream: An American Chronicle*. Boni and Liveright, New York, 1922 (German Jew).

Lewisohn, Ludwig, *Mid-channel*. Thornton Butterworth, Ltd., London, 1929 (German Jew).

Linhart, George, *Out of the Melting Pot*. Privately printed, 1923 (Czech).

Mattson, Hans, *Reminiscences: The Story of an Emigrant*. D. D. Merrill Company, St. Paul, 1891 (Swede).

McClure, Samuel S., *My Autobiography*. Frederick A. Stokes Company, New York, 1914 (Irish).

Mirza, Youell B., *Myself When Young*. Doubleday, Doran and Company, New York, 1929 (Persian).

Morgenthau, Henry (In collaboration with French Strother), *All in a Life-Time*. Doubleday, Page and Company, Garden City, 1922 (German Jew).

Mørck, Paal (O. E. Rölvaag), *Amerika-Breve fra P. A. Smevik*. Augsburg Publishing House, 1912 (Norwegian).

Morton, Leah, pseud. See Stern, Elizabeth G.

Muir, John, *Story of My Boyhood and Youth*. Houghton Mifflin Company, Boston and New York, 1913 (Scotch).

Mukerji, Dhan Gopal, *Caste and Outcast*. E. P. Dutton and Company, New York, 1923 (Hindu).

Nielsen, T. M., *How a Dane Became an American, or Hits and Misses of My Life*. The Torch Press, Cedar Rapids, Iowa, 1935 (Dane).

Panunzio, Constantine, *The Soul of an Immigrant*. The Macmillan Company, New York, 1921 (Italian).

Patri, Angelo, *A Schoolmaster of the Great City*. The Macmillan Company, New York, 1917 (Italian).

Peterson, Frank, *Life of Dr. Frank Peterson*. Conference Press, Chicago, n.d. (Swede).

Powell, Felix, *The Transformation of Felix*. Privately printed, Portland, Maine, 1915 (Italian).

Pupin, Michael, *From Immigrant to Inventor*. Charles Scribner's Sons, New York, 1923 (Serb).

Radziwill, Princess Catherine, *It Really Happened: An Autobiography*. Dial Press, New York, 1932 (Russian).

Rainsford, W. S., *The Story of a Varied Life: An Autobiography*. Doubleday, Page and Company, New York, 1924 (Irish).

Ravage, Marcus Eli, *An American In the Making*. Harper and Brothers, New York, 1917 (Roumanian Jew).

Rihbany, Abraham M., *A Far Journey*. Houghton Mifflin Company, Boston and New York, 1914 (Syrian).

Riis, Jacob A., *The Making of an American*. The Macmillan Company, New York, 1901 (Dane).

Rockne, Knut Kenneth, *Autobiography*. Bobbs-Merrill Company, Indianapolis, 1931 (Norwegian).

Saint-Gaudens, Augustus (Edited and amplified by Homer Saint-Gaudens), *The Reminiscences of Augustus Saint-Gaudens*. The Century Company, New York, 1913 (Irish-French).

Schurz, Carl, *The Reminiscences of Carl Schurz*. The McClure Company, New York, 1907–1908 (German).

Shaw, Anna Howard (With the collaboration of Elizabeth Jordan), *The Story of a Pioneer*. Harper and Brothers, New York, 1915 (Scotch).

Steiner, Edward A., *From Alien to Citizen: The Story of My Life in America*. Fleming H. Revell and Company, New York, 1914 (Austrian Jew).

Stern, Elizabeth, Gertrude, *My Mother and I*. The Macmillan Company, New York, 1917 (Polish Jew).

Stern, Elizabeth, Gertrude, *I Am a Woman—and a Jew*. J. H. Sears and Company, New York, 1926 (Polish Jew).

Straus, Oscar S., *Under Four Administrations, From Cleveland to Taft*.

Houghton Mifflin Company, Boston and New York, 1922 (German Jew).

Sugimoto, Etsu Inagaki, *A Daughter of the Samurai*. Doubleday, Doran and Company, New York, 1924 (Japanese).

Sutter, John Augustus, *Sutter's Own Story*. G. P. Putnam's Sons, New York, 1936 (Swiss).

Thomas, Theodore (Edited by George P. Upton), *Theodore Thomas, A Musical Autobiography*. A. C. McClurg and Company, Chicago, 1905 (German).

Thomas, W. I. and Znaniecki, Florian, *The Polish Peasant in Europe and America*. The Gorham Press, Boston, 1919, Vol. III; also Alfred Knopf, New York, 1927 (Pole).

Ueland, Andreas, *Recollections of an Immigrant*. Minton Balch and Company, New York, 1929 (Norwegian).

Van der Veen, Egbert, *Life History and Reminiscences*. Privately printed, Holland, Michigan. n.d. (Dutch).

Villa, Silvio, *The Unbidden Guest*. The Macmillan Company, New York, 1923 (Italian).

Villard, Henry, *Memoirs of Henry Villard, Journalist and Financier 1835–1900*. Houghton Mifflin Company, New York, 1904 (Bavarian).

Wing, Yung, *My Life in China and America*. Henry Holt and Company, New York, 1909 (Chinese).

Wise, Stephen S., *My Thirty Years' Battle*. Brentanos, New York, 1925 (Hungarian Jew).

Yankoff, Peter D., *Peter Menikoff: The Story of a Bulgarian Boy in the Great American Melting Pot*. Cokesbury Press, Nashville, 1928 (Bulgarian).

Youell, George, *Lower Class*. Caxton Publishing Company, Caldwell, Idaho, 1938 (English).

The Second Generation

BOOKS:

Bell, Reginald, *Public School Education of the Second Generation Japanese in California*. Stanford University Press, Palo Alto, 1935.

Bogardus, Emory S., *The Mexican in the United States*. University of Southern California Press, Los Angeles, 1934.

Brunner, Edmund deS., *Immigrant Farmers and Their Children*. Harper and Brothers, New York, 1929.

Brown, Francis J. and Roucek, Joseph S., *Our Racial and National Minorities*. Prentice-Hall, Inc., New York, 1937.

Carpenter, Niles, *Immigrants and Their Children*. Bureau of the Census, Washington, 1927.

Duncan, H. G., *Immigration and Assimilation*. D. C. Heath and Company, Boston, 1933.

Ferber, Edna, *A Peculiar Treasure*. Doubleday, Doran and Company, New York, 1939.

Gold, Michael, *Jews Without Money*. Horace Liveright, New York, 1932.

Ichihashi, Yamato, *Japanese in the United States*. Stanford University Press, Palo Alto, 1932.

Mariano, John H., *The Second Generation of Italians in New York City*. Christopher Publishing House, Boston, 1921.

Ornitz, Samuel B., *Haunch, Paunch, and Jowl: An Anonymous Autobiography*. G. P. Putnam's Sons, New York, 1933.

Rölvaag, O. E., *Peder Victorious*. Harper and Brothers, New York, 1929.

Smith, William C., *Americans in Process: A Study of Our Citizens of Oriental Ancestry*. Edwards Brothers, Ann Arbor, 1937.

Steiner, J. F., in E. B. Reuter, *Race and Culture Contacts*. McGraw-Hill Book Company, New York, 1934.

Strong, Edward K., *The Second Generation Japanese Problem*. Stanford University Press, Palo Alto, 1934.

Young, Charles H. and Reid, Helen R. Y., *The Japanese Canadians*. University of Toronto Press, Toronto, 1938.

PAMPHLETS:

Adams, Romanzo, *The Education of the Boys of Hawaii and Their Economic Outlook*. Institute of Pacific Relations, Honolulu, 1928.

Cassidy, Florence G., *Second-Generation Youth*. The Women's Press, New York, 1930.

Johansen, John P., *Immigrants and Their Children in South Dakota*. Brookings, 1936.

Smith, William C., *The Second Generation Oriental in America*. Institute of Pacific Relations, Honolulu, 1927.

ARTICLES:

Adamic, Louis, "Thirty Million New Americans," *Harpers*, XLXIX (November, 1934), 684–94.

Adams, Eustace L., "Second Generation," *American Magazine*, CXXI (March, 1936), 12–13.

Adams, Eustace L., "Thunder in the Valley," *American Magazine*, CXXII (August, 1936), 56–59.

Bogardus, E. S., "Second Generation Mexicans," *Sociology and Social Research*, XIII (January–February, 1929), 276–83.

Brody, Catherine, "A New York Childhood," *The American Mercury*, XIV (May, 1928), 57–66.

Fante, John, "The Odyssey of a Wop," *The American Mercury*, XXX (September, 1933), 89–97.

Kawai, Kazuo, "Three Roads, and None Easy," *Survey*, LVI (May 1, 1926), 164–66.

Lewis, Read, "Immigrants and Their Children," *Interpreter Releases*, Foreign Language Information Service, XII (April 30, 1935).

Lyons, Eugene, "Aliens," *Nation*, XCVI (April 25, 1923), 490–91.

McClatchy, V. S., "The Second Generation Oriental in America," *Pacific Affairs*, April, 1929, 200–03.

Marshall, James, "How the Schools Can Help to Solve the Second Generation Problem," *Interpreter Releases*, XII (May 13, 1935), 194–96.

Roucek, J. S., "Social Attitudes of Native-born Children of Foreign-born Parents," *Sociology and Social Research*, XXII (November–December, 1937), 149–55.

Schibsby, Marian, "Second Generation Problems," *Interpreter Releases*, XII (April 25, 1935), 159–70.

Sellin, Thorsten, "Crime and the Second Generation of Immigrant Stock," *Interpreter Releases*, XIII (May 23, 1936), 144–50.

Sleszynski, Thaddeus, "The Second Generation of Immigrants in the Assimilation Process," *Annals*, XCIII (January, 1921), 156–61.

Smith, William C., "Born American, But—," *Survey*, LVI (May 1, 1926), 167–68.

Smith, William C., "Second Generation Oriental Americans," *Journal of Applied Sociology*, X (November–December, 1925), 160–68.

Smith, William C., "Changing Personality Traits of Second Generation Orientals in America," *American Journal of Sociology*, XXXIII (May, 1928), 922–29.

Valentine, John, "Of the Second Generation," *Survey*, XLVII (March 18, 1922), 956–57.

INDEX

(1)